LOCOMOTIVE KIT CHASSIS CONSTRUCTION in 4MM

By IAIN RICE

WILD SWAN PUBLICATIONS LTD.

ISBN 1 874103 10 0

DEDICATION

To Don Leeper
in grateful recognition of his interest,
encouragement and support throughout
the protracted and laboured compilation
of this book.

Designed by Paul Karau
Printed by Amadeus Press, Huddersfield

Published by
WILD SWAN PUBLICATIONS LTD.
1–3 Hagbourne Road, Didcot, Oxon OX11 8DP

INTRODUCTION

I originally wrote this book back in about 1985, when Wild Swan Publications were barely out of the cygnet stage. It was combined with an extended treatise on whitemetal loco kit construction, which last appeared – duly ameliorated – in 1989, sans all mention of the vital underpinnings. This apparent insanity on the part of author and publisher is readily explained, for, while the whitemetal parts of whitemetal locos are much as they have always been, the mechanical elements have undergone a merciful and long-overdue transformation. My original text was out of date before ever Mr. Karau got at it with his large scissors and his pot of paste.

After an abortive attempt to save something from the wreckage, the first attempt was towed out to sea on a quiet Sunday, and scuttled in deep water. This is a totally fresh attempt to set out, I hope, in comprehensible form, my experiences of locomotive kit chassis construction. Unlike the original, this treatise is also relevant to the construction of the types of chassis associated with etched, as well as cast, locomotive kits. In view of the fact that the vast majority of loco kits now employ etched chassis of one sort or another, this is unsurprising. In fact, there now exists through much of the specialist trade a consensus as to what constitutes a soundly-designed chassis. Let us hope the rest of them catch up sooner rather than later.

While the emphasis is laid on the construction of what I might term 'state of the art' etched chassis, I have been careful not to overlook the fact that there are a goodly few older kits around, some still in production, and others lurking in dark, cobwebby corners of those famous store-cupboards of 'one-day' projects that we modellers are so fond of. So, in scope, we range from cast blocks through solid chunks of milled brass to the far more manageable etchings of recent times. What is described herein relates principally to 4 mm, which is where my experience mostly lies, but the design consensus transcends scales these days, and chassis in other scales now tend to be similar to the 'popular norm'.

Even my best friends have no hesitation in pointing out that, as an engineer, Rice would have a job justifying a place in the novice class, so I don't go too much on the engineering in these pages. Rather, it's a mixture of common sense (well, it makes sense

A good chassis kit is a sound foundation for any loco, be it a cast or etched kit superstructure, a moulded plastic R-T-R body, or, as here, a scratchbuilt model. My GWR '1366' 0–6–0PT sits on a slightly modified Peter K etched chassis kit, intended for the earlier GWR '1361' 0–6–0ST. It is powered by a Mashima 1224 motor driving through Ultrascale 38:1 gears. Wheels are by Sharman.

to *me*) and what might kindly be termed 'refined bodging'. This is not a book for the man who can't contemplate kit construction without the resources of a precision workshop behind him. A table and a modest selection of hand tools will see most modern chassis kits together and working, and that is the precept on which I've based this essay. My only qualification for writing the dratted thing in the first place is that I've somehow managed to build somewhere on the high side of 450 locos – not all from kits, admittedly – which have, in their fashion, worked reasonably, if not well.

There is no formal qualification in the railway modelling business, which is, on the whole, a blessing. But there are certain fundamentals which need to be understood in order to ensure that the mechanisms of our model locomotives function satisfactorily. Unfortunately, a good many such mechanisms have been designed by those who either didn't know any better, or if they did, couldn't care less. There have been some truly gruesome chassis designs foisted upon the loco-kit-buying public, responsible for sapping the confidence of many an aspiring builder. It is quite impossible to achieve satisfactory results with daft design and components awesome in their awfulness, and the only possible course of action with kits that ignore the dictates of common sense (leave alone those of sound engineering practice) is to eschew them. Spend the money on beer or fast women, for it is wasted on kits whose ultimate resting place is marked 'no hot ashes' on the lid. I describe several such abortions in these pages.

Fortunately, there are also plenty of people who *do* understand the makings of a good chassis, not least my old friend Mike Sharman, whose pioneering work on the 'Flexichas' system led Rod Neep to develop the influential 'Perseverance' range of chassis kits, from which the majority of current designs are descended. My own approach to chassis construction results from a near quarter-century of the Sharman influence, so I suppose that I'm fortunate in being, for once, 'in the swim'.

Whilst much of the concern with chassis construction is in ensuring the proper functioning of the thing, it must not be overlooked that the chassis is just as much a part of the model as the more obviously cosmetic superstructure. This has long been a hobbyhorse of mine, and one I have ridden a good few times since my original article on 'realistic' chassis construction – 'The Poor Relation' – appeared in the June 1980 *Model Railways*. And, leaving aside their manifold mechanical failings, most of the older loco kit chassis were aesthetic aberrations, bearing scant resemblance to their supposed subjects. Even otherwise satisfactory kits rarely looked right in the chassis department, and those occasional specimens that sat on properly-modelled handbuilt chassis were scarcely recognisable as having the same humble origins. The etched chassis has – or should have – changed all that, and nowadays we pay as much attention to correct detailing and finishing of the chassis as we do to the rest of the loco. That these cosmetic aspects are not neglected in these pages goes, of course, without saying.

It's probably about the only thing that *will* go without saying, mind, as most of what I write seems to come out bountiful rather than brief. Never mind, when it comes to chassis construction, there's plenty to write about, so perhaps all is not lost. It's taken six years and a few false starts to get this lot down in some semblance of sense and order, so here's hoping that no clever dick is about to make the etched chassis obsolete!

Iain Rice,
Chagford, Devon.
1992

CHAPTER ONE
SOME CHASSIS FUNDAMENTALS

'It is perfectly possible,' quoth the sage, 'to play the Moonlight Sonata without knowing how a piano works'. Well, that's as may be, especially in my case, when the simpler bits of Bach are enough to knot the Rice fingers, but there's no doubt that some understanding of the whys and wherefores of any mechanism do help you to get the best out of it. This is, I feel, quite valid in relation to those aspects of our model railway which actually have to function, as well as simply looking realistic. So, as has become my wont when embarking upon one of these treatises, I'd like to conduct a swift and reasonably flippant examination of locomotive chassis, both full-sized and modelled.

In the best traditions of our hobby, in which nothing is ever as straightforward as it seems, the whole business of model locomotive chassis design has been plunged into a dense fog of tortological debate, a fog compounded variously of factions, fictions, notions, opinions and theories, which has successfully served to obscure one or two rather important *facts*. Chief amongst these facts is a small matter of molecules, or rather, the properties which molecular structures impart to the materials they make up. Inconvenient as it may be, there is no such thing as a 4 mm scale molecule; a piece of metal incorporated in our models exhibits exactly the same properties as a bit of metal incorporated in a full-sized loco. In particular, it is no more flexible in the model application, and requires the same forces to deflect it – you can't scale down materials or their properties, however wishful the thinking.

Unfortunately, a good deal of the thinking that has been applied to model locomotive chassis design is decidedly on the wishful side, never more so than by the fundamentalist sect of the 'Scale-it-down-regardless' school. These well-known diehards argue that the only way to make a proper loco chassis is to make it exactly like a real loco chassis, only 76 times smaller. The logic, if I may so dignify it, runs along the lines that, if we use components dimensioned to scale, they will function in the same way as their full-sized counterparts. Never being one to argue with a soft theory when a hard fact is at hand, I would invite the protagonists of this notion to try a practical experiment; accepting that a typical etched chassis, with its frames of 18–20 thou metal scaling out pretty well spot on for typical prototype frame thicknesses of 1.125 in–1.5 in, is a pretty good rendition of reality in miniature, try bending it – laterally. Not so easy, that – especially when you realise that, to replicate prototype behaviour, the frames have to deflect in this way under the side thrust imparted on them by the track.

The point is that *all* model loco chassis constructed in any of the fashions or materials currently on offer are rock-solid rigid compared to the highly flexible and comparatively flimsy prototype. Don't believe it? Take a trip to a preserved steam line, and observe the real thing; note especially the clearance between the back of the driving wheels and the face of the frames – the 'side-play allowance' to enable the engine to round curves. If it is safe to do so (loco dead and cold), try inserting a finger into this gap – if you can. The conclusion is that real engines get round bends by bending; we need sideplay of considerable extent to do the same thing – our chassis does *not* behave in the same way as the real thing at all.

This is, of course, just one aspect of chassis behaviour, taken in convenient isolation. But it is symptomatic of the conclusion that must soon be reached if the examination is continued: that a small-scale model locomotive chassis, made of materials of far greater relative rigidity, electrically powered by means of a geared transmission, having little mass and almost nil inertia, in no way resembles a massive, flexible structure powered by a reciprocating steam engine. In other words, it calls for a totally different approach to design.

A real loco chassis is far from straightforward, as exemplified by LSWR 'Adams Radial' No. 488, happily preserved on the Bluebell line. Here seen at rest c.1970, No. 488 has a sprung and equalised front bogie with side control, sprung drivers and a compensating beam each side, a rear radial truck, power and manual brakes, and gravity sanding gear. And that's before you even consider the bits that actually make it go! GRAHAM WARREN

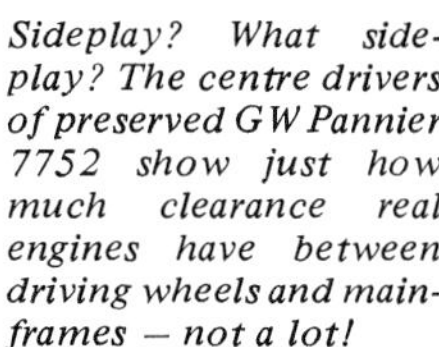

Sideplay? What sideplay? The centre drivers of preserved GW Pannier 7752 show just how much clearance real engines have between driving wheels and mainframes – not a lot!

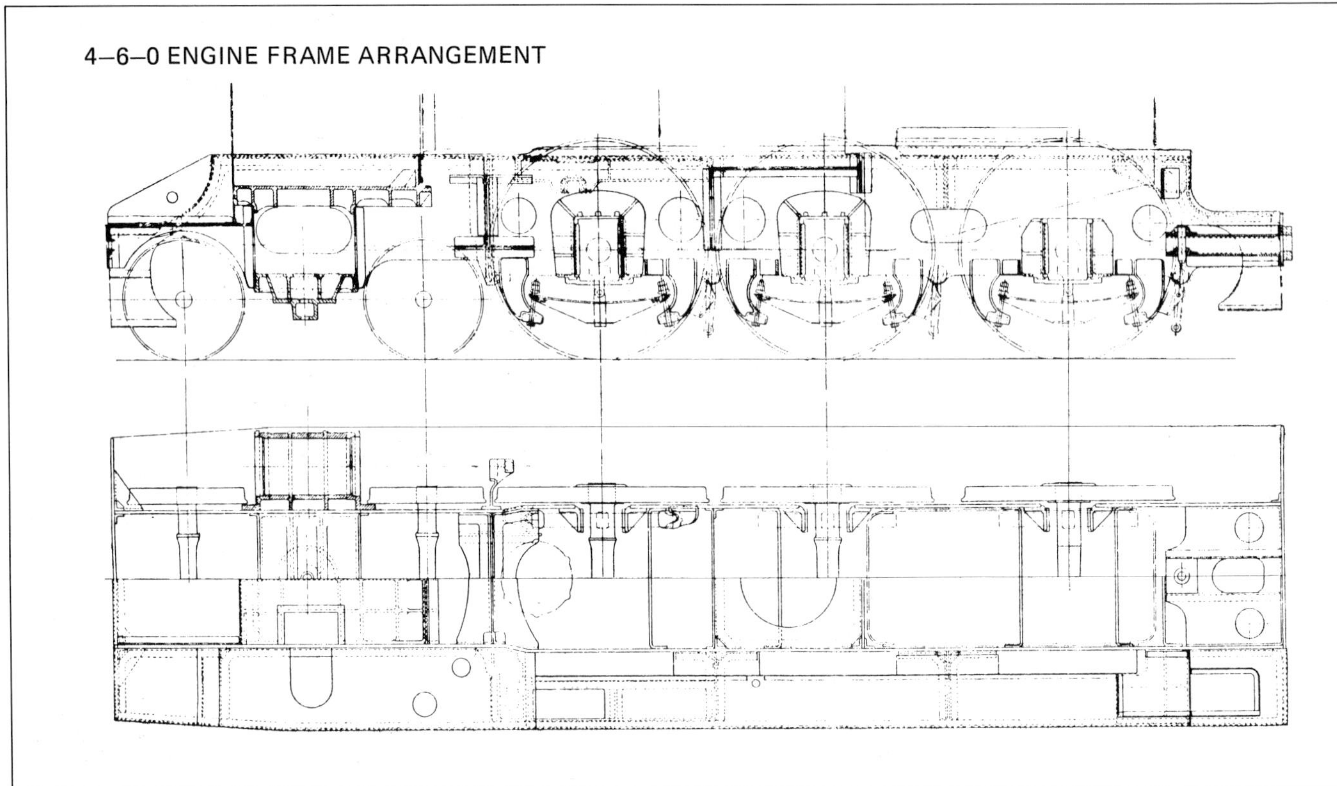

Nowhere is this more true than in the case for suspension systems, the aspect of model chassis design responsible for most of the fog. Leaving aside for a moment the pros and cons of the various 'model solutions' on offer, let us continue for a moment with our examination of reality. Whilst on your visit to the preserved railway of your choice, observe a locomotive in motion over the typical steam-age bullhead permanent way which we attempt to model for our historical model railways. What strikes one most forcibly is the amount by which the track 'gives' under the weight of the loco rolling over it (around 45 tons for a typical 0–6–0T – does your 4 mm model weigh 0.5921 tons, or 11.8 cwt – as the SIDR protagonist would argue it should, presumably?). It is this track deflection that forms the principal springing medium in the suspension of a real railway, *not* the loco springs, as is so often assumed. (Please note that I'm talking here of steam traction – modern diesels are fish from a very different kettle.)

So what of the springs? If not the primary means of suspension, what function do they have? Well, given that the constraints of the coupling rods, which limit vertical wheel travel on real engines to not much more than an inch (any further deflection being accommodated by those so-flexible frames twisting in cant), it is apparent that their role is secondary. They are, indeed, more akin to shock absorbers, accommodating the 'hammer-loading' resulting from such minor track inequalities as rail-joints and crossing noses, and helping to damp out the considerable oscillations that afflict a real steam engine on account of several tons of out-of-balance machinery flailing around – not a problem with the average well-regulated RG4! This is why most steam engines are 'sprung' by multi-plate leaf springs or coiled volute springs, types whose high internal friction renders them 'self damping'. Not much in common there with the coil-sprung hornblock much favoured by modellers!

Ken Northwood's 'King' – the uncompromising paradox. 2lb of lead, a big Pitman and 'sprung' track result in serious hauling power.

In fact, of the model loco suspension systems I have seen in action, one of the most generally effective has been that employed by my old mentor, Ken Northwood. Yes, you're right – Ken's loco chassis were as uncompromisingly solid as Grampian granite – but his flexibly-built track 'floating' on a soft road-bed of sponge rubber acted to a considerable extent like real track under the loadings imposed by Ken's locos, which aren't just solid, but seriously heavy. Those who have been privileged to see the Wills-kit-based *King Henry*

III start 'The Torreyman' – all sixteen heavy, metal-bodied, glass-glazed Exleys of it – from a stand on one of the North Devonshire Railway's 1 in 100 banks with barely a trace of slip and absolute smoothness of running, can be left in little doubt that a DC70 Pitman and a pound or two of lead in the right place are the equal of any amount of 1990s cleverness.

Of course, this is a solution that ignores a lot of factors, and is not without its drawbacks, notably in high mechanical wear and in current consumption. Start Ken's '72xx' with its '65 of mineral' on the drawbar, and lights go dim all over South Devon! The impressive results achieved are not entirely due to the efficacy of the motive power, either. Much care and effort has been expended in achieving great freedom of running in the rolling stock, Ken being a pioneer of the now-universal pinpoint bearing, while those stately Exleys roll on ball-bearing bogies. But the overall system works well, underlining the point that good design looks at the total system before examining any individual aspect in depth. A lot of people still prefer this simple, robust approach to model railway engineering, and, without doubt, it works well in the right application as Roy Jackson and the 'Dunwich' team continue to demonstrate.

Mike Sharman's infamous Flexi-chas demonstration track went to extremes to illustrate the spectacular track-holding potential endowed by the system (although only 4-coupled or single-driver types would negotiate the more fearsome of its dips, hollows and twists). The 'victim' in this case is one of several Mallard kit-based GWR '517' class engines that I built back in the late 1970s.

You will have noted that qualifier. As with all design solutions, it's a case of making the punishment fit the crime. The 'North Devonshire', 'Dunwich', Jim Russell's 'Little Western' and a host of other notable layouts have got along very nicely with never a hornblock on the property, due to a number of factors that may not apply in other circumstances. The first, most obvious point is that none of the aforementioned use modern finescale standards, either EMF or P4. The greater leeway permitted by the old BRMSB-based standards render a number of aspects of chassis design less critical than is the case with the more uncompromising approach now in vogue. The use of fine standards has, unfortunately, become somewhat associated with the didactic dictates of the 'Scale-it-down-regardless' school, which has tended to obscure the work and worth of that alliance of alternative engineers which I shall choose to call the 'Kitchen Table Pragmatists'.

This worthy band, amongst whose ranks I am pleased to number myself, take from the solid-chassis traditionalists, such as Ken and Roy, their insistence on a simple approach meticulously applied, whilst accepting that the closer adherence to full-size practice that lies behind finescale standards calls for an attempt to be made to replicate some aspects of full-sized chassis behaviour. Where the Pragmatic Party differs from the Scale-it-down-regardless Sect is in recognising that the replication of this behaviour will call for some quite unprototypical solutions, to get around the intransigence of our chassis when it comes to bending.

The 'chief Druid' of the pragmatists is Mike Sharman, never one to do anything the same way as anybody else ever did it. For all his little quirks (and to see just how quirky those are, just look at his nun's-knitting trackwork and weird-and-wonderful antique locomotives), Mike is both logical and methodical. And it is logic and method which lie at the root of the 'Flexi-chas' system which Mike developed, and which has now come to be the most widely-accepted form of non-rigid loco chassis. Unfortunately, it is also a widely-misunderstood system, which has led to some misapplications and misguided modifications; so I'm going to crave your indulgence for a brief and, I hope, comprehensible detour along these charmingly beamed-and-hornblocked byways.

The chief virtue of any successful suspension system applied to a model locomotive is that it will keep all of the wheels in firm and constant contact with the rails, to the great benefit of both traction and electrical pick-up. This, needless to say, the Flexi-chas system does without peer; but it has one further important attribute which is less well understood, and that is in its ability to compensate for the lack of flexure in the frames when traversing curved track, in that it allows for the vital independence of tilt between axles needed to accommodate the action of a coned wheelset (which all of ours now are).

I've already delved a bit into the action of coned wheels in my track book, so apologies to those who have been bored or baffled before. One of the chief purposes of the coning of railway wheelsets is to provide the 'differential' action needed when two wheels, of the same nominal diameter, both affixed firmly to a common axle, need to travel different distances whilst revolving at the same speed, which is the case when negotiating any curve in the trackwork. One of the properties of a coned wheel is that it can assume any diameter between the limits set by the minimum and maximum diameter of the coning, simply by moving sideways on the rail-head. Conveniently, with the opposed cones on the railway wheelset, a simple move to the outside of the curve brings an increase in effective diameter to the outer wheel, and a corresponding decrease in diameter on the inside. As a wheel of larger diameter will need to revolve fewer times to cover a given distance than a smaller wheel, then it can be seen that the wheelset will readily take up a position in relation to the track where no skidding of either wheel will take place while rounding the curve, *but only if the axle is free to tilt.*

Why does the axle tilt? Because the wheel at one end is now effectively bigger than the wheel at the other. And, if the design of the chassis does not allow independent axle tilt, as in 'solid' chassis or in those sprung or compensated designs where the axle-bearings can only move in the vertical plane (which is most of them), then the coning cannot work, resulting in skidding wheelsets, high levels of friction, and high side-loadings on the flanges, leading to a greater propensity for derailment. The prototype, of course, accommodates this small but necessary deflection by flexure of the track and the loco frames; the Flexi-chas bearing, with its V-section slot allowing each bearing freedom to adopt whatever angle is necessary in relation to the frames, compensates for our excess of rigidity in these components. The independence between axles ensures that, no matter what the situation of each wheelset is in relation to the track – on a curve or on a straight, traversing a dip or bump or whatever – the axle is free to take up the appropriate degree of tilt dictated by its circumstance, no matter what the rest of the chassis is doing.

The result is a chassis which runs more freely, develops more tractive effort, holds the track better, copes with inequalities and enables tighter curves to be negotiated without the need for excessive 'slop' or sideplay, either between the wheels and the frames, or between the wheelsets and the track gauge.

All this would be worse than useless if it called for a degree of skill and engineering sophistication way beyond that which is available to the average railway modeller. Which brings me on to the other shining virtue of the Pragmatic School's adoption of Flexi-chas – ease of use. By employing the coupling rods as jigs to set up the axles, any chance of waywardness in this vital correlation is greatly diminished. Even a scratch-built 'Flexi-chas' doesn't call for any great prowess at accurate measurement, marking or cutting-out. Building a modern commercialised kit version of the same system, as developed by Rod Neep in his influential 'Perseverance' chassis designs, is as easy as a good 'rigid' chassis, and a lot easier than a bad one, of which there are still plenty about. That the benefits more than repay the effort, whatever the scale or gauge, is something that I would argue strongly.

So what of sprung chassis, also to be found in commercial kit form? Well, I'm not going to say that they're an unworkable waste of time, as that patently isn't true. However, I would argue three points: firstly, that the majority of commercial sprung chassis don't work in the way that most people think they do, and that the proper design and construction of a truly effective sprung chassis is no simple matter. Doubters are referred to the writings in MRJ of Chris Pendlenton, who produces some remarkably effective examples of the breed, but not, be it noted, using any commercial coil-sprung hornblock. Mr. Pendlenton also comes from the North-East of England where, as is well known, they eat a lot of fish from an early age, which makes him,

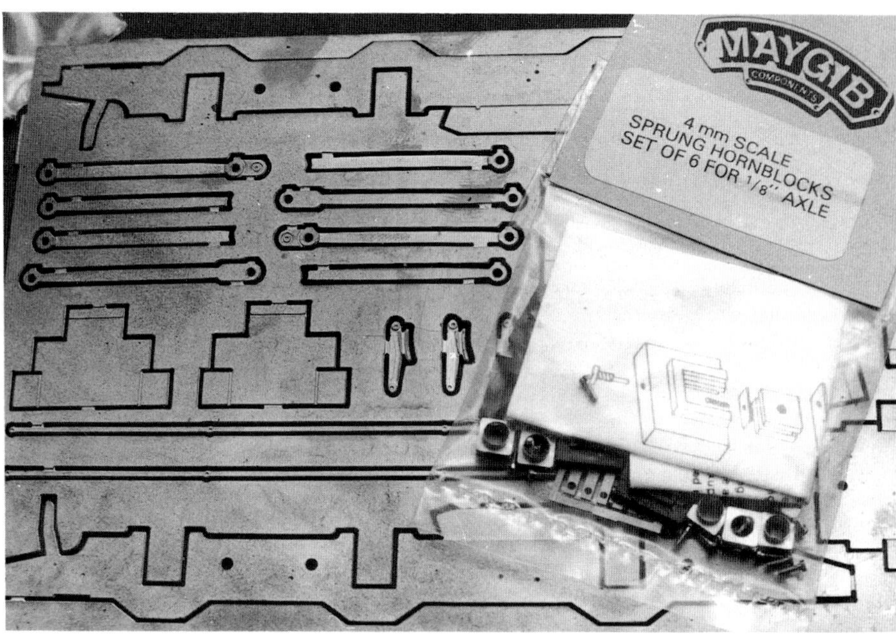

An early commercial sprung chassis kit by pre-Kean-Maygib, for the GWR '94XX'. The coil-sprung hornblocks were fiendishly fiddly and, having plastic hornguides, had to be stuck in place. Note also the holes in the frames for plunger pick-ups, which were part of the specification. High-tech stuff fifteen years ago.

like Jeeves, in need of a hat-size considerably above the average.

Secondly, I feel that commercial sprung chassis only address one aspect of the functioning of locomotive suspension, and don't attempt to compensate for any of the problems arising from the lack of flexibility in the track and frames. In particular, the lack of freedom in the tilting of axles seems to me to be no advance on a solid chassis, for a lot of additional complication. Thirdly, none of the commercial sprung chassis designs that I've come across so far address the 'ease of use' aspect. I've found a lot of them fiendishly difficult to install and set up. And, being possessed of but moderate ability in such matters, I'm always on the lookout for the easy way to do things.

So, for the purposes of this book, I'm confining myself to two basic chassis types, which, happily, predominate in the current generation of kits; the 'solid' chassis, preferably in etched metal, but not precluding the better cast or milled designs, and, hopefully, the increasingly widespread 'Son of Perseverance' chassis, capable of being built either as a rigid or, better still, as a flexi-chas compensated type. All this with the proviso that, as we now expect, I can apply the combination of motor, transmission, wheels and pick-ups that seem to me to best suit the occasion or the (usually parlous) state of my bank account.

Before getting down to the nuts and bolts of chassis construction, it occurred to me that a briefish 'historical review' of developments in model railway locomotive chassis design in the popular scale might prove instructive and possibly amusing. I'm a great one for recognising my heritage as a modeller, and in tracing the course of evolution that has led to the highly-developed contemporary 'state of the art'; it's also regrettably true that not a few of our kit-makers are stuck several rungs back down this 'evolutionary ladder', and that what might be termed 'mediaeval' design practice can still readily be found. But let's have a look at the starting point for all this tortuous development.

A BRIEF HISTORY OF THE AHERN LOCO CHASSIS

'In the beginning', we are told in the Good Book, 'was the Word'. The Word, in this case, being written by the late John Ahern, in the form of a modest little volume entitled *Miniature Locomotive Construction*, which for a good many years comprised virtually the entire literature upon the subject, at least in 4 mm scale. There are many remarkable things about this pioneering work, not least among which is the fact that nowhere in its 170-odd close-packed pages is there any mention of the importance – the absolutely vital, fundamental importance – of ensuring that the centres of the coupling rods and those of the axles that they are coupling match accurately. This is a dimension that the prototype quotes to tolerances of a few thou, and one whose relevance to a sweet-running model loco chassis can't be over-stressed.

I asked Ken Northwood about this, as a senior member of the hobby with experience going back to the late 1940s, when Ahern was writing. 'Ah,' said Ken, chuckling, 'I'm not surprised about that. I don't think Ahern knew much about things like that.' And, as a sotto voce aside: 'The old Madder Valley, it never ran very well, you know; not very well at all.' Indeed, re-reading Ahern, much of the mechanical side of his methods seem a touch dubious, although he's adamant about getting things square and meshing the gears properly. Strange, though, that his influence on chassis design lasted so long, and was so widely accepted without question.

Among the first loco kits (perhaps they were the very first?) to be marketed were the old Jamieson sheet-metal models, which were provided with 'pure Ahern' chassis – frames of 1/16 in brass with massive brass spacers, plain drilled holes for axle bearings, coupling rods from unadorned code 95 bull-head rail, the most approximate of outlines, and a total lack of any sort of chassis detail. Where they were in advance of Ahern was in their use of an accurate jig-drilling system to get the necessary exactitude in the relationship of coupling-rods to chassis. Generous frame cut-outs and hefty mounting plates (more 1/16 in brass plate) were provided to suit the contemporary motors by Romford and Zenith, Taycol or Jennings – motors of considerable heft but surprising refinement. With all this substantial brass about, (designed for solder-assembly using ordinary tinman's solder of about 240°C melting point) building a 'Jamieson' chassis called for *serious* heat, either the kitchen gas-stove or one of those 'Valtock' meths blow-lamps, ever an uncertain ally. It was not exactly easy to carry out minor adjustments, or to correct errors!

For the rest, Jamieson kits provided you with cast whitemetal cylinders and stamped-out nickel-silver valve gear with cast cross-heads – pretty presentable by the standards of the day. But that was as far as the cosmetics went; one looked in vain for such vital appendages as brake, sanding or springing gear, guard irons, ashpans and all the rest of it. The incorporation of such fripperies in 1/16 in brass plate is a pretty daunting prospect, so it's perhaps not surprising that intricate frame outlines, lightening and access holes and other such subtleties are also notable by their absence. This was all in accord with Ahern, although I notice from pictures that he wasn't above tacking on a guard-iron or two in his wilder moments.

Mind you, an original solder-assembled Jamieson chassis was robust in the extreme. Nothing short of a direct hit from a round of 88 mm HE armour-piercing would distort or damage the basic frames, while the jig-drilling and the use of pre-quartered (Romford) or jig-quartered (Hambling) driving wheels made for free running. The strength, rigidity and general accuracy of the chassis also made for good gear meshing, while with the use of flangeless centre drivers accepted as normal on six or eight-coupled chassis, not much sideplay was needed to get around typically confining model railway curves. Pick-ups were usually minimal on 2-rail chassis (a lot of 3-rail still around at this period), with insulated wheels on Romford-fitted locos being confined to one side. Even Hambling wheels – which had Bakelite spokes separating brass centres and rims – were often shorted out rather than using extra pick-ups. Most of the contemporary motors had only one insulated brush, so there wasn't a lot of point in trying to arrange an electrically-dead chassis.

So, the starting point for 4 mm chassis design practice was a mechanism of solid simplicity, functional but with little pretence to any aesthetic accomplishment. The next development to appear came with the birth of the whitemetal loco kit in 1957, when K's brought out the 14xx. These early K's chassis were also paragons of solidity, with a slotted brass sideframe screwed to a massive casting, which acted as a combined keeper

Model railway pre-history! Pre-dating any *kit is this entirely hand-made mechanism, which features fretted brass wheels, a chassis of channel-section brass, home-brewed motor, and a spur-and-bevel drive using clock gears. It still goes!*

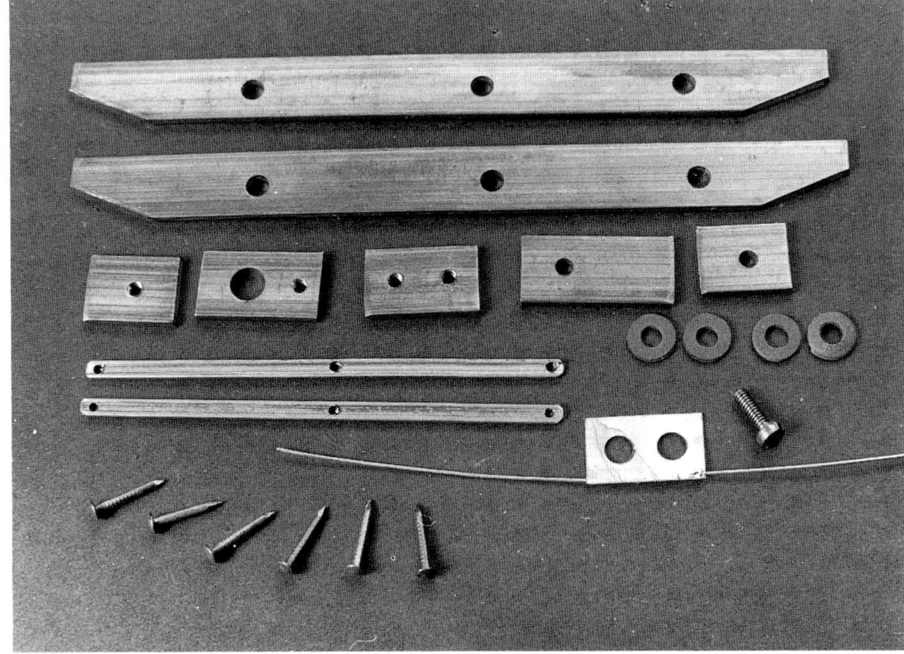

A Jamieson chassis kit for the '57XX' Pannier no less – an interesting comparison with the latest etched version from Puffers that figures elsewhere in this book. Reliable engineering in the Ahern tradition, if a trifle lacking in prototype fidelity!

plate and frame spacer-cum-motor mounting. This was good engineering, although the actual retention of the motor by a single 6BA screw was decidedly less than clever. But there were high quality steel-and-brass gears and some very nice driving wheels – nickel-plated brass with hub insulation on one side. These came pre-mounted on their axles, and chassis assembly was very simple. The coupling rods were of stamped nickel-silver, jig-drilled (not always too accurately, in my experience), running on very neat shouldered turned nickel-silver crankpins with 14BA retaining nuts, a distinct advance on the brass nail and turn of fuse wire then generally used with Romford wheels; Hamblings wheels were always superior in that respect, having turned brass crankpins with neat retaining washers.

Unfortunately, for reasons of cost or production expediency or whatever, K's soon compromised their chassis, and were responsible over the years for marketing some very dubious designs, including such blue-chip non-starters as fibre frames and single-point motor mounting on screwed frame spacers, offering just about nil gear-meshing restraint! Pity, for there was much to admire in many of those older K's bits. The chassis illustrated here is an EM Dean Goods mechanism – K's were EM pioneers – built by Pop Keyser himself for Pat Garland in about 1961; it ran for over 25 years before wear reached unacceptable levels.

When Bob Wills entered the fray with his 'Finecast' kits in 1958, he took a fresh look at chassis design, and came up with the one-piece cast chassis block fitted with brass top-hat bearings. The accompanying rods were either of stamped nickel silver or, later, cast in a special strong whitemetal alloy. Either way, the important thing was that both rods and chassis were accurately jig-drilled, and good correlation was always a Wills strong point. Mechanical design on most Wills chassis centred around the Rovex/Triang/Hornby (née Zenith) XO4 motor, a very sound piece of design among whose many good points were a proper 2-point lug-and-screw mounting system. Wills capitalised on this to give consistently accurate gear-meshing. The only real weak point in the Wills design was the pick-up system, a fanciful piece of whimsy involving an 8BA screw, two fibre washers and a tag to which the phosphor-bronze wiper strip was soldered. It worked considerably less well than the Soviet economy. Wills cast chassis were not as solid as the brass-framed designs, which made them less robust but a lot easier to add detail to.

A lot of subsequent purveyors of cast-whitemetal locomotive kits have copied the Wills-style cast block chassis, unfortunately usually without the refinement of design and care in manufacture that Wills brought to bear. In particular, the need for the accurate jig-drilling of chassis and rods was often not appreciated. Whitemetal castings are not dimensionably stable, tending to shrink on cooling by variable amounts. It is not possible to obtain reliable and accurate axle location by casting-in holes to frames, but plenty of people have tried, with results ranging from the simply dire to the absolutely disastrous. Any kit incorporating a chassis of this type should be viewed with the jaundiced eye of suspicion; any kit incorporating such nonsense as separate cast whitemetal sideframes either glued together or screwed to brass spacers should be left severely alone, at least so far as its chassis is concerned.

Vintage K's, c.1960. Cast block with brass sideframes, original K's Mk I 'long' motor, K's 35:1 gearset, and those nice nickel-plated brass wheels. Chassis for a Dean Goods in EM. Below: *Wills cast chassis block.*

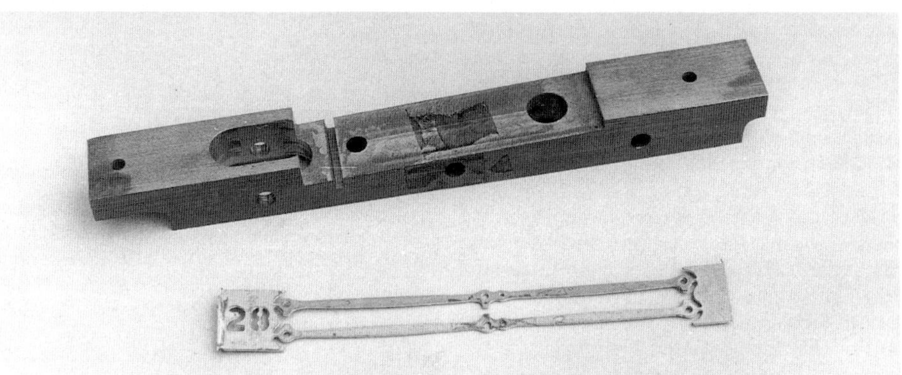

The most solid of solid chassis – a milled brass Cotswold effort, designed around the X04-type motor and Romford gears. The rods are etched in nickel-silver, and rod-to-chassis matching suffered from these disparate manufacturing processes. The prototype fidelity of this '16XX' Pannier chassis is no better than the early 1950s Jamieson '57XX', and certainly doesn't do the excellent cast body of this loco any favours.

The next departure in kit chassis design came from Cotswold, who acquired a hefty milling machine and set out to mill one-piece cast-style chassis blocks out of solid brass. These were the ultimate in rigidity, but were very crude in outline (not really surprising) while trying to solder on brake gear or other detail called for a small nuclear reactor. The accompanying rods were produced by the coming process of photo-etching; unfortunately, they didn't always match the chassis too well, a fundamental defect that torpedoes any hope of decent running with a direct hit in the engine room. These milled brass chassis are a good example of what can often happen in the model railway business when one aspect of chassis design is pursued without consideration of other factors, of equivalent or greater importance.

At much the same time as Cotswold were chewing out their solid brass lumps, the diametrically opposite approach was being

An early etched chassis, that of my first Mallard '517', c.1974 – OO gauge, rigid, with an Airfix 'Slimline' motor and Romford 40:1 gears. The forward mounting of the motor was an attempt to keep the cab clear, but it cost the daylight under the boiler. Oh for a Mashima 1224 in 1974! Compare this with the '14XX' chassis illustrated in Chapter 10 to see what progress the intervening 18 years have wrought. CHRIS CHAPMAN

evolved by those two pioneers of photo-etching, Fred Blackman at Mallard and Tony Dyer at Kemilway. Here was a revolution indeed! Chassis that were, like the prototype, of relatively thin plate, attached to fabricated spacers; chassis that could be put together with an ordinary soldering iron, which incorporated things like ashpans, guard irons and an accurate outline in their basic design, and made proper provision for details like brake gear and sandboxes; and, in the case of the early Kemilway efforts, chassis which incorporated suspension systems of fearful complexity. No matter, the Mallard 'Duke' chassis and Kemilway's 'Battle of Britain' design for the old Kitmaster/Airfix plastic kit were the first of the new breed. In the twenty or so years since, the etched chassis has effectively rendered all other types obsolete, and these days offers a near-ideal solution to the problems inherent in designing model locomotive chassis that work well, look right and are easy to build.

I have already mentioned Rod Neep and his 'Perseverance' chassis, which has been refined over the years and still sets a standard for sensible design allied to ease of use. The incorporation by Rod of 'Flexichas' into the Mallard/Kemilway style of chassis produced a system that offered a reasonable best of most worlds. The increasing sophistication of the etching process, allied to the introduction of computer-aided design and other state-of-the-art originating techniques, now gives the potential for simply-assembled, accurate and prototypical chassis. Allied to modern components – high quality wheels and crankpin systems, lovely delicate etched valve gears and rods incorporating proper articulation, super-smooth can or coreless motors and properly designed and produced fine-pitch gearsets – we can produce something that comfortably eclipses the performance of all

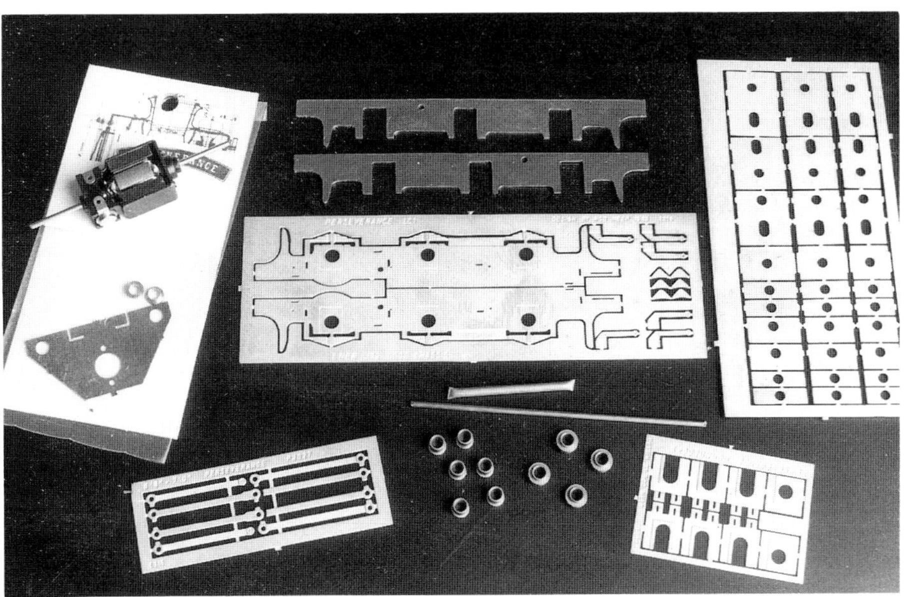

Two generations of Perseverance chassis, in this case for the LNER 'J72'. The upper set of frames has been cut from brass some 1mm thick using a profile-milling machine – a technique still used by Alan Gibson to produce frames for a very wide range of locos on a 'one-off' basis. These aren't really chassis kits, unlike the etched version also illustrated. This has all the features of the state-of-the-art kit – fully-detailed frames of correct outline, provision for rigid or compensated construction, fold-up L-section spacers, a free choice of motor and mounting system (recommended components were DS10 on fold-up mount illustrated), and detail refinements like brake gear. A long way from Ahern.

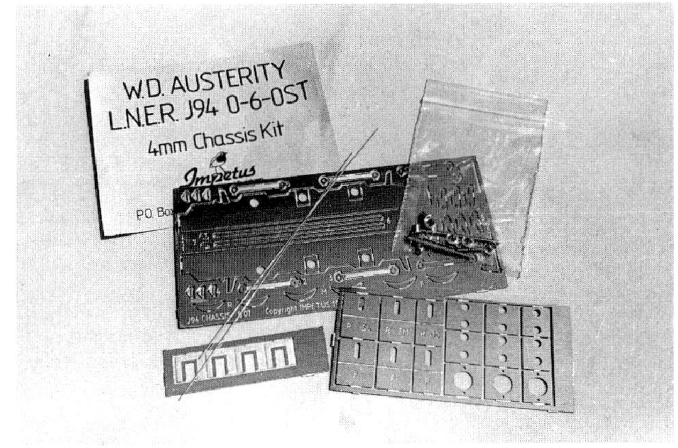

Son of Perseverance many other kitmakers have adopted the basic design precepts evolved by Rod Neep in his Perseverance range. Here is a typical and excellent example, the Impetus chassis for the Hunslet 'Austerity' 0–6–0ST. Etched in nickel silver with rods on the chassis fret, easy-to-remove hornblock cut-outs, fold-up spacers and a refined type of hornguide, it incorporates minor but useful improvements on the Neep original.

but the very best Ahern-type conventional chassis, and looks about three hundred per cent more realistic.

Note that I said modern production and origination give us the *potential* for these chassis; far too often, design ineptitude or plain sloppiness introduce anomalies and daft, unnecessary compromises that result in chassis that are nowhere as good as they quite simply could be. I illustrate a goodly few examples of such nonsenses in the coming chapters, and I find it disquieting that we still have to put up with poor design and lack of proper product development even today, when sound design principles are so well established. If we were a bit more discerning, a bit less afraid to be 'un-British' and moan a bit when we came across such 3-dimensional balderdash, then perhaps things might improve still further.

But there's much to be thankful for, and many truly excellent products to enjoy. We've come a long way from Mr. Jamieson's bits of stamped brass strip, and the chances are that we can provide most of our model locomotives with a chassis that will match in quality and appearance the truly excellent upperworks provided by both contemporary R-T-R makers, and by the majority of etched, cast, or composite loco kits. So, before departing for the practical realm of the workbench, I'd just like to summarise the end-result of the forty-plus years of evolution skimmed through in these pages by describing what I would consider to be the current 'state of the art' in model locomotive chassis design.

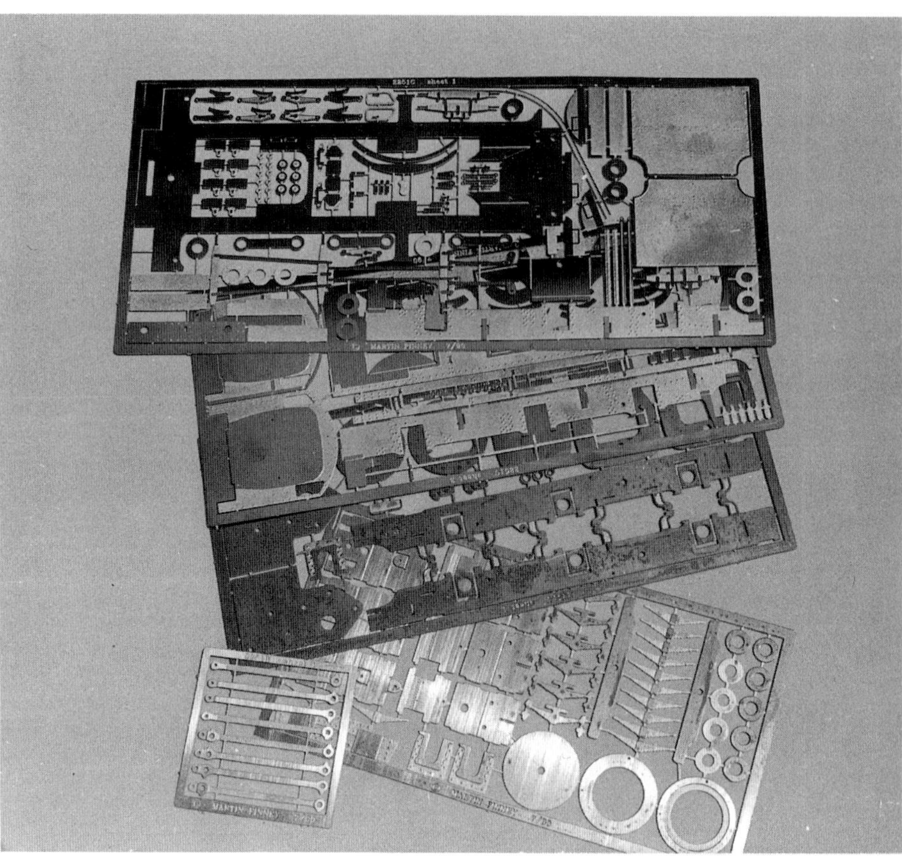

The cutting edge – chassis designs for the new breed of etched brass super-kit have introduced further refinements to the basic Perseverance-style kit. Here are the components and instructions for the chassis of Martin Finney's GWR '2251'. The provision of fully detailed frame overlays and a greater amount of applied detail make for considerable complexity. Even alternative gearbox sides for the recommended Escap/RG4 are included. Instructions are clear and comprehensive. Note alternative compensation schemes.

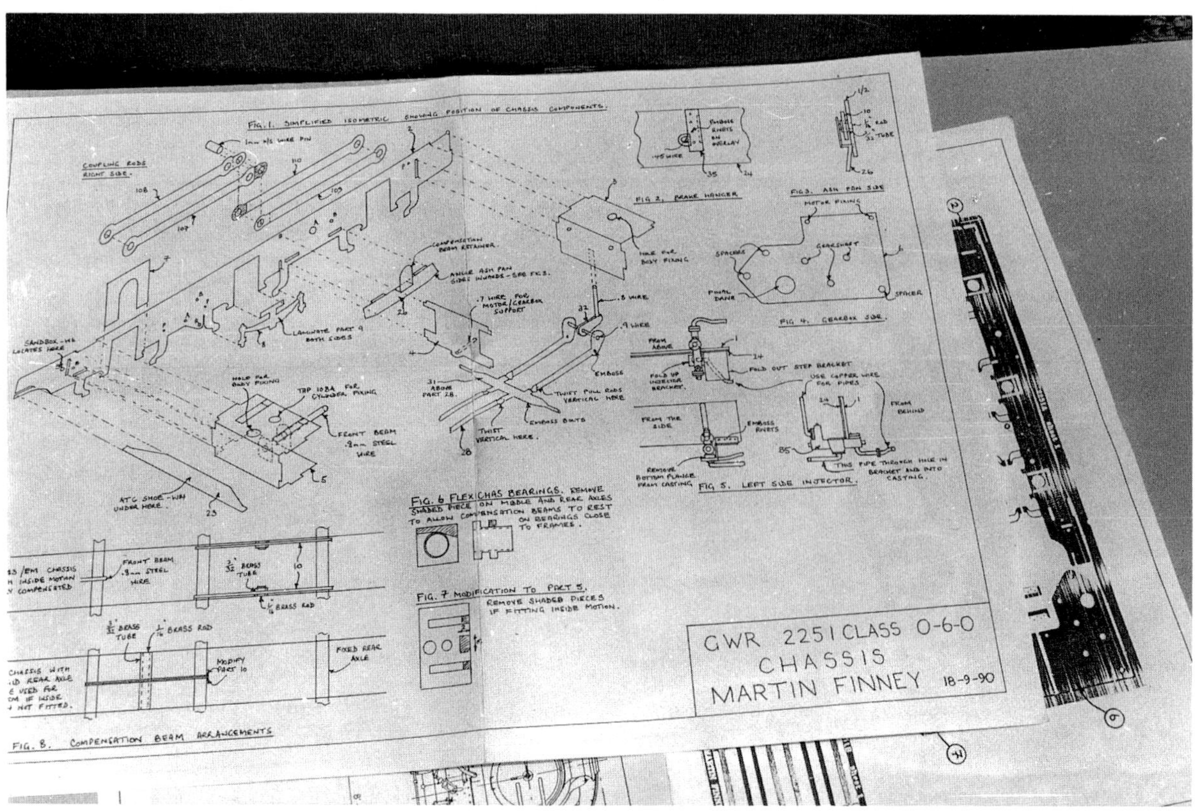

THE VERY MODEL OF A MODERN MODEL MECHANISM

That the best chassis kit is etched, preferably in nickel-silver now goes, I think, without saying. Why nickel silver? Not through any intrinsic virtue of the metal in terms of structure or properties, but rather because it is a reasonable colour to represent coupling rods; and, in the context of the basic 'solid option' which the modern chassis should seek to accommodate, I'm far happier seeing both frames and rods on the same etch, preferably in direct alignment, than separated. That way, the axle-centre/coupling-rod-centre relationship should be spot-on, the only possible starting point for a sweet-running chassis.

The coupling rods themselves are very important components, and their proper design is fundamental to a good kit. They should be in sections, jointed on crankpins for simplicity. Sectional rods are easier to assemble accurately, facilitate quartering and trouble-shooting, and make a model loco much 'easier' on curves, as well as accommodating the vertical wheel movement that will occur if suspension is applied to the chassis. But even on a rigid mechanism, they give better results than one-piece rigid rods; this is especially true on

Still with the '2251', the R-T-R Mainline version in this instance, we see the difference that a correctly-modelled chassis makes. Top: *the standard item, straight out of the box. The second photo is the same body moulding on a Perseverance chassis, to EM gauge, and fitted with Sharman wheels. The tender, too, has 'Percy' running gear.*

All of a piece. The modern loco kit, in this case an Alan Gibson 'J15', has a uniform standard throughout, giving a result that is pleasing and well-balanced. The chassis is in keeping with the level of detail and fidelity to prototype of the superstructure.

eight- and ten-coupled engines. Hornby, Fleischmann or Pacific Fast Mail would never attempt a multi-axle coupling rod, with all the high-quality manufacturing facilities at their disposal. Why a cottage-industry kitmaker with only the most basic of equipment thinks he can go boldly where these paragons fear to tread is one of the abiding mysteries of the business.

The frames themselves should, of course, be of accurate outline so far as their visible portions are concerned, and contain any lightening or access holes the prototype might possess. They should incorporate axle-holes designed to take a turned brass bearing, and situated in clearly-marked and easily removable 'lands' to facilitate the application of suspension systems if the purchaser so desires. There should *not* be any gaping cut-outs for motors; the 18–20 thou thickness of modern etched frames will give room for a wide selection of motors to go *between* the frames, even in OO. And the days of single-choice, take-it-or-leave-it motorisation designs are past. Most modellers these days have their own ideas on motors, and expect a number of viable options.

Frame spacers are also critical components, and need careful design to ensure accurate frame alignment and adequate support in both the vertical and longitudinal planes. These conditions are best met by the L-shaped spacer, preferably with either groove or tab-and-slot location in the frames. I do not like turned screw-in spacers – unless the screw-holes in the frames are an *exact* fit on the screws, then there is no accuracy of alignment, while the area of the end of the spacer in contact with the frames is often insufficient to provide adequate support. I also recall that that which is screwed is apt to unscrew – not too helpful for reliable longevity. The screw-heads look awful, too.

Choice – as wide as possible – should be the byword of modern loco kit chassis design: the freedom and facility to opt for a rigid, sprung or compensated version of the chassis; to build it for OO, EM or P4 at will, with the necessary spacers provided and clearances built-in; to fit the motor and transmission of the builder's choice (which does not stop the kitmaker pushing his preferred motorisation package in his literature); to accept any of the available wheel types; to have some provision for at least two alternative types of pick-up; and to provide a full and comprehensive range of chassis detailing components, which the builder can always choose to leave off!

Cylinders and valve gear are always a problem area, for both the designer and builder of the kit. There is no doubt that the trend to etched, fabricated cylinders gives a better result, but they are quite tricky to assemble when compared with the cast alternative. Similarly, fabricated as opposed to cast crossheads give superior results for greater effort, and may be one area where alternatives could be provided. Walschaerts valve gear has long been the 4mm scale loco-builder's *bête noire*, but good design, combined with modern high-quality etching, can make it as easy as possible.

Lastly, of course, the state-of-the-art-kit will contain state-of-the-art instructions, well-illustrated with clear diagrams, well laid out, and written in the Queen's English. Things are getting better, but this particular branch of the art is still woefully neglected.

To see just how the kit on the model-shop shelves measures up to this theoretical ideal, it's time to take the lid off the box and take a look at what you will actually be faced with...

CHAPTER TWO

ASSESSING A CHASSIS KIT

In an ideal world, all loco kits would have a chassis designed along the lines just described, and I wouldn't be writing this chapter at all. That they haven't goes, I fear, without saying, so I'm afraid you'll just have to plough through this lot unless you are fortunate to have lit upon a kit from one of our more enlightened makers. Those worthies known to me include Perseverance/Westward, South-Eastern Finecast, George Norton, Malcolm Mitchell, Martin Finney, Impetus, Steve Barnfield, Brassmasters, Kingdom Kits, London Road Models, Peter K, Albion, and some outfit called Riceworks. There are probably a good few others that I've missed off this impromptu list, to whom apologies.

So, given that we are dealing with less than the ideal, what in particular are we looking out for? Well, so far as our traditional coupled-driver steam loco is concerned, what matters above all else is the accurate correlation of coupling rod and coupled axle centres. As I've already stressed in the last chapter, and will stress again here, an exact match is VITAL. Nothing, no dodge, tweak or fiddle, no motor, however mettlesome, or wormgear, however worthy, will compensate for a mismatch in this fundamental relationship. One of the towering advantages of the Flexichas system is that, by setting the axle centres using the coupling rods as a jig, it ensures that this crucial relationship is correct. It is a problem that *must* be addressed by the kit designer, and watched over with hawklike vigilance by the manufacturer.

This is why, as I've already mentioned, I like to see etched frames and rods on the same fret, which means that they will have been drawn on the same artwork and photographed together in the production origination stage. Any error, whether in the measuring or the drawing, or in the optical and process sequence, will be common to both frame and rods, and their matching will thereby be ensured. However, many makers do consider it an extravagance to etch an entire chassis in nickel-silver (which is about 50% more expensive than brass of equivalent thickness) just to safeguard this aspect of the design, and have opted to etch the frames in brass but the rods in nickel or even, in one or two welcome cases, in steel. Given due care in the origination process, particularly using computer-generated artwork, there is no doubt that the necessary accuracy can be obtained, so that finding separately-etched rods and frames in a kit, while it may sound a warning bell, is not necessarily a cause for alarm.

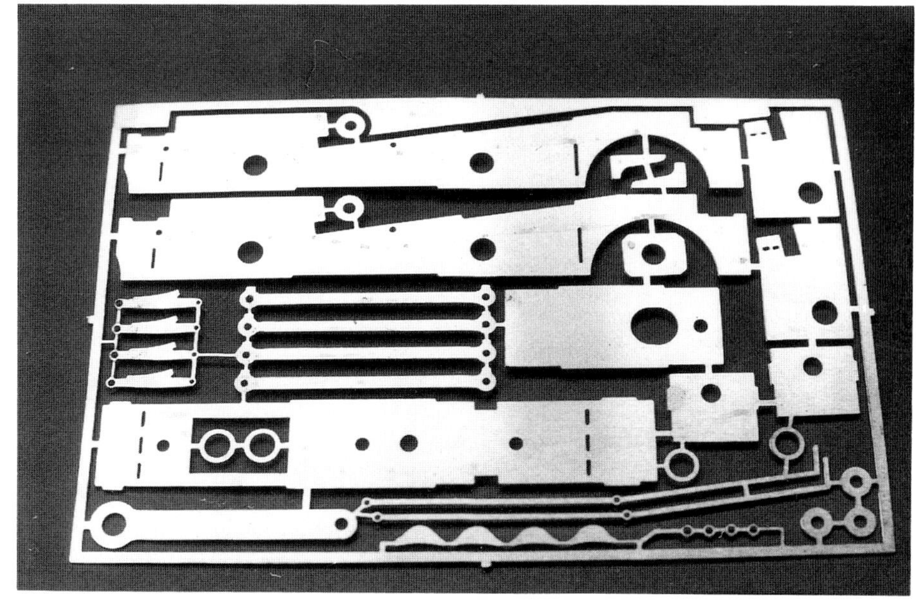

Good news and bad – the chassis of the Craftsman LNER 'C12' 4–4–2T. The good news is that the coupling rods are on the chassis artwork, in line with the axle holes. The bad news for EM and P4 modellers is the 'OO only' frame spacers, motor cut-outs for X04-type motors, reflecting the era in which it was designed. The brake gear made up nicely, though.

However, it does suggest the first and most elementary check that can be applied to any such chassis, which is simply to compare the coupling rods to the frames. There are a number of ways in which this can be done, but the simplest involves a pair of dividers. Set these so that the points are both touching the same side of the coupling-rod holes, ie., both to the front or rear; now offer up the dividers to the frames – the points should also just touch one side of the axle bearing holes. *Fig. 1* should make this clear. Repeat the check for all rod sections and pairs of axle-holes. This check will reveal any errors, and the extent of such errors. If the mismatch is

Fig. 2:1 USING DIVIDERS TO CHECK CHASSIS/ROD CORRELATION

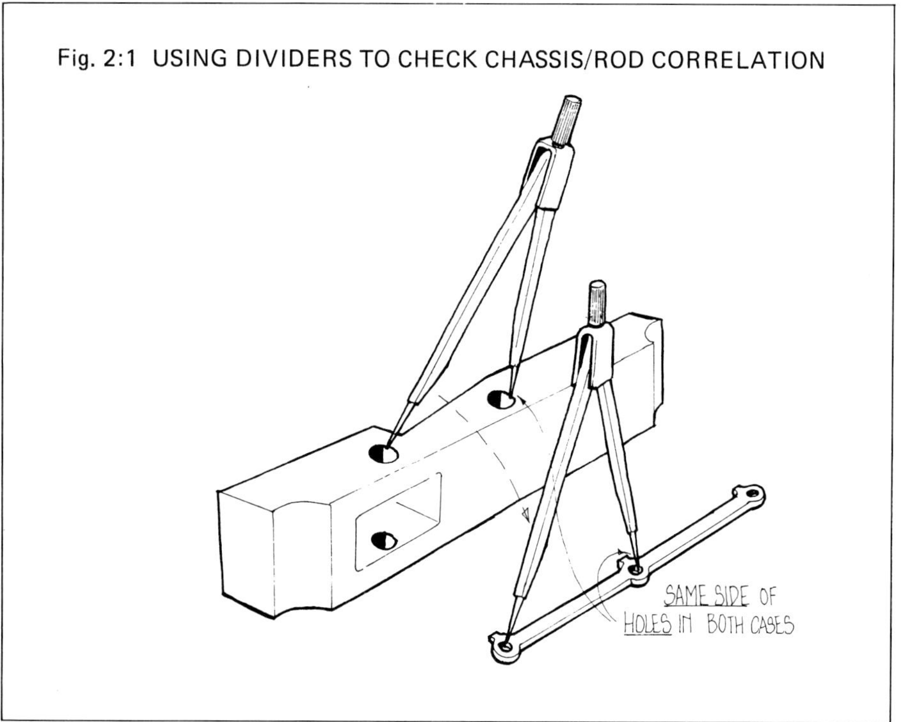

The DJH 'West Country' kit.

slight – a few thou perhaps – then it can be corrected simply. If it is greater – $\frac{1}{2}$mm or more – then it will be more difficult to put right, but should still be possible. If the error is gross – a millimetre or more – then I would consider the kit fundamentally flawed and not of merchantable quality. If, as I would advocate, you have taken your dividers along to the model shop or trade stand to assess the kit *before* purchase, you can then exercise one of the most fundamental of all chassis-building choices, by opting not to build the thing at all. If the body kit looks reasonable in spite of the dud chassis, order a superstructure-only kit if this can be obtained (it usually can). If, however, you get no joy in this direction, you are left with two alternatives: to buy the whole kit, and junk the chassis in favour of an alternative, or to walk away and buy something more worthwhile. These days, I usually exercise the latter option.

These strictures apply, of course, only to 'rigid' chassis kits, where there is no built-in facility to adjust either rod or axle centres. If you're going for a Flexi-chas, you can overcome errors of even the 'gross' proportion described above (although I would be most unhappy to have to do so!). I have to say that I find the frequency with which kits exhibiting such a fault reach the market most disturbing, as it can have only one explanation; the manufacturer either doesn't know, or worse, does know but doesn't care. Either way, he deserves a sharp kick in the pants, while those makers who take no action in the face of such abysmal quality deserve to make the better acquaintance of the local Trading Standards Officer, as their goods are most decidedly 'not of merchantable quality'.

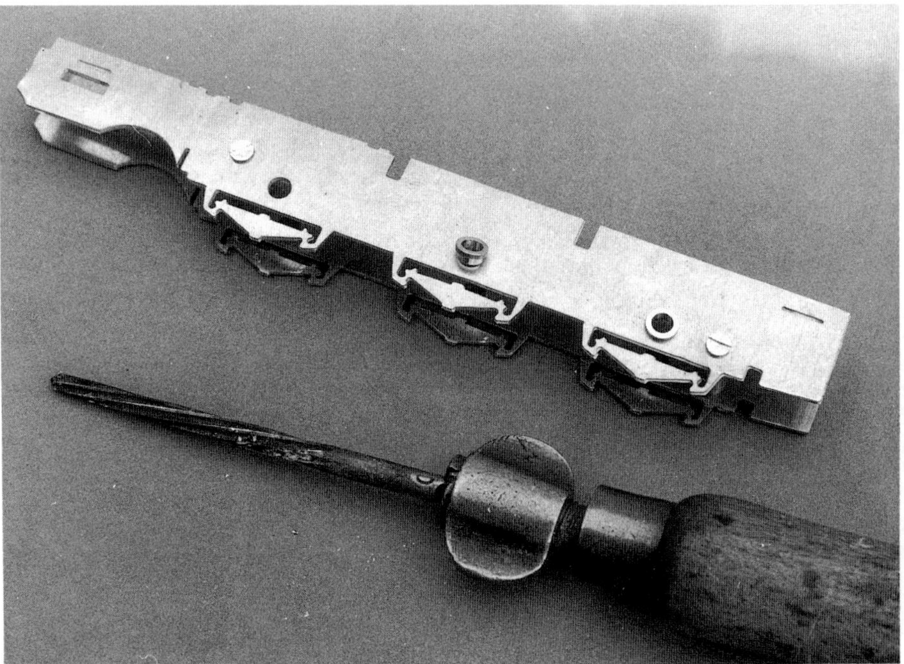

Not a fault – a hole too small for a bearing, as here, is no bad thing. It's a simple matter to ream for a fit, but an awful problem if the hole's too big!

I have gone on a bit about this business of rods matching frames, not only because it is so essential to the success of the chassis, but also because it is a pointer to the likely quality of the rest of the kit; if the makers can't get the basics right, what chance is there for the twiddly bits? The probability is that a kit which reaches the market with such a grievous shortcoming has not been properly developed. Indeed, I know a few chassis kits which have been placed on the market without a running test version ever having been built! Quite apart from the ethics of this sort of thing, I would have thought that, in the face of ever-tighter consumer protection legislation, such actions constitute a commercial folly of no small order. But still it goes on, and still I meet people who profess to being such poor modellers that they are quite incapable of putting together a chassis kit that is merely quite unworkable – for which shortcoming they blame themselves! The Americans wouldn't wear it, and on the Continent, one or two kitmakers have found themselves in court to answer for just such misdeeds. Me,

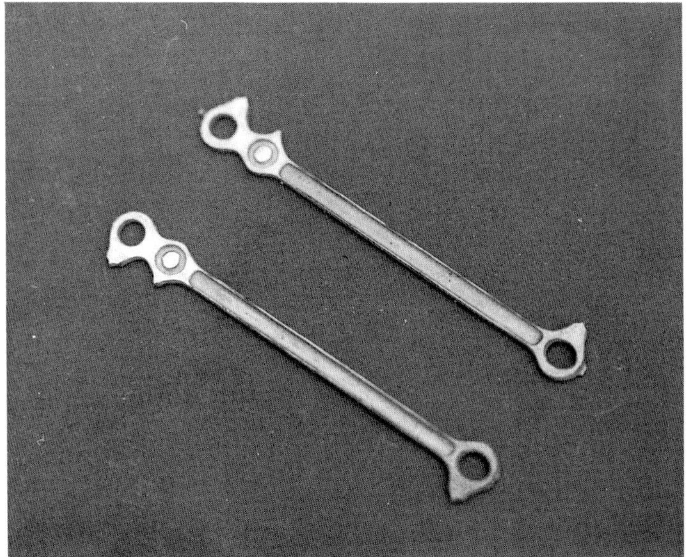

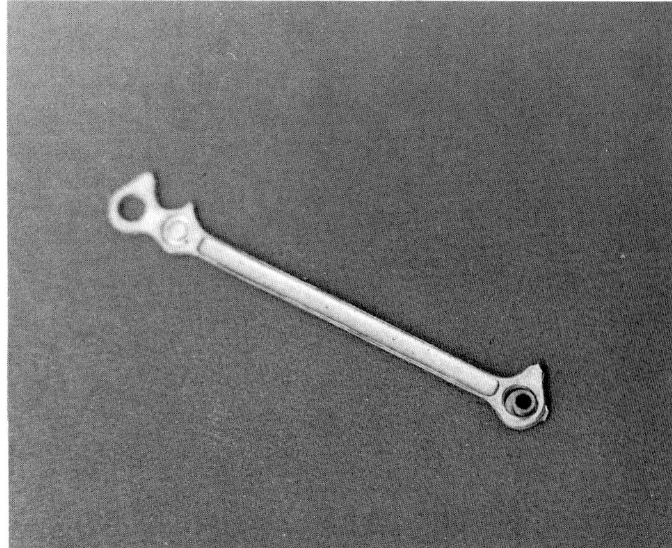

Horror story! These are the rods of the DJH 'West Country' as they came. And yes, that crankpin bearing is one of those supplied in the kit. This degree of slop, notwithstanding the odd shape of the holes, would render any chassis unworkable. I've got locos with 20 years of running behind them without this much slack in the rods! Unacceptable, but not, alas, uncommon.

I just fire off vitriolic letters, as one or two of our kitmakers will know; I suggest that you do the same in similar circumstances!

Right. Having got that lot off my chest, I'll move on to the other main factor that can easily render a chassis unbuildable and unworkable: holes. What can go wrong with a hole? Well, two things – it can be in the wrong place, and it can be the wrong size. Holes in the wrong place are self-explanatory, and are very largely what I've already been talking about. Holes of the wrong size really come down to one thing, holes that are too big. It is one of the most basic tenets of the most rule-of-thumb type of engineering that, while it is a simple matter to make a hole a bit bigger – or even a lot bigger – it's the very devil of a job to make it a bit smaller. Kit designers who have the least clue what they're about take good notice of this elementary bit of common nouse, and ensure that all holes, but most especially those for critical components like axle-bearings, crankpins, and screwed frame spacers, are made a touch on the tight side. The modeller can then gently ease the hole out until the required component is a nice exact fit. Unfortunately, a lot of etched kit-designers have a rather rose-tinted view of the accuracy of the process, and try and etch things 'dead to size'; while this is theoretically possible, given spot-on quality control, in practice the slightest degree of over-etching (which etchers tend to err in favour of, to ensure that all components are properly pierced-out) will result in the side-cut taking the hole oversize.

It won't take much reflection on the implications of, say, an oversized axle-bearing hole to realise that a sloppy fit can soon lose you that vital rod/axle centre correlation, landing you right back in the soup. Similarly, coupling rods that flop around on their crankpins with umpteen thou of float will make an utter nonsense of the most painstaking and accurate of wheel-quartering. About 5–7 thou of play is necessary and desirable – vital on compensated chassis – but 10 thou and more are a disaster. Just the other week I found a cast kit with nearly 40 thou (a full 1 mm or 3 in at full size) slop on the coupling rods! Utter rubbish – and that was a £100+ kit! Vitriolic letter duly sent...

To add insult to injury, the holes in these rods weren't just grossly oversize, but were far from round, resembling in shape some form of blighted pear. This was, I must say, a new one on me, and I would charitably infer some problem with the etching – dirt on the positives, perchance? Or some damage to the photo-tooling? Possible – but in view of the fact that not just one, but several of the holes were thus distorted, unlikely. Once may be misfortune, twice be coincidence, but three times smacks of downright carelessness; I had five funny holes out of six, which leads me to the inescapable conclusion that they were drawn like that on the artwork! I despair...

So, take a good look at your holes. Offer up an axle-bearing, and try it for fit; tight is great, hole too small fine, a wee bit of slop (1 or 2 thou) acceptable (see 'corrections' section in a page or two). Anything else is a waste of time. Strictly speaking, it is quite possible to rectify even the most grossly oversized of holes, by reaming them out, turning a bush, force-fitting or soldering it in place, and finally reaming it to be the size hole that you should have started out with in the first place. This does not, however, fall within the scope of the sort of kitchen-table workshoppery about which this book is based; and, let's face it, if you're skilled enough and well-equipped enough to undertake that sort of operation, then you're not going to waste time putting right some kit-maker's cock-up when you could build yourself something a great deal better!

If you find that coupling-rod holes are a very sloppy fit on crankpins, before calling down curses on the kitmaker's head, do just check that he hasn't included some nice little turned brass 'top hat' crankpin bushes to take up the difference, a sound design practice that is fortunately becoming more widespread. Mind you, these aren't an unmixed blessing, as you've got two lots of slop/tolerance to worry about – fit of bushes on crankpins, and fit of rods on bushes. Again, the maxim might be summarised as 'tight is good' in both cases.

Other holes that can have a critical bearing on chassis assembly and mechanical integrity are those relating to turned frame spacers, and anything to do with motor mounting and gear meshing. Screw-holes for turned spacers have a crucial role in accurately aligning the frames, and, once again, slop is bad news, as you can end up with lateral misalignment, with the axles no longer held at right-angles to the frames. I never rely on turned spacers as sole location and retention for the frames, as will be revealed shortly; but if the fit of the parts is so poor that they can't perform the primary function of basic frame alignment, what on earth is the point of the things in the first place? This is one of those cases, quite common in model loco building, where something that superficially appears easy to use is actually a potential problem; 'easy-fit' devices that don't fit are anything *but* easy!

The same can be said of quite a few of the super-clever fold-up etched motor mounting devices, which call for very accurate design and manufacture if they're to work well. Motor-boss and screw mounting holes that are sloppy fits are obviously unlikely to provide accurate and consistent meshing for the gearsets, and to work properly, worm-and-pinion gears need firm and precise location, as I shall hope to explain. Fortunately, the modern trend in chassis design is to provide the motor-mounting/transmission as a separate item, very often not included in the kit at all, which does at least enable you to go looking for a good one.

More DJH, in this case the frames for their BR Standard Class 3 Mogul kit, the upper portion of which is lovely. But the frames are thick etchings in 36-thou brass with, as can be seen here, a heavily-cusped edge and motor cut-outs.

FRAMES AND SPACERS

These are the very foundations of the whole loco, so their quality is obviously of paramount importance. Most modern kits use etched mainframes in material of some 18–20 thou thickness, set onto some form of fold-up spacers, which is basically a very sound design. Locating the spacer in either a half-etched groove on the inside of the frames or using cornflake-packet-model type tabs and slots will ensure accurate alignment, although once again we're looking for a 'tight' fit rather than loads of slop. It's also worth checking the frames against each other for an exact match; left and right frames should be photographically produced opposing twins, but some makers draw them separately, and errors can creep in.

The various one-piece chassis blocks, be they cast or milled, have the obvious advantage of combining sideframes and spacers in one indissoluble unit, which should be pretty accurate and wholly symmetrical. The big snag with one-piece chassis blocks, apart from their unprototypical appearance, is that only one width of chassis is possible. Which, obviously, is going to suit under-gauge OO, leaving EM and P4 modellers with frames that are palpably too narrow, which looks awful and calls for umpteen spacing washers on each axle. I have also yet to meet the solid block chassis that is compatible with any form of compensation, or offers a free choice of motor/drivetrain configuration.

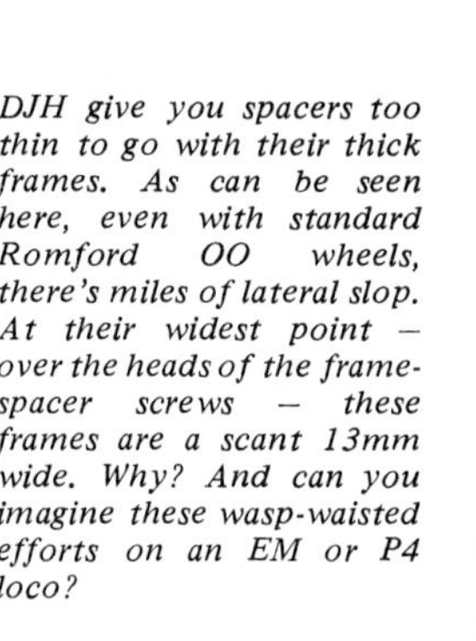

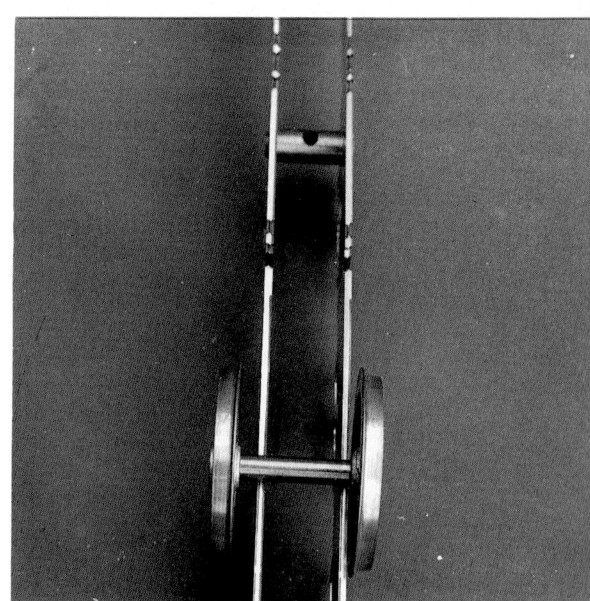

DJH give you spacers too thin to go with their thick frames. As can be seen here, even with standard Romford OO wheels, there's miles of lateral slop. At their widest point – over the heads of the frame-spacer screws – these frames are a scant 13mm wide. Why? And can you imagine these wasp-waisted efforts on an EM or P4 loco?

Mind you, the purveyors of one-piece cast or milled blocks don't enjoy a monopoly of daft frame-width dimensions. DJH, who like to style themselves our 'leading loco kit manufacturer' (which in some ways they may well be, producing some quite exquisite castings), provide only a single turned spacer of 10 mm length in their loco kits, the needs of EM and P4 modellers being evidently deemed of no account. They also, for reasons which I fail to understand, use frames etched in brass no less than 36 thou thick, characterised by cusped edges and side-cut in all the openings. A little arithmetic will give a total width for the frames and spacers of a bit under 12 mm, to which must be added the rather hefty collars of

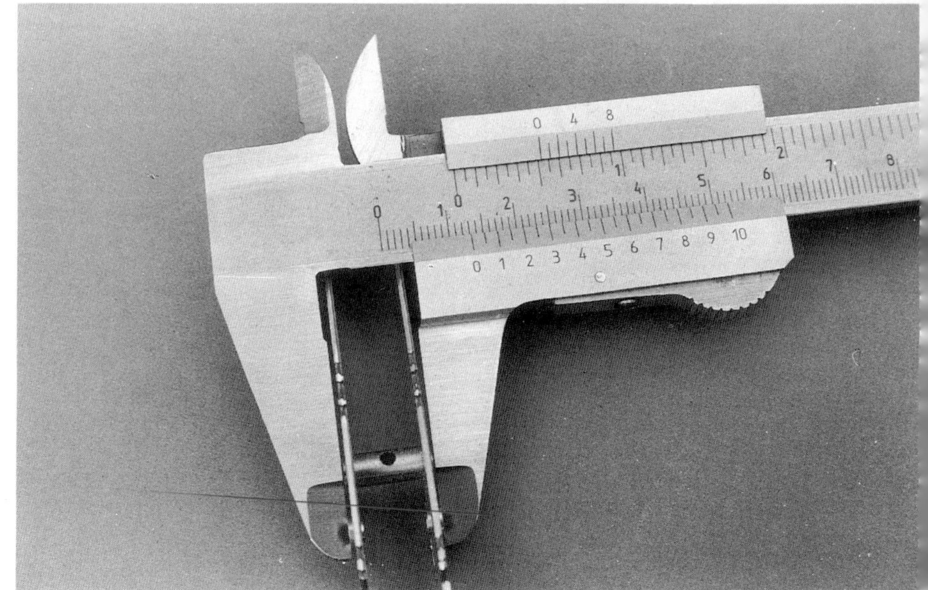

the top-hat axle bearings supplied. Even so, the result is still the thick end of 2 mm sideplay even with standard BRMSB-width wheels. One wonders what radius of curvature is envisaged as the 'design standard'. I have to say that I have been disappointed with the design of DJH chassis and experienced a number of problems with those I've built.

Quite a few makers do settle for one 'wide' spacer to suit both EM and P4, which is generally more acceptable, as the difference in dimensions is not nearly so marked as between coarse 'OO' – still on Ahern's half-inch frame width – and P4 purists on 17 mm, getting on for half as wide again. Fortunately, it's not too difficult to conjure up a set of home-made frame spacers of the simple 'L' type, as we see in a page or two – which is just as well, as there are still a lamentable number of kit-designers producing chassis which, while they may be made by using 1990s etching technology, are still designed along 1940s lines, OO only and full of compromises. There are quite a lot of one-piece 'fold-up' etched chassis around – M & L were very fond of them – which, like so many supposedly 'user-friendly' ideas, introduce as many drawbacks as they overcome, and pose a real headache for the EM or P4 builder. Again, I find myself amazed at this. With the strength and vigour of the 'finescale' end of the hobby, arguably the only sector that has shown consistent growth in the last decade, it is surely commercial folly for so many makers to ignore even their most basic needs?

Not as easy as they seem – screwed, turned spacers have a number of significant drawbacks to set against their apparent ease of use. Apart from being miles too short, these DJH spacers (typical of the breed) show just how little support, in terms of area in contact, they give to the frames. And look at that machining burr on the specimen at the right.

Other matters that might require rectification in the mainframe area include unwanted holes or cut-outs to be filled, clearances to be checked and adjusted, and cosmetic deviations to be corrected. It is difficult to generalise on these points, so I've described these sort of mods as I encountered them on the various chassis I built whilst preparing this manuscript. For

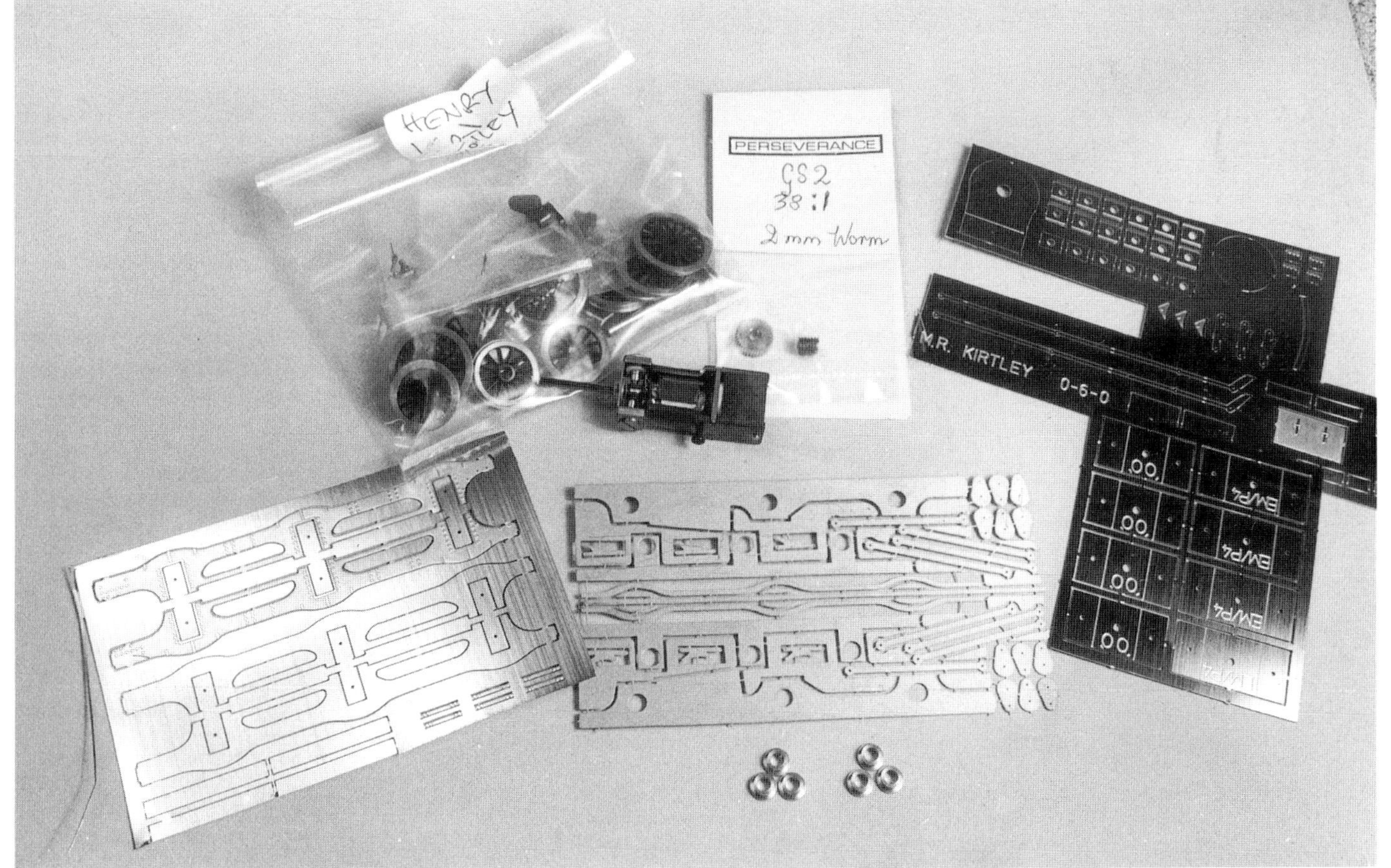

Another type of chassis that leaves a great deal to be desired – in this case by Falcon Brass for their MR Kirtley Goods 0–6–0. This, believe it or not, was supplied with screwed spacers, but no holes in the frames into which to screw them! Note the 'outside cranks', also arranged for 'DIY' (drill it yourself), the crude coupling rods, lack of any provision for compensation, and waste metal needlessly tabbed into the middle of the cut-outs of the outside frames. There were also, as can be seen, some nasty sharp pieces of fine fret waste attached to the edge of the outside frame etch, on which I duly stabbed my thumb. Is this a kit? And is it 'of merchantable quality'?

Time spent capturing the 'look' of cylinders and valve gear of a prototype like this 'Royal Scot' would contribute significantly to the character of any finescale model of such a handsome engine.
W. A. CAMWELL

the record, by the by, there were nearly a dozen 'guinea pigs', ranging from the Peter K '1361' GWR 0-6-0ST, through the Impetus 0-6-0 diesel shunter chassis and a Perseverance GW Mogul, to a DJH rebuilt 'West Country' Pacific, mostly in P4, but with some EM and a couple in OO, just to be catholic about it all.

CYLINDERS AND VALVE GEAR

There are many modellers of my acquaintance who, while they will happily churn out inside-cylinder 0-6-0s until the cows come home, quail at the thought of outside cylinders and, worse still, Walschaerts valve gear. However, as they can't all model the Midland in pre-Compound days, sooner or later most of them come face to face with a naked valve gear fret and a pair of cylinders. It is a fate that will befall us all, one day; so what is there to look out for?

Apart from general considerations of quality, there are a number of new pitfalls introduced where outside cylinders are involved, of which the most awkward and intransigent is clearance. Given that, on many a prototype loco, the head of the leading crankpin clears the back of a coupling rod or the rear of the crosshead by well under an inch (around 13 thou in 4 mm scale, if everything is to scale, which it isn't), the potential for problems on a model is obvious. Things would be bad enough if the kit designer took account of these matters, but I find that it's often not only ignored, but compounded by compromised design. It's Ahern and OO at the bottom of it again, I fear; at least it is in those cases where the clearances are all set up for 16.5 mm gauge, with no allowance for EM or P4.

I'll start by describing the ideal, and then I'll take you on a tour of the chamber of horrors. Ideally, any outside cylinders, with their associated slidebars and bracketry, should be designed as a separate, self-contained unit separate from the frames, so that vital dimensions such as overall width and cylinder centres are not affected by incorrect or differing frame spacings. Those kits so designed do at least ensure that the plane of operation of the crosshead is in the right place, where it will be well clear of undergauge OO wheels, and hopefully will also give enough room to sneak in wider

Cylinders bracketed direct off the frames, as on this DJH 'S15' in OO gauge, are OK until you need to alter the frame width – as for finescale OO, EM or P4. Then you gotta lot of filing to do . . .

The cylinders of a Blacksmith LBSC 'K' Mogul, made on a stretcher as advocated, but set at a spacing suited only to 'OO', and incorrect at that. Although there were slots in the cylinder stretcher for EM frames, the result of fitting the assembly to an EM chassis can be seen in the second picture. Negative crosshead clearance? Did anybody ever test-build this one, I wonder? How did they do it? The mind boggles!

gauges if the builder desires. After all, whether you like it or not, OO is the most compromised gauge for 4 mm scale, so logic would surely dictate that the OO gauge version of any kit will inevitably be the most compromised. Apart from anything else, too much clearance in OO can hardly be held to constitute a vice, and is often a virtue.

But what is this crookened and wizened thing crouching here in the blood-red light of the chamber of horrors? A cylinder bracketed off the mainframes? Hideous! Why? Because, if said cylinder is arranged to be at the correct overall width when fixed to OO frames, it will be miles outside the loading gauge when those frames are spaced appositely for EM or P4. Alternatively, it may be set the correct distance out from the frames to scale, which means that in OO the overall width will be miles too narrow, and not even the OO modeller will enjoy decent clearance. Oh death, where is thy sting? And what is this dreadful thing, abject and abandoned, in a dark corner? It is a set of fold-up cylinders and valve gear, replete with slidebars and brackets, exactly as advocated a paragraph since – except that these cylinders are set at the centres corresponding to scale related to a OO chassis, for all that they have locating slots for EM frames, where the wheels and the crossheads will be on almost exactly the same centres. Aaaaargh!

The application of a little logic to the design of outside cylinders and their associated components can minimise the problems, while there are one or two wheezes to sneak a few thou of extra clearance. The recipes will be found in Chapter 8.

Walschaerts valve-gear should, these days, be less of a problem than it was back in Jamieson's stamped-out days, and the result, using the best of modern etching techniques, can be absolutely superb. Sometimes, it is – but there are still some serious faults to look out for. The first of these is simply to check that the valve gear you've been given in the kit is actually the right valve gear for the loco in question. This may seem so obvious as to be accepted without question, but there are still some manufacturers operating on a 'near enough is good enough' basis, who believe that a valve gear is a valve gear is a valve gear, and so what if the lifting links end up halfway across the middle driving wheels, or the wrong length of radius-rod has all the levers at funny angles? There are alternatives, and I certainly wouldn't compromise a model for want of the correct valve gear. But then, in 1992, I shouldn't have to . . .

The other common faults with valve gears are an excess of chunkiness, easy enough to correct, and over-large holes, almost impossible to put right. So, take a look at the relationship between the valve-gear rivet or pin or whatever is provided, and the hole it is supposed to fit. And yes, I have found etched valve gears where the holes were so oversized that the entire rivet passed through, head and all! However, the best of modern etched valve gears are very good indeed, and things like the MRJ etched LMS gear (which also suits some BR standard types) are well worth paying out for even over and above the cost of the kit; for the 'fillip' they give to the look of the thing, it's money well spent.

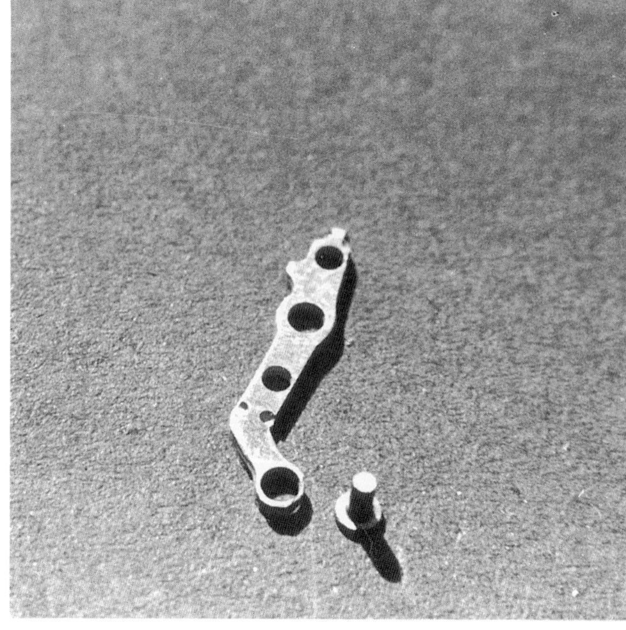

That DJH 'West Country' again, showing the considerable mismatch between the size of hole in the etched component and the shank of the rivet that is supposed to fit it.

MOTORS, GEARS AND PICK-UPS

Just the briefest of notes under this 'assessment' section, as this should be a matter of choice, and I shall have plenty to say on these matters in chapters devoted exclusively to them. However, when considering the motorisation of a loco, a couple of points are worth pondering. In all probability, there will be a suggested set-up, which will more than likely do the job. There is a tendency on the part of some makers to simply specify the pre-assembled RG4 coreless motor/spur gearbox set up – all well and good if you can afford it, and assuming that you have a suitable control system on the layout. But it's not everybody's cup of tea, and these days, comparable alternatives can be assembled at considerably less cost.

Do be aware, however, of potential mismatches of powertrain to model. Not a few of the makers suggesting coreless power for their model were advising the small, relatively low-powered Portescap 1219 motor (which is notoriously prone to 'sudden death' if overloaded) as suitable for big (like GWR 2–8–0 big) locos. Would you put a lawn-mower engine in a lorry? As a rule of thumb, the biggest motor that will conveniently fit is in all probability the most suited to the job in hand; but more, much more, on all this in due course.

Pick-ups are often either totally neglected or, at best, somewhat skimpily addressed, by most chassis-kit designers. As they are obviously quite crucial to the running qualities of any chassis, I have devoted a section in Chapter 11 to their provision, starting from the general premise that the kit gives you either nothing at all, or only something approximate. This will inevitably exhibit my own personal bias in this matter, so I'll come out now and nail my colours to the mast: I don't like plungers – at least, not any of the commercial versions you're likely to find in a kit – and I consider split-frame chassis to be a lot of complication for very little gain. So it'll be wipers plain and simple, with apologies to all those who may have bought this book solely to discover how all the other types might be made to work!

SUMMARY

This chapter has confined itself to the assessment of the mechanical and electrical aspects of a chassis design that are intrinsic in the design itself; the cosmetic success of the thing as a model is a matter of judgement, and some comparison with prototype reference material. As to such fripperies as the degree of detailing and the provision of cosmetic but non-working features, these are largely in the hands of the builder, and are certainly readily capable of improvement, addition or substitution. But that is again a tale for a later page; first, we must put right any fundamental functional ills.

CHAPTER THREE

CHASSIS CORRECTIONS AND CURES

I have been at considerable pains, in the last chapter, to identify the more prominent problems associated with locomotive chassis kits. As I hope will become apparent, most of these problems are capable of solution. As will also have become clear, I am strongly of the opinion that a great number of them should not occur in the first place, and the fact that they do is to a greater or lesser extent an indictment of the kit-makers, many of whom have, it would seem, never built a model loco in their lives. So, the first step in putting right the ills found in the box may well be a decision not to bother, but rather to look elsewhere for chassis components for the kit in question. This is an increasingly valid option, with firms like Perseverance, Comet, Impetus and Gibson producing chassis either for other people's bodies, or of general application.

Certainly, I have produced a good many model locos over the years by combining components from different sources. The old Maygib (now Gibson) MR '3F' 0–6–0 chassis, for instance, would suit virtually any post-Johnson Midland or LMS 0–6–0 tender loco, and I built things as diverse as Somerset and Dorset 'Scotties' and BR-period Stanier '4Fs' (from, respectively, K's and Wills body parts) on this utilitarian underpinning. Even now, there lurks on my workbench a GWR '57XX' pannier, with a 1965-vintage K's body sitting on a 1991-vintage Perseverance chassis, a combination producing a most pleasing result. The only snag in this approach may be an economic one, where you are already in possession of a less-than-satisfactory kit chassis where the kit comes complete. In which case, the question must be posed: 'Is the compromised result that will arise from the use of an indifferent kit chassis worth the saving in cash from not buying something better?' Or, to put it another way, is it not better to have a good chassis powered by a simple motor and gearset than an utter dud with an RG4?

However, we're not always dealing with utter duds, so with luck it may only amount to putting right a couple of trifling defects to turn a slightly dodgy chassis into a good bet. It is with this sort of attainable correction that I now intend to do battle, taking the faults in the same order in which I described them. Which brings us at once face-to-face with the most fundamental fault of all – the coupling rod/chassis mismatch.

CORRECTING ROD-TO-CHASSIS ERRORS

There are obviously two basic approaches to this problem; one can either make the rods match the chassis, or vice-versa. On the face of it, the former may seem the simpler option, but, assuming that the rods are otherwise OK, and that the chassis employs modern etched frames, I have found the reverse to be true. There is not much material to play with in the boss of the average 4 mm scale coupling rod, whereas mainframes give you plenty of scope to shift things about without 'coming out the side'.

Fig. 3:1
RICE TAPERED JIG AXLE

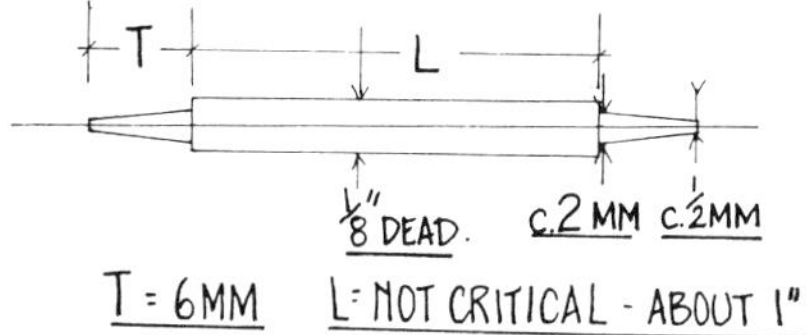

The key to this operation, and to a goodly few others to be described, is the 'jig-axle', a simple gadget that I think originated in the fertile cranium of Rod Neep. I have long had my own version of this, which differs from the Neep original in having tapered rather than parallel, fixed-diameter ends. A drawing of this simple gizmo appears alongside, and, with luck, by the time this book hits the shelves, a commercial version will be on sale; it is, I suggest, sorely needed.

The sole purpose of the jig-axle is to enable chassis and rod centres to be set-up and aligned exactly. Originally, it was conceived for use when constructing chassis along best Sharman principles, but I find it just as valuable when building rigid chassis. In the present case, we can use it to re-set the axle centres in the frames, by enlarging the etched axle-bearing holes slightly, and then using our coupling rods and jig-axles to get the bearings in the right spot, when they can be soldered in place. I generally find it easier to do this with the chassis assembled, when I proceed as in *Fig 3:2*.

Fig. 3:2. CORRECTING AXLE CENTRES IN A CHASSIS

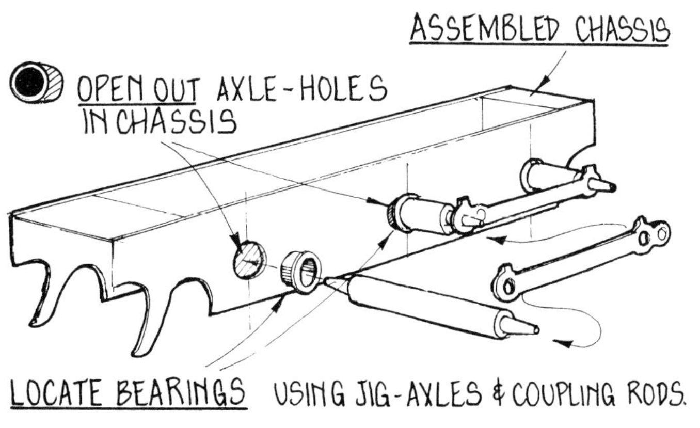

ASSEMBLED CHASSIS
OPEN OUT AXLE-HOLES IN CHASSIS
LOCATE BEARINGS USING JIG-AXLES & COUPLING RODS.

At least a pair of the invaluable jig-axles are needed, and in the case of six-coupled engines with one-piece rods, three are advisable. Before assembling the frames, I select one axle to act as the 'datum', which will not be touched. Where the error is of reasonable proportions (around the ½mm mark) I use an 'end axle', usually the rear, which is almost always the one I opt to drive. If the error is on the large side, it might pay to 'fix' the centre axle and spread the adjustment out both ways, to minimise the amount by which any individual bearing will need to be moved. Anyhow, so far as datum axle is concerned, it will simply be a matter of easing out the holes, should they (hopefully) need it, to take a pair of bearings, which are soldered in place. The remaining axle-holes are then carefully filed-out with a rat-tailed needle file to provide sufficient space to get the remaining bearings into the required locations. The rod/chassis comparison described at the beginning of the last chapter should give a pretty fair indication of the amount by which the offending bearings need to be moved – I find it useful to make a little thumbnail note to remind me, as in *Fig 3:3*.

Whilst correcting a rigid chassis by the use of jig-axles shares the virtue of spot-on

Fig. 3:3 NOTING AXLE CORRECTIONS

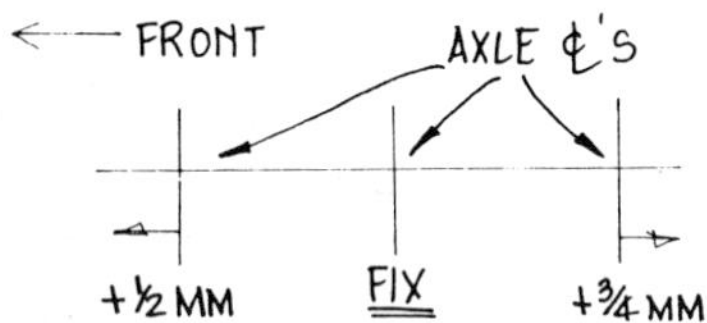

Fig. 3:4 SETTING CENTRE AXLE HIGH

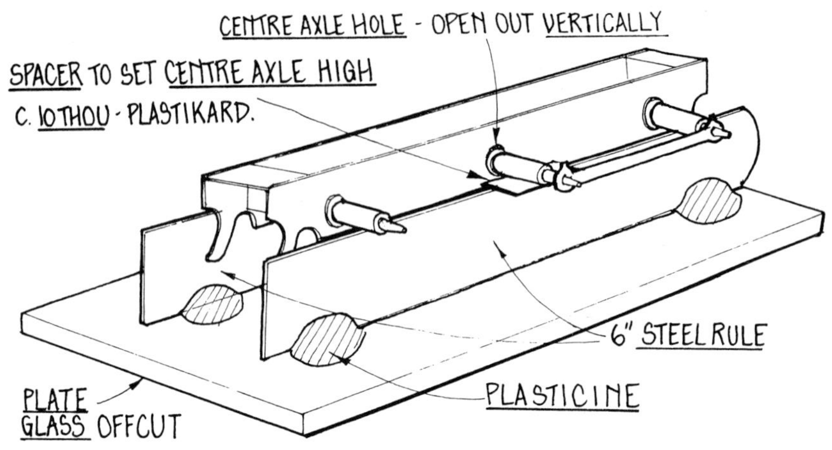

longitudinal accuracy with the same method used to align a 'Flexi-chas', it does not address the other critical alignment essential to the proper working of fixed-axle mechanisms – vertical alignment, which is, of course, of no consequence when the axles are free to move in this dimension. Specifically, what is to be avoided is the situation where the centre axle of a six-coupled mechanism ends up a trifle on the low side, which results in the whole chassis teetering about the middle wheels like a fat lady on stilettos after her fifth gin. There was for many years a sort of 'reverse tradition' of setting centre axles a fraction high, and I notice that some kit-makers still do this. Strictly speaking, it's bad practice, as it effectively makes any chassis no more than an 0–4–0 most of the time. But it is very much the lesser of two evils, and it is advisable to take steps to either get the axles dead in line, or to play safe with 10 thou or so of uplift in the middle. This I achieve by use of the simple cobble-up sketched in *Fig 3:4*, whose main ingredients are a pair of identical steel rulers and a bit of plate glass.

Figs 3:2 & 3:4 together should give the bones of the whole business of chassis-setting by this method. The jig-axles are lightly oiled to ensure that the solder doesn't make a bid to gum the works solid; I keep meaning to make myself some aluminium ones for this purpose, but ⅛in aluminium rod doesn't seem to grow on any trees in these parts. That is really the only possible glitch in the system, and it is certainly 100% effective at producing an accurate chassis. Really, I'm jumping ahead of myself a bit, in that it's an operation best carried out after the basic chassis has been assembled, and that's not on the slate until Chapter 4, but you don't really expect all this horse's-mouth stuff *and* a logical sequence, surely?

Given the comparative ease of shunting bearings about in an etched chassis, I would never contemplate trying to alter a set of coupling rods in preference. However, if the rods supplied are less than satisfactory in other respects as well as in their mismatch to the chassis, then a number of courses are open once we have opted to modify the frames. One of the simplest is to obtain a better set of rods from another source, and set the chassis up to match these. There are a pretty wide selection of good etched

Comparison of the coupling rods of the finished MR Kirtley Goods, built from the Falcon kit, with the raw items illustrated in the last chapter will show the benefit of a little titivation as described in Fig. 3:6. *The Sharman moulded-nylon outside cranks are also a pretty substantial improvement on the etched 'wishful thinking' provided by the kit. For good etched outside cranks, look to the Impetus 08 chassis.*

coupling rods on the market from a number of sources (see appendix) and, given the prevalence of standardised wheelbases on many railways, it's not difficult to find something suitable. The alternative, should you be building a kit for something a bit obscure, is either to bring the kit rods up to a satisfactory standard, as I did, for instance, with the 'Falcon Brass' M.R. outside-framed Kirtley goods that makes occasional appearances in these pages, or to make some new rods from scratch.

Whilst you're at the business of improving coupling rods, or acquiring some better commercial alternatives/brewing your own, it's well worth taking the trouble to divide the rods into two-axle groups, as described in Chapter 1. Even in the context of a rigid-axle chassis, the benefits in ease of running on curved track, and simpler quartering and chassis tuning, are well worth having. Strictly speaking, to follow full-size practice 'to the letter', we should not joint our coupling-rod sections on crankpins (at least, not for more modern locos; older designs often did just that), but should produce a working 'knuckle joint', either just in front of, or just behind, the crankpin. Some of the new generation of 'Hi-Fi' loco kits, such as the Martin Finney GWR 'Collet Goods' illustrated, do incorporate proper knuckles, but there's no doubt that a dummy knuckle-joint and a simple overlap on the appropriate crankpin is a lot easier to produce on our hypothetical kitchen table.

The actual improvements that may be applied to unsatisfactory etched rods come into several categories, both practical and cosmetic. In the practical context, apart from having holes of the right size in the right place, it is the small matter of strength that is of prime concern. One of the frequent failings of a lot of etched chassis kits is an attempt to 'get away with' coupling rods consisting of only a single thickness of 18 or 20 thou nickel-silver. Such rods, apart from looking decidedly undernourished (prototype rods are typically around $2\frac{1}{2}$–3 in thick, or about 30–40 thou at 4 m scale), will be flimsy in the extreme, and will inevitably get bent if the chassis is handled (and it will be; most of us soon learn to pick up our locos by the underpinnings rather than erode all the paint off the footplate edges). I've also discovered that several chassis apparently etched in relatively sturdy nickel-silver are actually horribly soft nickel-plated brass – not good at all for robust rods!

There is no doubt that a rod consisting of a sandwich of two layers of frame-thickness nickel with a filling of solder is several orders of magnitude stronger than any single-layer rod not milled out of solid steel of a roughly similar thickness, or fabricated out of substantial rolled section (ie rail!).

I think that I'm right in saying that virtually all the etched coupling rods now on offer conform to the desirable specification where two layers are laminated together, with a single-layer 'halved joint' at the appropriate place or places. Provided it's of authentic outline, such a rod will be quite satisfactory in service, and is not hard to use; just sweat the two halves together and clean up (see the section covering this in Chapter 6). Single-layer rods can be brought up to this specification in two ways. Where the rods are supplied as a separate etching, try asking the kitmaker for a second etch. The rods can then be cut and joined in a similar way to the purpose-designed article – again, this is covered in Chapter 6. If you don't fancy divided rods, or it's only a 4-coupled loco, simply solder the two sets of rods together. The second way is similar, but more bothersome, in that it involves soldering the rods to a second layer of metal of suitable thickness, which is then trimmed and filed to size, and drilled for the crankpins as appropriate (see the sketch). This is tedious but effective.

Cosmetic shortcomings are generally easier to address. The most usual one – rods too fat – is the simplest to correct, with a spot of judicious filing down, taking care to keep (or impart) the correct outline. The

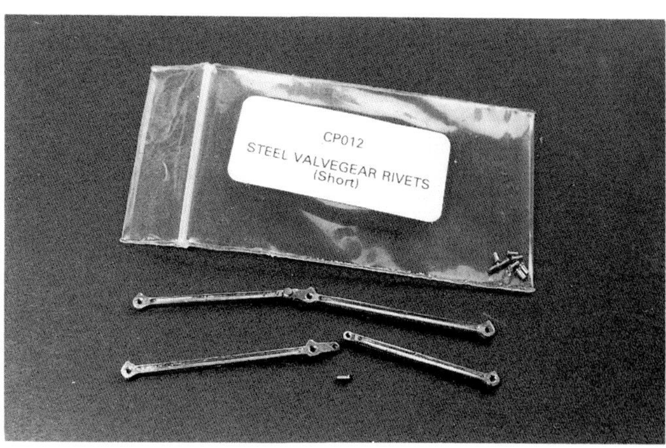
CP012
STEEL VALVEGEAR RIVETS
(Short)

Proper knuckle-jointed rods, ex-Finney '2251' kit. I prefer to rivet the joint with a valve-gear rivet, such as the Exactoscale items illustrated.

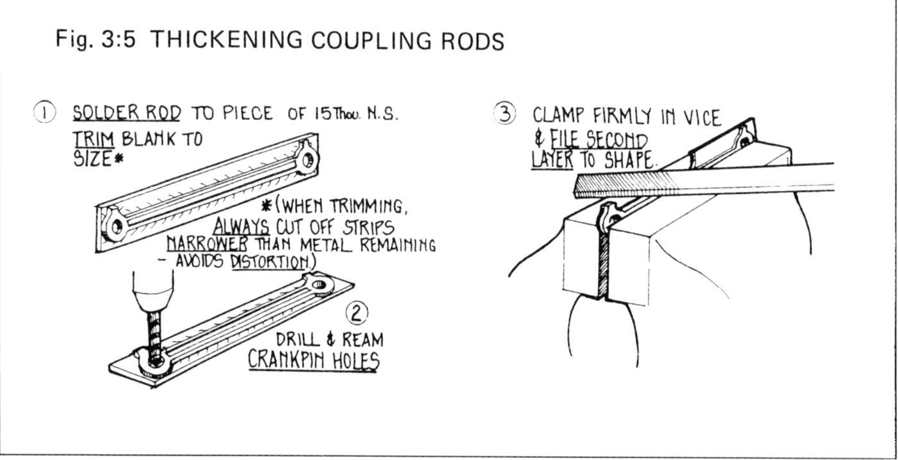
① SOLDER ROD TO PIECE OF 15Thou. N.S.
TRIM BLANK TO SIZE*
*(WHEN TRIMMING, ALWAYS CUT OFF STRIPS NARROWER THAN METAL REMAINING - AVOIDS DISTORTION)
② DRILL & REAM CRANKPIN HOLES
③ CLAMP FIRMLY IN VICE & FILE SECOND LAYER TO SHAPE.

Fig. 3:5 THICKENING COUPLING RODS

A little slimming can make a big difference to the look of an etched coupling rod, as these 'before 'before' and 'after' pictures of the long-suffering '14XX' should show. Many rods in current kits incorporate a 'finish filing' allowance, and look far too chunky if not dressed down in this way.

opposite problem, where the rods are too thin (quite inexcusable, but still quite common) is much more of a pain, as the only practical solution is a new set of rods. Skinny rods don't only look awful, they will also inevitably be knock-kneed. In the context of a modern chassis with etched rods, I would deem missing fluting (common in stamped-sheet days) unacceptable. It is possible to add fluting, but it's not easy, and I opt to replace the rods with something better, after sending the usual postal raspberry to the kitmaker.

This really leaves missing detail, usually in the boss area, to be added, as I did for the aforementioned Kirtley goods. The rods in this kit (OK for basic outline and general design, but having only simple circular 'dog-bone' ends) may be taken as typical of 'a suitable case for treatment'; the sketch shows how I went about adding the necessary 'meat' and detail to the bosses, with the aid of a few 12BA washers and some strip. The end result may not be perfect, but it is a lot more convincing than the originals. Mind you, why the originals were like this in the first place is a point to ponder.

It is only a relatively minor step from adding bosses and oil-boxes to some unadorned etched rods, to adding the same bits to suitable strip or section, pre-drilled at the appropriate centres, to create a set of rods from scratch. Bullhead rail has long been a traditional material from which to make fluted rods, and provided you're looking to reproduce rods with a depth of around 5–6 in, then code 75 does quite nicely as a starting point. As 5–5½ in is a very common coupling-rod dimension, I use rail quite often, filing the larger 'running' head down to match the smaller foot, giving a nice symmetrical 'I' section which is true to prototype. I also stick to prototype in using steel rail, which gives rods the right basic colour. The prepared strips – whether filed-down rail or suitable section nickel-silver – are tack-soldered in pairs for drilling, which needs doing carefully, in a vertical drill or drill press for preference, and then separated for finishing. Plain rods may need to be filed to 'fish-belly' outline, while all will need the 'halved' lap-joint(s) and recesses to accept the bosses and knuckle-joints. Once again, it's easier to draw than to describe – so I have. Cocktail sticks, of the tapered wooden variety, can be useful for centring the washers uses for the boss onto the drilled crankpin hole in the coupling rods. However, I usually put the washer on the bench, lay the rod on top, and locate the strip for the oil-box, holding it all in place with lumps of Plasticine while soldering. Another sketch will unravel this tortology. Any misalignment of washer with

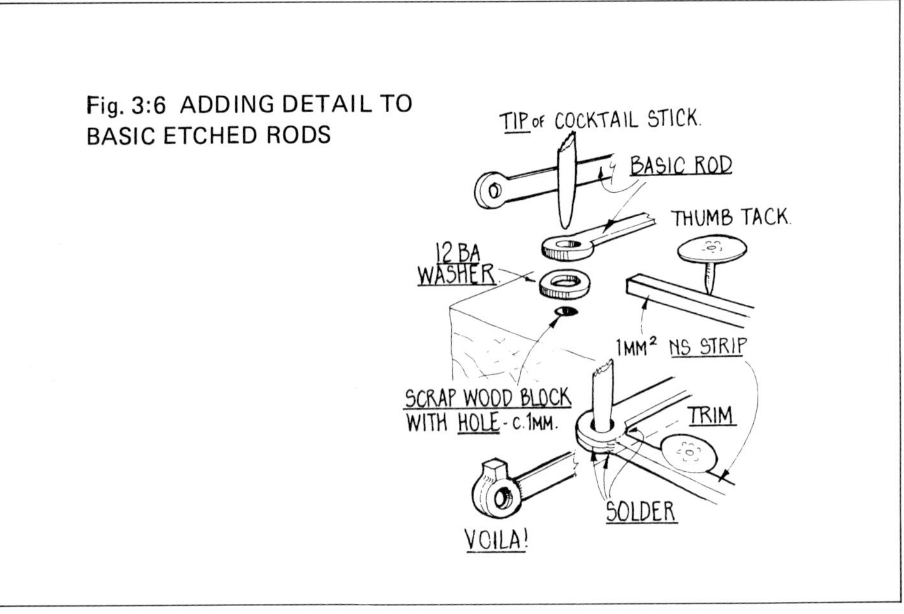

Fig. 3:6 ADDING DETAIL TO BASIC ETCHED RODS

Fig. 3.7 REALISTIC COUPLING RODS FROM BULLHEAD RAIL

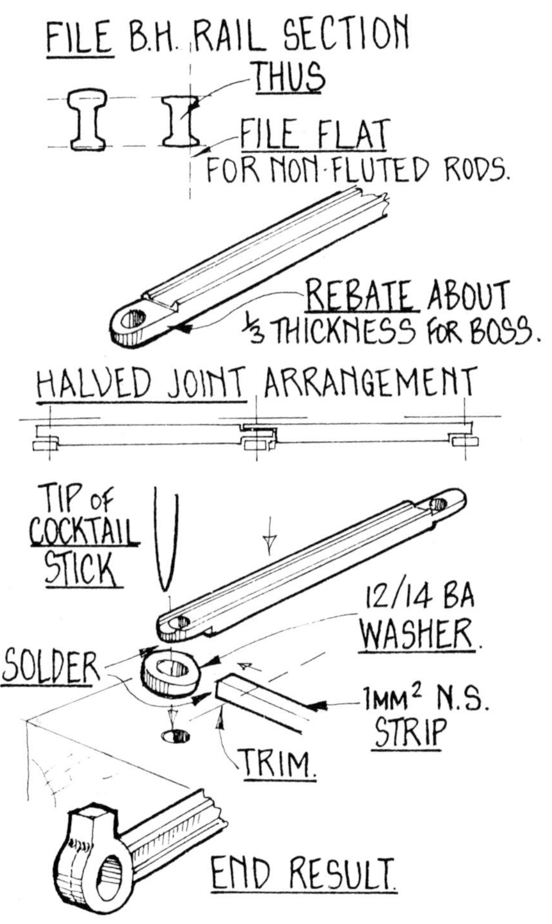

crankpin hole is corrected when I ream these to their final size, having, of course, obeyed my own basic engineering dictum and drilled them undersize!

CORRECTING COUPLING ROD CENTRES

Thus far, I have assumed that we are dealing with a modern etched chassis employing inserted top-hat axle bearings, where moving a bearing location is relatively simple. If, however, you're faced with a solid block chassis and a pair of discordant coupling rods, then this is an option which simply isn't open to you. In this situation, it will be necessary to make the rods fit the chassis.

How this is best achieved will depend on the nature and extent of the error, determined, once again, with the trusty dividers and duly noted in sketch form. We may alter (slightly!) the position of the crankpin hole in the boss of the rod, using a crankpin bush or washer soldered to the rod, with the existing incorrect hole filed to accommodate the correction, much as for the top-hat bearing in the chassis. If the rods are too short, we may 'stretch' them (again, slightly – we're talking in single-figure 'thou' here) by dressing them with a hammer. Or, if all else fails or the error is gross, we will once again need to resort to our own devices with some home-made rods made to match the chassis.

The key to the first two of these dodges is our old friend the jig-axle. In the first method, we discard the original hole by enlarging it, and then regain our centres by bushing. The best option is to use a top-hat crankpin bush, of the sort supplied with some of the crankpin systems sold for use with finescale wheels. Sharman wheels have a small brass version that is most suitable, as do DJH (supplied in many of their kits). If you can't get a 'top-hat', it's quite possible to use brass capillary tube (see suppliers index), provided it's a good enough (ie tight enough) fit on the crankpin. Remember, 5–7 thou is the acceptable level of 'running clearance' (slop, if you want it in plain English!). Use of a top-hat or tube bearing is determined by the amount of 'meat' in the coupling-rod boss; there must be enough metal to take the necessary enlargement of the crankpin hole to accept the bush, plus the allowance needed to offset it to get it in the right place. Rods that are designed to take a bush in the first place, such as DJH's, are obviously the best bet for the application of this particular 'cure'.

If you find that there's just not enough metal in the boss to get a bush in, bearing in mind you need a reasonable amount of material around the edges of the bush to avoid the rod distorting while you work on it, then the best bet is to enlarge the crankpin

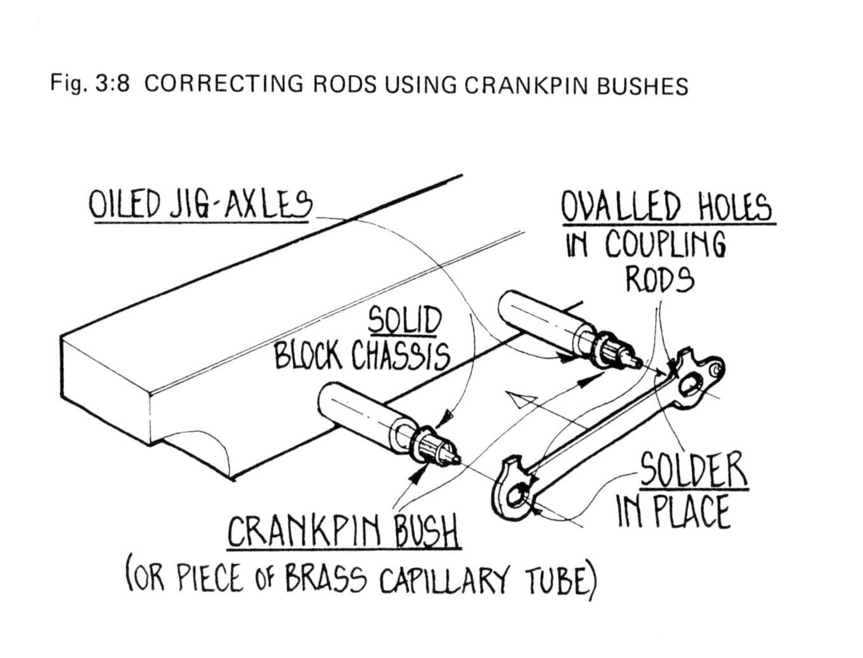

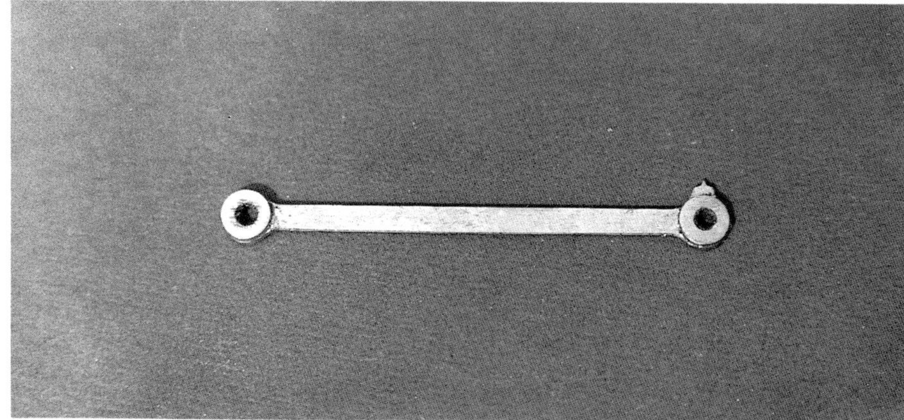

Washers soldered to the rear of a defective etched rod (one of those from the DJH 'West Country') to try and correct over-large and misshapen holes. I abandoned this bodge when the estimable Chris Challis produced a set of appropriate rods by Alan Gibson, which were fine.

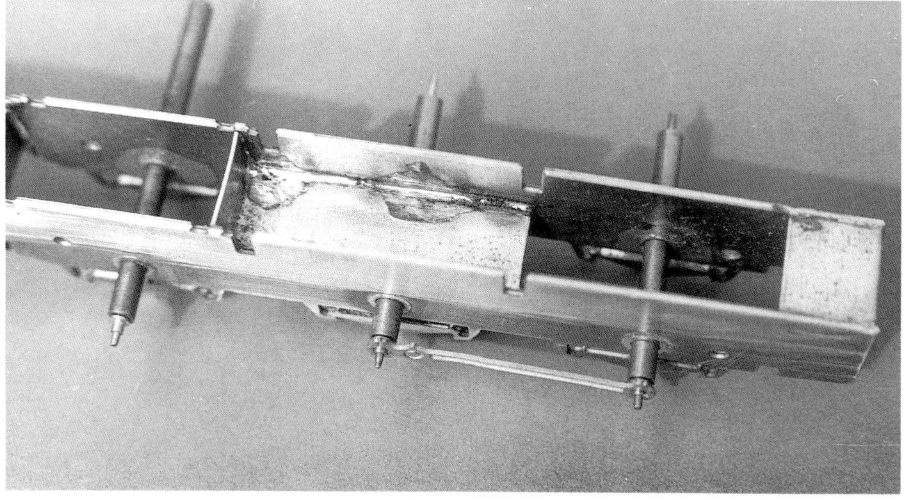

Here are the re-worked and washered DJH rods being set up on jig axles inserted in the chassis.

hole only far enough to accommodate the error. The centres are then reset by soldering on a suitable (ie 14BA) washer. Ideally, you want a washer on each side, but I've yet to manage that, and find that one on the 'inside' of the rod next to the wheels is adequate.

Locating the washers/bushes in the right place is down, once again, to the jig-axle. Place these in the chassis bearings, and spread a thin layer of grease (Vaseline will do, high-temp. is better) on the tapered ends. Offer up the rods, with the enlarged holes over the axle ends – as with the chassis mod, we will obviously need to select one axle as 'datum', keeping to the original crankpin hole on that axle as a reference point. The washers/bushes are then soldered in place, taking great care not to solder the whole shebang to the end of the jig-axle – a small iron, paste flux or solder cream, and a minimum of applied solder are the rules. Once again, there is a diagram of sorts to illuminate these dark and cloudy words.

By comparison with the above, the stretching of rods (or sections of rods) that are a few thou too *short*, by imitating the village blacksmith, may seem appealing. This is a bona-fide engineering practice of considerable antiquity, and works like magic. The only real snag is that it's a one-way process – you can make your rod longer, but you can't make it shorter. So softly, softly, bit-at-a-time is the required approach. In other words, use a little hammer – a $1\frac{1}{2}$oz pin-hammer is plenty heavy enough; use it with circumspection, and *keep checking*. Have the jig-axles in the chassis as a reference, and keep tap-tap-tapping away until you can just drop the errant rod over the tapered ends. The top of a small vice is fine for an anvil, so other than that all you need is patience and restraint. Try to dress the rod evenly over its entire length, avoiding too much aggro in any one spot. Even with care, you may find the outline of the rod gets a bit wavy and distorted; tidy it up with files once you're through with the smithery.

These dodges are always worth trying where the error in the rods is of modest proportions; after all, if the rods don't fit you've nothing to lose, and if these cures fail you're still no worse off than you would be if the kit rods were totally NBG in the first place – you're making your own. However, whilst the actual manufacturing process, from rail, strip or whatever, is much as described a page or so since, the difference is the need to get the crankpin holes in exactly the right place – which isn't so easy. There are two methods, one rather hit-and-miss, one sure-fire but less accessible.

Method 1 is simply to measure the axle centres as accurately as you possibly can, and to transfer these measurements to a piece of scrap metal, working, as always, on 4-coupled 'sections' at a time (see sketch). This marked-out trial piece is then drilled a suitable size (crankpin diameter less a bit, say, about 0.7 mm) and offered up to the jig-axles in the chassis. If it fits, fine; if it doesn't, observe the error, and try again, and again, until you eventually score the elusive double and can start the game. I told you it was trial-and-error! Once, however, you've got two holes in a bit of metal the right distance apart, you're home and dry, for you've got an accurate jig with which to drill the rail or strip for your coupling rods.

This erratic and laborious process can be short-circuited if you can make or obtain the gadget shown in my next sketch, a $\frac{1}{8}$in diameter centre punch. It was Martin Brent who first wrote up this method of transferring axle-centres accurately to coupling

Fig. 3:9 CORRECTING COUPLING RODS USING WASHERS

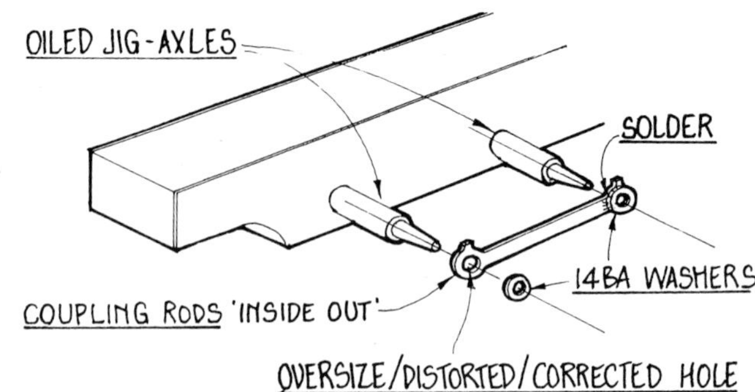

Fig. 3:10 COUPLING ROD CENTRES ESTABLISHED BY TRIAL AND ERROR

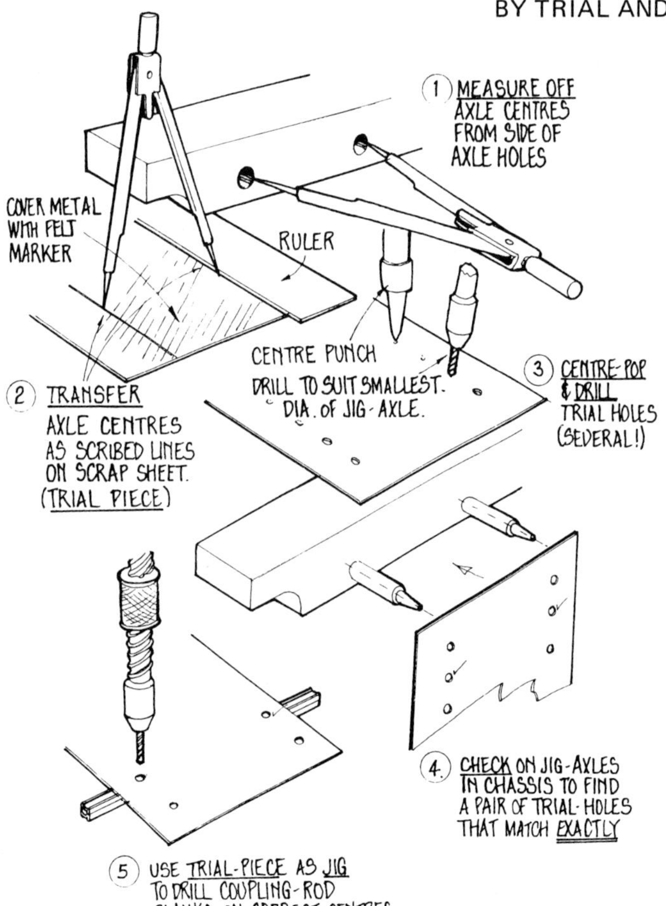

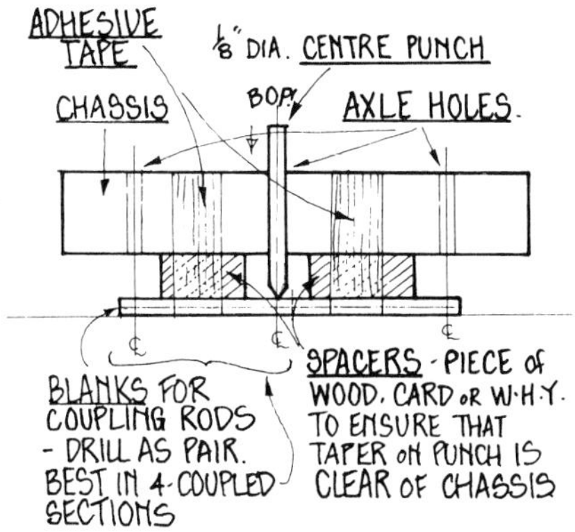
ADHESIVE TAPE
1/8" DIA. CENTRE PUNCH
CHASSIS
BOP
AXLE HOLES.
SPACERS - PIECE OF WOOD, CARD OR W.H.Y. TO ENSURE THAT TAPER ON PUNCH IS CLEAR OF CHASSIS
BLANKS FOR COUPLING RODS - DRILL AS PAIR. BEST IN 4-COUPLED SECTIONS

Fig. 3:11 USING CHASSIS AS JIG WITH 1/8in DIA. CENTRE PUNCH

rods, and I think that the diagram should say all that needs saying about this obvious and foolproof operation which is actually pukka engineering practice. The only snag is the difficulty in obtaining a $\frac{1}{8}$in diameter parallel-sided punch; any toolmaker out there listening? I turned mine in the lathe from a bit of $\frac{1}{8}$in silver steel, but that's not an option for many people, and it could really do with a hardened tip to be durable in use.

This process has a secondary use, by the by, in that it enables you to make a set of replacement rods to accurately match *any* chassis, rigid or suspended, should wear or damage require such drastic remedial action. Once again, your chances of ending up with a truly accurate set of rods are greatly improved if the job is tackled in 4-coupled sections, which means that there's only one place for error to creep in, rather than the three possibilities inherent in a single set of six-coupled rods. (End to end; front to centre; rear to centre. I won't even speculate on the opportunities for accumulated error in undivided 8-coupled rods!)

I have dwelt on this matter of coupling rods and axle centres at some considerable length, as it is at the heart of any sort of running quality for a coupled loco chassis. I have seen, over the years, some quite hideous suggestions for overcoming deficiencies in this fundamental relationship. Gentlemen, oval holes in coupling rods will never, ever put right errors in the rod/chassis match; all they will do is to compound the felony by negating the quartering as well – they are simply tantamount to introducing a massive amount of slop in one dimension. And yes, I do know that some types of R-T-R use either very sloppy rods, or rods with oval holes – but only in conjunction with driving axles geared together, where the rods are purely decorative. For most 4 mm locos, they need to perform their prototype function, transmitting the drive from driven to undriven axles. In the proper performance of this function, accuracy and restrained running clearances are vital, and unless you take the trouble to get this right, all else is a waste of time. Possibly the chief virtue of the Flexi-chas system is that precise setting of this critical dimension lies at the heart of it – which should commend it even before considering its other strengths, already discussed.

OVERSIZE HOLES

These can be a real headache if the degree of excess is greater than about $\frac{1}{2}$mm on diameter. The first thing to look at is the consequences of any misalignment – for some things, it just doesn't matter, but any hole intended to take an axle bush, to locate frame-spacer screws, motor mountings or other critical components *must* be a good fit.

Where the most critical of these holes, those for the axle bearings, are too big then a real problem is in prospect, which may call for drastic cures. If the degree of slop is slight, then it is usually possible to centre the bearing in the hole by running a fillet of solder all round the periphery. Hold the iron in contact long enough to heat the whole job to a temperature sufficient to keep the solder fillet fully molten for a few seconds. This will enable the solder to flow all round the bearing, filling in the offending gap, and, by the action of the surface tensions within the molten solder, to centre accurately the bearing in the hole. It's important when trying this dodge that the bearing is free to move about in the hole and hence find its own location. I support the job as in the sketch, crouching on the floor if needs be to observe the action of the solder!

Another solution to the oversize-bearing-hole dilemma is simply to swap the bearing supplied for one that's a bit fatter, and thus a better fit in the hole. If you can find one that's a bit too fat, even better, as you can then ream the offending hole out slightly for an exact fit. I have a little store of $\frac{1}{8}$in bearings from umpteen different makers to increase my chances of being able to match bearings and holes more accurately than the kit-makers seem to manage. Of course, if you're fortunate enough to have access to a lathe, and can drive it, then you don't have a problem, as it will simply be a matter of making a suitable bearing, whatever the misfit the kitmaker has foisted on you. But, once again, hardly a 'kitchen table' solution.

This brings me to a couple of rather more drastic dodges – or, in the first case, to an appalling (in engineering terms) but surprisingly effective bodge. Put crudely – and there's no other way to put it – the idea is to solder all the bearings into their oversize holes at 'top dead centre'. The diagram explains this, and shows how I accomplish it. If the axle-holes are in the right place, this preserves the rod/chassis alignment with surprising accuracy. The snag with this is,

Fig. 3:12 CENTRING BEARINGS WITH SOLDER

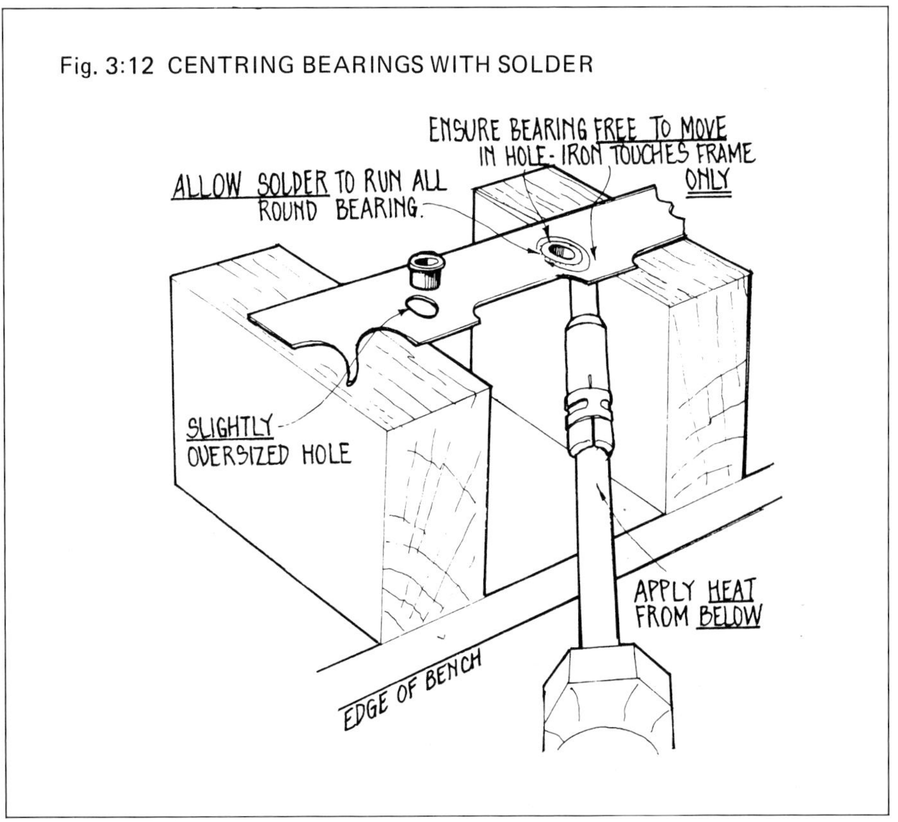
ENSURE BEARING FREE TO MOVE IN HOLE: IRON TOUCHES FRAME ONLY
ALLOW SOLDER TO RUN ALL ROUND BEARING.
SLIGHTLY OVERSIZED HOLE
APPLY HEAT FROM BELOW
EDGE OF BENCH

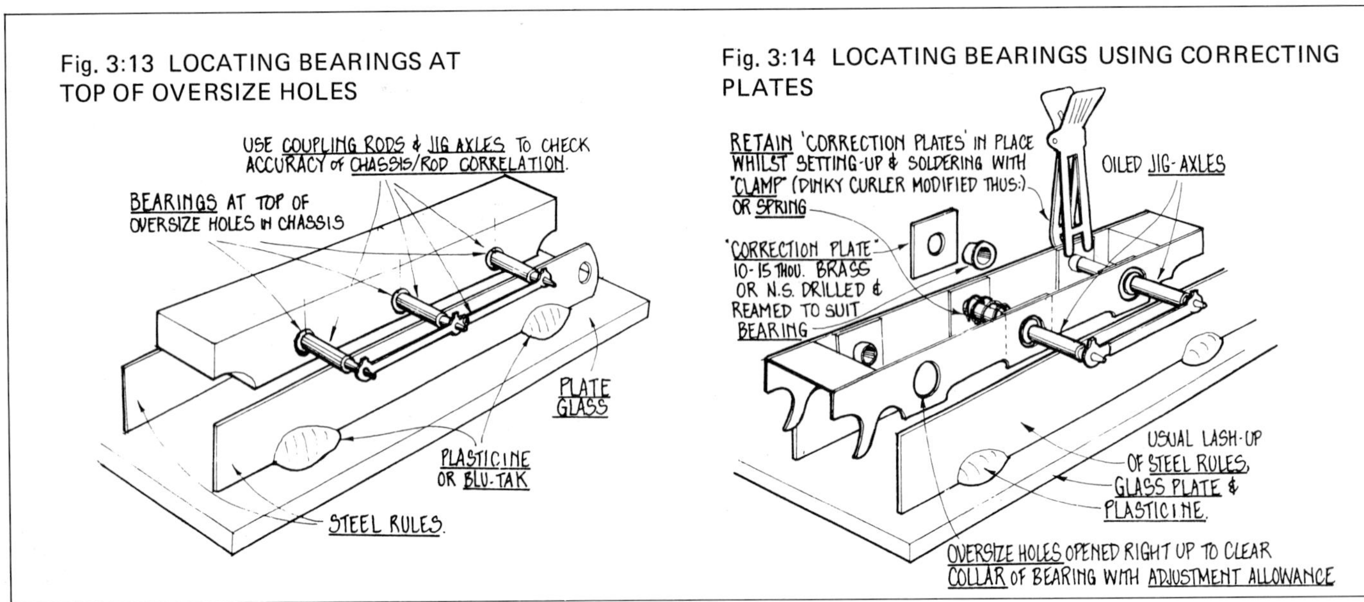
USE COUPLING RODS & JIG AXLES TO CHECK ACCURACY OF CHASSIS/ROD CORRELATION.
BEARINGS AT TOP OF OVERSIZE HOLES IN CHASSIS
PLATE GLASS
PLASTICINE OR BLU-TAK
STEEL RULES.
RETAIN 'CORRECTION PLATES' IN PLACE WHILST SETTING-UP & SOLDERING WITH 'CLAMP' (DINKY CURLER MODIFIED THUS:) OR SPRING
OILED JIG-AXLES
'CORRECTION PLATE' 10-15 THOU. BRASS OR N.S. DRILLED & REAMED TO SUIT BEARING
USUAL LASH-UP OF STEEL RULES, GLASS PLATE & PLASTICINE.
OVERSIZE HOLES OPENED RIGHT UP TO CLEAR COLLAR OF BEARING WITH ADJUSTMENT ALLOWANCE

Fig. 3:13 LOCATING BEARINGS AT TOP OF OVERSIZE HOLES

Fig. 3:14 LOCATING BEARINGS USING CORRECTING PLATES

of course, that you lose the vertical alignment of the bearings in the frames, and the chassis ends up riding too low. A bit of extra packing between the top of the chassis and the body will restore drooping buffer heights, and unless the error in the hole-size is really gross, then the effect should be slight.

A slightly more pukka approach is to use the jig-axles and coupling rods to align the bearings in the holes, when they can be soldered in place with an accurate correlation – in other words, the axle-centre correction dodge. One can take this a stage further, and fit the bearings into little correction plates, soldered in place behind the frames, which have the errant holes either greatly enlarged, or the hornguide lands cut out, as for a 'Flexi-chas' conversion. Mind you, if you go to those lengths, you're 7/8ths of the way to a compensated chassis anyway (*Fig 3:13* explains).

FRAME SPACERS

As will, I think, have become apparent in my preamble, I am no lover of the type of turned, screw-fixed frame spacers that K's originally pioneered in their second-generation 'keyhole' chassis – not amongst the designs that I can admire. I've already listed the drawbacks to the screwed spacer, so what can it be replaced or augmented with? My own preference is, and has always been, the L-section spacer, which has a number of significant advantages.

The first, and probably most significant, advantage is that a properly-designed L-shaped spacer provides support and alignment in both the longitudinal and vertical planes – support essential if the chassis is to be 'square'. The design is simply varied to obtain the desired proportions of the 'L', enabling an 'L' spacer to be sneaked in just about anywhere without getting in the way. Adapting an 'L' spacer to act as a motor or pick-up mounting is simplicity itself, and it performs both functions admirably; it is also easy to arrange 'L' spacers to accommodate body-mounting systems. An 'L' spacer will also do a pretty good job of replicating the prototype, and is far less likely to get in the way of things like brake gear, AWS shoes, vacuum cylinders and other chassis detail. Lastly, it's stunningly easy to make, in any width that might be required; it's quite possible to optimise the over-frame width for any loco, in any gauge, to any standards, simply by working backwards from the wheel back-to-back dimension.

So, faced with any other sort of frame spacer – not only screwed, but such corking examples of non-design as the etched-out bits of flat strip that were supposed to be the frame spacers of the Falcon 'Kirtley' – I have no hesitation in consigning the kit spacers to the scrap-box and brewing a set of my own. The material used isn't that critical, although I find it's better not to use metal (usually nickel-silver) of a really hard grade, which won't take too kindly to right-angle bends. Being of a thrifty nature, I use waste etching metal, usually 10 or 12 thou brass. Many kitmakers sell this in bundles at shows for a few pence – it has many uses. Otherwise, it'll be a case of buying some suitable sheet metal – John Flack sells a softish 10 thou nickel-silver that I have found answers very well (see suppliers index).

WORKING OUT FRAME SPACER WIDTH

Generally speaking, all the frame spacers for a given chassis will be of the same width. The exceptions are those types – usually of the 2–4–0, 0–4–2, 2–4–2T and 0–6–2T wheel arrangements – where the frames are designed to 'step in' behind leading or trailing wheelsets; this is usually much better than making the whole chassis far too narrow, and most of the better chassis kits for this type of loco will incorporate such a step. With luck, you'll find you've got some decent spacers to go with these chassis. Where you haven't got a good chassis kit – which means either that no provision has been made for adequate sideplay, or that the leading or trailing wheels are cobbled into some form of unprototypical pony truck (and I can't think of many British 4-coupled locos graced with a pony truck, although quite a few 0–6–2Ts are thus endowed), then it's worth adapting the chassis if this is possible.

To work out the optimum frame spacer width for a given loco, we need to know three things: the thickness of the frames, the back-to-back dimension of the wheels being used, and the amount of sideplay required. The first two can be measured, the most suitable tool for the job being a vernier calliper gauge – a generally useful tool in the armoury of the model loco-builder. Don't forget that we have to ensure that there is adequate clearance between the wheel-back and the frames to accommodate our less-than-perfectly-true (wobbly!) drivers, and to keep apart frames and wheel-tyres that may be electrically opposed. I find that, where 'top-hat' bushes are used, the collars of these provide the $\frac{1}{2}$mm or so a side required. 'Flexi-chas' locos may need washers to provide the necessary gap, while 'Romford' drivers incorporate a cast 'boss' on the wheel-back which provides about $\frac{1}{4}$mm a side – so I allow another $\frac{1}{4}$mm to be on the safe side. Lastly, we do need a touch of 'running clearance' to stop the backs of the wheels binding on the fronts of the bearings on non-sideplay axles, provided by the use of spacing washers of slightly less than the

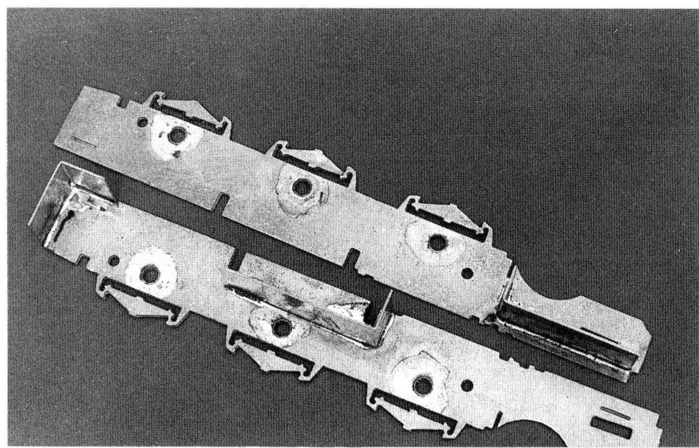

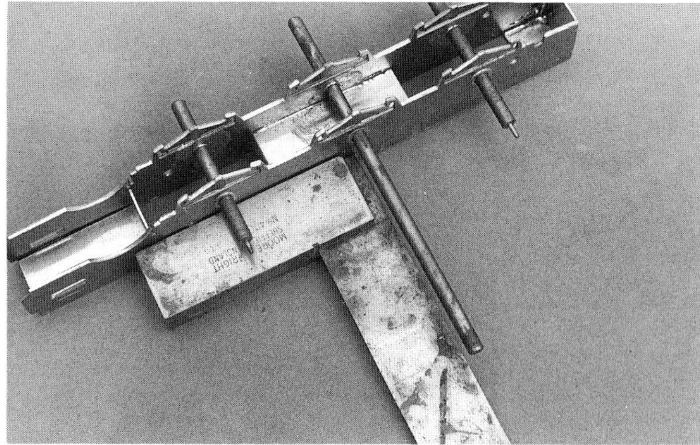

Fitting home-made L-section spacers to the DJH 'West Country' chassis. At this stage I was intending to drive the rear axle, hence the large centre spacer. However, I'd failed to check against the footplate casting, which only permits centre-axle drive. The moral is obvious! The second picture shows an alternative method of setting up frames where a full chassis jig is not available. A flat surface and a square will suffice.

sideplay allowance on these axles – a couple of thou a side will do, 5 thou is plenty.

The only vague variable in this little lot is the sideplay allowance, needed on the centre axle of six-coupled, on alternate axles of eight- or ten-coupled, and at the ends of four-coupled 2–4–2T 'radials' and the like. Plain four-coupled locos, as in 2–4–0, 4–4–0 and the sidetanked reversals of these same arrangements, do not need any sideplay, other than running clearance, on the driving wheels; indeed, it's undesirable, leading to a chassis that 'hunts' on the track. So, how much sideplay do you actually need? Not as much as you might think, I've found, especially in 'OO', with a full 1 mm of running clearance between the faces of the flanges and the insides of the rails. For reasons expounded in Chapter 1 (axle-tilt and all that), 'Flexi-chas' locos also need less sideplay, while the 'finescale' EMF and P4 standards have gauge-widening on curves to help things along. So how, in the face of all these variables, do you decide on a suitable amount of sideplay for a particular chassis?

In point of fact, quite a few such variables cancel each other out, while the effect of most of the rest is of such small significance that they can be disregarded. The only two factors that I have found to have a direct effect on the sideplay requirement are the length of the fixed wheelbase, and the limiting radius of curve that must be traversed. Obviously, a long-wheelbase engine – by which I mean a six-coupled chassis having axle centres in excess of, say, the MR/LMS standard of 8 ft + 8 ft 6 in – will need a touch more sideplay than a more modest locomotive. My LNER 'J39' in P4 (wheelbase 8 ft 0 in + 9 ft 0 in) needed nearly 1.5 mm of sideplay to get it around the flange-flaking 22 in radius curve on my old 'Butley Mills' layout, a curve that the modestly-proportioned 'J15' traversed on just half this amount. This was a pretty extreme case, mind you, and I find I rarely need to exceed 1 mm total sideplay.

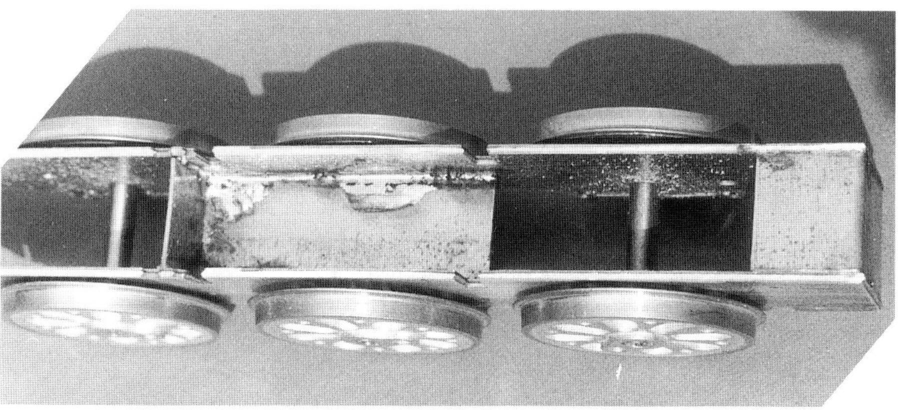

The re-spaced frames exhibit a more realistic and reasonable relationship with the wheels – or so I like to think. These are the original DJH 'Ersatz Romfords'; I later substituted a set from Alan Gibson's range.

So, to some rule-of-thumb figures. For OO, it's going to be a curve of dire proportions and a wheelbase of inordinate length to call for more than 1 mm of sideplay; that much should certainly see almost any six-coupled loco around a 24 in radius curve, bogie-swing and other such factors permitting. Coarse EM is a bit more of a problem, with the smaller running clearance, and here I find that 1.5 mm often isn't out of the way. EMF and P4, with their bias towards much more prototypical curve radii, plus, often, the incorporation of compensation into the chassis, can get by on less sideplay altogether, and I generally end up with around 0.75 mm – or, rather, 30 thou, set with an ordinary feeler gauge (1 thou = 0.0254 mm, so 30 thou = 0.762 mm).

So, to relate all this lot into a generally-applicable formula for calculating frame spacer widths, we work to:

$$F = B - (T + S + C)$$

where F is the frame spacer width, B is the distance between the wheel backs, S is the sideplay allowance we have settled on, and C is the clearance dimension, normally the collar thickness of top-hat bushes inserted in the frames (and hence a useful 'adjustment device', in that a wipe or two on these with a file wins you an extra thou or two of sideplay or running clearance).

In the best traditions of maths textbooks, I provide a couple of worked examples. I have taken the thickness of a pair of 18 or 20 thou frames (40 thou = 1.016 mm) as 1 mm, the extra 4 thou resulting from 18 thou frames being a bonus. So, for an EM chassis with 20 thou etched frames and Romford wheels, allowing 1 mm of sideplay and assuming $\frac{1}{2}$ mm collars to the bearings, I feed it all in and come out with:

$$F = 16 - (1 + 1 + 1) = 13\,\text{mm}$$

An alternative example, in OO with DJH's armour-plate 36 thou frames, gives the following depressing answer:

$$F = 14 - (1.8 + 1 + 1) = 10.2\,\text{mm}$$

which is how, I suppose, DJH arrived at their 10 mm spacer. As most of the modern 'slimline' motors call for 11 mm clearance, I'd start filing down top-hat collars and squeezing the sideplay to find a few more fractions of a mm, aiming for an 11.5 mm spacer, the dimension I used on the rebuilt 'West Country' chassis illustrated in this book. It does illustrate graphically just what a problem 36 thou thick frames can be in a 4mm context, losing nearly a whole millimetre of valuable inter-frame space, and calling for unsightly motor cut-outs which could be avoided using 18 or 20 thou metal. I rest my case...

I'm sorry if all this lot seems heavy going, but in the context of a book, I do have to cover every eventuality, and come up with solutions which are as universal as possible in their application, hence the formula. If, however, you're content to rest on the fruits of the Rice labours in years past, then I find that the following frame-spacer widths seem to serve pretty well in the vast majority of cases – say, wheelbases up to 8 ft + 8 ft 6 in and curves of 30 in radius in OO/coarse EM, 36 in in EMF and P4.

With 20 thou thick frames:
OO – 12 mm
EM – 13 mm
EMF – 14 mm
P4 – 14.5 mm

With 36 thou frames
OO – 11 mm
EM – 12 mm
EMF – 13 mm
P4 – 13.5 mm

In the context of a kit, many makers supply a single 14 mm spacer for both EM/P4, which is quite acceptable, a ½mm difference not being of great consequence. Where P4 spacers are supplied, these may well be to a 15 mm width – OK on curves of 3 ft 6 in or so, but tight for smaller radii. A similar stricture applies to 'EM' spacers supplied at 13.5 mm (both dimensions taken from Perseverance chassis) – OK for EMF, being a bit less than my dimension, but tight for 'coarse' EM using Romford wheels. The golden rule is, of course, if in doubt, err on the narrow side; one can always slip in a washer or two to take up excess, but once you've filed the collars off the bearings, finding more sideplay calls for drastic action! 'Percy' is a bit mean with his OO spacer, only 11 mm; certainly, with non-Romford wheels, you can put a full mm on that, as not having those clearance bosses to allow for gains you ½mm straight away.

MAKING L-SECTION SPACERS

Probably the hardest bit of making an L section spacer is deciding a suitable value for 'F' in the foregoing forehead-furrowing farago. Once you've lit upon the magic number, it's simply a matter of producing a strip of metal to the correct width. The easiest way to do this is with a 'scrawker', a device invented, I believe, by Mike Sharman. This is simply a form of hook-knife ground out of old hacksaw-blade to the approximate shape shown in *Fig 3:15*. It is used to 'score' metal along a line, such that it can simply be snapped, giving an accurate straight cut free from distortion. I start off by finding a piece of suitable metal with a straight 'datum edge', from which I can measure off the required width of strip. I then carefully align a steel rule on this dimension, and scribe a line with a normal engineers' scriber. Once you've established the scribed line, make a couple of further passes with the scriber to deepen the scribe-mark, then go over to the scrawker. This is drawn toward you, as in the sketch, cutting a deep V-groove in the metal along the scribed alignment. Keep going until you're nearly through the metal, then, placing the line over an edge, break the metal along the groove. Sounds crude, which it is, but it works.

If you don't have access to a scrawker, or the wherewithall for making same, then you can actually arrive at the same result, albeit more slowly, by keeping going with the ordinary scriber. Alternatively, if your patience fails you, scribe a good, deep line and then resort to a pair of scissors – better than snips or shears in this instance – which *should* follow the scribed line accurately. Just make sure that you don't use the best dress-making scissors which, while they suit our purpose well, tend to cause unaccountable ructions in the velvet fabric of the happy home...

Once a strip of suitable metal cut to the appropriate width has been produced (a bit about 3–4 in long will do most 4 mm chassis, although I tend to keep 12 in lengths of my 'standard widths' in stock for speed and convenience), then turning it into individual, tailor-made spacers is the work of moments. The only essential is a small engineers' square – an item, I suggest, that is a toolbox 'must' – and, once again our scriber and scrawker. To make the spacer, one simply scores a line accurately at right-angles to the strip with square and scriber, deepened with a pass or two of the skrawker or a pass or several with the scriber. To ensure a clean bend, I make a final couple of passes with the tip of a triangular needle file. The result should be that the strip can be simply and cleanly bent through 90° (or other angle as appropriate to location – see next paragraph) to give a square and accurate 'L', as in the photo-sequence.

Fig. 3:15 MAKING AND USING A SCRAWKER

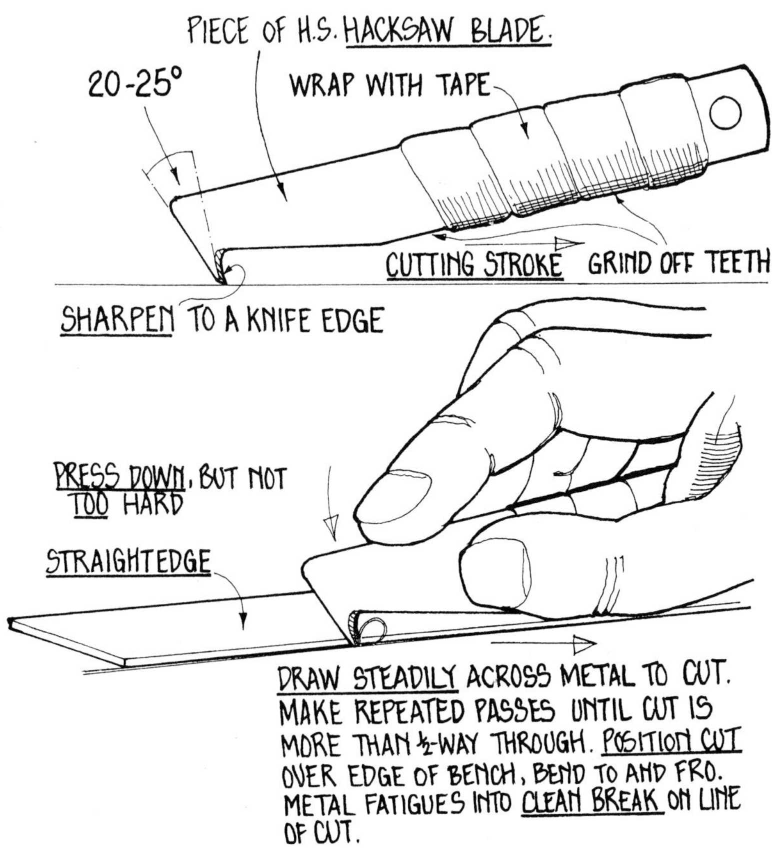
PIECE OF H.S. HACKSAW BLADE.
20-25°
WRAP WITH TAPE
CUTTING STROKE
GRIND OFF TEETH
SHARPEN TO A KNIFE EDGE
PRESS DOWN, BUT NOT TOO HARD
STRAIGHTEDGE
DRAW STEADILY ACROSS METAL TO CUT. MAKE REPEATED PASSES UNTIL CUT IS MORE THAN ½-WAY THROUGH. POSITION CUT OVER EDGE OF BENCH, BEND TO AND FRO. METAL FATIGUES INTO CLEAN BREAK ON LINE OF CUT.

DESIGNING SPACERS TO SUIT CHASSIS

Some kit-makers, such as Perseverance, design all their chassis around one universal set of fold-up etched 'L' spacers, augmented with a few 'flat' spacers for body and pick-up mounting, all located by tab-and-slot. Nothing wrong with that approach, provided that the rest of the chassis design isn't compromised thereby. However, when producing a set of spacers to suit a specific chassis, it's handy to have a few 'first principles' to go on. Certain things have to be borne in mind when deciding on the shape, proportion and location of spacers, on which it is possible to generalise. The first point is that frames are a lot longer than they are deep, so a lot more bracing will be required in the longitudinal direction than in the vertical, suggesting unequal 'L' spacers with a lot more in the longwise leg of the 'L'. The second point is that the frame spacers actually need to do rather more than just space and brace the mainframes, such as provide suitable mountings for pick-ups, loco/tender couplings, body mounts and perhaps motors or gearboxes. The third point is that they mustn't get in the way of the mechanical aspects of the chassis, so allow room for gears, compensation beams, bogie pivot arms and so on. Lastly, they may need to perform a cosmetic function in representing such prototype chassis features as cylinder or valve chest covers, firebox fronts, spectacle plates (internal slidebar brackets) or – surprise, surprise – frame spacers.

While I obviously can't provide a universal formula to suit any possible permutation or application, most loco chassis conform to one of the three basic types I've drawn, which should give a fair idea of how I go about proportioning and positioning my 'L's in these three basic instances. Variations from this will be dictated by particular considerations, such as cylinder stretchers or motion brackets, alternative wheel arrangements and drive configurations, and the need to mount the body, of which more in a moment. Really, the whole thing is down to applied common sense, which is possibly why a good few kit designers find it all beyond their ken.

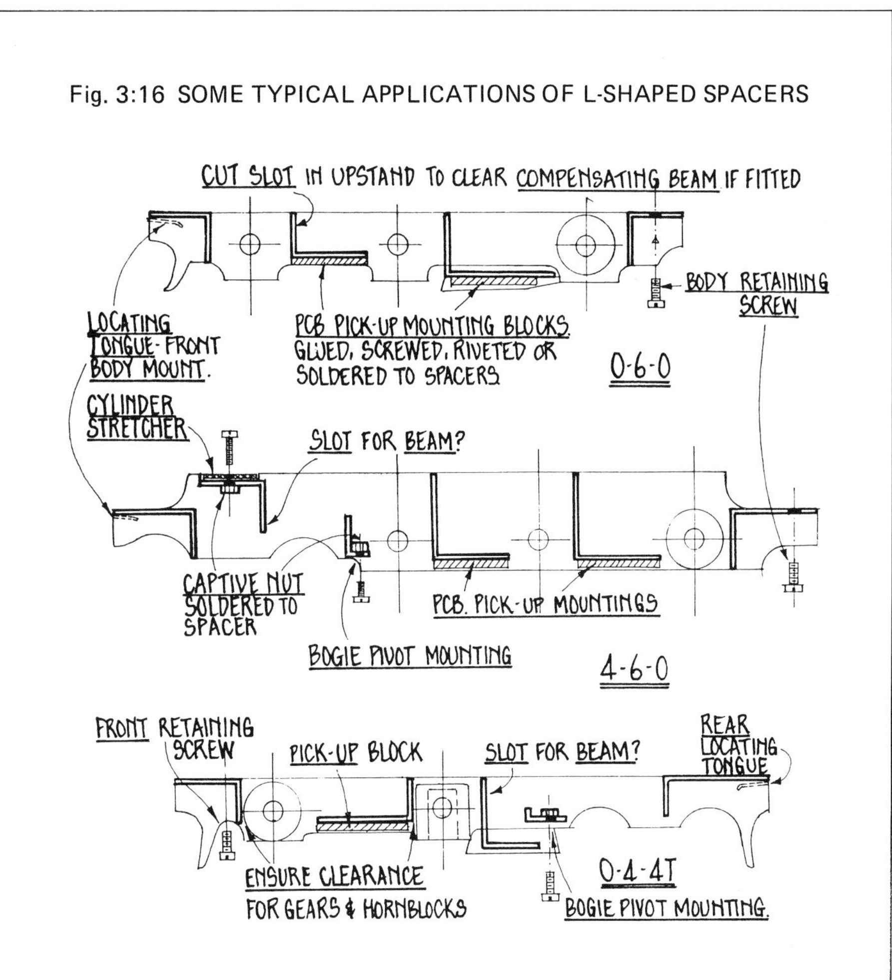

Fig. 3:16 SOME TYPICAL APPLICATIONS OF L-SHAPED SPACERS

BODY MOUNTING PROVISION

Simple, says tradition – two screws, one each end. Not so simple, say I, and only one screw should ever be entertained. Why? For a number of reasons, principal among which are the small matters of alignment and noise transmission. The first of these should be self-evident, in that to enable the chassis and superstructure to be clamped together by a pair of screws, then total accuracy of alignment will be required if the clamping operation isn't to distort the chassis or the superstructure or, probably, both. How many times have I heard regaled the mysterious tale of a chassis which 'ran like a dream' on its own, but degenerated into a nightmare when united with the body? And how many times have I conducted the simple 'wonder cure' of slackening off the body-fixing screws, allowing the frames to unwind and the axles to re-align themselves one with another and hopefully with the track?

From this bit of sorcery it may readily be deduced that attempts to clamp the chassis into the body are a Bad Idea – which is most certainly so, for it brings in its train the other evil to which a lot of 4 mm locos, especially with plastic or etched-brass superstructures, are prone – horrid grumbling noises, which, given that a lightweight, thin-walled hollow structure such as a loco body is a pretty effective sounding-box, is not surprising. What may be less generally appreciated is that a 'tight' interface or connection is an efficient transmitter of sound, whereas a loose fit between two components is a poor transmitter (but can

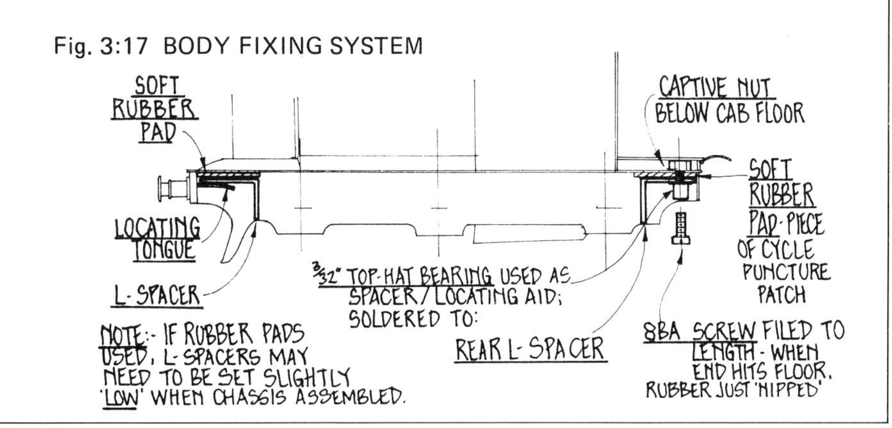

Fig. 3:17 BODY FIXING SYSTEM

cause buzzing vibrations by resonating the whole body), while a resilient mounting both dampens the sound transmission and stops resonance. A small piece of soft rubber (cycle puncture repair patch) glued to the bottom of the footplate where the chassis mounts, along with a 'loose' locating system, can work wonders.

So, enter Rice's preferred body mount, by lug-and-screw, as in *Fig 3:17*, which attempts to answer the case in this respect although – whisper this quietly only to your best friends – a lot of my locos have their chassis attached by even less, in the form of a couple of blobs of Blu-Tak. Yuk! But it works well, especially if your layout does not call for a great deal by way of stock handling. Certainly, there's no way that a lump of Blu-Tak is ever going to transmit any applied torque, so there's absolutely no danger of anything getting distorted. It is not, I will agree, an elegant solution in strict engineering terms...

OTHER CHASSIS CORRECTIONS

In the sort of preliminary vein which I have, until now, been quarrying, further work amounts really to the correction of cosmetic trifles such as the re-shaping of curves or cut-outs and the precise matching of frames one to another. If faced with a DJH heavyweight, I spend a happy half-hour or so 'de-cusping' the edges, while quite a few chassis will need holes drilling for brake-hangers, beam pivots and the like where these are not etched-in or otherwise provided for. If you are electing to apply the 'Flexi-chas' system to a kit chassis not providing for it, you may also be involved in hacking-out the required hornguide openings, as described in Chapter 6.

This, however, leaves untouched and uncured the various maladies affecting cylinders and slidebars, valve gears, motors, gears and pick-ups so luridly described in Chapter 2. These I will deal with under their respective topic headings – fault-curing being very much part of the assembly process, rather than a preliminary to it as with the operations I have just been describing. This chapter is anyway bidding fair to eclipse even my Tolstoyan tendency to go on a bit, so before we all get a headache I think that it's time to change tack, and actually start putting things together.

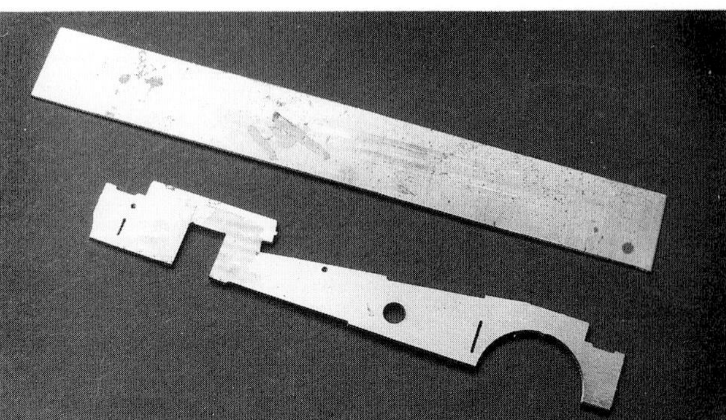

Filling in unwanted motor cut-outs, such as these intrusions in the frames of the Craftsman 'C12', is an irksome job. A piece of waste etch metal of appropriate thickness is soldered in place, trimmed down, and the result cleaned up – which is when you will discover that Craftsman chassis are not the nickel-silver they appear to be, but are actually plated brass.

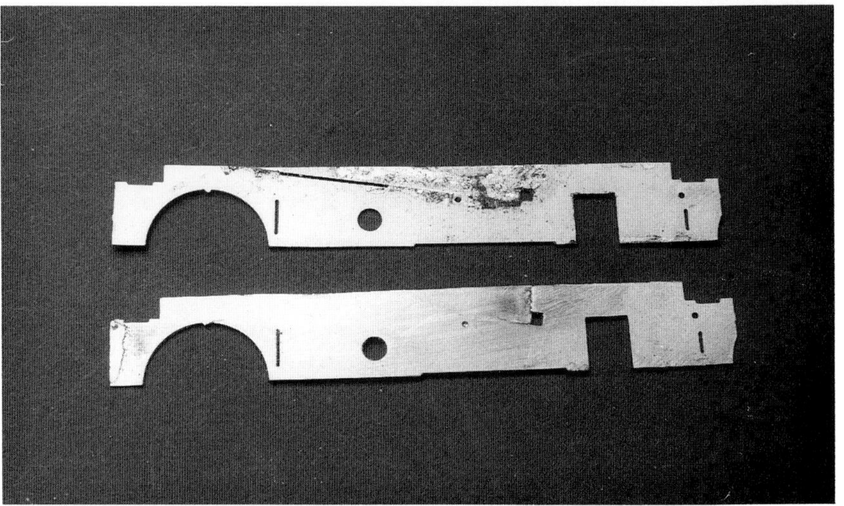

At a later juncture in the building of the 'C12' chassis, I added these little 'cheat' overlays of 10-thou brass, in an effort to suggest the correct frame outline above the firebox sides. Note that the unprototypical cut-outs for the trailing axle (in reality a radial) have also been backed to make them less conspicuous.

CHAPTER FOUR

BASIC CHASSIS CONSTRUCTION

TOOLS, EQUIPMENT AND TECHNIQUES

I usually devote an entire chapter to this topic, but it has now reached the stage in this series of books where I shall start repeating myself. As the construction of model locomotive chassis does not, by and large, call for techniques or equipment that are not also needed to build the rest of the loco, then I'm going to refer in the main to the chapter 'Tools, Techniques and Materials' in *Etched Loco Construction*. Included in this chapter was a fairly comprehensive tool list, to which the rigours of chassis construction will add little – so I'm only adding a small supplementary list here. Otherwise, I carry on with the same armoury of basic hand tools, and the same techniques.

Soldering is obviously the main operation involved in putting together an etched loco chassis, so I'll concentrate on that for a moment. As an aside, it is interesting to note that most of the other designs of loco-kit chassis – cast or milled blocks, keyhole frames on screwed spacers or best durum pasta stuck together with egg-white – were devised to *avoid* the poor inept modeller having to solder anything together. I think that it is now generally accepted that a mastery of simple soldering techniques is a prerequisite for assembling most modern kits. I've written a lot on the subject now, in both the *Etched Loco Construction* and *Whitemetal Loco* volumes of this series, so I'm limiting myself to a swiftish summary of my approach to the job, which I describe by the mock-technical term 'low input' soldering.

SOLDERING FOR CHASSIS ASSEMBLY

The whole basis of my approach to soldering lies in the use of relatively low melting-point 145°C solder, sold by Carrs and others as 'detailing solder'. I have long argued that the use of higher melt solders, such as normal 185–210°C 'tinman's' has no virtue in the context of small-scale sheet metalwork, as in building models from etched components. Obviously, to get 210° solder to flow properly and produce a strong, smooth, fully-formed bond, requires a lot more heat than is needed to achieve the same result with 145° alloy. This greater heat requirement makes for greater difficulty in (ouch!) handling the job, causes far greater problems with thermal expansion, heat-soak and consequent distortion on cooling, and calls for much heftier soldering equipment. The end result is often poor, dull, grey, 'dry' joints, blobs of solder hither and thither, and a model that has buckled and cockled everywhichway.

By contrast, the use of 145° solders means that the whole job stays much, much cooler, with greater ease of handling and a marked reduction in expansion and cooling problems. Excellent results can be achieved with a low-powered iron, which is much smaller and lighter, and thus much easier to use. Not only that, but the 145° solders are very high in tin and bismuth, which means that they flow much more readily than tinman's solder, with its greater lead content. And, as it's far easier to achieve working temperatures well up the melting scale of the solder, the chances are that a properly-formed joint will result, rather than the imperfect joints that are apt to result if higher melt solders are used at the lower end of their working range.

In the dozen or so years that I have been teaching modelling skills, both in the context of formal residential and weekend courses, and as a demonstrator and lecturer at shows, I have consistently found that soldering is the skill which causes most angst; I have also found that introducing modellers who are experiencing difficulties with soldering to the use of 145° solders and phosphoric acid fluxes provides a real breakthrough in proficiency in over 90% of cases, for the simple reason that this is a soldering system suited to the job in hand, not one devised to enable tinkers to fettle stewpots a century or two before the etched loco kit was invented.

The use of phosphoric acid as a flux has long been associated in most modellers' minds with the assembly of whitemetal loco kits with 70° eutectic alloy, sometimes called 'whitemetal solder' or 'low melt solder'. While effective with these alloys (they are not, strictly speaking, solders, being of different chemical composition, and suited only for joining lead-based alloy castings together), phosphoric acid is also an ideal flux for use on brass, nickel and other modelling metals. Ideally, it should be at a greater strength than is usual for use with whitemetal – about 12% by volume, rather than the 6–7% dilution normal in fluxes such as Model Aids 'Super Flux' sold for whitemetal work. 12% phosphoric acid flux is sold by Martin Brent as 'Phosflux 12', and it is to be hoped that other sources will soon appear. It is easy to make in quantity, as described in *Whitemetal Locos*. The weaker brew, such as 'Super Flux', still works pretty well, and if you're desperate on a Sunday, Coca-Cola contains a high enough concentration of phosphoric acid to solder with!

These soldering materials, which I have advocated in the construction of etched loco kit superstructures, are just as effective in the context of chassis work. By and large, I find that I can get away with the same small soldering iron – the 15W Antex or similar 18W SRB type 1 – that I use for more delicate modelling operations. A large-framed chassis in 20 thou brass, with more metal of high thermal conductivity, may call for a touch more grunt in the iron; a DJH battleship job definitely will – so for these heavier jobs I wheel on the 25W Antex, still a small and dainty iron, but one that packs a hefty punch. These days, I can also call on my resistance soldering equipment, which, even in the 'lower register' of its six power levels, will make short work of any chassis soldering job. Nice, but not necessary.

The actual soldering technique differs not a jot from that already described and dissected in the earlier books. This might be described as a 'standard modeller's', rather than 'correct', approach; that is, the solder is carried to the (generously pre-fluxed) job on the tip of the iron. In my heretical view, the correct technique in any application is that which is most effective in getting the job done – which is probably just one of the reasons why I'm a failed fifth-rate pianist! The only provisos with regard to successful soldering are those not limited to my low-temperature approach – the need for cleanliness, and a proper tinning of the iron. Cleanliness means not just buffing up the job and keeping the bit clean (try a wodge of wire wool in a little holder, as in

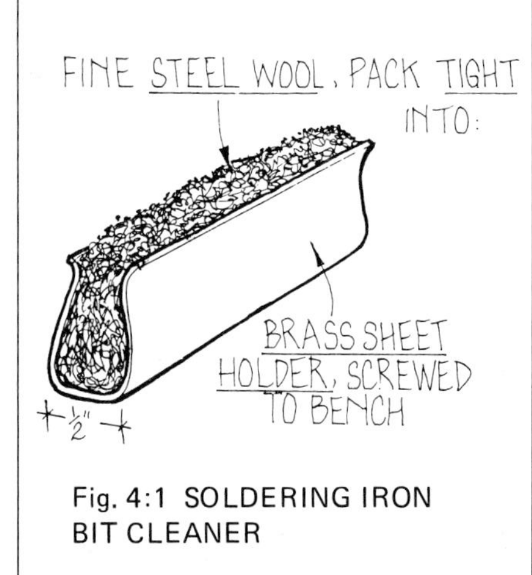

Fig. 4:1 SOLDERING IRON BIT CLEANER

the sketch), but also the necessity of making sure that the *solder* is clean – which it often isn't.

As, believe it or not, I do try to avoid repeating myself, I shall say no more about soldering and soldering equipment here. I devoted an entire chapter of the *Etched Loco* book to a fairly detailed and far-reaching analysis of the whole business of soldering etched bits together, and this is precisely what we'll be doing in assembling the vast majority of modern loco chassis kits. So, I'm afraid, I shall resort to the oldest and most transparent of marketing ploys, in suggesting that those of you who don't have a copy of *Etched Locos* but still want to read more of Rice on the Laws of Phosphoric and One-forty-five, take steps to rectify so gaping an omission in your libraries . . .

SPECIALIST TOOLS FOR CHASSIS CONSTRUCTION

There aren't too many of these, so here's the 'short list' I promised a page or so ago, which should be read in conjunction with the more basic and far-reaching list propounded in the *Etched Locos* book, also reproduced alongside. A lot of the 'specialist tools' aren't at all grand, barely qualifying as tools as such, while the rest are of general utility and complement my basic tool selection in a much broader sense.

A CHASSIS-BUILDER'S TOOL LIST

For measuring and marking:

1 A pair of dividers or screw callipers.
2 A 6in steel rule, metric, with ½mm divisions. Rabone Chesterman No. 64. Keep away from phosphoric flux, which stains.
3 A vernier calliper gauge – a basic engineering tool that is worth spending a few bob on, although you don't need digital read-outs to six decimal places. Mine came from a government surplus store for £15.
4 Engineer's scriber – Eclipse No. 227.
5 Small engineer's square. Moore and Wright No. 400, 3¼in × 1⅞in.
6 Permanent felt marker.

For cutting, fettling and fitting:

1 A 'Scrawker' – see description in Chapter 3.
2 Set of tapered jig-axles, preferably 3 off.
3 Two or three lengths of ⅛in steel rod, for chassis alignment. Try Steve Hodgson at Sharman Wheels.
4 Chassis assembly jig – see this chapter.
5 ⅛in diameter centre punch. A problem to find at the moment, and I regret no commercial source known to Rice. The chap who can undoubtedly make you one is Ken Cottle at KGC Engineering, 4 Harbury Dell, Luton, Beds., LU3 3XH. 0582–572420.
6 Set of jeweller's screwdrivers, ranging from something big enough for 8BA down to something small enough for a Portescap gear grubscrew. Lots about – those sets sold at shows in blue plastic boxes with clear lids for about £2 are fine.
7 Piercing Saw – the good old Eclipse PS50, plus a selection of blades – M6/0, 4/0 and 2 cover most things. To go with this, some sort of saw table is required – see the text and *Fig 4:3*.

A brief perusal of this pithy little selection will, by now, contain a lot of familiar ground. The measuring/marking gear has, of course, far wider relevance than merely in assessing the worth and accuracy of etched chassis, or making frame spacers and rods. The dividers don't need to be anything special – a rather nicer alternative to school geometry-set items is a pair of old-fashioned straight-leg screw callipers, which often turn up at flea markets and 'antique fairs'. Steel rules are much of a muchness, really, though if you lash out on a rustless chrome steel one it'll be easier to keep clean. The vernier calliper is probably the most useful all-round measuring device for the modeller, and if you intend to progress beyond the basics will be well worth acquiring. CK make a tolerable cheapy, but the nice ones all come from Japan, made by Mitutoyo, and cost about £20 upwards. Keep an eye open, though – they turn up secondhand, or, as in my own case, at Government surplus outlets, if you don't mind WD arrows all over your toolkit.

The scriber, square and felt marker are all basic marking-out tools that are just as relevant to building wagons in Plastikard, structures in card and locos in brass. If you're ever going to do more in the modelling line than shake kit-boxes, you'll need them. The rest of the list, with the possible exception of the ⅛in centre punch (which isn't, anyway, an essential), can be cobbled up at home or from scrap. Commercial jig-axles are available, from Perseverance, and I'm trying to persuade someone to market my taper design, preferably in aluminium. Watch press for details, as they say. The alignment rods can be ⅛in brass, which John Flack sells, and I seem to recollect that aluminium knitting needles of this diameter are available, but I'm afraid I don't know the number. Which leaves the grandly titled chassis assembly jig, which is actually dead simple. *Fig 4:2* really says all there is to say about this exceedingly low-tech bit of kit. The jeweller's screwdrivers are pretty ubiquitous, and turn up at every model show for very little money. You do need a tiddler for gear grubscrews and motor mount metrics.

The jeweller's piercing saw is a very basic item in the scratch-builder's tool kit, but it does have far wider applications than the purist fretting of delicate components from the virgin metal. It's a trimmer-off of odd bits par excellence, a chewer-out of openings or slots, and a precise etching de-nibber. It's also the ideal tool for chomping out hornguide openings in etched chassis should you be dabbling with a spot of compensation. It is best used in conjunction with a simplified saw-table of some sort, and the modest effort sketched in *Fig 4:3*, intended to sit in our ordinary engineer's vice, will serve for most jobs.

Otherwise, everything you'll ever need, with the possible exception of a Romford axle-nut screwdriver, is on the 'general' list. The only thing that got missed off last time round was a brace of craft knives, but I've added them here. Of special relevance to chassis work are the taper broaches and the reamer; this last will be essential to do a proper job of opening out holes etched in frames to take bearings, while the broaches are invaluable in easing out crankpin holes in coupling rods, or rivet-holes in valve gear. The broaches also cut down the need

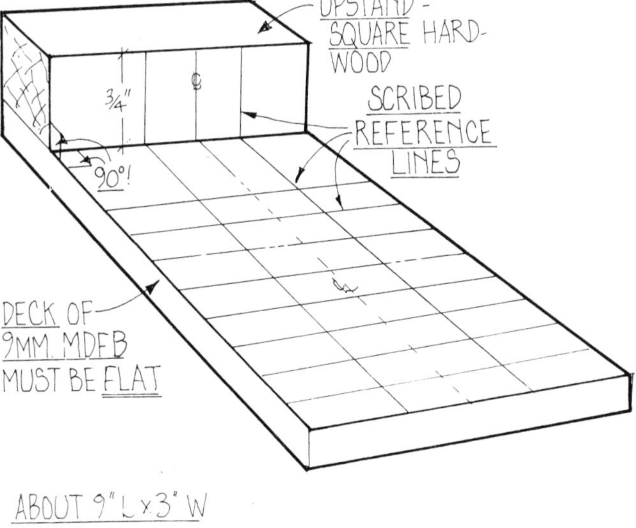

Fig. 4:2 CHASSIS ASSEMBLY JIG

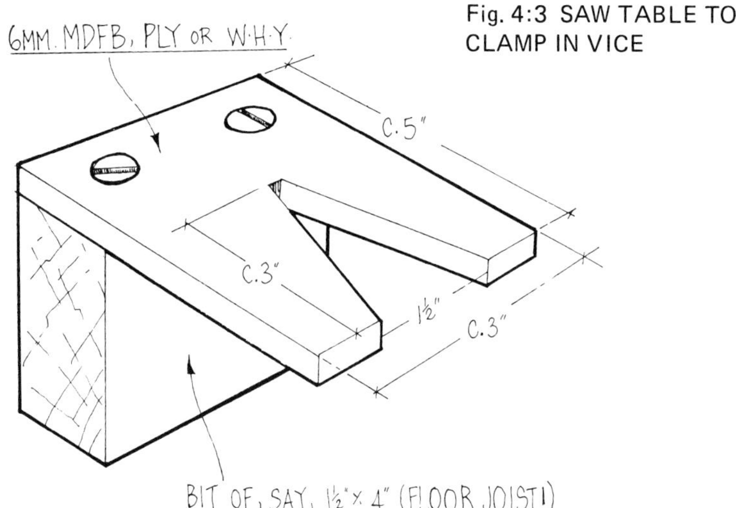

Fig. 4:3 SAW TABLE TO CLAMP IN VICE

for a wide selection of (very expensive) small HS twist drills – simply drill holes undersize and broach out to the required fit.

On the materials front, as well as the soldering necessities described earlier, we shall need some form of locking compound to secure gears or wheels onto axles, and to prevent nuts unscrewing. 'Loctite' is the generic and trade name for these chemicals – they are not, strictly, adhesives, and two are of particular value in chassis work. No. 601 'Retainer' is the real beastie for securing the gears and wheels, while No. 242 'Nutlock' does just what it says (sources in suppliers index). Please note that 'Superglue' is not suitable for these applications. Superglue is also a lousy lubricant, but it doesn't know this, and does its level best to nip into gearboxes and bearings if you let it anywhere near a chassis. What is much more useful is a good, non-degrading clock oil, such as J. R. Windle's (prize medal, Paris, 1867), and a low-viscosity grease – I use high-tech Teflon-loaded 'Tri-Flow' from A.R.M. lubricants (sources, again, in index).

PREPARING AN ETCHED CHASSIS FOR ASSEMBLY

The first operation to be undertaken in the assembly of any kit, be it for a chassis or anything else, is to study the instructions and the kit contents, in the undying hope that you will be able to relate the one to the other, and thus gain some insight into how the thing is *supposed* to go together. I haven't said too much about kit instructions in my 'assessment' chapter, mainly because most of what I'd like to say is probably unprintable. An exploded diagram is a ray of hope, but clear, concise and logical instructions are rare. DJH try, but make things convoluted by continually referring you to an involved parts list, everything being described purely by part number. I often find reading and understanding the instructions the most difficult stage of any kit assembly, and I'm afraid that I often abandon the manufacturer's 'party line' in favour of the dictates of common-sense and experience.

In the case of chassis, there is a degree of general conformity in the way the basics fit together, and I find that so long as I'm clear as to the identity of the various parts, then I can generally make a pretty fair stab at putting them together in a logical sequence. I often find myself at variance with the intended method of assembly anyway, as will have become apparent in my comments earlier in this book! So, I'll usually end up by discarding screwed spacers in favour of L-section fold-ups, or in fitting the cylinders supplied to my own stretchers and bracketry to ensure that the centres make sense. My own long-standing preference for 'Flexi-chas' compensated chassis also frequently finds me modifying frames to accept this system.

In point of fact, the most common basic chassis assembly sequence isn't really affected by the inclusion or otherwise of compensation, as in simple terms all that we're doing is to align the frames and spacers accurately, and solder them together. I've started here by illustrating a very plain chassis, the current 'Perseverance' item for an 0–6–0 tank (the ubiquitous GWR '57XX' pannier, as it unsurprisingly happens). This does at least include decent fold-up spacers, and as depicted is being built with a straight bat, absolutely out of the packet. The rigid version would be identical, except that I would not have cut out the hornguide openings for the front two axles.

As with most modern chassis kits, this Perseverance item does not include motor,

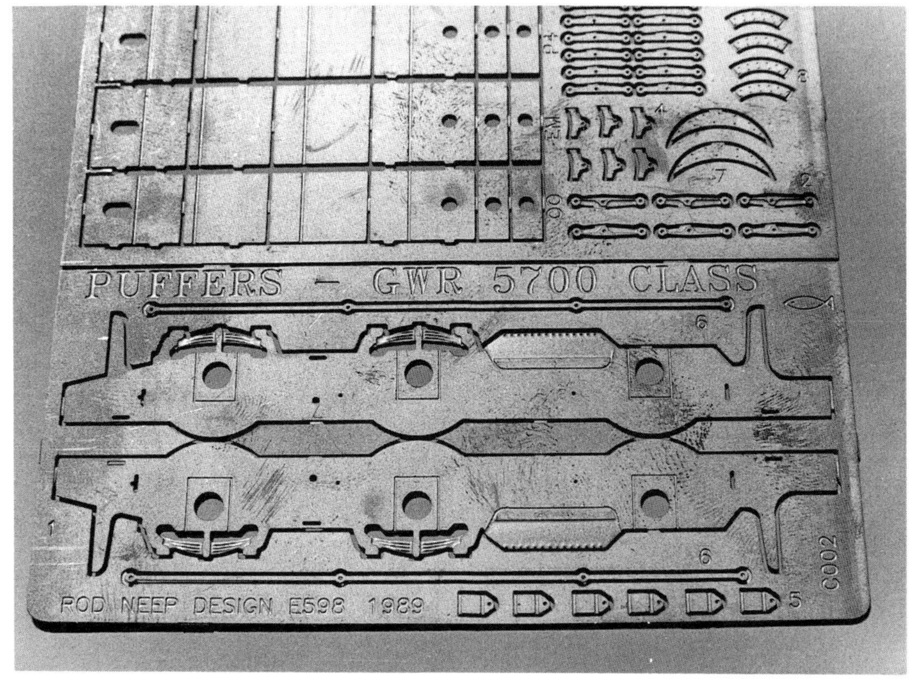

Starting point: here is the basic frame etch of the Puffers/Perseverance '57XX' chassis kit in its latest incarnation.

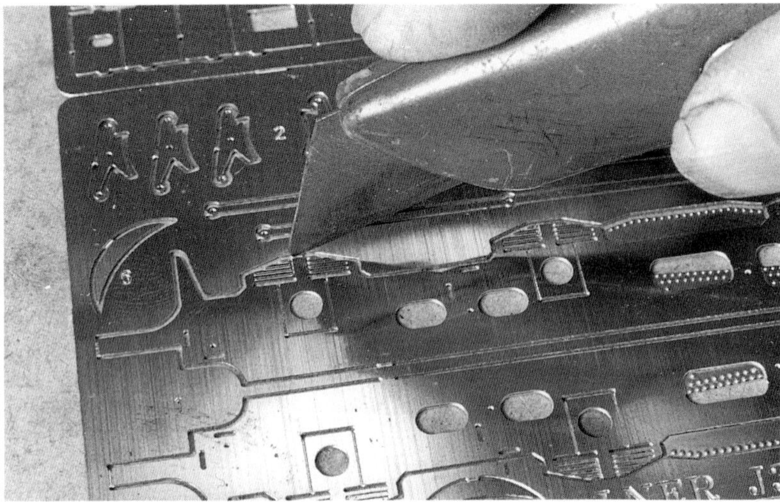

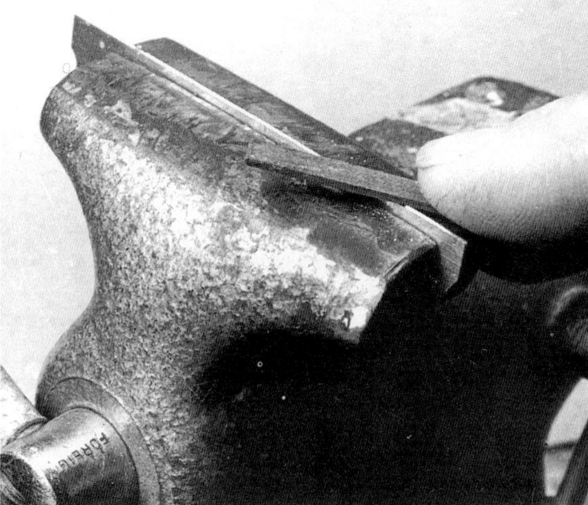

Left: *Cutting components from an etched fret without distorting them calls for care, firm support and a suitable tool. Here, an ordinary Stanley No. 199 knife with a heavy-duty blade is being used to cut out a Finecast 'J39' chassis etch. Try to cut as close to the component as possible to minimise the amount of cleaning-up required. The job is being supported on an offcut of MDFB (medium density fibre board) – the popular self-healing vinyl mats are* not *suitable, as they 'give' quite a lot, which leads to distorted etchings.* Right: *Filing off etched attachment 'nibs' also calls for care to avoid distortion. Use a fine file, work 'along' the job rather than across, and support the component by clamping in the (smooth-jaw) vice, as here.*

gears and wheels, leaving these to individual choice and the dictates of the modelling standards in use. While I shall have plenty to say on these matters in the appropriate chapters, it's obviously a good idea to decide on such things before you start building the chassis. For the record, the '57XX' was intended for my P4 'Trerice' china-clay layout, so had a set of Sharman wheels to this standard, and used the appropriate set of spacers provided in the kit.

Once I was happy that I knew what went where, and had settled on the rest of my 'spec', then I could start building. First job is to part the various etchings from the frets, which I did with a good hefty craft knife, supporting the fret on an offcut of MDFB (Medium Density Fibre Board) as a cutting-block. At this initial stage, I'm only interested in basic components – the mainframes, and the requisite frame spacers. Once they are freed from the rest of the etch, they can be 'cleaned up' to remove etching cusp marks and attachment nibs. These etchings are a touch on the soft side, and are easily distorted, so handle with care and support with a vice when filing. The photos in the first little sequence should make this clear. At this stage, I also cut out the hornblock openings on the leading two axles – a process described in the 'compensation' chapter.

The next step is to bend up the various frame spacers, and check them for fit. The wide etched fold lines go, as is general, to the inside of the bend; the edge of the vice jaw is a useful reference edge and folding aid. On trying the various tabs in their appropriate slots in the frames, I found that they would not enter cleanly. As a good, tight fit is desirable, this is to be preferred to the alternative, slop. However, it's one of the virtues of the tabbed L-section stretcher

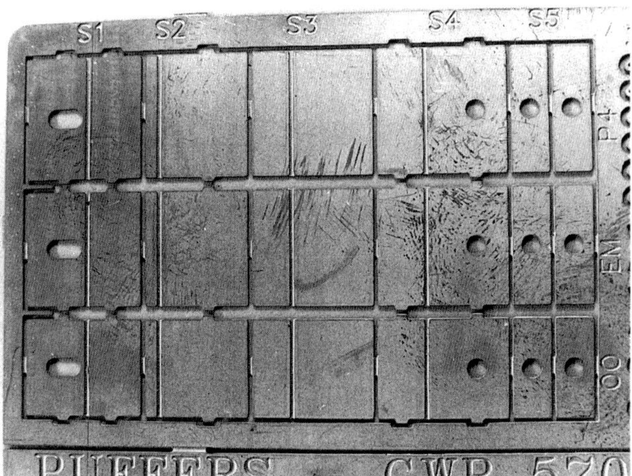

Frame spacers. The fold-up 'L' spacers of the '57XX' come in three widths suited to the popular gauges. The 'S5' flat spacers are intended for use as body-mounts. I used them as motor mounts instead!

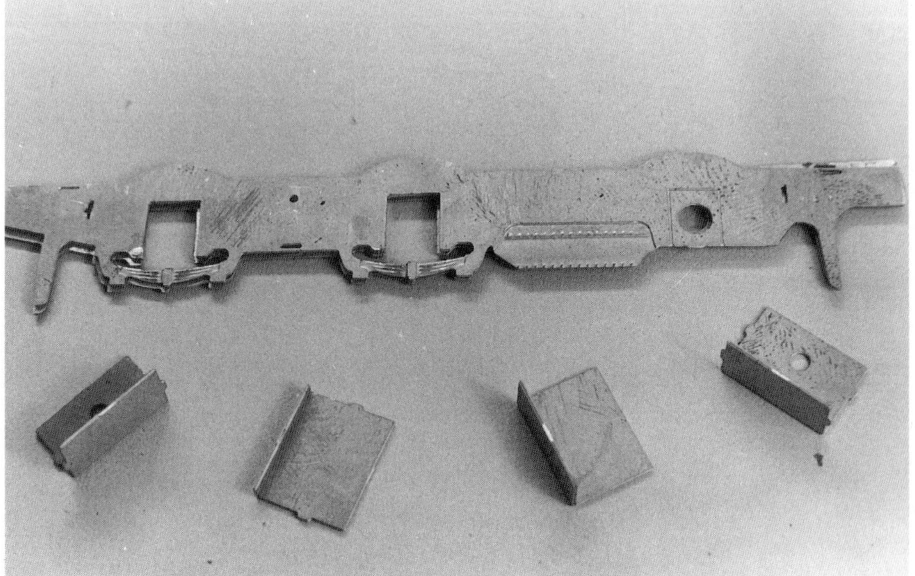

The '57XX' uses four L-spacers shown here folded to shape and related to the prepared frames, which have had the openings for the hornguides cut out.

that the tab on each leg of the 'L' limits the movement of the tab on the other leg, so even a slightly loose fit shouldn't cause problems – especially as we're 'backing up' the stretcher location with the chassis assembly jig and the alignment rods. In the case of 'tight' tabs, as here, I find it easier to carefully file down the tab, rather than trying to open out the slot in the frames.

If, as I have occasionally found, the tabs and slots don't line up, then more drastic action is called for. I simply cut the offending tabs right off, and proceed as for plain, home-made L-section spacer using the jig and alignment rods to get things together accurately and 'in square'. One of the virtues of the use of the 'jigged' approach to chassis erection is that we are no longer dependent upon the spacers to align the frames, but can set the chassis up empirically, and simply insert the required number of spacers to keep it all in shape after assembly. Of course, my little jig isn't the only means by which this desirable end may be achieved. There are one or two commercial jigs on the market, most especially a natty turned aluminium job from the Kean-Maygib stable, which is designed to locate in the hornblock cut-outs of a compensated or sprung chassis. It works well, with the proviso that you need frame spacers of a width exactly equal to that of the jig – not always easy to achieve. My little gadget is of universal application, and I've built the odd 7 mm chassis on it among all the 4 mm tiddlers.

I'm jumping ahead a bit here, with all this talk of frame erection and inserting spacers. Before this can be done by my system, there's a further important preliminary – the fitting of the axle bearings. In a well-ordered world, this would be the work of moments – a touch with the reamer, the pushing home of the bearing, and a touch of solder to retain it. This was, fortunately the case with both the Perseverance and DJH chassis that appear in the pictures – but if you're faced with nasty oversize holes, then you'll be doing battle with one of the remedies suggested in the last chapter. Whatever the degree of error, and however drastic the measures needed to overcome it, I'm afraid that this is the time at which the job must be tackled, unless you are intending to locate and solder the bearings into the holes using jig-axles and coupling rods, as described for correcting axle centres. That is best done after the basic chassis is assembled.

With the bearings located and soldered into the frames – either the full set for a rigid chassis, or those of the fixed 'datum' axle on a Flexi-chas – we have taken care of the mechanical prerequisites for chassis assembly. However, before rushing off to clap it all in the jig and attack it with a soldering iron, it may be worth attending to one or two cosmetic details, and checking that there is a sufficiency of holes to accept the various bits and pieces we may need to tack on to make it look right. I would hope that most modern chassis kits would make provision for brake gear, not only by providing suitable etched, cast or moulded components, but by including the necessary locating holes for brake pivots in the frames. However, some older kits do lack such refinements, which will call for the acquisition of suitable components, preferably etched, and for the drilling of any necessary holes. And for that, now is the time! Tack the frames together with solder, and mark and drill them as a pair. The position of such brake-hanger pivots, you will, of course, be able to determine from the superlative scale drawing with which the kit maker has embellished his instructions... Or, more likely, you'll be proceeding on the rule-of-thumb lines sketched in *Fig 4:4*.

Other cosmetic trifles that may engage you at this time include the pushing-out of any rivet or bolt heads intended to be reproduced by the 'dimple in the back' system, calling for judicious use of a blunt scriber. The current trend is to include a far greater amount of chassis detail of this type, which is welcome. But it does need consideration during the assembly sequence, not only where embossing is concerned, but in the addition of overlays and small detail fittings, which may well be easier to fit with the frames lying flat on the bench. I think that, when tackling these 'new wave', all-singing, all-dancing chassis kits, it's important to get away from the old approach of 'make it work first, bung a bit of detail on later'. Integration is the name of the game, nowadays.

ERECTING AN ETCHED CHASSIS

With all the necessary preparation completed, the actual erection of a straightforward etched chassis only takes a few moments. I never try and solder all the frame spacers in at one 'hit', for a number of reasons. The fundamental alignment of a chassis in plan is really determined by the relationship of the frames to the foremost and rearmost spacers, so I initially set out to fit just these. As the photos of the embryo '57XX' show, I solder the fore spacer to one frame, and the aft to another. This is

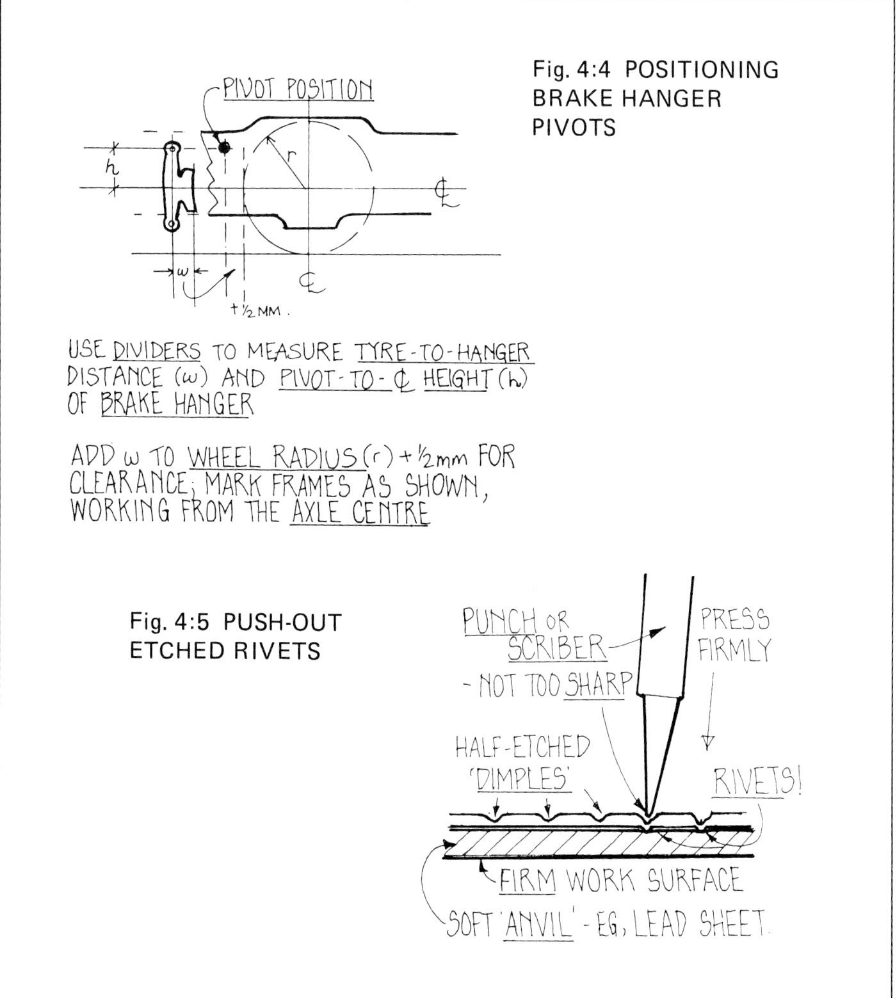
PIVOT POSITION
h
r
w
+½ MM
USE DIVIDERS TO MEASURE TYRE-TO-HANGER DISTANCE (w) AND PIVOT-TO-℄ HEIGHT (h) OF BRAKE HANGER
ADD w TO WHEEL RADIUS (r) + ½mm FOR CLEARANCE; MARK FRAMES AS SHOWN, WORKING FROM THE AXLE CENTRE
PUNCH OR SCRIBER
- NOT TOO SHARP
PRESS FIRMLY
HALF-ETCHED 'DIMPLES'
RIVETS!
FIRM WORK SURFACE
SOFT 'ANVIL' - EG, LEAD SHEET

Fig. 4:4 POSITIONING BRAKE HANGER PIVOTS

Fig. 4:5 PUSH-OUT ETCHED RIVETS

not just me being cussed, but represents an attempt to prevent uneven heating of the frames during final assembly, by making one joint at each side, rather than both joints on the same side. This, hopefully, avoids the all-too-common result of a banana-shaped chassis, caused by cooling of an assembly in which one side has expanded rather more than the other.

With these two 'foundation spacers' in place, I offer up the frames to the jig. Normally, I build chassis 'upside down', as the top side, designed to mate with the body, is usually a lot less bumpy than an underside cluttered up with springs and so on. The chassis is aligned in the jig by pushing the nose (or tail – you can start either end) of the frames against the upstand, and by lining them up with the longitudinal guide-lines. The lengths of steel or brass rod used to check chassis alignment are then passed through such of the axle-holes as are fitted with bearings – all of them, in the case of a rigid chassis such as the DJH 'West Country', or the single 'datum axle' on a 'Flexi-chas' such as the Pannier tank. These rods are carefully compared with one another, and with the scribed reference lines on the chassis jig. The objective, obviously, is to have all axles exactly parallel to each other, and at a true right-angle with the frames.

These checks should be made carefully, as the fundamental accuracy of the chassis depends upon them. If a discrepancy in these crucial relationships becomes apparent, it must be rectified before any more progress can be made. 'Axles out of parallel' is a pretty basic fault, and will call for jiggery-pokery with the bearings in the frames, as described in Chapter 3, using the jig-axles to set things up again from scratch. If you have already done this once, it may be worth checking that the coupling rods that you have been using to jig-set each side of the chassis are themselves a pair. Discrepancies are not unknown. The lack of right-angularity between axles and frames is a much simpler matter to put right, and will usually be found to have its origins in slight inequalities in the ends of the frames butted against the upstand of the jig. True them up with a file, and re-erect the chassis.

Once you are happy that all is aligned as it should be, the first of the two soldered joints is made. I generally go for the one at the end of the chassis closest to the upstand of the jig – in the case of the guinea-pig pannier, the alignment rod was a nice tight fit in the bearing-holes, so the back of the chassis was being held nice and square. Once I had got a proper, fully-flowed joint at the fore end of this chassis, I tack-soldered the rear spacer in place, and re-checked for alignment in all possible planes – frames sitting firmly on the deck of the jig, frames vertical and parallel (the small square is a good check here), and frames straight, parallel and in correct relation to the axle in plan. Any necessary adjustments are made by unsoldering and re-tacking the joint of this second spacer. Care at this stage, and a stern resistance of any temptation to hurry the checking, will pay rich dividends in a sound and square assembly. Only when I've kidded myself that it's all where it should be and all's right in the world do I 'flow and finish' the joint of this second frame spacer.

Now is a good time to wander off and have a brew-up. By the time you get back with a mug of the fragrant and steaming, the chassis will have cooled naturally and developed any kinks or other little wayward traits, which should be apparent. You can also cast a fresh eye on the job to make sure that you've got it as square as you think you have. If you haven't, then I'm afraid it's time to unsolder that joint and try again – but if you've taken the right

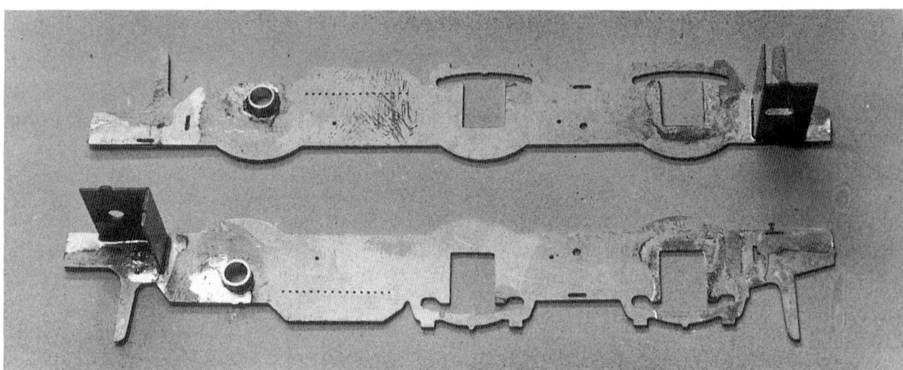

The '57XX' frames ready for final erection, with the two end spacers in place on opposite frames. Note the 'dimples' for the rivets on the lower firebox sides, pushed out with a scriber as described. The bearings of the fixed axle are also in place to act as location for the 'reference rod' during final assembly.

The chassis jig, in all its primitive glory – MDFB base, hardwood 'up-stand', reference lines ruled on with a Rotring pen. Sorry about the shadows – a sunny day!

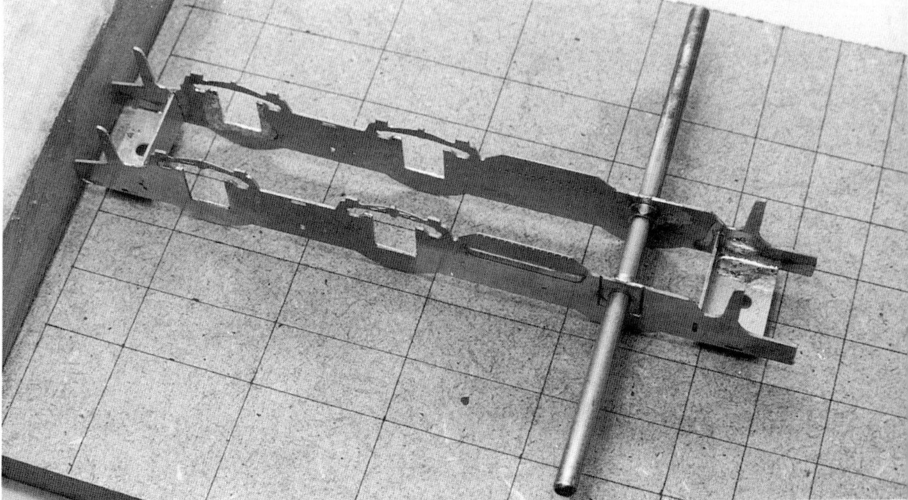

The chassis in course of erection on the jig – spacer tabs located in frames, reference rod through fixed axle bearings, ready for tacking, checking and final soldering.

trouble at the right time, all should be well. If you find that the frames have developed a slight twist in 'wind' (front and rear spacers not quite vertically aligned), you can usually sort that by giving the whole chassis a good 'tweak' in the required direction, but if the frames have gone out of square or assumed their Fyffes impersonation, unsoldering is the only answer, I'm afraid.

Fig. 4:6 CHASSIS DISTORTED IN WIND

GIVE IT A GOOD TWEAK
THUSWISE
NOT PARALLEL

Assuming that all is well, then you can congratulate yourself on achieving a true and sound foundation for a model locomotive. Being a cautious sort of soul, though, I always like to run a few verification checks on rigid chassis at this time, by fitting the jig-axles and offering up the coupling-rods to ensure that I've still got my vital agreement between their centres. It's rare for anything to shift, unless a frame-spacer joint is very close to a wheel-bearing soldered into an oversize hole. This possibility is obviated by my preferred order of doing things – frames first, bearings second – when that particular bodge is called into play. Once I'm happy about all these fundamentals, I fit the rest of the frame spacers – it's easy enough to 'spring' the frames by the small amount necessary to enter any tabs into their slots.

That completes the basic chassis assembly, but another job I like to sort out at this juncture is the fit of the chassis to the loco superstructure, and the means of locating and retaining it. A lot of cast kits come with the footplate as a single casting, but I do undertake any necessary building up of footplate assemblies needed to enable me to carry out both the check, and to devise and install the body retaining system. Points to note in the check include the obvious one of ensuring that the chassis actually fits – especially lengthwise between the bufferbeams, as well as such less obvious correlations as axle-centres with splasher centres. Don't always assume that butting the front of the frames up against the front bufferbeam will give you an exact relationship here – the chassis may have to be adjusted 'fore and aft' to get everything lined up. Lined up it must be, though – driving wheels that don't quite 'match' their splashers look awful, and a small error is surprisingly obvious.

I discussed body-fixing systems briefly at the end of the last chapter, and *Fig 3:17* set out the principles to which I adhere. With whitemetal superstructures where the body fixing screw can be located into a reasonable thickness of material, I quite often make use of a small self-tapping screw ($\frac{1}{4}$in No. 4) rather than either trying to cut a fine BA thread (not easy in whitemetal – it binds the tap badly, calling for lots of lubrication and the clearing of swarf every quarter-turn) or solder on a nut. Again, the emphasis on quick and easy body removal goes back

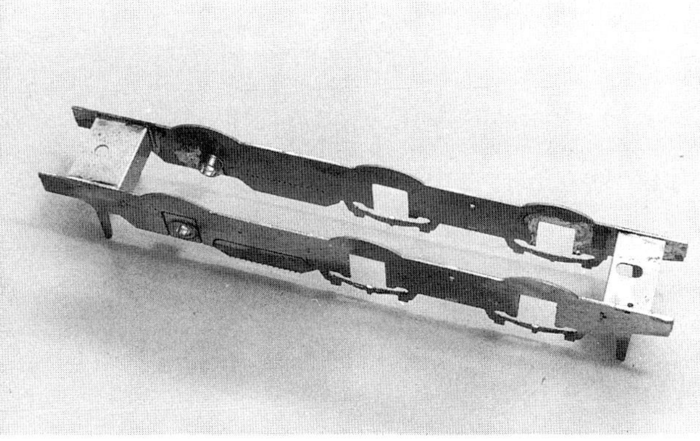

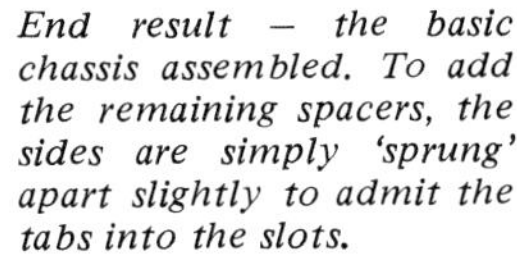

End result – the basic chassis assembled. To add the remaining spacers, the sides are simply 'sprung' apart slightly to admit the tabs into the slots.

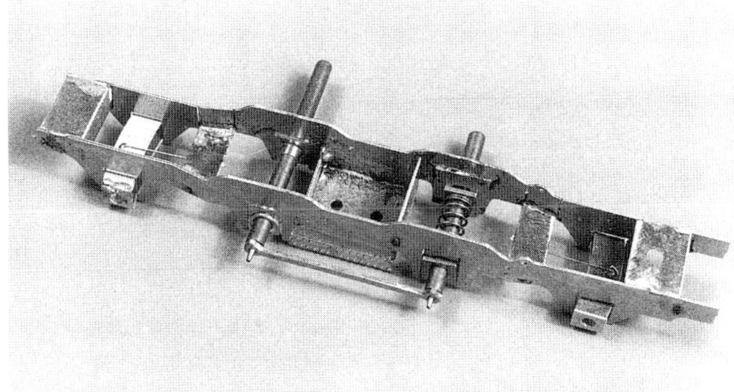

Here is a fully assembled set of frames, for the LNWR 4ft 6in 'Radial Tank', with all spacers in place, not to mention the radial trucks and hornblocks. Note that this chassis is 'stepped-in' at the ends to give a greater sideplay allowance to the leading and trailing wheels. The reference lines on the chassis jig are very useful in getting such frame 'joggles' symmetrical.

The frames of the DJH 'West Country' have been erected onto a full set of home-made 'L' spacers of a more generous width than DJH's turned efforts. This makes a very strong chassis.

to Ahern and the days of motors needing frequent maintenance, cleaning or adjustment. By contrast, there's not much you can do for a modern enclosed 'can', even less for a coreless. I find that I take loco bodies off once or twice a year at most, while a lot of my 'old stagers' haven't had their mechanisms touched for five years or more. So a self-cut thread and self-tapping screw are a perfectly valid fixing in such an application.

CAST AND MILLED BLOCK CHASSIS

These don't, of course, require any assembly, and so long as they are properly designed and well made, will come out of the box at a stage roughly equivalent to the etched chassis after assembly. This isn't to imply that nothing should be done to them before moving on to the fitting of wheels, motors and gears. Assuming that any necessary corrections needed to sort out the match with the coupling rods have been carried out, there will not, at this stage, be any mechanical work to do; but it is possible and well worthwhile to do something about the look of the thing, especially if it's being built for EM, or has gaping motor cut-outs or other expedient eyesores. A set of cosmetic overlays is the answer to a number of ills.

Actually, it amazes me that no kitmaker (that I know of) has come up with the rather obvious notion of combining a 'solid' mechanism block, with it's built-in accuracy and solder-free assembly, with a set of etched overlays to make a chassis that looks right. As these would have no mechanical significance, accuracy would not be critical, and they could be simply stuck in place. Such a chassis would still be markedly inferior to the modern all-etched designs in terms of flexibility of mechanical specification, but it would look 100% better than any unadorned cast block. Back in the days before I decided to stick to a policy of using only etched or homebuilt 'thinframe' chassis, I would produce overlays in Plastikard or thin sheet metal to disguise my Wills or K's unaesthetic chunks, especially in my brief EM phase about 1967–8. The improvement in appearance (and the saving in spacing washers) was quite dramatic. I have sketched the basic arrangement I used to use in *Fig 4:6*.

Other than these cosmetic embellishments, there's not really much you can do to a block chassis without getting drastic. So the only other operation that will need undertaking at this juncture is the establishing of the body/chassis relationship and the provision of mountings, exactly as described for the etched versions.

Fig. 4:7 COSMETIC OVERLAYS FOR SOLID CHASSIS

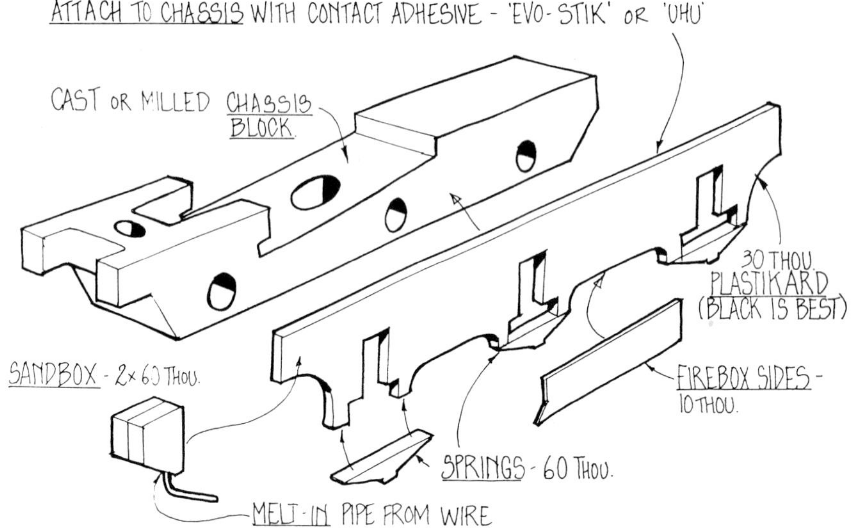

SCREWED CHASSIS ASSEMBLY

My dislike for chassis designed to be assembled onto screwed spacers – and the reasons for such an antithesis – has been well-aired in earlier chapters. I would never contemplate a chassis held together solely by a couple of screws each side into measly brass cylinders. I should expect to find some additional means of holding the thing together, such as DJH provided in the case of the 'West Country', where etched spacers intended to locate the body onto the chassis are provided. These are designed to be soldered in place, using tab-and-slot location – which immediately begs the question: if the modeller is deemed capable of soldering these in place, then why not provide a full set of such tab-and-slot spacers? In my opinion the use of the screwed spacers seems pointless in such circumstances. And, as I can't resist drumming home, it would be a simple matter for DJH then to cater for the EM and P4 modellers who presumably form a significant proportion of their customers.

I hope that I have managed to convince you that the answer to screwed-spacer chassis is to provide them with a set of decent fold-up 'L' spacers, as I did for the 'West Country' illustrated. The chassis can then be set up in the jig and soldered together exactly as described for the all-etched Perseverance 'Pannier' kit. However, if you're not convinced, then I suppose that it would be possible to set up the chassis and screw the frames to the spacers, which are used rather as a jig. Additional spacers, à la DJH, can then be soldered in, or solder run into the joint between screwed spacer and frame. I used to do that with the old K's 'Keyhole' chassis, filling in the slot of the screwhead with solder at the same time for good measure. Screwheads sticking out of the frames, a scale foot or so in diameter, are not to be tolerated in the context of a modern, high-quality, super-detailed superstructure. Assuming that solder hadn't infiltrated the screw-threads, the offending screws could be removed once the chassis had been permanently joined together, while if you opt for the sort of cosmetic overlays advocated for solid block chassis the screwheads could be thus decently concealed from view.

SUMMARY

That is all there is to putting together the bare bones of a chassis. The process is the same, no matter what the prototype (I speak here of British locos, not US bar-framed wonders, Shays or other geared locos, French metre-gauge compound Mallet tanks and Sharman-type Neanderthal Cramptons), the number of axles, the disposition of cylinders, valve gears and associated brackets, and the presence of bogies and pony trucks. These are all addenda to the basic chassis, and will be considered in due season, starting with the first last, just to add a little confusion and to continue with my logically illogical sequence.

CHAPTER FIVE

A BRIEF SKIRMISH WITH BOGIES AND PONY TRUCKS

INTRODUCTION

It was a bit of a job deciding on the right order of business for this book. Of all the awkward topics that needed to be fitted in somewhere, bogies and their kin were the most awkward – only right, really, being wholly in keeping with the awkwardnesses they can display in practice. I mean, something pretty drastic has to be wrong somewhere to derail a simple 0–4–0; but tack on a bogie before or behind, and you have a recipe for an engine that likes to dip its toes in the ballast at the least excuse. I've known a good few model locos of both the 4–4–0 and 0–4–4T persuasion that functioned a great deal better without the bogie than they did with it – which exposes an apparent conflict between the cosmetic and practical roles of bogies on many model engines.

To my way of thinking, the heart of the problem lies with the consideration of bogies as merely cosmetic additions to otherwise straightforward four or six-coupled mechanisms. This is an approach that seems to have gained great credence among the kitmaking fraternity, who rarely seem able to grasp the functional nature of such accoutrements – an aspect of chassis design that Ahern *did* address back in 1948. The result of this negation of the proper workings of bogies and pony trucks is the reduction of all model locos so fitted to a toy-like quality of running, characterised by riding over curves and pointwork more akin to a dodgem than a 'Duchess'. As I hope will have become apparent, I think it important to engineer model locomotive chassis to take account of all the functions of the real thing – which means that bogies need to *work*.

PRACTICAL CONSIDERATIONS

As with all aspects of model chassis design, it's first helpful to gain some understanding of the functioning of bogies and other carrying trucks at full size, before setting out to decide which aspects we need to replicate in the model, and how best to achieve the correct effect. Let me tell you, it's not always easy! And, as with so many other aspects of chassis design, while we can learn much from full-size practice, there's no way we can simply scale it down into our model, and expect it to do the business. We need original and apposite design solutions to achieve the desired result. Desired result? To produce, I suggest, a model locomotive that has proper weight distribution over the driven and carrying wheels, and one which receives proper guidance and restraint over the entire length of the chassis, so that it negotiates curved trackwork in a smooth and prototypical manner.

The function of a bogie or trailing truck, leading pony or radial axle at full size is quite critical. Get it wrong, and a loco can be a killer, as the GWR found out with its troublesome '3521' class 0–4–4Ts. The prototype suffers other, less obvious problems – there is a school of thought, for instance, that ascribes the relatively poor performance of the solitary BR '8' Pacific, *Duke of Gloucester*, to defective design of the trailing truck, leading to a harmonic vibration afflicting the firebox. This caused the fire to shift and settle, thus impairing the steaming. At least that's one worry we don't have to cope with! A real engine has additional carrying axles for two basic reasons – to support a proportion of the locomotive's weight, and to provide guidance to the extremities of the loco chassis,

Far from just being decorative additions, real bogies and pony trucks earn their keep. The bogie of this LMS de-streamlined 'Coronation' carries some 20% of the loco weight, being loaded through the pads and slides visible below and just to the front of the cylinders. Visually, it is very much 'of a piece' with the rest of the loco chassis. Separating it with a lot of unprototypical daylight doesn't help the look of a model. AUTHOR'S COLLECTION

Troublesome truck – here is the trailing truck of Duke of Gloucester, *held by some to have defective suspension design, leading to rough riding and poor steaming. It has a massive cast steel frame with fabricated sideframes and coil springs, carrying 16 ton 3 cwt of the engine's total weight of 101 ton 5 cwt.* AUTHOR'S COLLECTION

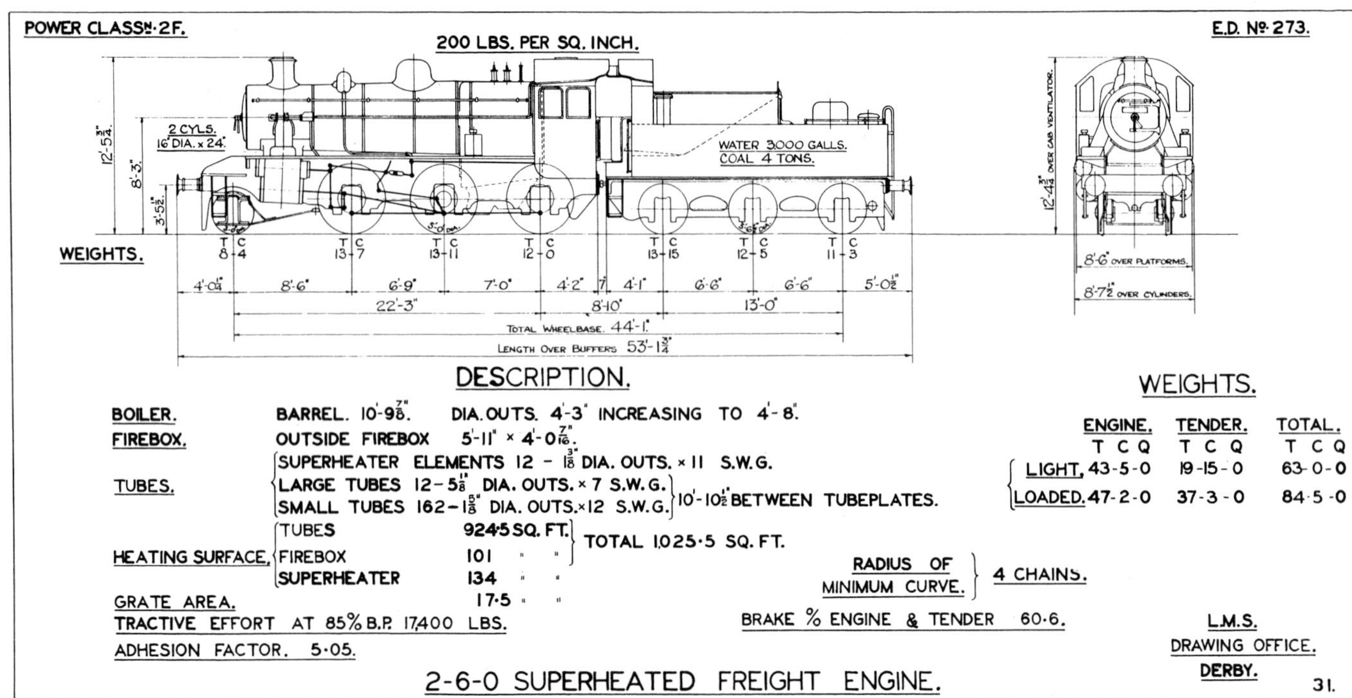

The weight diagram – here, the LMS drawing for the Ivatt lightweight Class '2' 2–6–0 – is an important aspect of prototype loco design. The Civil Engineer will want to see this before he accepts a loco for traffic, and it will determine the route availability of the loco.

WHEEL ARRANGT.	LOCO TYPE.	WEIGHT OF LOCO		WEIGHT ON BOGIE -OR- LEADING TRUCK		% OF TOTAL		WEIGHT ON TRAILING BOGIE OR TRUCK		% OF TOTAL	
		TON	CWT.	TON	CWT.	ACTUAL	* MODEL	TON	CWT.	ACTUAL	* MODEL
4-2-2	GWR DEAN SINGLE	49	0	18	0	37%	30%	13	0	26%	15%
4-4-0	GWR 'BULLDOG'	49	4	17	6	35%	30%				
4-4-0	S.R. 'SCHOOLS'	67	2	25	2	37%	30%				
4-4-2	G.N.R. 'LARGE ATLANTIC'	69	12	16	12	24%	20%	13	0	19%	15%
4-4-2T	LSWR ADAMS 'RADIAL'	54	17	16	8	30%	25%	10	13	19%	15%
0-4-4T	LSWR ADAMS 'T1'	53	0					17	17	34%	40%
0-4-2T	GWR '517'	27	2					7	17	29%	30%
2-4-0T	GWR 'METRO' (SMALL)	39	10	11	5	28%	30%				
2-4-2T	LNWR 4'6"	45	18	10	1	22%	20%	9	1	20%	20%
2-4-0	GWR 'BARNUM'	42	10	13	8	31%	30%				
2-2-2-0	LNWR 'DREADNOUGHT'	45	0	18	10	41%	30%				
0-4-2	LSWR ADAMS 'JUBILEE'	42	7					10	13	25%	30%
2-6-0	GWR '43XX'	62	0	9	8	15%	20%				
2-6-0	BR. STD. CL. 4 '76XXX'	59	15	9	6	16%	20%				
2-6-2T	GWR '45XX'	57	0	6	10	11%	15%	7	0	12%	15%
2-6-4T	LMS STANIER '4P'	85	5	13	2	15%	15%	21	10	25%	20%
2-6-2	LNER 'V2'	93	2	11	0	12%	15%	16	10	18%	15%
4-6-0	LMS STANIER '5P5F'	72	2	17	17	25%	25%				
4-6-0	GWR 'HALL' 49XX	75	0	18	10	21%	25%				
4-6-0	GWR 'KING' 60XX	89	0	21	10	24%	25%				
4-6-2	LNER GRESLEY 'A'	92	9	17	1	18%	20%	15	8	17%	15%
4-6-2	LMS STANIER 'CORONATION'	105	5	21	10	20%	20%	16	16	16%	15%
2-8-0	LMS STANIER '8F'	72	2	9	0	12%	20%				
2-8-0	LNER O2	78	13	9	6	12%	20%				

DATA COMPILED FROM RLY. Co. OFFICIAL WEIGHT DIAGRAMS — * RICE'S SUGGESTED COMPROMISE.

Fig. 5:1 TABLE OF WEIGHTS

particularly the 'steering' of the front of the engine into curves, and in damping out lateral oscillation caused by the alternating action of a two-cylinder steam engine.

WEIGHT ON BOGIES

Once again, the visit to the favoured preserved line (or the NRM at York) might suggest just how these things are made to work. A moment's thought whilst looking at a real bogie loco – particularly of the 4–4–0, 4–6–0 or 4–6–2 persuasion – will serve to indicate that there's actually quite a concentration of weight at the front end, over the bogie. Those cylinders and their associated steam chests are solid iron or steel castings, weighing several tons, all of which is confined within a few feet of the engine's total length. That weight is almost entirely borne by the bogie. Consulting the BR weight diagram for the aforementioned Class '8' Pacific, which I actually managed to find when I looked for it, tells me that, of a total 'full' weight of 101T 5 Cwt, 19T 2 Cwt was on the leading bogie; in other words, nearly 20%. (For interest, there were 22T dead on each driven axle, and 16T 3 Cwt on the trailing truck.) The value of ascertaining the actual weight carried by each axle or truck in a model loco is only just beginning to receive any real attention, but I've long found it relevant and have reached the conclusion that trying to get about the right proportion of weight onto a loco bogie or truck is helpful in maximising trackholding.

Consulting a few more weight diagrams gave me some rough rule-of-thumb figures to play with. The figure of around 20% of the total weight on the leading bogie of a Pacific seems not untypical (ranging from about 16% on a Gresley 'A3' to about 22% on a Stanier 'Coronation', with over 21T on the bogie). For a 4–6–0, the figure is typically a bit more – the 'Jubilee' has 19T 11 Cwt out of a total of just under 80T, about 25%, a corollary of 3-cylinder design, as does the 'Scot', with an even higher 22T out of 83T, and the 'Sandringham', also 22T but now out of only 77T 5 Cwt. With the ever-troublesome 4–4–0, the figure takes a further leap. A Gresley D49, clocking in at 65T 11 Cwt, has no less than 23T 11 Cwt of that on the leading bogie – slightly more than a third. So, to summarise these earth-shattering researches in a few lines, I would suggest that a Pacific, by and large, calls for 20% of the weight on the front bogie, and around 15% on the rear truck to replicate prototype weight distribution. A 4–6–0 calls for about 25% on the bogie, and a 4–4–0 a full third. Rather than expand this section to tedious lengths with a full analysis of the proportional weight distribution apposite to all manner and types of locos, I have set my own particular conclusions out in tabular form in *Fig 5:1*. Make of these what you will, but the point must be made: in order to function correctly, model locomotive bogies need to carry an appreciable proportion of the total weight of the model, or to be weighted within themselves to something around that proportion.

Transferring the appropriate degree of loading to a bogie is not, it must be said, the easiest trick in the book. Ahern advises simply making the bogie itself as heavy as possible, so that it will hold the track with a sufficient degree of surety to enable it to carry out its other main function, that of guidance. This is, in terms of the model, the more critical aspect of bogie design, as we have the freedom to weight our locos so that there is nil load to be carried by bogies or trucks – which, in the quest for maximum adhesion and tractive effort, has become something of a tradition. To cite an extreme example of this approach, Ken Northwood's 'King', already figuring back in Chapter 1, turns in at 2 lb dead on the scales, of which no less than 1 lb 15 oz is on the driving wheels. (Bear in mind that this is in relation to a train weight of something over a stone, not something many of us have to cope with!) The fact that Ken's 'King' runs beautifully in all respects in spite of what might seem a very small proportion of the total weight on the bogie, might seem to scupper Rice's theory, but the arrangements for this loco are a good deal more subtle than most, and careful springing can feed progressively greater loadings onto the bogie when circumstances require.

However, most of us don't have to emulate the sort of haulage feats that the 'North Devonshire' imposes on its motive power, and are usually possessed of an excess of motor power and grip over requirement. For reasons discussed in the 'Powertrain' chapters, it's important to ensure that our model locos can slip in extreme circumstances, and particularly in the context of a coreless-powered loco riding on a compensated chassis, we can develop high levels of tractive effort with a considerably lower loading on the driving wheels. It is rarely necessary to ballast a loco to the sort of degree that Ken has, where every crevice is used for weight addition, which gives us freedom to add the weight where it will not only achieve the required 'bite' on the rails, but will also give the best weight distribution over all axles of the loco. This is an operation that well repays the trouble of carrying it out, a process I'll come to in a page or two.

GUIDANCE

If you can crouch low enough – or, better still, get in the NRM's pit with a bogie loco atop you – you will see that real bogies locate onto a massive central pin. You will also, more than likely, see an equally substantial side-control spring either side of this pivot. If you can't see any springs, then you may be looking at a loco using ramped slides for guidance – but the point is, a real bogie isn't free to float sideways unrestrained as is so often the case with a model. Most real loco bogies can move for only fractions of an inch before they come up against the restraint of spring or slide, when

Side-control springing is an important aspect of prototype bogie design. The retaining plate and cap of the long progressive-rate coil springs used on the 'Schools' class are a prominent feature of the bogie sideframes, on the mid-point of the wheelbase. AUTHOR'S COLLECTION

they will start to take the rest of the loco with them. Even then, there won't be a lot of travel – there doesn't need to be, given that the loco chassis will flex in its entirety, while the track will also deform to accommodate the antics of the loco. When I was building my GW outside-framed 'Dukedog' a couple of years back, I came up against the rather constraining factor of the top of the outside frames of the bogie being inside the forward end of the outside frames of the driving wheels. This was a touch puzzling, so I went off to have a look at *City of Truro*, which happened to be at Swindon that summer. There, I found that the clearance on the real engine was less than $\frac{3}{4}$in; hence the maximum bogie deflection possible was no more than $\frac{1}{2}$in or so – in model terms, the engine was to all intents and purposes a rigid-framed 0–8–0. Certainly, when I tried to endow my 4 mm version with a prototypical arrangement, it wouldn't look at anything below about 6 ft radius, and then it complained. I had to chop the top of the bogie off flush with the bottom of the outside frames before it would cope with even the 4 ft radius of its intended home.

The point of all this is that we require our model bogies to have a good deal more lateral movement that real ones ever do, which is why we experience so many clearance problems that the prototype ignores. However, I would suggest that an arrangement whereby the bogie only moves slightly before it starts to take the rest of the loco with it, is less likely to produce a conflict between bogie wheels and such impedimentia as steps, outside cylinders, slide-bars and crossheads. I have also found that, whilst replicating the prototype arrangement of a central pin acting through side control springs can be made to work, it's a lot easier to use the more normal model arrangement of a double-pivoted swinging link to carry the actual bogie, guidance being imparted by springing the link to centre so that it can only deflect sideways by flexing the spring. This was basically Ahern's suggested method of side-control springing, so it's pretty well-proven! My only modification to Ahern's original scheme is to take the spring *forward* to its anchorage point on the chassis, so that the steering action is imparted to the loco as soon as possible when entering a curve.

However, in order that any of this highly desirable interaction between the bogie and the rest of the loco can take place, it is necessary to ensure that the bogie can generate sufficient sideforce to do the business with the spring – which is where the requirement to put a decent amount of weight down through the bogie wheels comes in. There's no way you're going to steer a loco through side-control springs if it's easier for the flange of a bogie-wheel to climb over the rail than it is for the bogie as a whole to move sideways and flex the side control spring. So this is another area where it isn't really a good idea to follow prototype practice too far, by arranging to spring the bogie wheels within the bogie. In the days when I used to try and do everything 'by the book', I got into all sorts of pickles with sprung bogies (as opposed to unsprung or equalised *spring-loaded* bogies, which are quite a different thing), particularly with

Fig. 5:2 PROTOTYPE BOGIE WITH SIDE-CONTROL

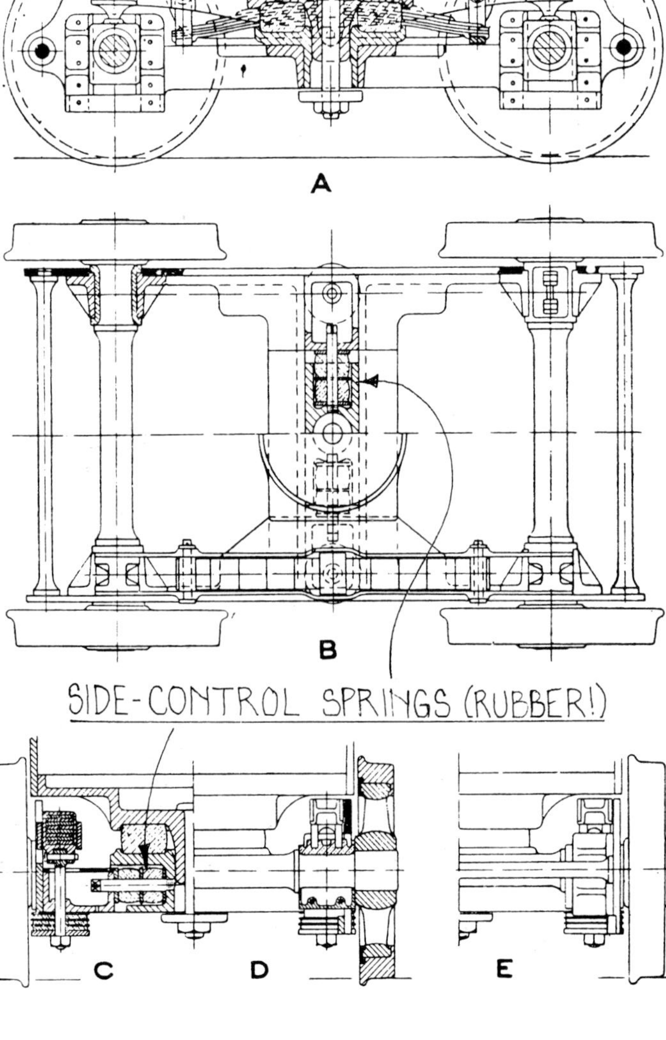

Prototype arrangements on the GWR outside frame 'Dukedog' allowed so little bogie swing that the model would only go in straight lines. Those bogie sideframes should go up behind the valances, but had to be cut off to get the engine around 4ft radius curves.

Not much side-control on this bogie! The unrestrained swinging-arm arrangement used on this chassis is typical of traditional 4mm scale cosmetic bogies without steering action.

bogie-axles tending to tilt on the springs rather than deflecting the bogie and bringing the side-control into play.

However, getting the required weight-loading onto the bogie without impeding the lateral action is not the easiest trick in the book. The prototype uses a system of slides and pads, and if you are using some form of suspension on the driving wheels, then the same system will work on the model. But in the context of a rigid chassis, all that happens is that the bogie will lift the drivers clear of the track when it encounters a hump, and will cease to take any load if negotiating a dip (see *Fig 5:4*). So it is necessary, once again, to look to a non-prototypical solution, by either using a spring or a compensating beam to apply the load directly to the centre pivot of the bogie (*Fig 5:3*). This works fairly well, but it does have the disadvantage of feeding the weight in on the centreline of the bogie, rather than over the frames, which can, once again, result in the bogie attempting to tilt under the sideforce generated in a bend. So there are perhaps rather more factors to consider in this traditionally neglected area than might at first be apparent; certainly, I've found that going to the trouble of confecting the arrangements sketched in *Fig 5:5*, which endeavour to load the bogie as close to the plane of the sideframes as possible, is well worth while. The sprung version of this arrangement isn't hard to scheme out, and can be very simply adjusted by tweaking the spring wire up or down a bit.

So, to summarise all this rather convoluted examination of bogie function into some simple, rule-of-thumb guidelines that can be applied to the sort of bogies found in loco kits, what we are aiming to achieve is a bogie which effectively steers the fore end into (or the aft end out of, in the case of tank engines with trailing bogies) curves in the track, and that supports a due proportion of the loco's weight. In simple terms, we will probably end up with a rigid bogie as supplied in the kit, suspended from a swinging link of some sort, controlled by a simple wire side control spring, and loaded through the pivot, again probably by a

Fig. 5:3 BOGIE WITH SIDE-CONTROL SPRING, LOADED THROUGH CENTRE PIVOT

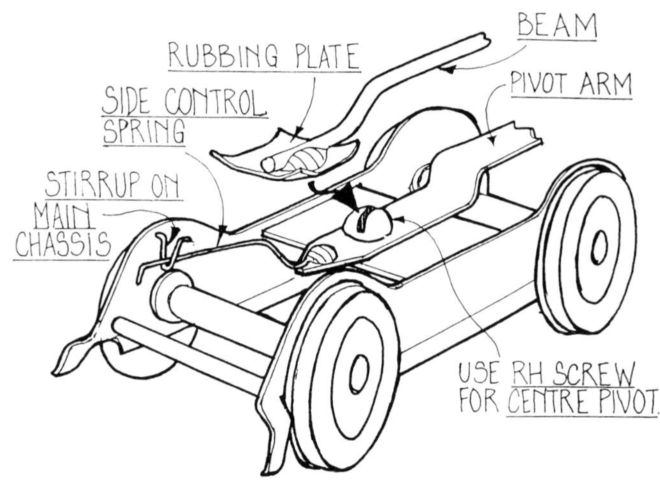

Fig. 5:4 WHY FIXED BOGIE PIVOTS ARE NOT A GOOD IDEA ON RIGID LOCOS

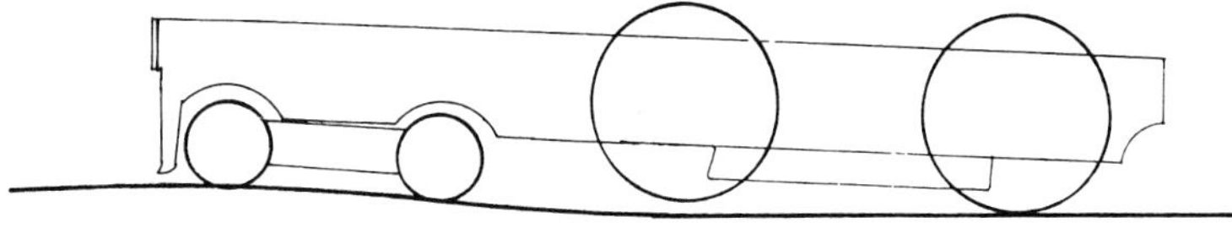

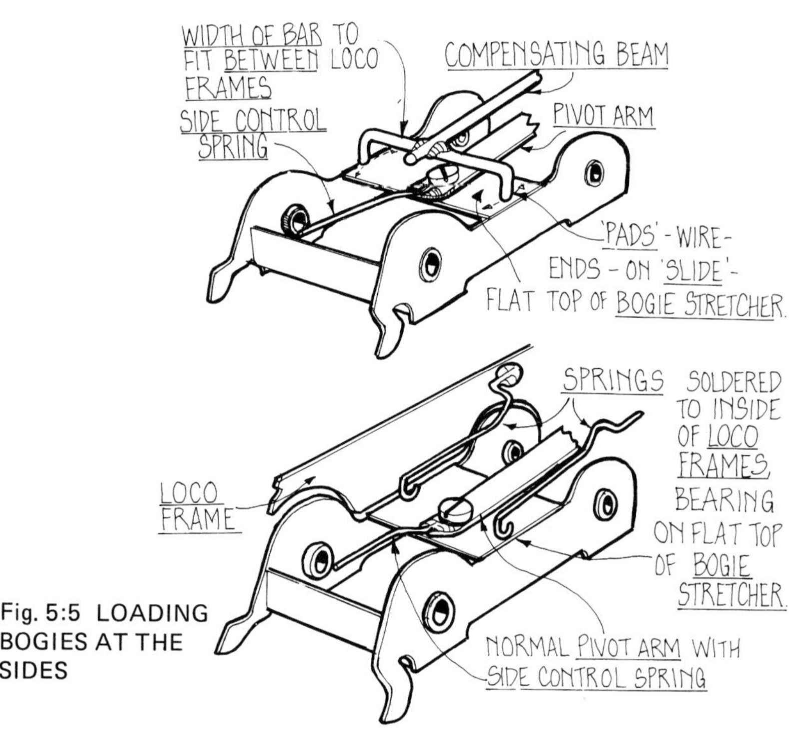

Fig. 5:5 LOADING BOGIES AT THE SIDES

spring – in which role the flat strip shown is effective. This basic arrangement is drawn in *Fig 5:6*, and is of pretty universal application. It's also easy to make, and can usually be simply adapted from the bits provided in the kit, as I did for the DJH 'West Country' illustrated.

Fig. 5.6 A SIMPLE SPRINGING AND GUIDANCE SET-UP

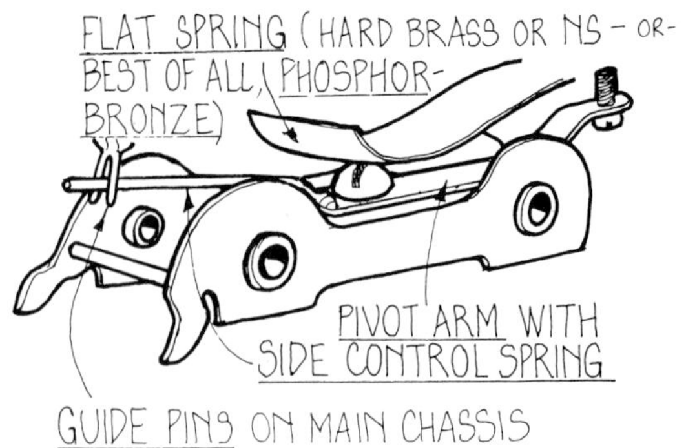

PONY TRUCKS

These perform exactly the same function as a bogie in prototype terms, but are an awful lot easier to cope with on a model. It's rare to come up against the sort of sideplay limitations that can cause such headaches with a bogie. A pony truck is pivoted some way aft of its axle, and is free to move in an arc of that radius – although, of course, once again limited by side-control springing. This arc is of surprisingly short radius – measuring off the LMS official drawing for the Ivatt class 2 ('Mickey Mouse') 2–6–0 gives a pivot arc of just 6 ft, in the context of a total wheelbase of 22 ft 3 in. The side control on this engine is by a pin running in a slot on top of the pony truck, under the influence of side control springs mounted in the truck itself. The pin also bears on a slide atop the truck, and loads 8T 4 Cwt of the total loco weight of 47T 2 Cwt onto these carrying wheels.

We don't need to go to these lengths (though the loading system isn't that hard to replicate), and the same basic approach as I suggested for the bogie can be employed with profit; a simple wire side-control spring on the pivot arm of the truck, and the flat strip spring to load it vertically. The snag

The leading pony performs much the same function on this LNER 'L1' 2–6–4T as would a bogie. It carries 11 of the 91 tons total loco weight, and has a vital guidance role in steering this big, heavy engine on curved track. Side control followed LMS practice, using helical springs in an effort to improve guidance over Gresley's double sprung link design, held to be responsible for several derailments of the 'V2' 2–6–2 engines. The trailing bogie, carrying 20 tons, had coil spring side-control allowing a maximum of 4 in side travel overall – less than 1.5mm in 4mm scale!

AUTHOR'S COLLECTION

And here are the side-control arrangements on a typical kit-built 2–6–4T, the DJH 'Fairburn' – in essence an 0–6–0T with very long overhangs

Fig. 5:7 SIDE-CONTROL SPRING BEHIND PIVOT OF PONY TRUCK

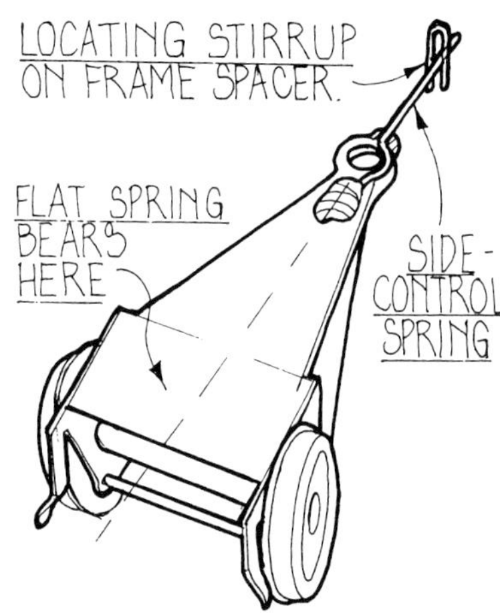

in this instance is that the two can get in the way of each other, so I modify the arrangement to that drawn in *Fig 5:7*, where the side-control is applied at the pivot end of the truck. As I've just noted, these pivots are a lot closer to the end of the wheelbase than the inboard pivot of a bogie swinging arm (which is, in any case, purely a modelling convenience – no real loco bogie uses such an arrangement), so the guidance is still being applied well out towards the end of the loco, which is the important thing. This can all be seen in the pictures of the leading truck of my GW Mogul, which should surface somewhere about here.

WHEN IS A PONY TRUCK NOT A PONY TRUCK?

Not all locomotives containing a '2-' prefix or '-2' suffix in their wheel arrangements are riding on pony trucks – although this fact seems to have escaped some kitmakers! Many locos with a 2–4–0 or 2–4–2T wheel arrangement use radial trucks or simply axleboxes with a touch of sideplay, as do most 0–4–2Ts; 0–6–2Ts can use either of those or a pony truck (the ex-GE/LNER 'N7' 0–6–2T class was split, half having radial trucks and half pony trucks), while some 2–6–2Ts had radials either end (L & Y), some had a leading pony and trailing radial (GWR large Prairie), and some had pony trucks both ends (small GW Prairie, Ivatt '2' and BR '3' 2–6–2T. I can't see any justification at all for making a 2–4–0 or 0–4–2 as anything other than a simple all-in-one 0–6–0, as it were; the old K's arrangement with their '14XX' of having a trailing pony truck is really an awful nonsense, and it's interesting to note that the Airfix R-T-R version, which has no difficulty on R-T-R curves, makes do with a touch of sideplay in a simple chassis.

Radial axleboxes also work, effectively, in an arc as for a pony truck, but the effect is achieved by allowing the actual axlebox to move in a set of curved slides. It's quite possible to replicate this action in a model, and Rod Neep introduced a simple etched version in his chassis design for the GW large Prairie, as illustrated in the photo – this chassis is the same as the GW Mogul, as it was, effectively, in reality. I put optional radial trucks into my own design for the Perseverance LNWR 4 ft 6 in 2–4–2T, which are a slightly more complete version, as can be seen in the illustrations of that chassis.

I think that working radial trucks are a perfectly practical proposition in 4 mm scale, and more and more kit designers are slipping them in. Of course, to do any good, they need side-control springing and enough weight on them to make it work, just as for any other type of leading or trailing truck; the arrangement can be seen in *Fig 5:9*. As I mentioned way back in my introductory chapter, locos with radial trucks call for frames narrowing at the ends to give the necessary sideplay.

Fig. 5:8 PONY AND RADIAL TRUCKS

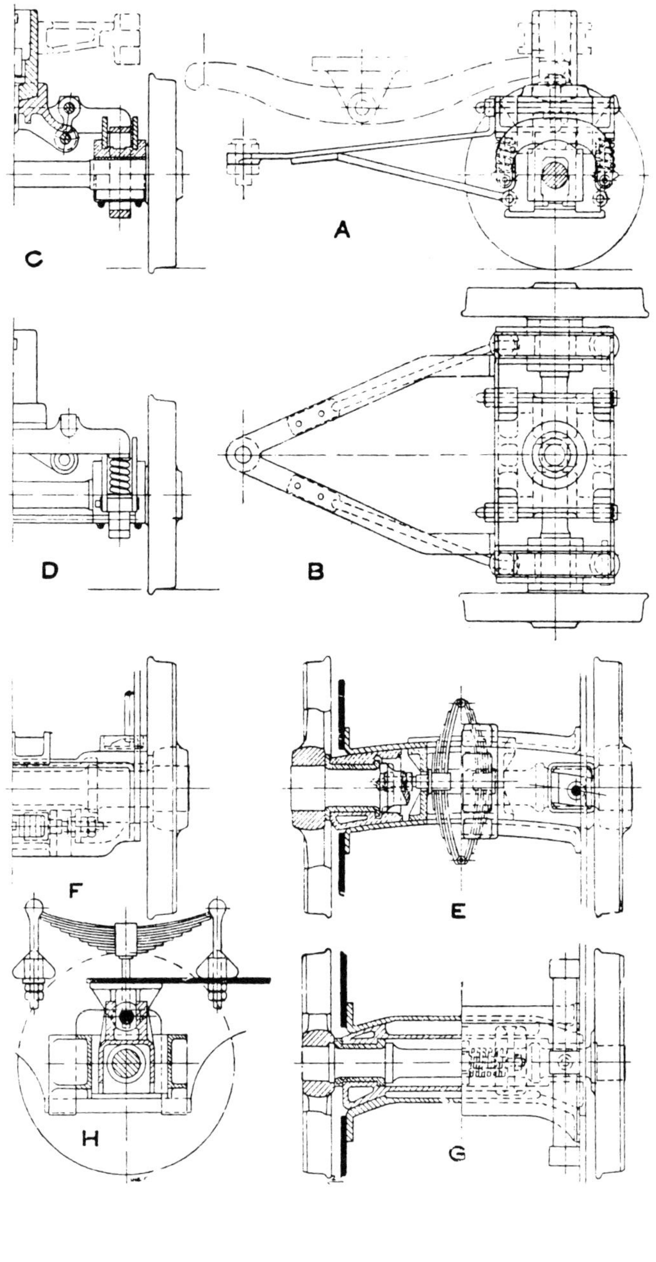

Radial trucks in model form, here on the Puffers/ Perseverance kit for the LNWR Webb 4ft 6in 2–4–2T. Note side-control and vertical springing arrangements, as in Fig. 5:9.

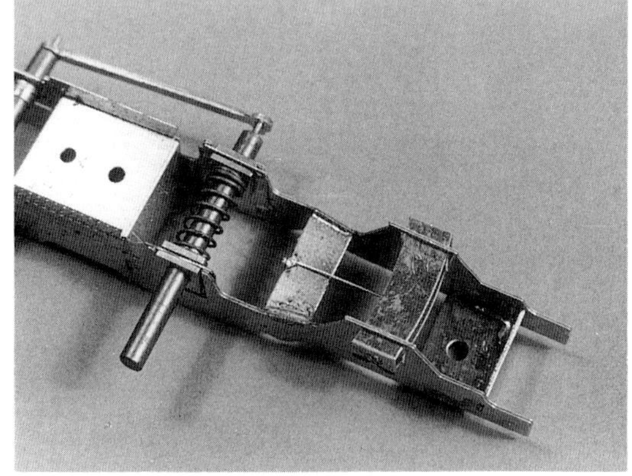

Close-up of radial truck, showing the way it slides through the sideframes. The side-control spring is 0.33mm dia. hard brass wire.

Fig. 5:9 SPRINGING FOR RADIAL TRUCK

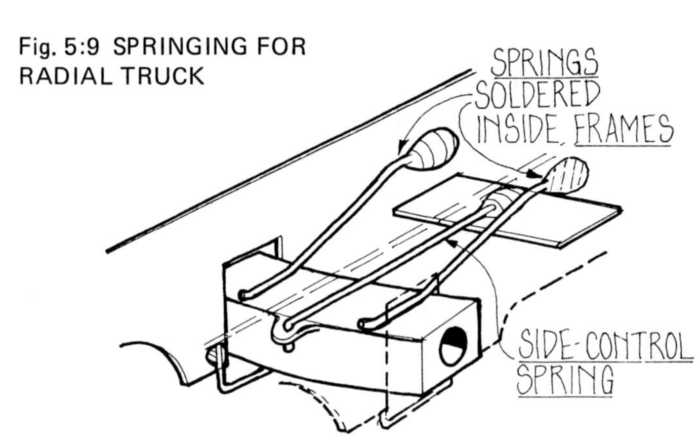

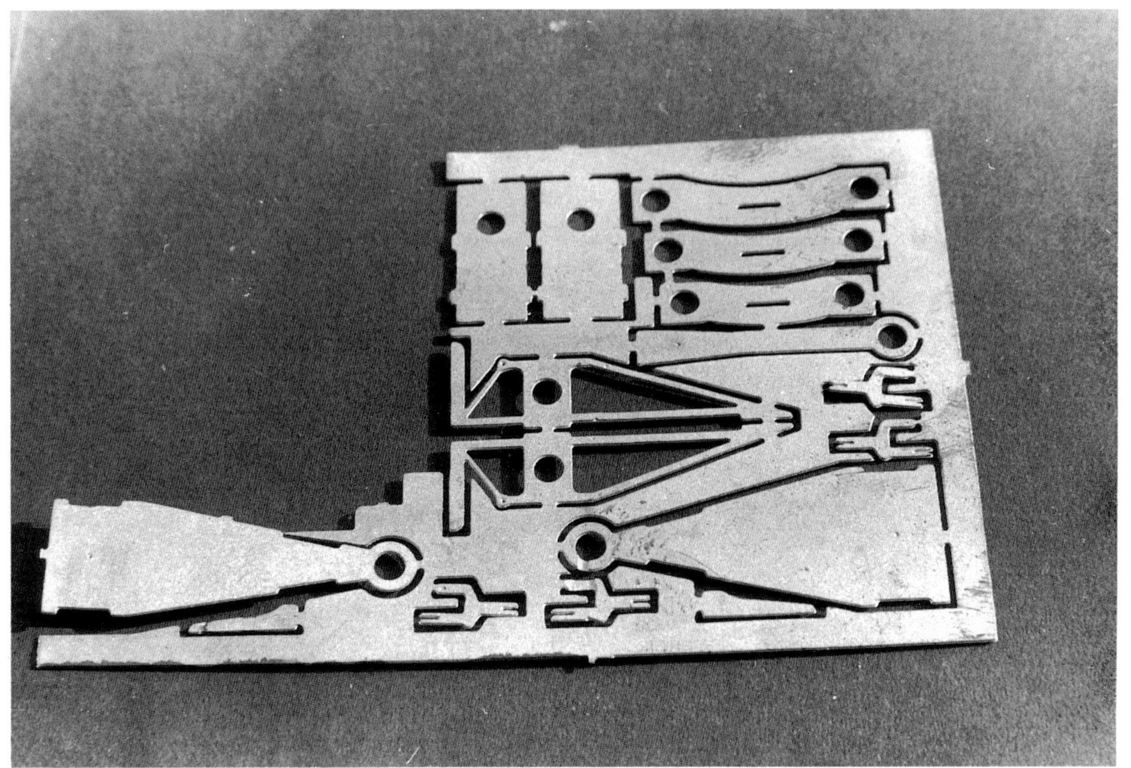

Parts for both pony and radial trucks on the Puffers / Perseverance chassis for the GWR '61XX' large Prairie.

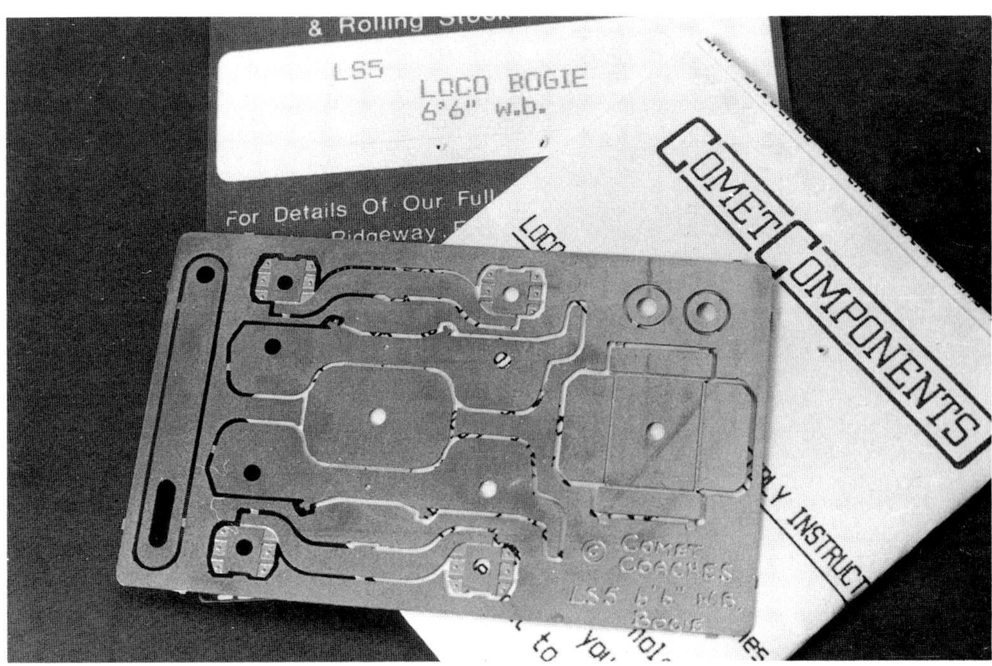

After-market etched bogies, such as this LMS/BR pattern 6ft 6in wheelbase type by Comet, are a valuable substitute for poor kit bogies.

BUILDING BOGIES AND PONY TRUCKS

Sideplay is, of course, the one thing you most certainly don't want when it comes to wheelsets running in bogies or pony trucks. There's absolutely no point in cluttering the loco up with side control springing and all the other gubbins intended to make the bogie or truck steer the engine, if the wheels can move a millimetre sideways before anything happens. So I'm always looking to make the frame of the bogie or pony truck as wide as possible within the constraints of the back-to-back measurement – which, in turn, will often find me making a new bogie stretcher, given that a lot of kit bogies are decidedly lacking in this respect. If the kit bogie is an assembly (rather than a one-piece casting), then it's not too difficult to get the width right. Etched bogies will, hopefully, come provided with a number of alternative stretchers to give bogie widths suited to OO, EM and P4. Now and then, however, one comes up against the odd bogie which is unadaptable in this respect, and is almost certainly designed for OO use.

Whilst full consideration must be given to making the bogie earn its keep, the appearance of the thing shouldn't be overlooked. Again, the right width of bogie in relation to the wheelsets will look a great deal better than something far too narrow with half-a-dozen spacing washers on each axle. If you are faced – as is still quite likely – with a bogie which neither looks the part nor fits the bill, there are a number of options open. Simplest of these is to adapt the same dodge that we applied to too-narrow, unlovely solid block chassis – fit some cosmetic overlays, which will both improve the look of the thing, and take up the excess clearance behind the wheels. Plastikard is very suited to such a purpose, being easy to work and to add detail to, and having insulating properties that can be useful when wheel-flanges and sideframes are in close proximity. The sketch in *Fig 5:10* shows how I set about producing these cosmetic wrappings for a plain cast bogie block.

An alternative is to find a better bogie from another source. Several of our better kit-makers can provide bogies as separate units, and I'd have no hesitation in putting a Malcolm Mitchell GW bar-frame bogie under the front of any GW 4-6-0 thus endowed. One or two other kitmakers can provide suitable bogies for other popular designs – firms like South Eastern Finecast,

Fig. 5:10 PLASTIKARD OVERLAYS FOR CAST BOGIE

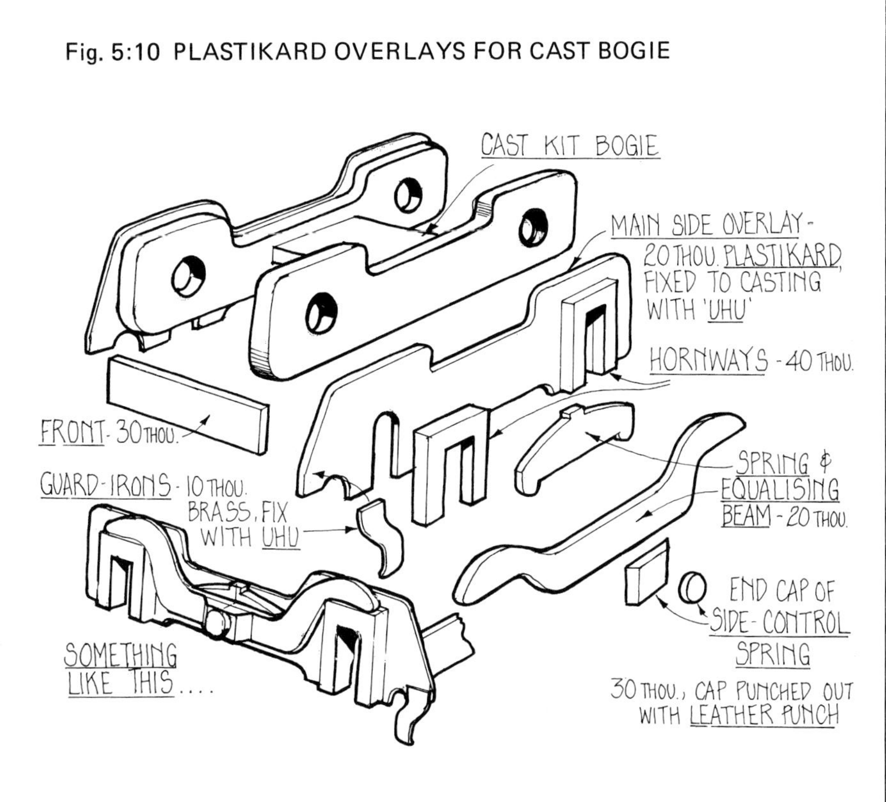

Fig. 5:11 HOME-BREWED BOGIES

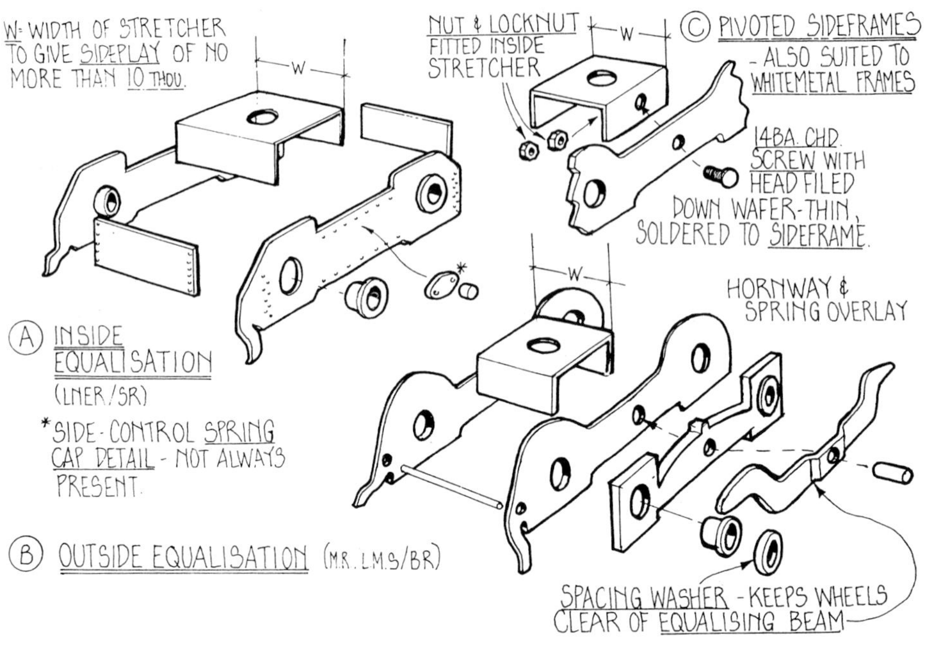

who have some very good cast bogies in their range, can usually be prevailed upon to supply castings separately. The availability of such things does depend, though, upon the way that kits are tooled, so it isn't always possible to obtain individual components economically. The manufacturer who says 'no' isn't necessarily being bloody-minded!

If you're prepared to have a crack at a home-brewed bogie, then you can overcome any deficiencies in the kit in the most satisfactory manner possible. Building a bogie from scratch isn't that daunting a proposition, unless it's one of the aforementioned GW bar-frame efforts – but that is one you needn't tangle with. Plate frame bogies – which is virtually all other types – come in two basic varieties; inside equalisation, and outside ditto. The former is the simpler, and stars in *Fig 5:11A*. These are found on a lot of more modern locos such as the Bulleid 'Pacifics', all Gresleys, the later GWR types such as the Modified 'Hall' and 'County', and the numerous LNER 'B1' 4-6-0s. The actual equalising beam and the spring providing bogie suspension are hidden inside the frames, where we can ignore them.

Outside-equalised bogies were favoured by the LMS, in succession to the Midland and LNWR, both of whom adopted this design. All the LMS 'Standards' had such bogies, except the Stanier and Ivatt 'Pacifics', which used a GW-style bar-frame design. Fortunately, the kits for these locos provide something appropriate! The outside-equalised design also featured on the BR 'Standards', which generally followed

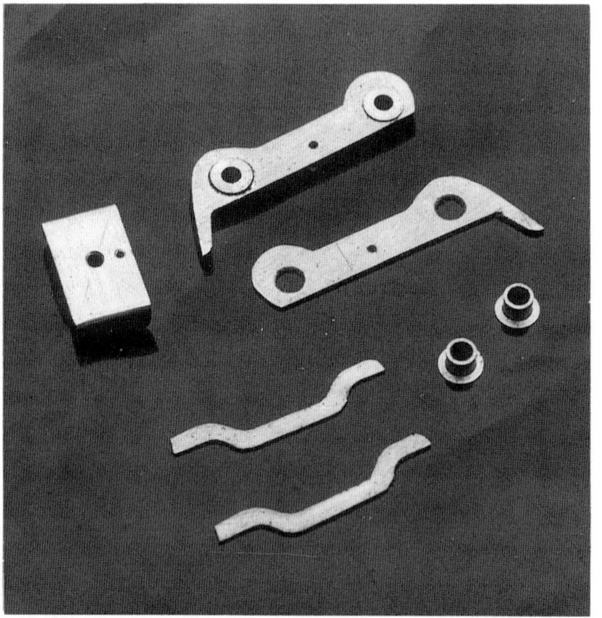

Ingredients for a home-made bogie – in this instance for an 'H' class 0-4-4T. Frames and stretcher in 10-thou brass, with Sharman 3/32in 'top-hat' bearing bushes.

LMS design practice. The construction of a typical outside-equalised bogie is shown in *Fig 5:11B*. It is not necessary to make the whole thing in metal, and the spring and equalising beam can be readily made in Plastikard and stuck in place with suitable adhesive – epoxy or thick cyano.

If this book isn't to stretch to an impossible length, I must skimp a little on precise detail as to scratchbuilding techniques. But, in outline, to make a bogie – either the whole of an 'inside' type or the guts of an 'outside' – the process goes roughly as follows:

Ingredients: Some suitable metal – 10 thou brass etched kit waste is quite adequate. Some axle-bearing 'top-hats' of the right diameter for the axles being used (see 'Sources' appendix).

Tools: Felt pen, scriber, scissors or snips, files, drill & reamer or broach soldering kit.

Method: Cover a sufficient area of metal for the sideframe with permanent felt marker. Measure off total length and height, the vertical centreline, axle height and axle centres. Mark the bogie outline. Scribe a simple rectangle which just encloses the bogie frame. Cut this rectangle out with

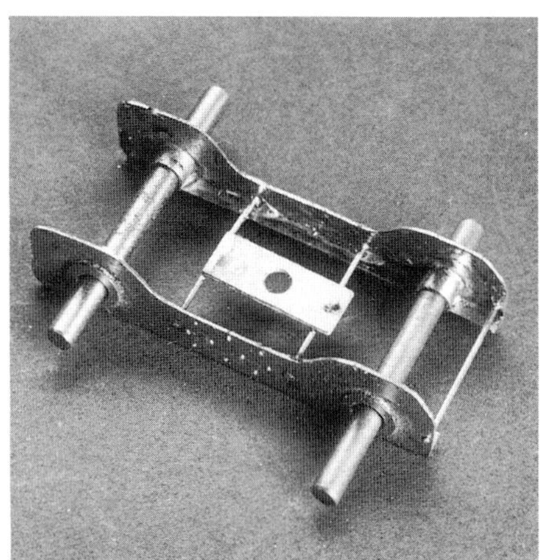

A new leading bogie being built for a Craftsman 'C12' 4–4–2T, using Dick Ganderton's scheme of a torsion-bar 'flexible stretcher' to provide equalisation. Once again, 10-thou brass and Sharman bearings are the essential ingredients.

scissors or snips, cutting off strips narrower than the 'bogie blank' to avoid distortion. (The narrower piece of metal will always distort when cutting with snips or shears).

Solder this 'blank' to a second layer of metal, and trim that to size. Centre-pop the axle centres – pushing with the end of the scriber will do the trick – and drill undersize: about 2 mm. Clamp the frames in the vice, and attack with files to make the shape. This is a lot easier than it sounds. Clean up with fine wet-and-dry, unsolder sideframes to make a pair. Make fold-up stretcher exactly as described for making L-section frame spacers back in Chapter 3. Erect on chassis jig as described for frames – ream holes, fit bearings, and use bogie axles to locate – and solder together. Finish off with a front and rear stretcher of suitable strip. Bingo! One bogie. Add detail to taste. Honestly, it's not that difficult.

Etched kit bogies go together in exactly the same way as just described, fitting the bearings and using the axles to align them on the stretcher. Cast bogie sides can be fitted to a home-made brass stretcher to correct inadequate width. If you're not happy about soldering whitemetal to brass, then make the alternative type of stretcher shown in *Fig 5:11C*, and attach the bogie sides with a suitable adhesive, or by bolting them in place with small (14BA) nuts and bolts. Try and locate these out of sight behind the wheels – countersinking may be called for. You may need to make the holes in the stretcher side a tad oversize on one side to give a spot of adjustment when the bogie is bolted together, once again done on the chassis jig with the axles as alignment rods. It's essential that bogies are dead square, so take the trouble to set things up 'just so', and if you're bolting together, lock the bolts with epoxy, especially on the 'adjust' side.

Pony trucks are generally an awful lot easier to build than bogies, but the same remarks and techniques still apply. There are still a few kits about which include dreadful cast 'ponies' that bear no resemblance whatever to the (usually bar-framed) prototype. Again, substitution is the only answer, with the slight complication that pony trucks are less easy to come by from trade sources, though not impossible. Getting a pony 'dead square' isn't quite so important as with a bogie, so long as the pivot is central. Plate pony trucks are made exactly as described for plate bogies. The assembly of a typical etched bar-frame pony truck, that of the GWR mogul, is illustrated somewhere alongside this epic, while a cast trailing truck, the other popular beastie, is illustrated by the rather complex DJH assembly for the 'rebuilt Bulleid'; most examples are a good deal simpler than this.

Here is the pony truck of the '43XX' Mogul, made up from the etched parts included on the Perseverance 43/63/61XX chassis kit, illustrated a page or so ago. Forward-facing side-control spring not yet bent to final shape.

A cast trailing pony, from a DJH kit. Nothing wrong with this at all – add a touch of side-control and it will do very nicely, being (deliberately) quite heavy within itself.

C. J. LANGDON

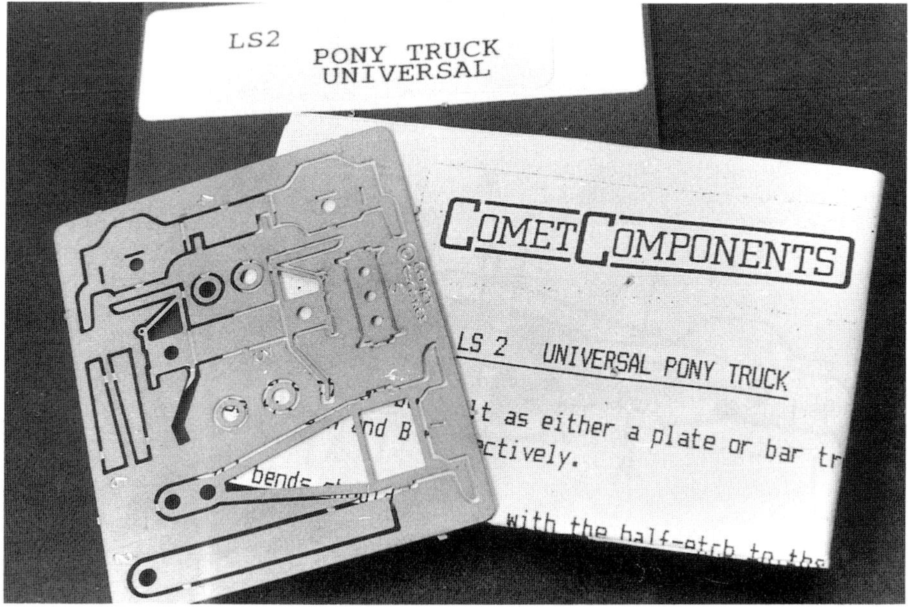

Comet's 'universal' pony truck etch gives you both plate and bar-frame options, and can be simply adapted to suit the vast majority of locos. Very useful, if needing a touch of widening for EM or P4.

SETTING UP BOGIES AND PONY TRUCKS

This is, really, jumping well ahead, as there aren't any wheels on our chassis yet! But it seems logical to keep all the basic information and description on carrying trucks in one place, so I'll plug on here. These operations will, by and large, be carried out once the basic 4, 6, 8 or 10 coupled mechanism has been built and is functioning, but some preparatory work is needed at a much earlier stage.

The provision of suitable mounting points for bogies and pony trucks will, we hope, have been addressed by the kit designer when the chassis was being laid out. However, in view of the rather more sophisticated requirements imposed by our endeavours to get the bogie functioning properly may call for some modification of these provisions, or for additional anchorage points for side-control springs and the like. However, these are generally very simple to provide; if you're concocting your own frame spacers, then suitable mountings can be 'designed in'; generally, though, it's easier to either tack some sort of bracket onto an existing spacer, or to add a separate small spacer just to provide a mounting point. The diagrams illustrating the various bogie loading/suspension systems should give some pointers as to what might be required in these directions, while the illustrations covering such examples as the West Country Pacific, the GW 'Mogul' and the 'Dukedog' will suggest a few more. Really, this is pure bodging; fit something, try it out, alter it if needs be. Classic trial-and-error, in other words.

One snag with etched bogies or pony trucks is their very low 'unsprung weight'. The GW bar-framed pony trucks of Malcolm Mitchell's gorgeous '45XX' tank kit come with little brackets designed to take ballast weights, a neat alternative to spring-loading for reliable tracking.
R. G. WILLIAMS

RESTRICTING BOGIE SWING

For reasons already noted some way back in this rather lengthy brief skirmish, we may find that the rather greater swing associated with model loco bogies (and, in some rarer instances, pony trucks) may bring them into conflict with fixed portions of the locomotive's anatomy, particularly front footsteps and outside cylinders, slidebars and crossheads. This is one of the oldest problems in the book, especially where we're dealing with curves a very great deal tighter than the real loco could ever have negotiated.Whilst it cannot provide a complete and universal solution, the offsetting of the bogie pivot from the midpoint of the bogie wheelbase can reduce the swing at one end of the bogie – at the expense of greater swing at the other end. Hornby-Dublo were the great masters of this, and Hornby locos did exhibit a surprising moderation in the matter of bogie swing even when the 'Duchess' or 'A4' was charging around a 15 in radius curve at some breakneck speed. The general principle is illustrated in *Fig 5:12*, and I often leave myself the option to do this by drilling a series of possible pivot holes when I'm making bogie stretchers.

A chassis for an old Wills wide-cab 'T9', a notorious nose-heavy cast 4–4–0. This is based on the Westward/Perseverance 'T9' chassis kit, using a beam to load the leading bogie via the pivot. Note the waisting-in of the frames behind the leading bogie wheels, but also the lack of any unprototypical 'daylight' around the bogie.

Fig. 5:12 RESTRICTING BOGIE SWING BY MOVING BOGIE PIVOT

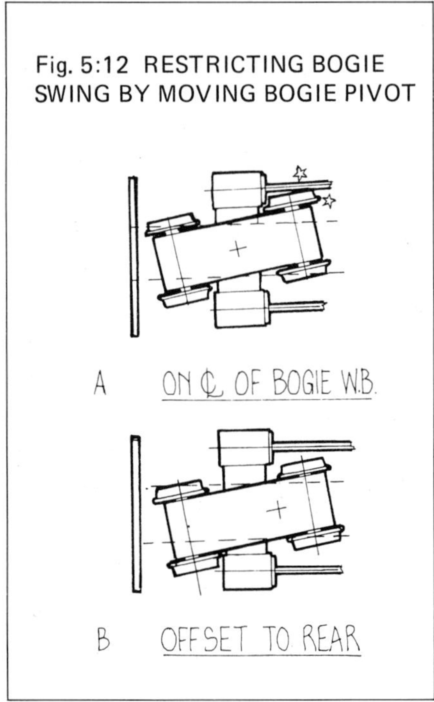

WEIGHTING OF BOGIES AND TRUCKS

The importance of ensuring that carrying trucks bear sufficient load to ensure reliable trackholding has been expounded, at not inconsiderable length, earlier in this chapter. Likewise, the means by which weight might be transferred from the rest of the loco onto the bogie have been outlined, or will be in the next chapter, when compensating beams are considered. Which only leaves a couple of overcooked brussels sprouts on the plate of life's Sunday roast to be toyed with: how to obtain the right weight in the right place, and how to find out whether it *is* the right weight.

Actually ballasting a loco isn't too much of a problem – one just bungs in the Cerrobend, lead-shot-and-Plasticine or whatever one's favourite means of adding avoirdupois is. The snag comes when we want to balance out the loco so that the right amount of weight comes in the right place. This is yet another strength of the 'Flexi-chas' system, where, by shifting the beam pivot points, we can control within very exact limits the proportion of the total loco weight being carried by each axle or truck. Real locomotives employ real compensating beams for exactly this purpose. However, weight setting on real locos is greatly aided by the ability to accurately determine the actual load carried by individual axles – something to which little attention has ever been paid in model locomotive constructional circles. Chris Pen-

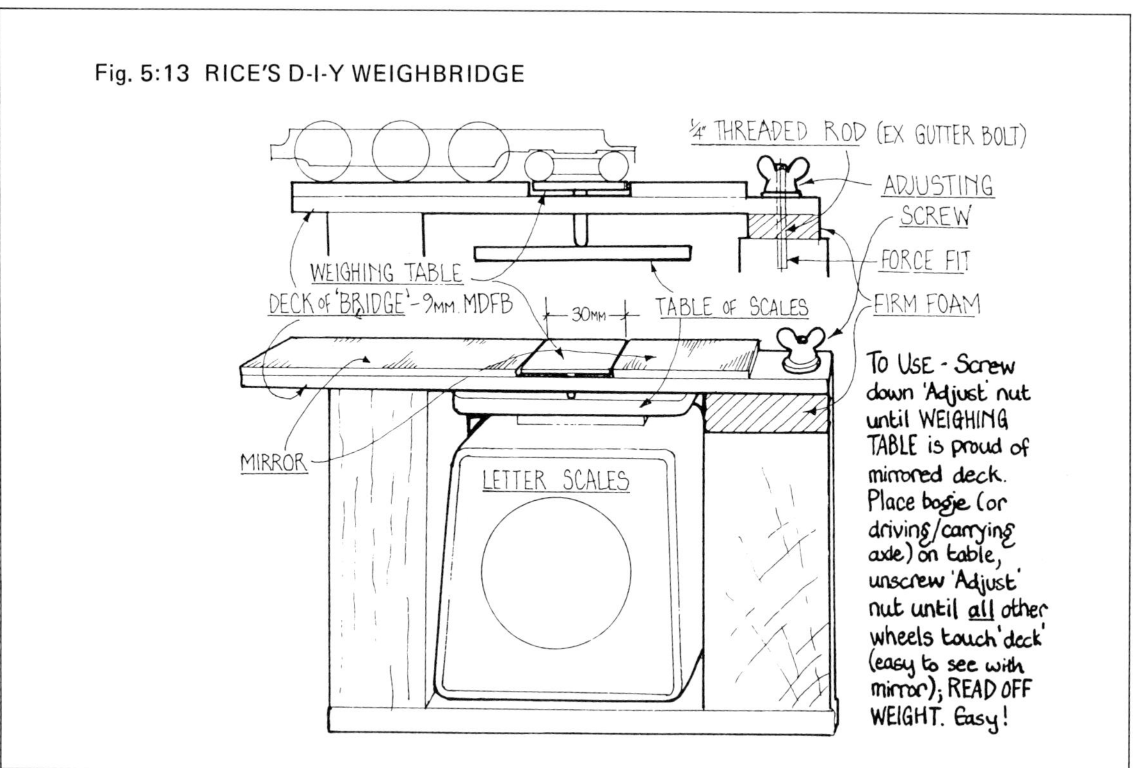
Fig. 5:13 RICE'S D-I-Y WEIGHBRIDGE
¼" THREADED ROD (EX GUTTER BOLT)
ADJUSTING SCREW
FORCE FIT
FIRM FOAM
WEIGHING TABLE
DECK of 'BRIDGE' - 9MM. MDFB
30MM
TABLE OF SCALES
MIRROR
LETTER SCALES
To USE - Screw down 'Adjust' nut until WEIGHING TABLE is proud of mirrored deck. Place bogie (or driving/carrying axle) on table, unscrew 'Adjust' nut until all other wheels touch 'deck' (easy to see with mirror); READ OFF WEIGHT. Easy!

dlenton, in the context of his properly-defined leaf-sprung loco chassis design, has devised a means of assessing axle-loading. Derek Genzel, of the Scalefour Society, recently unveiled 'Genzel's Gizmo', a very accurate and sophisticated bit of kit which uses a sensitive load-cell to measure this elusive figure.

I don't run to any of this sophistication, relying instead on the typical Rice lash-up illustrated, which took the better part of five minutes to design and make; the miracle is, it seems to work, and is surprisingly sensitive and consistent – probably more of a reflection on the quality of the Waymaster 424 LD letter scales than on any cleverness on my part! These letter scales cost me £4 at a secondhand shop, but other small and relatively sensitive scales, such as the ones that 'Weightwatchers' sell to aspiring slimmers for around thirty bob, will do. Don't forget, we're only interested in finding out roughly what proportion of the loco weight is being carried by the various axles, bogie, trucks, etc. As any error should be consistent, it won't matter in this application.Failing the availability of any sort of weighing device, then I'm afraid it's back to our old friend, trial-and-error.

The actual adjustment of the load carried by individual parts of the loco chassis is accomplished by two means. Weight is added and taken away from suitable locations in the loco body, or the spring (by means of which weight is loaded onto a bogie or pony truck) is bent a bit in the appropriate direction to either increase or decrease the load carried. If you're proceeding by trial-and-error, I'd suggest you start with a light loading and gradually increase this until the bogie tracks reliably, by adding weight over the bogie and bending the spring down. I wouldn't try to achieve the necessary downforce by one of these means alone – they need adjusting in tandem. At the end of the day, if the loco runs reliably, with the bogie tracking consistently and guiding the loco over curved track effectively, you've achieved the desired result; the actual weights and loadings involved are of only academic interest.

Thus far, I've been concentrating on locomotives having simple rigid chassis for both mainframes and bogies. When we introduce compensation, the whole ball-game changes, so that's where we had better go next.

ESCAP
RG4

A suitable case for treatment! Even without the cast body, this chassis (for an EM 'M7' 0–4–4T) is tail-heavy. Getting the weight distribution right calls for careful ballasting of the complete loco, aided by an offset pivot on the compensating beam linking the rear bogie with the trailing coupled axle. This rests on the spacer bar of the RG4 gearbox at the 'inboard' end. The chassis is based on EM Gauge Society/Alan Gibson milled brass frames. The bogie has pivoted sideframes as in Fig. 6:7 in the next chapter.

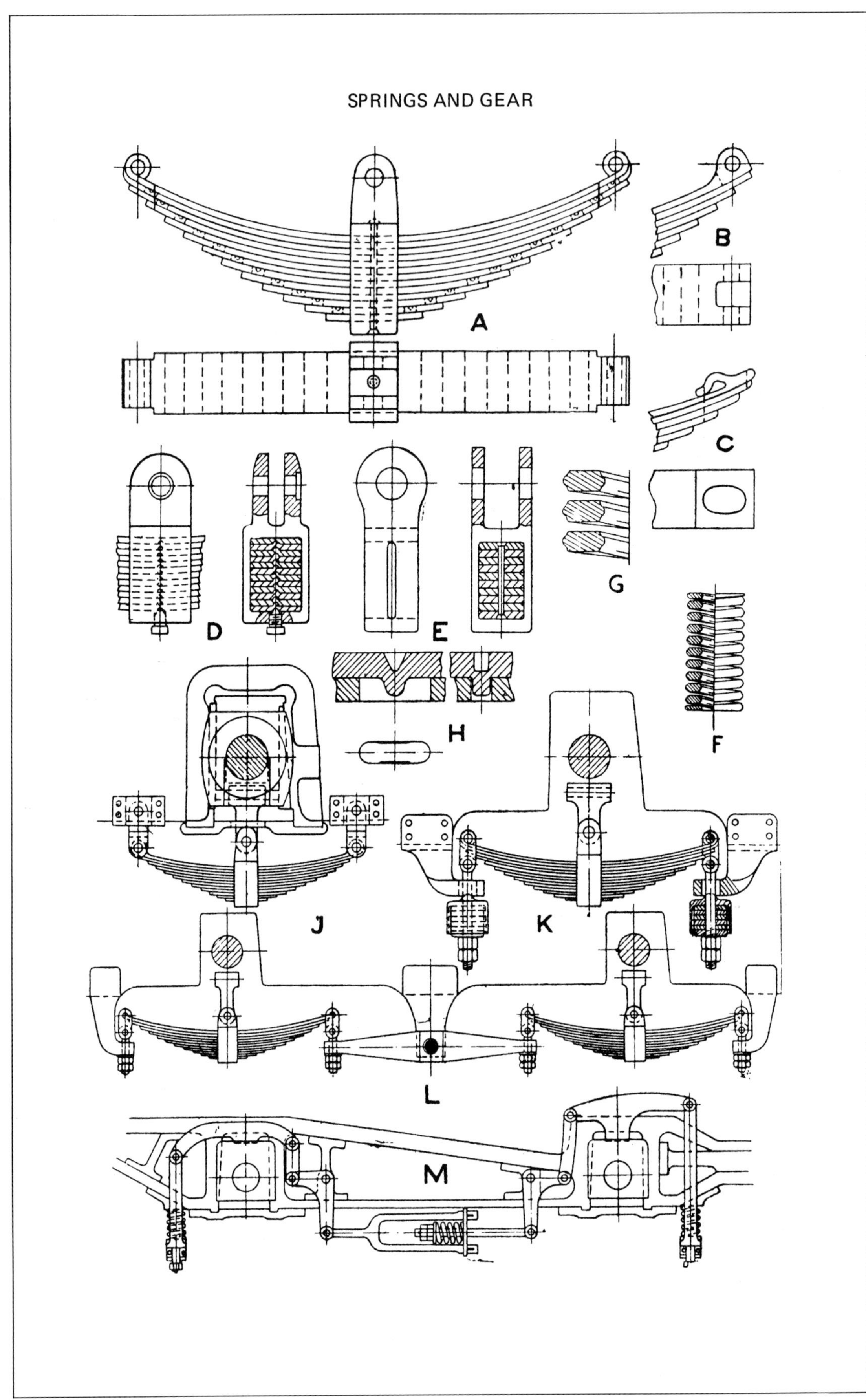
SPRINGS AND GEAR
A
B
C
D
E
G
F
H
J
K
L
M

CHAPTER SIX
COMPENSATION

Here, just to frighten you all to death, is the compensation system of Malcolm Mitchell's '45XX', which is a heavy-duty variant of the Flexi-chas system originally developed by Guy Williams for Pendon, and 'productionised' by Malcolm. The rocking axles run in brass tubes, which replace the Flexi-chas bearings. These are located by nice broad guides, made to resemble prototype axlebox hornways, and are loaded by an etched version of the normal compensating beam. The objective is to achieve far greater bearing areas for a long and trouble-free life under the arduous conditions at Pendon.
A. E. SMITH

IN AT THE DEEP END?

If I had a crinkly folding portrait of HM the Queen for every time that my favourite contention – that it's often easier to build a compensated chassis than it is to tackle most rigid chassis kits – has been greeted with a sharp intake of breath and a shake of the head, then I too could afford a stud of Portescap powered Mitchell/Finney paragons. As it is, poor but unrepentant, I make do with a mix of rehashed R-T-R, cheapo kits and ropey Rice scratchbuilds – compensated, every one. Leaving aside the functional superiority of a properly-compensated chassis (which is as apparent in the coarsest OO context as in the most esoteric of P4 creations) it's the built-in accuracy and ease of adjustment of the Flexi-chas system that so appeals. You can get it wrong but put it right – without going near any of the desperate bodges paraded in Chapter 3.

I did toy, at this point, with the notion of devastating you all with a brilliant exposition of the theory and rationale of the three-point compensated loco chassis in all its logical glory. But wiser counsels prevailed; this book is getting longer by the page, and anyway, if I give away too much now, no-one's going to buy my 'Pragmatic Guide to Loco Building' when I eventually get around to writing it, are they? So, for the moment, I'll concentrate on the differences twixt rigid and compensated chassis kits, while urging the doubters to throw caution to the winds, pick a simple prototype to try, and dip a toe in the waggly-wheel waters.

DIFFERENCES BETWEEN RIGID AND COMPENSATED CHASSIS

As we agreed at the end of Chapter 1, the best of modern loco kit chassis are designed for basic assembly as a simple rigid version, with the option of a compensated alternative at the behest of the builder. So, just what is involved in going to this 'next stage'? Part of the answer has already been provided, in the shape of the 'Perseverance' '57XX' pannier tank chassis that figured in the frame erection sequence back in Chapter 4, which I was building in the compensated version in accordance with my normal practice. If you fancy a dabble in the lovely warm compensatory waters, I would strongly recommend that one of these 'Percy' chassis form the subject of a first essay, as they contain both a full selection of

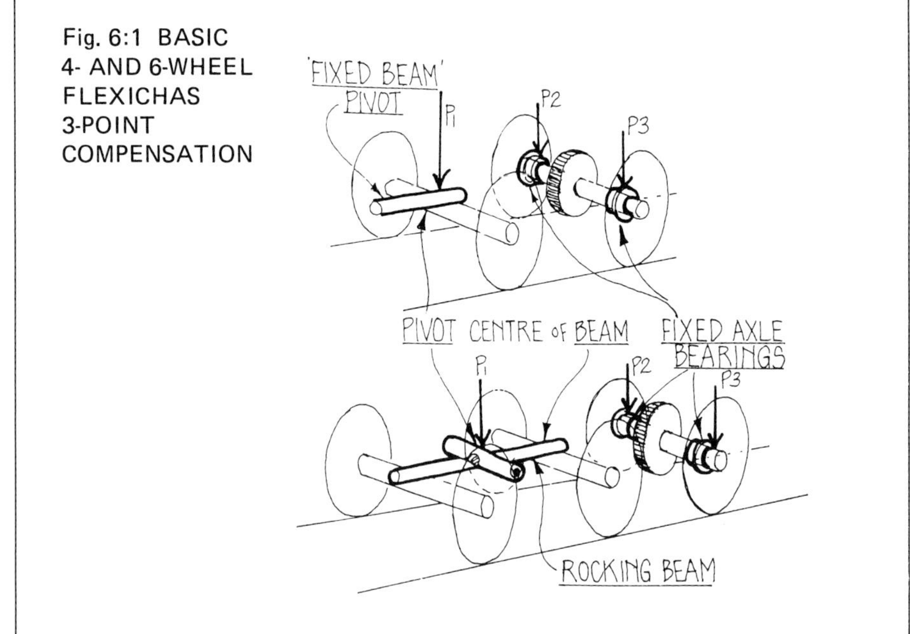

Fig. 6:1 BASIC 4- AND 6-WHEEL FLEXICHAS 3-POINT COMPENSATION

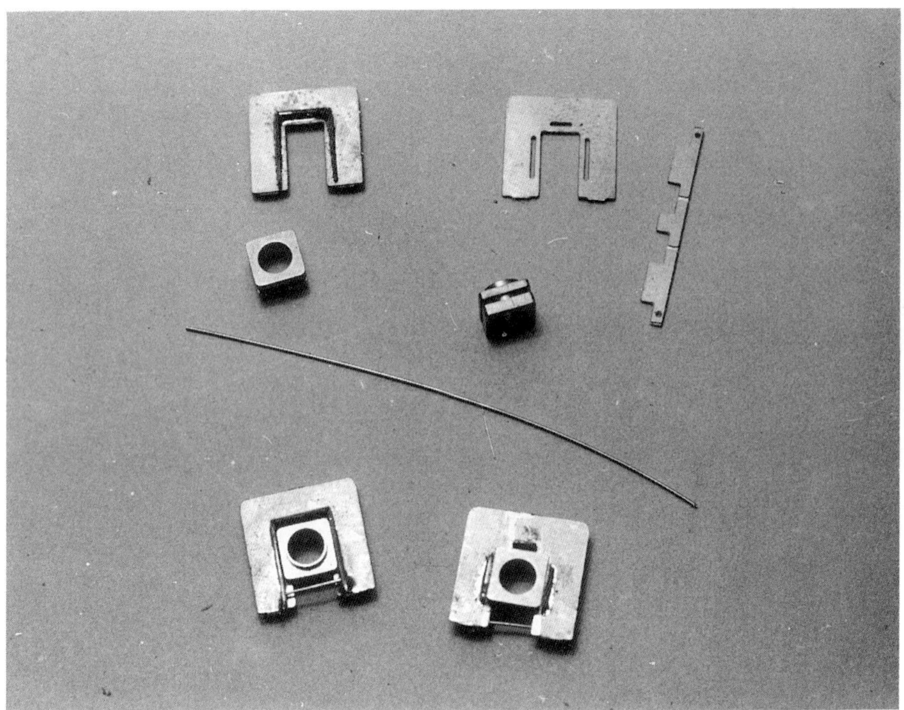

The key component of the commercial versions of the Flexi-chas system is the hornblock assembly. These are the latest version of the Perseverance design drawn in Fig. 6:2. The MJT type is virtually identical, while London Road Models have just produced a lost-wax cast brass version. These are the actual hornblocks that came with my guinea-pig '57XX' chassis kit.

Fig. 6:2 ANATOMY OF A HORNBLOCK ASSEMBLY

components, and some pretty comprehensive instructions. Taken in conjunction with this chapter, you won't go far wrong.

The basic principle of the Flexi-chas compensation system is that of the three-legged stool, where all three legs will always be on the ground. In the case of the simple six-wheeled chassis such as the 0–6–0T illustrated in the photo sequence, these three 'legs' are the two bearings of the 'fixed' axle (which is also, for convenience, the driven axle) and the centre pivot of the beam linking the other two axles. Thus, it will follow that the fixed axle (the rear, in this case; it must always be an outer axle) is identical to any axle of a rigid chassis, while the other two axles are carried in hornblocks, which allow them to move vertically, *and to tilt*. The significance of this freedom to tilt was explained fully in Chapter 1, you may recollect. The actual hornblocks comprise a 'square' bearing, with a broad groove around all four edges, riding in an etched 'hornguide'. In the latest (and best) hornblock systems, this hornguide is made up of a flat plate incorporating the 'hornway' – simply a parallel-sided slot in which the bearings slide – and a 'fence' to stop the bearing from rotating, this being a second etching located by tabs and slots. This 'fence' has a second vital function, in that it provides a broad face against which the bearing can slide, reducing friction and wear, and providing accurate lateral location. *Fig 6:2* should make this convoluted anatomy clear. The 'fence' lies to the inside of the loco frames, with the tails of the tabs providing location in the hornblock cut-out. There is, fortunately, a convention on hornblock design which means that they will almost all fit a standard opening, within which context they will give a proper ride height with the bearing at mid-travel. This convention calls for the cut-out in the frame to be 6 mm wide, with the top of the opening 4 mm above mean axle centreline; what happens *below* the axle centreline is basically irrelevant to these criteria.

These hornblock assemblies replace the fixed axle bearings in the rest of the chassis, which will, therefore, need the appropriate cut-outs providing. Virtually all of the better kit makers now allow for this, with at least

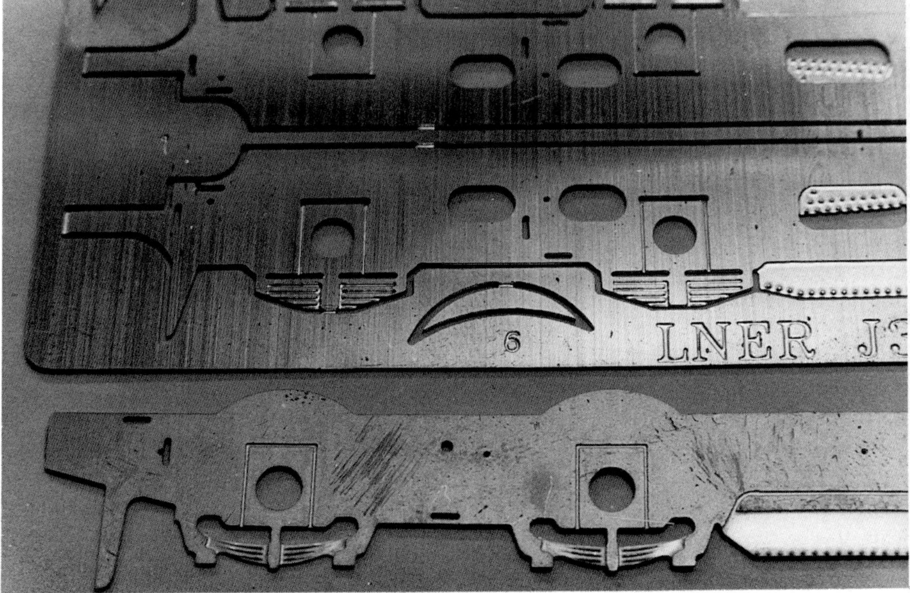

Making provision for hornblocks is a key feature of most modern loco kit chassis. Here are two examples – for the Finecast 'J39' (top) and the Perseverance '57XX' (lower). The Finecast frames make life just a bit easier for the would-be compensator by etching a slot right through above the axle position, simplifying the cutting-out of the hornguide opening. Others please copy!

a half-etched guide line to help you cut them out. The best design practice goes a bit further than this, and gives you a slot across the top of the opening, leaving the half-etch guides at the sides for a very simple 'snip a side' to open out the whole clearance. One or two chassis are appearing with the bias in favour of compensation and here the openings are etched-out clear, leaving the fixed-bearing man to solder in a 'blanking plate' to locate his bearings.

The other main difference between rigid and compensated chassis is the need to fit a compensating beam. This is simply a stiff rod lying along the chassis centreline over the compensated axles it is linking, and resting on top of those axles. The rod is in turn fixed to a lateral pivot, lying across the chassis parallel to the axles, and usually midway between them (which gives an equal weight distribution on each axle). The weight of the loco not being carried by the fixed axle is passed to the compensated axle by the beam – the square sliding bearings in the hornguides carry no part of the loco weight; they are there to cope with the fore-and-aft reactive loads of the coupling rods.

The compensating beam of a simple 0–6–0 Flexi-chas – a rod, bearing on the centre of the rocking axles, pivoted on a tube running across the frames.

A lot of people get very worried by this business of the side bearings not carrying the loco weight, and go to all sorts of lengths to make them do so. In trying to effect this totally pointless modification, they usually end up by impeding the freedom of the side bearings to locate the axle accurately while allowing it to tilt freely and unhindered. In other words, they effectively negate the whole system. While one round bar (the compensating beam) resting on another (the axle) at right-angles does not resemble any conventional bearing traditionally associated with either real or model locos, it is actually a most effective arrangement, with exceptionally low friction. It works exceedingly well, has been proven over many years, and should be left well alone! Keep it lightly oiled and it'll last for ever; all that any wear will do is to lower the ride height of the loco by a thou or two, which has no significance whatsoever in either the functioning or appearance of the loco.

I'm going to stop there for the moment in my description of the bones of a compensated chassis. There are further ramifications to consider when we come on to locos with bogies, trailing trucks and what-have-you, although in a good many instances, it is often possible to ignore a leading pony or trailing radial, applying simple spring-loading as for a rigid chassis.

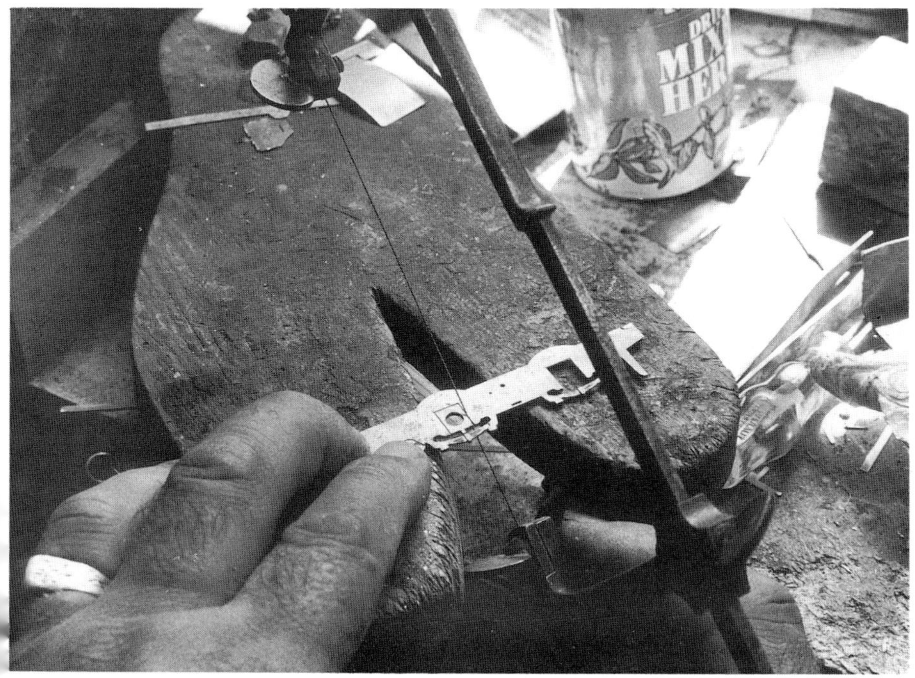

Cutting out hornguide openings in the frames of the '57XX'. The best tool is the piercing saw as shown. The frames are tack-soldered together as a pair, enabling both sides to be cut at once.

PREPARING FRAMES FOR COMPENSATION

In the context of our initial, simple example, then the only additional operations we need to carry out in preparing the frames before assembly are concerned with providing the necessary cut-outs to accept the hornblocks, and ensuring that we have the pivot-holes for the compensating beam. The Perseverance (now made by Puffers) '57XX' chassis is an example of a kit with half-etched guide-lines defining the hornguide cut-out, a bit more difficult to cut out than the 'snip-a-side'. In fact, the easiest way to do this is to make use of that grand old modeller's standby, the jeweller's piercing saw that creeps in at the foot of the tool-list. Fit a fairly fine blade – about M4/O, and cut the representation of the spring-loading rod first, then carefully chase the half-etched guide-line around the cut-out. The blade will follow the etched guide quite accurately so long as you don't try and force it. A little lubrication of some sort on the blade will help, and the job will need to be firmly supported on our suitable cutting table! If you haven't got one, the complex and sophisticated item illustrated in *Fig 4:3* should take, oh, the better part of five minutes to confect. Clamp it in the vice, and make sure that you've got the blade in the saw so that it cuts on the down-stroke. It's really quite a simple business, and if you want to speed things up a bit, tack-solder the frames back-to-back and cut them both at once.

Once you've got the sawing out of the way, the cut-outs can be cleaned-up with files if necessary, and attention turned to the beam pivot holes. The '57XX' chassis has these etched-in, so it's just a case of opening them up to the required size, which I do with a taper broach.

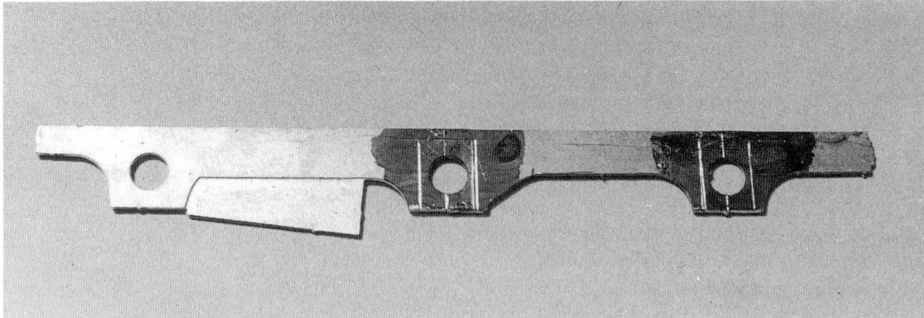

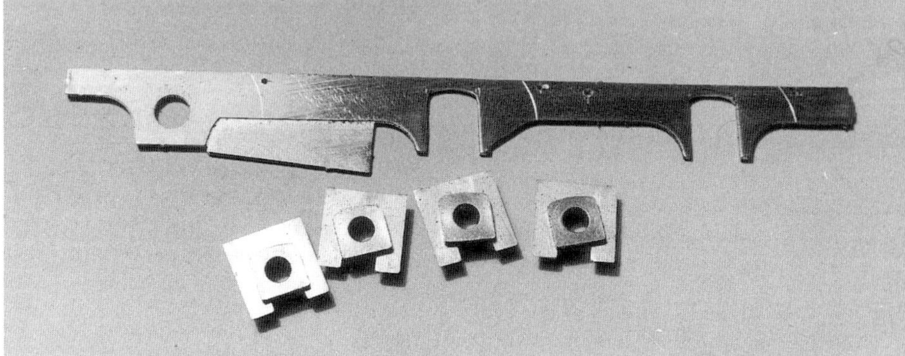

Not all kit chassis make provision for hornguide openings, so it may be necessary to mark and cut these yourself. I had to do this in the case of the Falcon Brass 'Kirtley' shown here. A patch of permanent felt marker helped the scribe-marks to show up. The cut-outs were 6mm wide, with the top 4mm above the axle centre. The openings were cut out with the piercing saw, just as for the '57XX'. Making the top of the opening 'arched' does not impair the hornblocks, and makes it easier to turn the saw. The holes for the beam pivot and the brake hangers were also drilled at this stage. The work was done with the frames tacked together as a pair. The hornblocks shown are an older design by Impetus.

HORNBLOCK ASSEMBLY

This is really pretty self-evident both from the anatomy drawing, *Fig 6:2*, and from the hornblock instructions. The only point to check is that the bearing slides freely in its slot before you start fitting the guide fence. As with all other 'fits', the hornguide should be etched a trifle on the 'tight' side, so a stroke or two with a fine flat file might well be needed to get things sliding smoothly. Don't for goodness sake go mad here, as a sloppy fit between bearing and guide is not a good idea. If you do overstep the mark, don't despair, as you get a spare set of hornguide blanks in this instance, and hence a second chance. These Puffers hornblocks incorporate a simple wire retainer in the bottom of the 'guide fence', which, when fitted, makes the whole thing a self-contained unit. Simple!

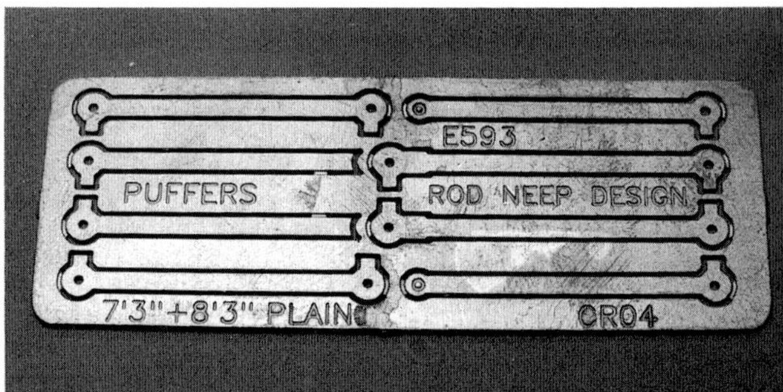

Two-part coupling rods for a compensated chassis, once again from the Puffers '57XX' chassis. The first shot shows the basic etch, in 18-thou nickel silver.

COUPLING RODS

As I think I've made clear by now, it's the proper relationship between coupling rods and frames that underpins any sweet-running mech. On a compensated chassis, we also need those rods to be capable of articulation in the vertical plane, which we normally accomplish by the simple (but usually incorrect) expedient of overlapping the various sections of the rods onto a convenient crankpin. No section of rod ever covers more than an adjacent pair of axles, and the actual overlap is by means of simple halved joints. The basic arrangement is sketched in *Fig 6:4*, and the actual construction figures in the next of our little photo-sequences – these are, once again, the rods for the '57XX'.

The assembled rods will need cleaning up with files and fine wet-and-dry to remove any excess solder, and to dress the exposed edges of the rods so that the 'layers' are lost, and the finished item looks as if it has been hewn from a single chunk of metal. Both Finney and Puffers rods are etched a bit oversize on depth to give you some allowance to play with; the '57XX' rods also called for a bit of refining and shaping to reproduce the characteristic GWR 'fish-

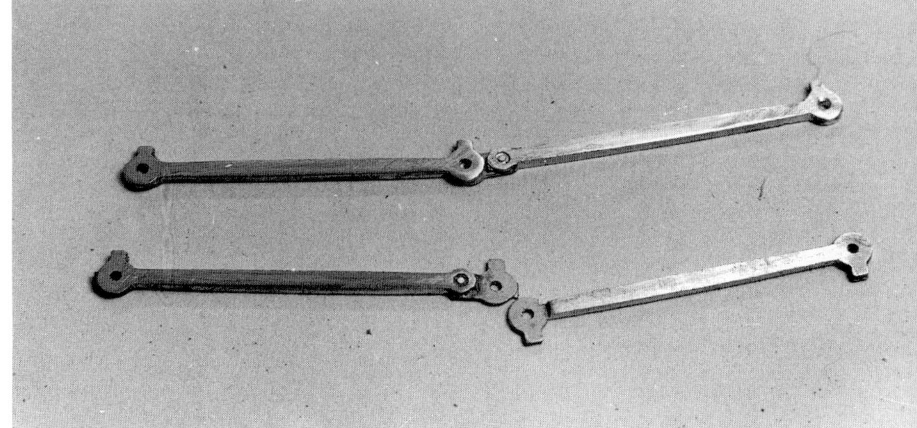

These rods are designed to overlap on the centre crankpin of this 0–6–0, so are assembled to give the required 'halved joint', as in Fig. 6:4.

belly' rod profile, which the Finney rods already incorporated. The last job in preparing the rods is to ease the crankpin holes out to a good tight fit on the jig-axles being used, if these are of the parallel-sided (rather than Rice tapered) design. The Puffers (née Perseverance) jig-axle has two diameters, to suit 'crankpin' and 'crankpin + bush' size holes, some rods being etched to this latter dimension. The advantage of the tapered type of jig axle is, of course, than *any* size of hole will locate accurately somewhere along the taper.

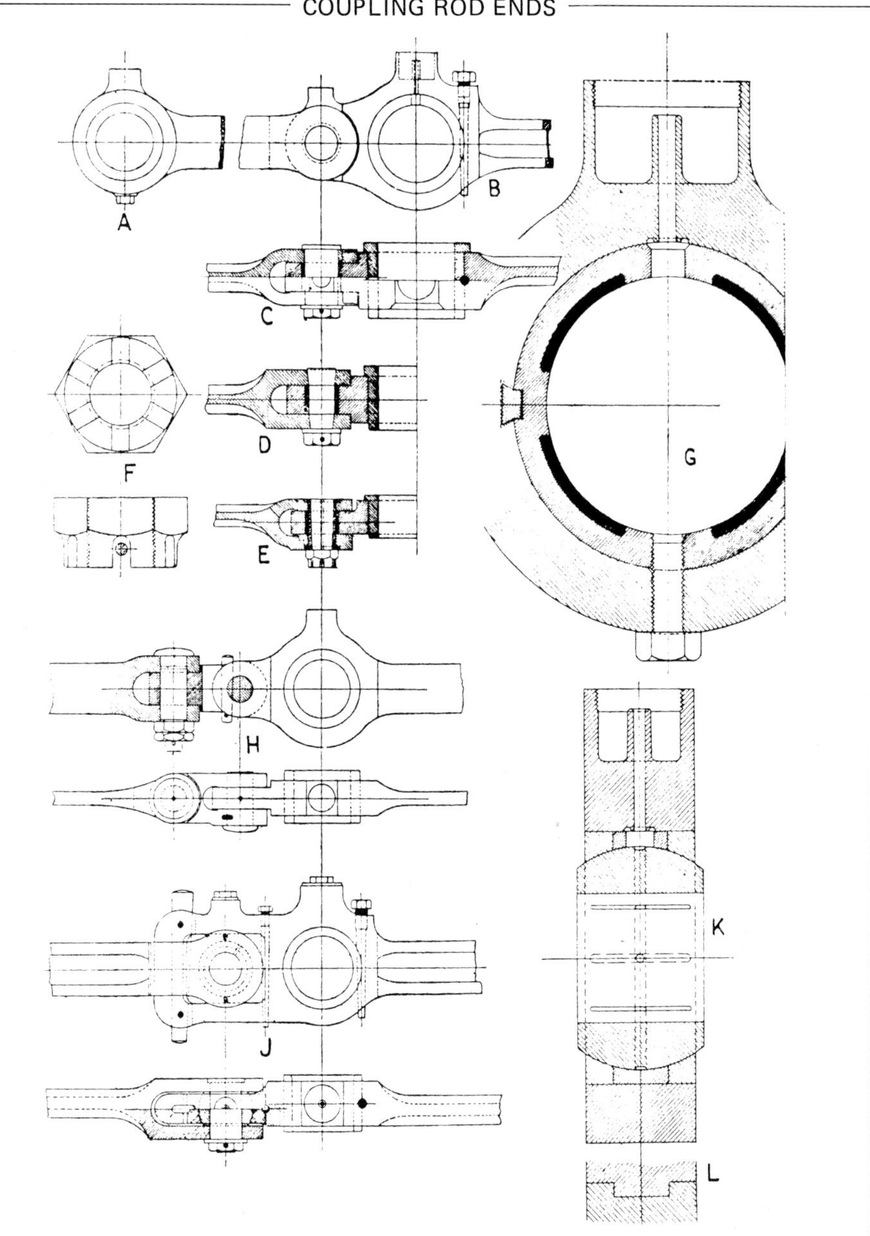

Fig. 6:3 HALVED COUPLING-ROD JOINTS ON CRANKPINS

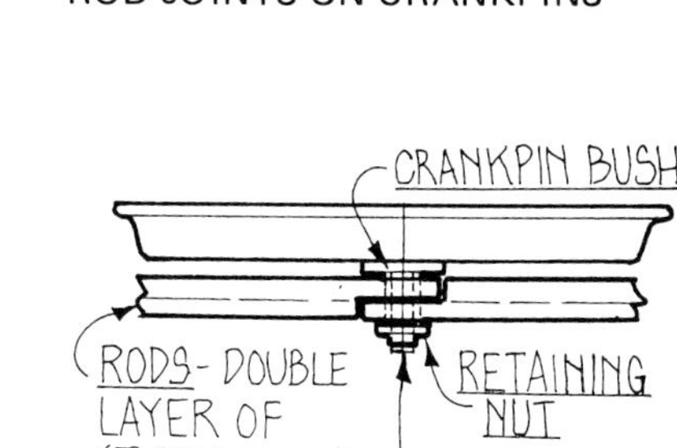

The completed arrangement should be apparent from the photo of the completed rods duly installed on the chassis.

JIGGING A CHASSIS

We now come to the operation at the heart of the Flexi-chas system of chassis assembly – setting-in the hornblocks to the frames using the coupling rods as a jig. The vital tool is the jig-axle, together with some means of retaining the hornblocks in the frames while adjustments are made and soldering undertaken. With the commercial jig-axles, you get some coil springs which, threaded over the jig-axle between the hornblocks, will press these out against the frames when the whole assembly is in place in the chassis. The alternative is a simple spring clamp, and I have found that either aluminium 'Dinky' hair-curlers or small Bulldog clips will do the job quite nicely.

There is no reason, given a sufficiency of jig-axles, springs and clamps, why one should not set up the whole chassis in one go, both sides and all sections of rod. Sometimes I do that, but usually I prefer to take things a step at a time, setting up one four-coupled group, getting that right and fixed before moving on to the rest of the coupled axles. It is essential to work out from the fixed 'datum' axle, so I start by inserting a jig-axle in the bearings of, usually, the rear axle, as in the good old '57XX' still figuring in the photographs. The centre jig-axle now receives the hornblocks and retainer springs, before going into the chassis. And then, well, it's really too simple, and should be apparent from the photo-sequence. The only point to make is that I only ever tack-solder the hornblocks into place, usually on diagonally opposite corners. This makes it easier to unsolder them should the need ever arise – usually for 'refit' purposes when the loco has clocked up a good big mileage, which a lot of mine seem to!

Once I'm happy that it's all spot-on, the jig-axles, springs and clamps are removed,

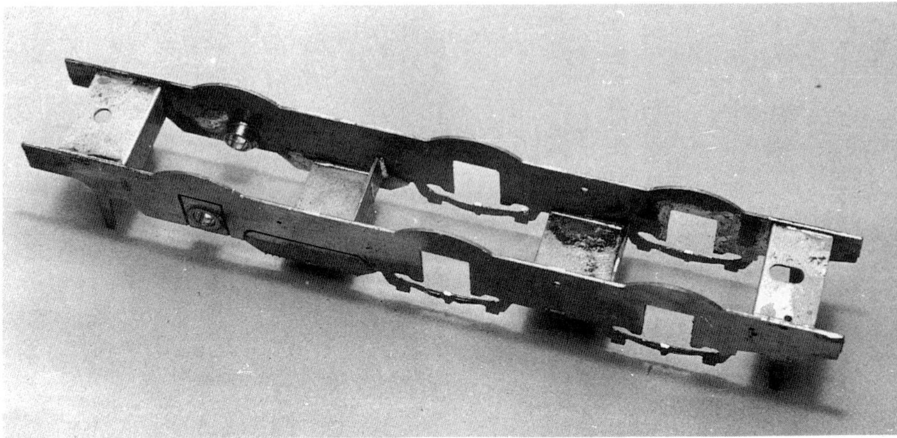

Ready for the hornblock assemblies, here are the prepared '57XX' frames duly erected with a full complement of frame spacers.

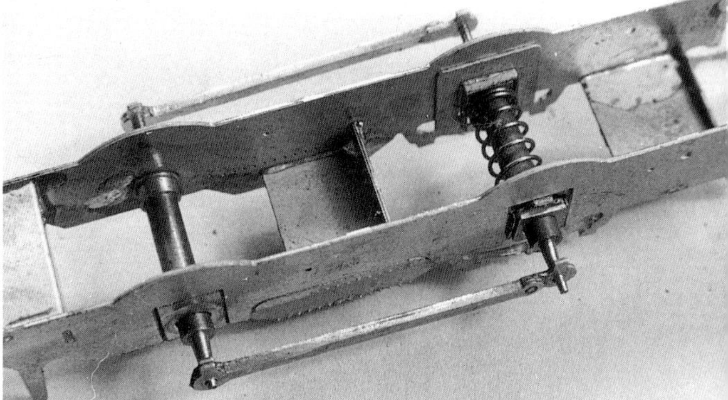

Left: *The hornblock assemblies are threaded on to a jig-axle either side of a spring (supplied with Puffers jig-axles) and located in the frames.* Right: *The coupling rods are then offered up to the jig-axles, and the position of the hornblock assembly adjusted to match the rods.*

Left: *An alternative to the spring for holding the hornblock assembly in place on the frames during setting-up is the modified (chopped short) Dinky hair-grip shown here.* Right: *Once everything is lined up, the hornblock assemblies are then tack-soldered into the frames as described in the text. Here is the end result – the '57XX', still.*

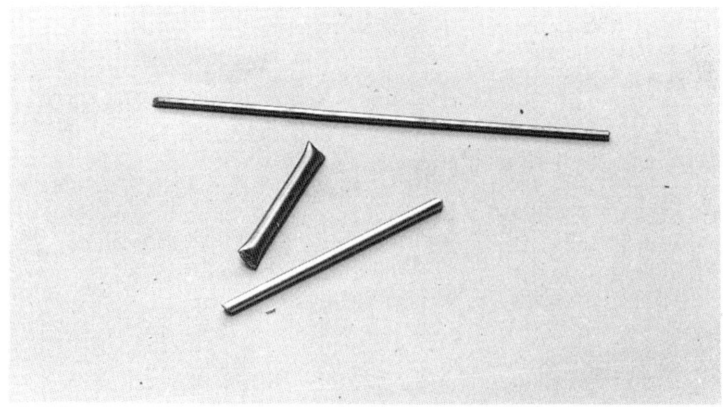

Left: *Making and fitting the beam. Puffers supply rod and tube in the '57XX' chassis kit. I found the 'beam' supplied (1/16 in brass rod) a bit hefty and awkward to 'tweak' if needed, so substituted some of John Flack's 1mm dia. nickel silver rod.* Right: *The pivot tube runs on a piece of the 1/16 in rod soldered across the frames. Care is needed to ensure that you don't solder the whole thing solid. The paper spacers shown here help avoid such a mishap. An alternative is the 'clench-fix' beam as in Fig. 6:5.*

and the chassis receives any necessary cleaning-up. I usually reckon to fit the beam pivot at this stage, even if I leave the beam itself until later. It's also a good time to fit some frame detail, such as brake pivots and guard irons, together with any inter-frame twiddly bits. Some chassis kits provide the springs as separate add-on etchings or castings, and now is a good time to solder them in place. I can only generalise, but if the wheels are likely to impede access, then now is the time to fit it. There's also a strong argument for painting the chassis at this stage – more on that in Chapter 12.

Installing the beam itself – cropped to length once it is soldered in place. It may be necessary to 'tweak' the beam up or down to adjust the ride height of the chassis. The '57XX' was, fortunately, right as built.

MAKING AND FITTING THE BEAM AND PIVOT

I'm still with my simple six-wheeled chassis here (although I'm illustrating an 0–6–0, a 2–4–0 or 0–4–2 would be similar, although in the latter case the leading axle would be the fixed/driven one) and so can, for the moment, duck around compound beams and other such seemingly-fearsome bits that appear when bogies cloud the issue. A simple chassis has a simple beam, which is, naturally, simple to make and install. Perseverance/Puffers give you a bit of $\frac{1}{16}$ in ID brass tube, and a bit of $\frac{1}{16}$ in rod to pivot it on. The idea is that the tube is squared-off and filed to the length apposite to the width of chassis being built. The holes in the frames are opened out to a *tight* fit on the $\frac{1}{16}$ in rod, which is then passed through the frames and the tube, as in the sketch in *Fig 6:4*, and retained by being soldered in place. This is the only dodgy bit of the operation, calling for the precautions shown in the sketch. Making the frame hole a tight fit lessens the chance of any solder trying to nip through and gum up the tube, while oiling this joint helps to repel any that does manage it; the paper also interferes with this undesirable possibility.

If all this talk of things soldering themselves solid rather than pivoting in approved see-saw fashion has you worried, may I commend Rice's 'dry' alternative, shown in *Fig 6:5*? Here the tube is reduced to a retaining sleeve clenched onto the rod, which now pivots in the chassis holes – same effect, different method. In both cases, the beam is simply soldered in place at the mid-point of the tube, and as parallel as possible to the frames. This beam is bent up and down to set the ride height of the chassis, in which application I find the $\frac{1}{16}$ in rod Puffers supply a bit on the hefty side.

Fig. 6:4 CROSS-SECTION OF PIVOT TUBE AND BEAM

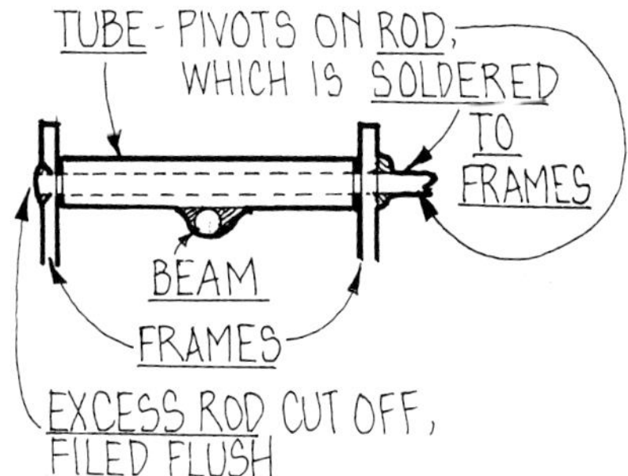

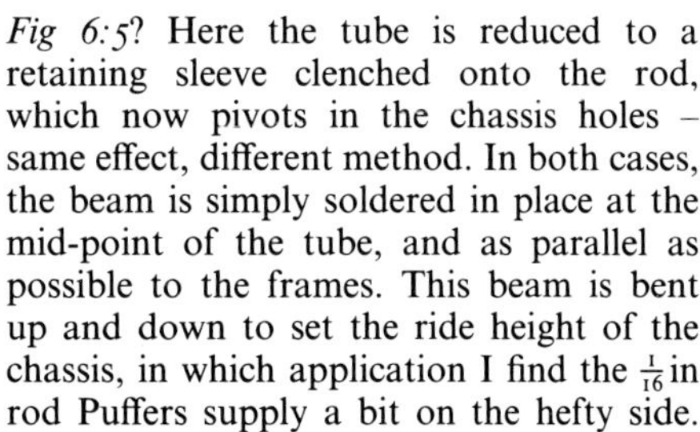

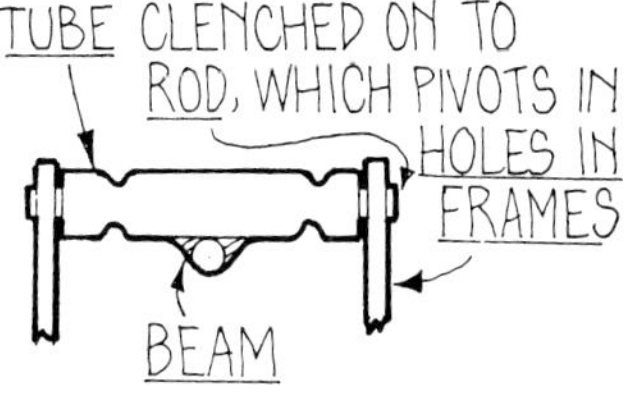

Fig. 6:5 CLENCHED TUBE PIVOT

As the weight of the average compensated 0–6–0 isn't going to be any where near the sort of level at which a $\frac{1}{16}$ in beam would be needed, I beg to differ and fit one made of something a good deal slimmer – about 0.9 mm brass wire slim, or, not infrequently, straightened-out paper clip. And that's about it, apart from the aforementioned touch of beam-bending in best Yuri Geller style to get the loco sitting level, which I do once the wheels are on, the next state in chassis construction whether wobbly or rigid.

MULTI-BEAMS AND OTHER DELIGHTS

It is a regrettable fact of life that not all locos are 0–6–0Ts – life would be a lot easier if they were, and this book would be a good deal shorter. Unless you are, like me, content for a bit to build a Cornish china-clay branch entirely motivated by 0–6–0PTs (a '1336', two '57XX', a '16XX' and a '74XX', if you must know...) then sooner or later you will need to grasp the nettle and have a go at a bogie or trailing truck, a bar-framed leading pony or, worst of all, some behemoth with umpteen coupled axles *and* a truck or two. The very thought of a '9F' gives me palpitations... Actually, I'm over-dramatising, as usual; it's not that difficult once you've grasped the principles and can apply them. If you're using a properly-designed chassis kit, then the problems will, of course, have been solved for you in advance ... won't they?

However, before leaving our simple 0–6–0, time must be found for a mention of the twin-beam method of compensating even so basic a chassis, as makers such as Martin Finney are already incorporating this in their designs. As can be seen from the general layout in *Fig 6:6*, based on the Finney 2251 0–6–0, the three points of the suspension have now wandered about a bit. We have dispensed with the fixed driven axle, so that we must be looking to fit an axle-hung motor – no problem, these days, as the now-universal motor + fold-up mount/gearbox amounts to just that, as does the RG4 if you can run to it. Instead, we now have two beams, fitted immediately inside the frames between the rear pair of axles, both of which ride in hornblocks. The pivots of these beams are now two of our 'fixed points', replacing the bearings of the datum axle in the simple version. The third point is a simple pivot sitting on top of the mid-point of the leading axle, which, also being carried in hornguides, is free to rock about it.

The method of jigging-up the axles in this instance involves an extra stage, in that the driven/datum axle must now also be installed in the frames, which will have hornblock cut-outs for all the axles. This is accomplished by the same basic means as is used to set in the remaining axles, except that the job is undertaken with the chassis back in the erecting jig, and with an alignment rod in place of the jig-axle. Once this first axle is in square to the frames, matters proceed exactly as described for the simple chassis of the '57XX', except for the obvious difference with respect to the installation of the beams.

Back in my purist days, I started out compensating locos on this multi-beam system, which does have the advantage that, with no 'fixed axle' to 'lurch' the loco over bumps, the riding is a touch smoother. Does your track have bumps that bad? Not even mine does, as a rule; and real locos, with their unyielding springs, are pretty much apt to lurch anyway, so it has ceased to worry me too much. Nowadays I generally don't bother with twin-beams on 0–6–0s; where they truly come into their own is with bogie engines, when they can allow us to avoid the dubious delights of compound beams, on which more in a moment.

As usual, I'm getting ahead of myself, so before embarking on the beamy byways of bogies and their compensation, I'd like to do my best to avoid any unnecessary complications, by considering the simpler option already outlined, viz., compensating the coupled wheelbase and spring-loading such sundry carrying axles as might be jogging along for the ride. To take some concrete examples, consider for a moment that paragon of usefulness, the Mogul. In this instance, a GW '43XX' – but no matter, it could easily be the Ivatt 'Mickey Mouse', a Southern 'Woolwich' or something elegant and purposeful by Gresley. Consulting the table of weights back in Chapter 5 will show that leading pony trucks don't usually carry too much weight, as the mass of the cylinders, etc, will be shared between the truck and the leading driven axle. In the case of the '43XX', it's only about 10 tons out of a total of something over 60; the weight bias is firmly on the drivers. So, a simple pony truck, lightly sprung, gives us the required effect. This is what Rod Neep did

Fig. 6:6 3-BEAM 0–6–0 CHASSIS

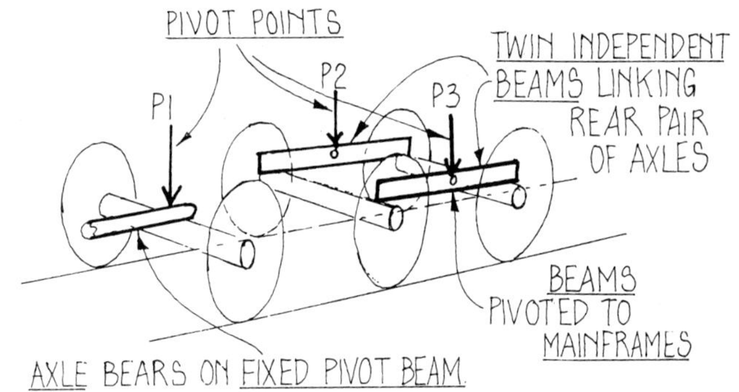

Twin-beam compensation applied to an 0–4–4T – the 'H' class built by the MRJ 'regulars'. This had twin beams between the drivers and a single beam to the bogie.

in designing the relevant chassis kit, and it works perfectly well.

The same could also be said of the very similar case of an 0–6–2T, not to mention 2–6–2s of all persuasions. I rarely bother with full compensation on any of these types – even the BR Standard '4' 2–6–4T illustrated has the simple combination of a basic 0–6–0 'Flexi-chas' with sprung leading pony and trailing bogie. It's when you come on to those troublesome twins, the 0–4–4T and the 4–4–0, that the compensated bogie comes into its own. The reason is, of course, that both these types have, to put it kindly, an unfortunate weight distribution. This is especially true of cast whitemetal kits, which often end up with a lot of mass right where you least want it – over the bogie.

The chassis for the '43XX' Mogul is compensated as a simple 0–6–0, with spring loading applied to the pony truck, as described in the last chapter.

The imposing BR Standard Class 4 2–6–4T, which I built from a modified DJH kit, has a simple six-coupled compensated chassis with weighted and sprung leading and trailing trucks.

COMPENSATED BOGIES

There are really two aspects of this arrangement to consider; compensation within the bogie itself, and compensation between the bogie and the coupled wheels. These problems can be considered separately, so I'll start with the former.

Bogies can be compensated in two basic ways, which I will summarise as pivoted frames and rocking axle. The first of these is drawn in *Fig 6:7*, which should show just how easy it is to construct. Basically, the bogie sideframes, together with any necessary detail, are bolted to the stretcher with a single central bolt each side, which acts as a pivot and enables the sideframes to rotate on the stretcher, keeping all the wheels on the track at all times, and, most importantly, under equal load. This is well worth doing, even in the context of an otherwise rigid chassis; it is very similar in execution to the system suggested for fitting cast bogie sideframes in place without solder, described in Chapter 5. Snags? Only one, really, in that as the sideframes need to be capable of independent movement, it's not possible to attach the bogie front and rear to them. My solution to that little problem also appears in *Fig 6:7*. It *is* possible to pivot one sideframe and fix the other, which can then carry the end stretchers, but I prefer the fully-equalised version.

The alternative type of compensated bogie is one treated in the same way as a 4-wheeled wagon, having one fixed and one rocking axle. The layout is shown in *Fig 6:8*, which shows the rocking axle running in simple slots in the bogie side, with a short fixed pivot sitting on top of it to provide a fulcrum and set the ride height. It also shows the rocking axle as the *rear* axle of the bogie, and this is important if unwanted axle tilt is to be avoided. This is a problem

Fig. 6:7 PIVOTED FRAME BOGIE

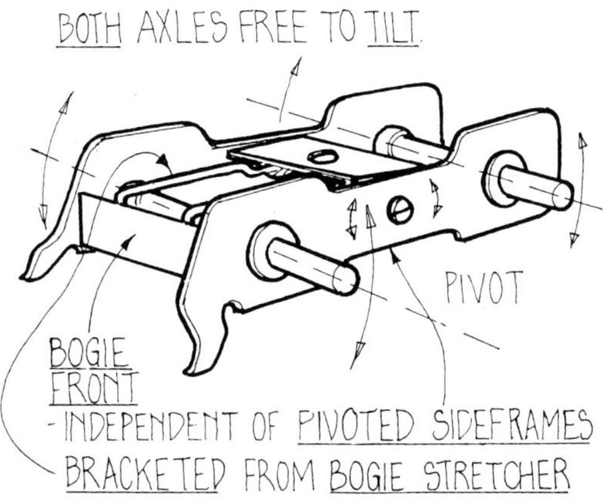

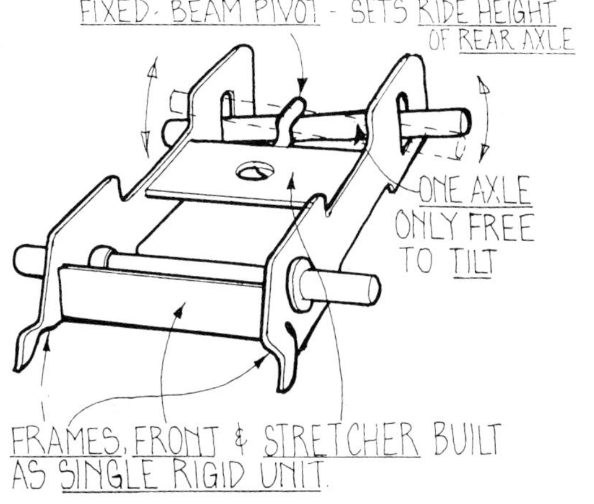

Fig. 6:8 ROCKING-AXLE BOGIE

I've already mentioned in connection with bogies incorporating sprung suspension, which I used to try and make. It occurs on the *leading* axle of a locomotive or other multi-axle vehicle entering a curve, when the side-loading imposed by the action of the coning/flange on the railhead overcomes the vertical restraint of the axle and, rather than deflecting the axle sideways and thus 'steering' the loco into the curve, tilts the axle instead. This is particularly prone to happen with a long total wheelbase, or when the axle is being loaded by a beam or wire spring bearing on its mid-point – exactly the case with the rocking axle of our bogie.

This is why the pivoted bogie axle needs to be to the rear, and is also why any sprung leading axles – as in, say, a 2–4–0 or the radial-fitted 2–4–2T, often need a spring at each side. I've occasionally experienced the effect with a simple 'Flexi-chas' 2–4–0 with a beam on the front two axles, in which case a twin-beam and pivot system provides a cure. However, generally speaking, 2–4–0 types have a short wheelbase, and the sideloading on the flange of the 'steering' axle is directly proportional to the distance of that axle from the next fixed point of the wheelbase. Hence, most 2–4–0 (and 0–4–2) types 'get away with it', especially if the sideplay is on the middle, rather than leading, axle.

Leaving aside that aside, I think that my preference for a bogie equalised by pivoting the sideframes is evident, and this is what I generally do. In the case of GW outside-framed bogies, it is straightforward to construct a simple equalised 'inner bogie' to achieve this, with the outside frame simply bracketed off the stretcher. I converted the bogie of my 'Dukedog' – originally built with a rocking axle – to this system, with a dramatic improvement in its reliability into curves and through pointwork as a reward for my trouble. There are also various, rather more fanciful, versions of the basic pivoting frame design, but in the context of this book, adapting the average kit bogie to the simple form is probably the best bet.

There are also one or two 'universal' bogie compensating kits about, most notably the ingenious but rather fiddly 'Perseverance' item. This is basically a rocking-axle design, based on a long bolt which both forms the pivot of the rocking cradle carrying the axle, and is used to adjust the wheelbase, by means of nuts run along its thread. This design of bogie suspension was intended for use with a compound beam system, with the bogie hung direct from the beam. I prefer, if possible, to keep the bogie pivoting/steering system separate from the beam, but there are circumstances where a bogie pivoted from the end of a compensation beam can work well. Generally, these are instances where little, if any, bogie swing is required – in other words, short wheelbase engines such as the little NBR 'R' 4–4–0T, or similarly compact 0–4–4Ts such as the wee Highland 'Strathpeffer Pug' or the LSWR Adams 'O2'. On easy curves, there's no reason why a slightly longer wheelbase couldn't be accommodated in this way – but the relationship between the loco and the layout needs to be carefully determined; it certainly can't be recommended as a universal solution.

COMPENSATION BEAMS FOR BOGIES

Which is where we return to our old friend, the swinging link bogie discussed at some length in the last chapter. I described a couple of methods for 'loading' such bogies briefly there – mostly in the context of transferring the load from the beam or spring to the bogie in the most effective way, without interfering with the important guidance function. What I am concerned with here is the other end of this loading system – the beam, and its relationship to the rest of the locomotive's wheelbase.

There are two types of beam that can be used in this application; the simple beam, used for four-coupled bogie engines, or on six-coupled where a twin-beam system is used for the rear pair of coupled axles; and the compound beam, used on six-coupled types with a 'fixed' axle. Both are drawn in *Fig 6:9*, from which it will be evident that the compound beam is considerably the more complex animal. Put bluntly, this is a

Fig. 6:9 SIMPLE AND COMPOUND BEAMS FOR BOGIES

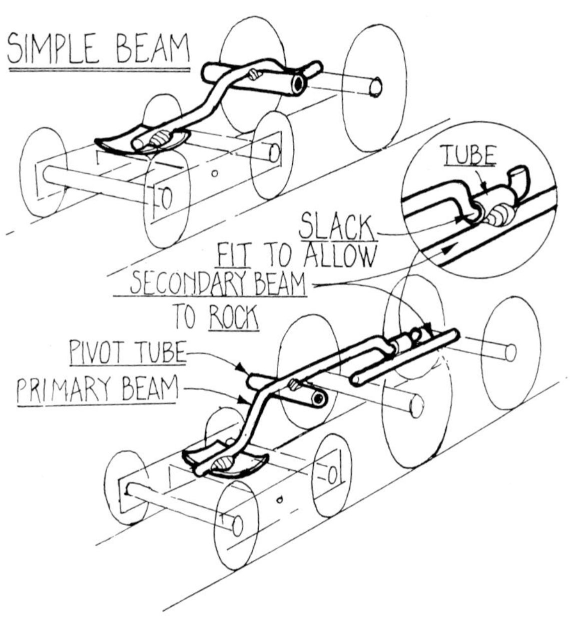

Fig. 6:10 PIVOT FRAME BOGIE AND 3-BEAM CHASSIS

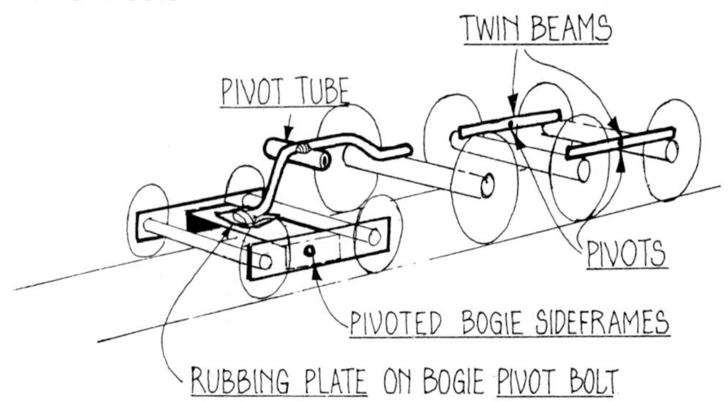

beam off a beam – in other words, the beam linking the front pair of coupled axles, rather than being pivoted off a tube-and-shaft running across the frames, finds itself dangling from the nether end of a second beam, linking the front pair of coupled wheels to the bogie. It is the pivot of this second beam that forms the 'third point', with the fixed bearings of the rear axle forming the remaining two. The system by which the two beams are joined is shown in the enlarged detail circled out of the diagram.

I have never been a great lover of the compound beam, although I've always found that it works well enough, especially the etched version developed by Perseverance. It's bulky, takes up room that is otherwise needed for cylinder stretchers and so on, and is a fiddle to make and set up. The combination of a 'twin beam' coupled wheelbase and a simple beam linking the leading coupled axle to the bogie is, to my mind, a distinctly superior system, and I'm glad to see that kit-designers are increasingly adopting it; all the Mitchell/Finney GW 4–6–0s are thus endowed. So, to bring all this together into one clear and concrete recommendation for providing compensation between leading bogies and coupled wheelbases, I would suggest that the set-up outlined in *Fig 6:10* will serve most needs. This combines a pivoted-frame bogie, loaded through the pivot by a sliding plate atop the bolt, with a simple beam resting on the pivot at one end and on the leading coupled axle at the other. If the engine be a 4–4–0, then the remaining coupled axle is simply fixed; if a 4–6–0, then twin beams link the rear coupled axle pair. 4–4–2 or 4–6–2 types get a sprung rear truck for simplicity. Trailing-bogie tank locos are simply the same thing backwards. End of story – except for the small matter of positioning the beam pivot to determine the load on the bogie.

PROPORTIONAL LOADING

Lor, don't it sound grand? Actually, it's extremely simple; a compensation beam is like a see-saw in reverse. A see-saw with the same weight each end will balance; a compensation beam with the pivot in the middle will likewise balance, by applying the same load at each end. Move the pivot, though, and you put more load onto the end of the beam nearest the pivot. The relationship is absolutely linear – if the pivot divides the beam two-thirds and one-third, then two-thirds of the weight will apply to the end of the beam one-third of the length away from the pivot. So, if you want to apply, say, 25% of the weight of a 4–4–0 onto the bogie and 75% onto the drivers – about right according to Rice's first theorem – then you do a simple sum: without the bogie, a 4–4–0 is an 0–4–0. If it is balanced about that wheelbase (ie, the nose isn't resting on the deck), then you can reckon the weight on each axle is about the same. If it doesn't balance, make a rough determination of the centre of gravity by standing the thing (complete with body, of course) on a bit of wood over a pivot (a ruler on a pencil is fine). Now move the ruler along over the pivot until the thing just tips the 'other way'. The point at which it just goes from tipping one way to tipping the other is the centre of gravity. Note, approximately, where it is in relation to the wheelbase.

This is exactly the same business as the see-saw and the beam, and the same law applies; if the c of g is one-quarter of the wheelbase aft of the leading axle (fairly typical for a model 4–4–0), then three-quarters of the total weight is on that front axle. As we want 25%, ie one-quarter, on the bogie, then it's simply a case of arranging the pivot of the beam linking coupled axle and bogie to be nearer the coupled axle in the ratio 1:2, placing two-thirds of the load on the axle and the remaining third on the bogie. Simple, isn't it? And what a convenient example! In point of fact, great accuracy is not required, as these are all ball-park figures and so long as you get somewhere near the right amount of weight onto the bogie, then all is well. I cheat by drilling myself three or four sets of pivot holes in the frames when I'm building the loco, to keep my options open; or I suspend the beam from an adjustable pivot, as sketched in *Fig 6:11* – a simple arrangement bracketed off the cylinder stretcher or some convenient frame spacer. It may all seem a little complex and fiddly, but believe me, it's a regular 'miracle cure' for dog-on-the-scent 4–4–0s and 0–4–4Ts that refuse to get off their behinds!

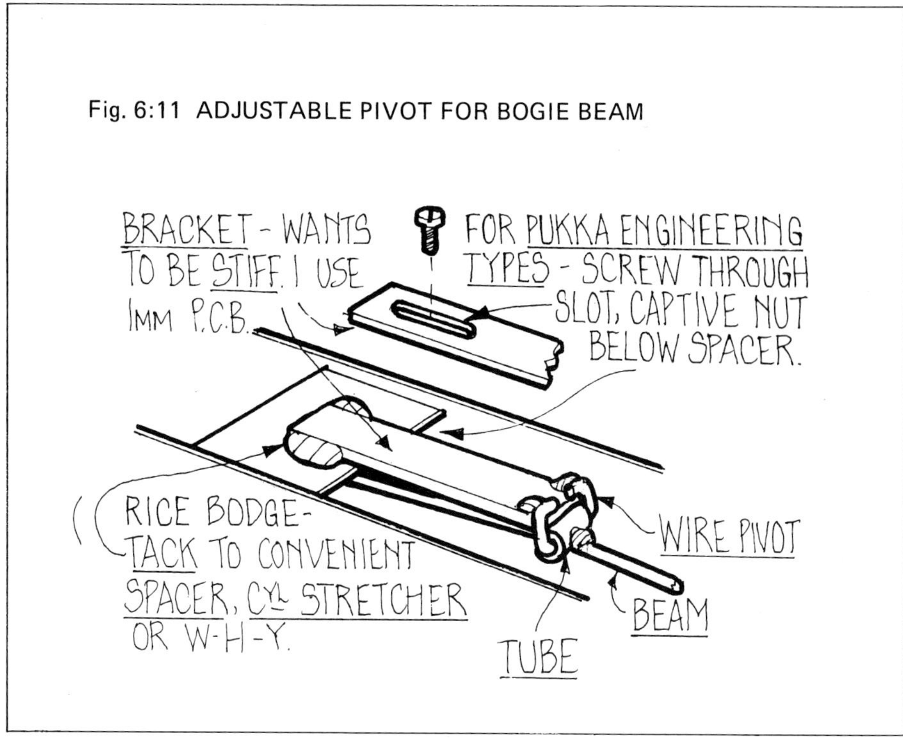
BRACKET - WANTS TO BE STIFF. I USE 1MM P.C.B.
FOR PUKKA ENGINEERING TYPES - SCREW THROUGH SLOT, CAPTIVE NUT BELOW SPACER.
RICE BODGE - TACK TO CONVENIENT SPACER, CYL STRETCHER OR W-H-Y.
WIRE PIVOT
BEAM
TUBE
Fig. 6:11 ADJUSTABLE PIVOT FOR BOGIE BEAM

SUMMARY

I could write an awful lot more about compensation, and the ways and means of designing compensated chassis for any and every application, but this isn't the place – it's a topic almost worth a book on its own. But, to bring all this together in the context of locomotive kit chassis construction, I hope that I have shown that applying straightforward 3-point compensation in a very great number of cases is simple and worthwhile. Any 0–6–0, 2–4–0, 0–4–2, 2–6–0, 0–6–2, 2–6–2 or 2–6–4 will normally be susceptible to the simplest form, with a fixed axle and single beam. 4–4–0 and 0–4–4T types have much to gain from compensated bogie systems. 4–6–0 and 4–6–2 designs will also benefit from bogie compensation. For more complex 8 and 10-coupled types, it's still possible, but the exposition would be lengthy. If you are building a kit for such a loco, it is to be hoped that the necessary compensation will have been designed-in. If not, I will have to refer you, for the moment, to the 'little blue book'; no, not Ahern, but Mike Sharman's original treatise that started the whole thing off: *Flexichas; A Way to Build Fully Compensated Model Locomotive Chassis*. Well, you don't think that I made it all up, surely?

A glimpse of the real thing – Stanier '8F' 2–8–0s being built at Swindon. NATIONAL RAILWAY MUSEUM

CHAPTER SEVEN
WHEELING-UP AND QUARTERING

GENERAL CONSIDERATIONS

This is the point in this divergent and rambling narrative where all the threads come together once again. For the rest of this book, what I have to say relates to any chassis, from the most uncompromising of solid blocks to the most sophisticated state-of-the-art compensated job. They all need wheels; cylinders and valve gear are always a headache; motors, gears and pick-ups are universally required to make 'em run; and at the end of it all they need painting, if not covering in twiddly bits. However, before going on, I always like to pause and take stock. This is where I think we've got to – where we *need* to get to, before there's any possibility of fitting the wheels.

Firstly, and most importantly, we will be quite clear about our specification, especially such mechanical basics as the motor and drive-train we intend to fit, the make and standard of wheel we favour, and the nature and location of the pick-ups. In most instances, of course, much of this will be decided for us by the kit-designer, provided we find him a fellow of wit and perception. However, it's always best to develop and depend upon your own judgement – kitmakers' recommendations are far from sacrosanct and not infrequently far from sanity. There's a lot to come on motors and gear-trains, and given that it's difficult to change your mind once the wheels are on, now is the time to check that the favoured set-up is practicable. Which means that you need at least the bones of the body together, to check that motor X will actually fit between the firebox sides of kit Y...

Secondly, we need to be sure that no task that is best done before the wheels go on still remains undone. The frames are erected, and all spacers are in place, including bogie or pick-up mountings. The wheel bearings or hornblocks are installed, and their alignment with the coupling-rods ascertained and corrected if need be. The arrangements associated with any bogies, pony trucks, radial or carrying axles have been decided upon and, so far as is possible in a wheel-less state, installed. Certain cosmetic details may need attending to while the chassis remains naked, while provision may need to be made for brake gear or outside cylinders. Solid chassis that are being provided with cosmetic overlays need to have these fitted at this point (unless the axle clearance in these is slotted, when they can be kept out of the way while any rough stuff with the wheels is taking place). And, of course, it is often prudent to paint the basic chassis at this juncture, especially where the wheels and frames are different colours.

Fitting the correct wheels is an important contribution to the correct overall look of a model. The highly distinctive Bulleid-Firth-Browns (BFBs) of the 'West Country' are a vital element of the engine's character. Fortunately, even in 'OO', as here, there is a reasonable choice of suitable types. These are Alan Gibson's version.

Fig. 7.1 MEASURING WHEEL DIAMETER

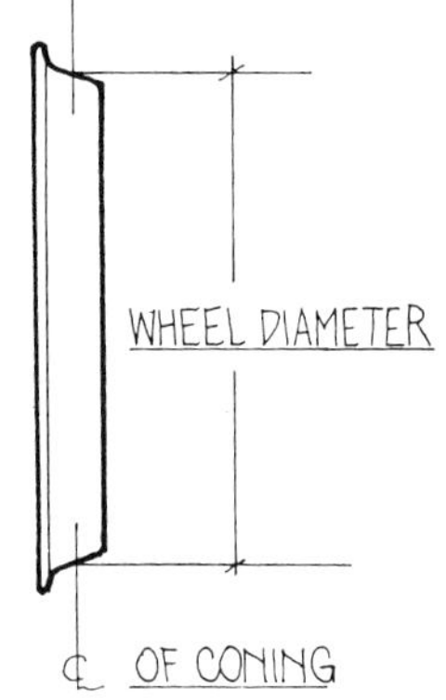

Thirdly, we need to be sure that the wheels that we're intending to use are actually suitable for the loco in question. This is a point upon which kit instructions are all too often mute, or so vague as to be meaningless. Back in the days when the range of driving wheel sizes and configurations was limited to a handful of 'round number' diameters, no choice of spoke numbers, crank throw or crank position, and only one profile, this *laissez faire* attitude was understandable; these days, it's unpardonable. The relevant prototype information is now readily available – thanks, once again, to Mike Sharman and his *Wheel Specifications for the Modeller*; so a suitable starting point for wheel choice is no problem. However, leaving aside the question of fidelity to the prototype for a moment, there are some practical considerations to take into account.

WHEEL COMPATIBILITY

Prototype driving wheel diameters are quoted 'on the tyre'; that is, if a loco is given as having a 5 ft 6 in driving wheel, this will be the diameter of the tread at the mid-point of the coning, and is often described as the 'nominal diameter'. It's nominal for three reasons – there's a 'manufacturing tolerance'; the wheel is, as just noted, coned, and thus exhibits a range of diameters; and there is an inbuilt 'turning factor', which permits the tyre to be re-profiled in a wheel lathe to accommodate wear – resulting in a reduction of diameter that may eventually reach as much as 3 in below the nominal figure.

Model locomotive wheels have likewise normally been quoted by a similar on-tyre 'nominal' size, originally giving the *actual* diameter in millimetres, latterly the scale equivalent at full size. So, where are the pitfalls? Well, in two areas – those of overall diameter and wheel configuration, both of which have a critical impact on the workability of models. The first of these might seem obvious – but it is frequently overlooked. A real driving wheel will be profiled to one basic standard, an important element of which will be a flange depth. Model wheels (I'm really talking 4 mm scale here, but other scales also suffer) can employ any one of a number of wheel standards, with a variation in flange depth that may result in *overall* wheel diameters for the same *nominal* size varying by over a millimetre. The potential for splasher clearance problems, fouling of cylinders, slidebar brackets, and brake gear, and even for adjacent wheels touching, is obviously considerable if this anomaly is overlooked.

Every locomotive drawing published by that grand old guru of the model railway world, F. J. Roche, had a note on it that ran thus: 'Wheel treads and flanges are drawn to R.C.H. dimensions, and clearances must be made for B.R.M.S.B. standard wheels …' It is one of the fundamental decisions that a kit designer has to make when he sets out on his long and rocky road: does he make his splashers to scale diameter, and correctly locate cylinders, slidebar brackets and so on – accepting that those modellers not working in P4 are going to have to fit wheels of a nominal diameter less than true scale? Or does he compromise for overscale flanges by moving things about and introducing errors in the model? Or (all too often) does he simply fudge the issue and leave the poor old modeller to find out the hard way that a 6 ft 6 in Romford driver has the same overall diameter as a 6 ft 9 in P4 wheel, and won't fit scale 6 ft 6 in splashers?

I must apologise if the tone of this book is starting to sound a bit grouchy, but really I think it's about time all this woolly thinking and abdication of basic design responsibility on the part of so many kitmakers was exposed and done away with. I get furious when I find such fundamentals as wheel sizing haven't been properly addressed, leaving me – as a P4 modeller – with splashers too big by a mile, or brake gear so far from the wheel-tyres that it would need a foot of pull to apply it. I'd be equally peeved if I was building for OO and found that 'scale size' wheels, often bought from the 'parts required to finish' list, fouled and shorted every-which-where. It should be firmly and unequivocably stated on the instructions whether the kit is designed for wheels of correct overall diameter or compromised for oversize flanges. In 1992 the former is, I suggest, the correct approach.

The chances are, you'll be left to work this out for yourself, so investigate the body to assess wheel clearances. I've already advocated some 'bare-bones' assembly before chassis construction gets too far advanced, and conducting clearance trials for the wheels you intend to fit is greatly facilitated if any splashers are already in place on the footplate at this juncture. While

The trouble with Romfords – at least when you fit the 'correct' size of wheel in situations where the prototype has a close centre-to-centre spacing. This calls for fitment of wheels 'a size down' to get the right clearance. GW 'Castle'/'Star' chassis.

I'm lambasting poor kit design in respect of wheels, splashers and clearances, I'll also spare a spot of invective for those hapless kitmakers who design and 'engineer' (if I may so debase the term) their kits with splasher-settings only suited to OO gauge and overscale wheels? I think that it is reasonably obvious that a OO wheelset in an EM/P4 (and hence prototypical) width splasher will prove a problem to nobody; but an EM wheelset in a OO splasher is an impossibility.

So, to clarify and summarise this whole business: locomotive wheels need to be considered in terms of their *overall* diameter – that is, nominal diameter plus flange depth. It is the overall diameter that is the determinant in wheel application, and the compromise must surely rest in the area of the overscale flange, where an underscale – *nominal* diameter will be needed to obtain a scale *overall* diameter. Most of the time, the required deviation from true nominal diameter is still within the turning allowance of the prototype tyre, so no real offence should be caused. But the importance of these factors is a 'fact of life', and can't go on being ignored.'

THE IMPORTANCE OF CONFIGURATION

Unfortunately, problems with wheel compatibility don't end just with the overall diameter; there is also the knotty problem of crank throw to consider – which, once again, it frequently isn't. Prototype crank throw – the total distance by which the coupling rod moves up and down (or fore-and-aft – it's actually a circular motion) – is a critical factor in many ways. For modellers, it poses two problems that can have drastic effects – footplate clearance, and crosshead travel. Model wheels that deviate from the correct scale dimension in this respect can render a loco quite unworkable – and, if you're not careful, you'll only find out when it's too late to take corrective action with tearing the job apart. Now is the time to check.

The problem is most acute where the prototype used a very short crank throw, such as the 18 in of many Drummond locos, both Scottish and LSWR types. Just such a case was my little 'R' class 4–4–0T, which, as can be seen from the picture, has a very small clearance inside the rear coupling-rod splashers. The Sharman wheels on my model incorporate this short throw to scale, so all is well; fit Romfords, with a scale 24in crank throw, and pow! two total seizures per revolution. Again, this is a poser for the kit designer; does he assume the builder is fitting a wheel correct in all particulars, or should he design to take the overscale throw of the popular 'Romford'? In the case of the 'R', I elected for the former, with a note in the instructions to that effect. Fitters of Romford wheels needed to provide a bigger coupling-rod splasher.

The problem of overscale crank throws can be equally acute when it comes to crosshead travel, which is identical to the crank throw, and hence the cylinder stroke of the prototype engine. Obviously, crossheads trying to put in a 24 in stroke on an 18 in or 20 in slidebar set are going to clout either the back of the cylinder or the front of the slidebar bracket or, quite frequently, both. This situation is most prevalent on small-wheeled industrial locos, or shunters like my GWR 1366, where the need to position the slidebar bracket between the fore and centre drivers tends to limit the length of the slidebars to the minimum; 1369, which has correct-throw Sharman drivers, uses virtually the entire slidebar length on each wheel revolution.

The full gamut of crosshead-travel problems and their associated solutions occupy a pithy paragraph or two in Chapter 8, but it's easier to avoid such difficulties in the first place by fitting the right wheels.

Other factors affected by incorrect crank throws include the fouling of steps and outside pull-rods for brake gear, sundry bits of sub-footplate plumbing, and clearance difficulties within slidebar brackets. I have often found that, if you get a problem in one area, such as footplate clearance, the chances are other things will be affected as well. The best answer, for both cosmetic and practical reasons, is to fit the correct wheel, or as close to it in terms of overall diameter and crank throw, as can be obtained. These days, with five major ranges and several hundred wheels to choose from, this is normally no problem, although I'm afraid that workers in the old coarse BRMSB OO and EM standards, to whom the newer ranges of plastic-centred wheels are denied by too fine a profile, will be limited in this respect. For the rest, working to 'finescale' OO, the modern EM standard or, of course, to P4, then fidelity of wheel type should be second nature; why compromise when you don't have to?

The total wheel configuration, which is what we're attempting to match in the choice for our model, is defined by four basic parameters – wheel size, wheel type, number of spokes, and crank position and throw. Nowadays, these are quoted as prototype dimensions, and provide a reasonably complete description of the wheel, though not taking account of such peculiarities as hub flare and individual fitments like balance weights. Thus, to take a few concrete examples, the good old '57XX' requires drivers of 4 ft $7\frac{1}{2}$in nominal diameter, plain rim and spoke profile, 14 spokes, and a crank between the spokes with a 24 in throw. The 'West Country', of course, requires a very different set of wheels: bogie and trailing truck wheels of 3 ft 1 in diameter, Bulleid-Firth-Brown cast steel centres; drivers of 6 ft 2 in diameter, BFB centres, cast-in crank between lightening holes, 24 in crank throw. The wee Drummond 'R' tank is different again – 2 ft 6 in diameter disc wheels on the bogie, and drivers of 5 ft 0 in diameter, plain rims, 16 spokes, crank between spokes and 18 in throw. As a final contrasted pair, a Webb 'Coal tank' needs drivers of 4 ft 5 in diameter, H-section spoke

The NBR Drummond 'R' class has a very short (18in) crank throw, as this picture of my 4mm model shows. Fitting wheels with too great a crank throw will bring conflict with footplate, steps and brake pull-rods.

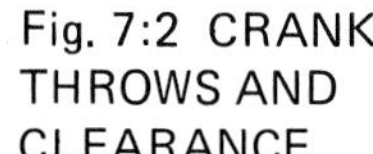

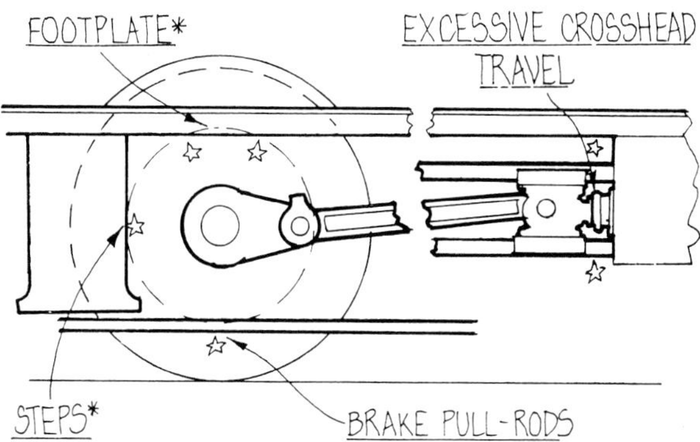

Another danger area for locos with wheels having incorrect crank throws is crosshead travel, as on my GWR '1366' 0–6–0PT. That crosshead is fag-papers away from the slidebar bracket at 'back dead centre'.

'Grand old stagers'. I built this 'B1', out of a much-mauled Jamieson kit, back in about 1976. It is OO gauge, and the Romford drivers have been considerably improved by some simple cosmetic additions – correctly-sized and shaped balance weights and 'axle ends' of Plastikard, knocked out with a leather punch, and glued in place over those giveaway cheesehead nuts. Insulated wheels are fitted all round, while the bogie wheels are Ultrascale.

centre, 12 spokes, crank between spokes and of the common 24 in throw, with 3 ft 9 in 10-spoke trailing wheels to match, while the Ivatt '2' 2–6–0 has bevel-rim wheels throughout, 3 ft 0 in with 9 spokes on the pony, and 5 ft 0 in 15-spoke drivers with the cranks, once again, between the spokes and of 24 in throw. The good old Romford with its 24 in throw is a canny attempt at an average, although to be really typical the pin should be between, rather than on, the spokes.

WHEEL CHOICE

I hope that I've said enough by now to suggest that there's quite a bit to be considered and checked when deciding what wheels are to be fitted to a loco. But there are yet more factors to be considered in a great many cases – such as cost, ease of use, compatibility with coupling rods, crankpin systems and the minor matter of standards. Before you reach for the gin-bottle or head off for the darkened room, the couch and the cold compress, I would like to allay one fear which might have raised a nagging doubt; all the wheels on the market today – certainly for 4mm scale – are of good or excellent quality, and exhibit no fundamental faults; and that most certainly wasn't the case a year or ten ago!

Romfords

I'll start with the simplest option first – the fitment of those grand old stagers, Romfords, the only choice for the modern coarse-scale worker. Coarse scale? A relative term, as always, and, in 4mm scale at least, not necessarily indicative of gross steam-roller wheels as with Tri-ang or Trix of yore. Modern 'coarse scale' OO is actually the 'scale of OO' of not very many years since, and is the standard now adopted by most R-T-R manufacturers. It is associated with the normal (as opposed to 'Finescale') Peco Streamline track, and is the basic level at which the bigger kit-makers like DJH are aiming – hence their inclusion of Romford wheels in their kits. These days, Romford offer a much wider spread of sizes than they used to, even stretching to such esoterica as the 8 ft 0 in driver for a Stirling Single. The basic wheel design goes back to Ahern's day, with a cast mazak (lead/zinc/aluminium alloy) centre locating onto a square-ended axle with a 10BA slotted cheese-head nut retainer. The tyres are turned nickel-silver to a modified BRMSB profile, with insulation by means of a thin band of material between the tyre and the centre. These days, the crankpin holes are drilled and tapped to take a crankpin which is identical to that fitted to the old Hamblings plastic-centred wheels, long extinct though respected in their day. Romford are unique in offering an uninsulated wheel, although the modern version does have a nickel tyre to match the insulated wheels; the originals were all-mazak, and collected dirt like mad.

So, if you're using Romfords, then you can't do much about things like spoke numbers or rim type, or, of course, crank throw. Visually speaking, they are some way off the mark, but they are well-engineered and of good quality, and win a lot of friends in the 'ease of use' stakes. The only point to consider when choosing a set of Romfords is that small matter of overall diameter – just keep your fingers crossed on the crank-clearance aspects if your chosen prototype deviates from Romford's median 24 in. (That's why Wills made the wide-splasher 'T9' (a Drummond 18 in-throw 'twiddler') rather than the far-more-common narrow version...) I'm not trying to be elitist in any way when I assert that a compromised gauge and compromised wheel standards are apt to result in a compromised model.

Kean-Maygib and Gibson

These two makers represent the next basic approach to wheel-making, with a turned steel tyre pressed onto a moulded plastic (nylon) centre. Their wheels, in common with all the 'finescale' ranges, are available in two profiles – fine OO/EM or P4, are designed for press-fitting to plain 1/8 in axles, and need to be gauged and quartered by the modeller. Neither of these two types of wheel come fitted with a crankpin, but both supply a crankpin system separately, using fine machine screws with turned collars and crankpin bushes. Both these ranges are 'high fidelity' wheels, with accurate modelling of spoke profile, rim section, and crank shape. The only drawback that I've experienced is an occasional propensity for the tyres to come loose on the centres, not difficult to cure with a spot of Loctite 601 or a smear of epoxy resin. The only real visual difference between them is that Kean-Maygib chemically-blacken their steel tyres, while Gibson's are untreated. The blackening cleans off easily, but is helpful in keeping paint on tyre-edges.

Sharman and Ultrascale

The remaining two makers both opt to mould their wheel-centres into pre-turned tyres, steel for Sharman and nickel-silver for Ultrascale. This makes for a true-running wheel with a tyre that will not shift on the centre under any circumstances. The moulding material is reinforced nylon, that of the Sharman wheel being specially formulated to exhibit a torque/grip characteristic intended to keep the wheel tight on the axle, while permitting it to be adjusted. This natty little trick is accomplished by having a very slight (1°) taper in the centre hole, and by using a plastic brew that will release its grip under a high level of torque – Joe modeller giving it a hefty tweak to shift the quartering – but will re-establish that grip once the torque is released. Ultrascale wheels don't have this taper or the happy-handshake nylon brew, but are a very smooth close-tolerance fit on the axles, and are easy to lock if required with a spot of '601'.

There are two main differences between these two superficially similar ranges. The Sharman wheel has a moulded-in crankpin, in the form of a 14BA steel screw, a definite ease-of-use plus. Ultrascale, on the other hand, opt for a very refined version of the inserted crankpin, à la Gibson/Maygib, characterised by the use of a very precise double-ended collar which both locates the pin accurately in the wheel, and provides a crankpin bush – an item which Sharman supplies as a separate turning. The other main difference is one of prototype fidelity, which is, in turn, determined by the method used to produce the moulding dies. Brian Rogers at Ultrascale uses conventional high-quality die-cutting techniques to give a very fine and subtle result, which makes these the ultimate 'high fidelity' wheels, complete with correct spoke profiles, beautifully (and protypically flared) hub-spoke and rim-spoke junctions and accurate rim cross-sections. Sharman, on the other hand, produced tooling by far more expedient means, but means that were not capable of producing some of the subtleties that Ultrascale capture so well. This isn't to say that Sharman wheels are inaccurate or unrealistic, but they do lack the 'ultimate

The Gibson range has been developed from the old Protofour wheels, and includes quite a few 'specials' such as this '03' diesel shunter wheel. The use of a 2mm dia. axle for smaller wheel sizes was a feature of the Protofour range, perpetuated by Gibson. Note the matching 'fly crank' for the jackshaft drive common on diesel-mechanical types.

The Kean-Maygib wheel looks very well, and it's a pity the range isn't a bit wider. These are MR-pattern 5ft 3in 16-spoke wheels fitted to an EM chassis for an S & DJR 'Armstrong'. Loctite fitting to the axle is recommended.

Left: *Here are the Sharman wheels for the guinea-pig '57XX'. Moulded-in crankpins are a bonus, but die codes and injection 'pips' on the back call for some preparation work.* Right: *Ultrascale wheels have very fine spokes and are preferred by some builders for their delicacy and authenticity. Here are a GW 5ft 8in dia. 30in crank wheel (GW Mogul), the 4ft 8½in Stanier bevel-rim wheel for the '8F', and a GW 4ft 1½in 12-spoke tender wheel, all in EMF profile.*

fidelity' of the Ultrascales. The corollary of that is that the Ultrascale range numbers a bit over thirty types, while Sharman's exceeds two *hundred* and thirty!

Other Factors Affecting Wheel Choice

On the face of it, it may seem a matter of 'yer pays yer money and...' If you are shopping for wheels for a 'Jinty' or '57XX', that may be so, as these are in all four ranges. However, given that Sharman has getting on for twice as many wheels as the other ranges added together, then very often there *is* no choice if you want something apposite – it's Sharman or nowt. I think that Mike – and, latterly, Steve Hodgson (who took the range over when Mike finally retired, and has continued to develop and refine it) do deserve the recognition and thanks of all modellers for, in effect, expanding their horizons by making such a wide selection of wheels available. The commercial viability of the whole enterprise has always depended on a high degree of 'self help', and an awful lot of kits – my 'R' class being a classic example – would not have been practicable without the appropriate wheels conveniently appearing in the Sharman range. Latterly, Brian Rogers of Ultrascale has followed the same path by providing appropriate wheels for some Malcolm Mitchell and Martin Finney kits, where, once again, there's effectively no choice. Which leaves the coarse OO man, as usual 'out in the cold' – though, I would suggest, building a Mitchell or Finney kit to such standards would anyway be as pointless as it would doubtless be impracticable.

So it comes down to ease of use, and choice of tyre material. Ease of use I have found to be pretty consistent across all these finescale ranges, with the moulded-in Sharman crankpin perhaps giving them a slight edge now that you get your axles cut to length. Coupling rod location and retention and quartering are all identical, while outside cranks, where appropriate, are all push-on nylon mouldings, with Sharman once again scoring a couple of extra brownie-points for moulding-in the crankpins. Axle lengths are also generally good, checking against the back-to-back gauge appropriate to the standard in use rarely showing more than a thou or two of discrepancy. (Do bear in mind that some real axles have ends proud of the wheel, which the model should replicate if possible.) In other words, when you've got a choice of source for a given wheel, as I did for my '57XX', you can more or less discount user-friendliness – all these wheels are just dying to shake you by the hand and slap you on the back.

Tyre material is the only real variable – apart from cost. In both cases, it comes down to Ultrascale, the only nickel-tyred wheel amid the steel alternatives and, by the time the crankpins are included in the equation, the priciest. The question I would pose is: do you consider the extra cost justified in terms of quality – particularly quality of appearance – and can you overlook the nickel tyre? Rice, poor but fond of steel, usually opts for a slight loss of fidelity (not a quality my locos are often noted for at the best of times) and plumps for Sharmans. Fond of steel? Definitely – for two reasons; it looks right (because it is right), and, in my hands at least, it works better. I have found that steel wheels, particularly in combination with steel rail, grip better and keep cleaner, aiding haulage and electrical pick-up.

Special wheels for a special kit – these are the distinctive small-boss GW 4ft 1½in drivers of the '44XX', specially produced by Ultrascale to go with the Mitchell kit. Note reduced diameter of axle ends.
R. G. WILLIAMS

WHEEL FITTING AT LAST!

Just in time to allay all your well-founded fears that I have forgotten what I'm supposed to be writing about, I think that I've dissected all there is to dissect; it's time to get on and fit a few wheels to whatever type of chassis has engaged our fancy. There is a fortunate concurrence about the most suitable diameter for driving wheel axles in 4 mm scale, still resolutely imperial at 1/8 in. The accompanying bearings will therefore also need to suit such an axle, which convention tells us can be assured by reaming them to size with a 1/8 in parallel reamer.

Bearing Preparation

You may have noticed that nowhere in my various tool lists does this particular item figure, although widely deemed essential. Well, if you want to ream holes to *exactly* 1/8 in, it is – but a 1/8 in diameter axle in a 1/8 in diameter hole is a nice, tight push fit – and that has never struck me as ideal for a free-running chassis. What we actually need is a bearing reamed to 1/8 in + about 2 thou, to give some running clearance. I've yet to find a source of 0.127 in parallel reamers (though they quite probably do exist, as reaming a 1/8 in running fit is not peculiar to 4 mm scale loco chassis construction), so I use a drill for this purpose, taking comfort from the knowledge that an engineer needing an exact 1/8 in hole would never drill it with a 1/8 in drill because no drill, however sharp, ever drills a hole exactly corresponding to its nominal diameter. The error quoted with a new drill of small (below 1/4 in) size is of the order 2–3 thou oversize. Bingo! I keep an ordinary 1/8 in HS drill, bought new, especially for this purpose. It usually does the business used in a pin-vice and rotated by finger power. Several passes may be needed.

While I'm at preparing the bearings, there are a couple of other little touches to consider, both in the cause of low friction and freedom of running. The first is to look at the actual length of the bearing – some top-hats supplied with kits are 5mm and more long. In other words, there's a very large bearing area. Were I building a Ken Northwood style lead-loaded behemoth, I'd be happy to see that; indeed, I used to put

Fig. 7:3 RELIEVING FACES OF BEARINGS

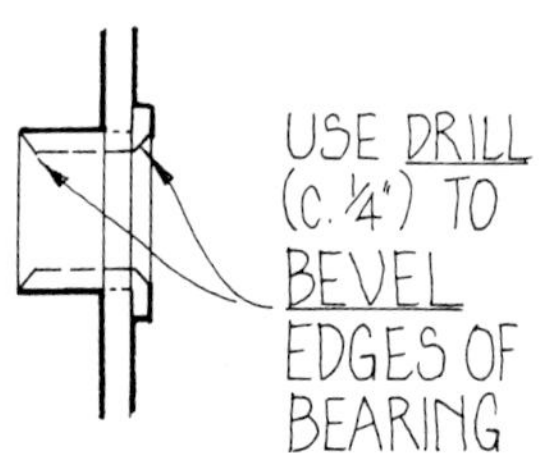
USE DRILL
(C. ¼") TO
BEVEL
EDGES OF
BEARING

thumping great oilite sintered bronze bearing bushes in my solid-chassis locos of fifteen years since, and some of them are still running with no discernible wear in spite of all the lead. But, in the context of a modern lightweight model, with an etched brass or plastic body (and often with a lot of whitemetal kits, which are nowhere near as chunky as they used to be), I'll file the bearing bush down a lot shorter, as the low bearing load doesn't justify all that contact area.

The last job I always do to bearings – and I'm not distinguishing in any of this between top-hat and square block sliding types – is to relieve the front and rear of the actual bearing holes with a 45° (or thereabouts) mitre, as in the sketch. This gives, in effect, a small oilway at each side of the bearing, and helps keep the lubricant where it's wanted. This mitre can be cut with a larger drill (about 1/4 in) used in the fingers.

I have described all these bearing preparations here, as I do this once I have finished setting-up the chassis, but before trying to fit the wheels. The reason for this is that the bearings are a critical part of the jigging procedure by which the chassis is accurately set up – and in that context, a nice, tight fit on the 1/8 in jig-axles and alignment rods is a Good Thing. So I'm never sorry to find my bearings a bit 'stiff' as they come – better that than slop in the jig-axles.

Axle Preparation

Most of the axles supplied with current production wheels are ready for use, and need no general preparation. For those with a stock of older Sharman wheels, which came with uncut axles, I've inserted a brief run-down of axle-trimming under the section dealing specifically with those wheels. Otherwise, the only bit of preparatory work that may need to be carried out on an axle before fitting is concerned with the provision of grubscrew lands or 'flats' on driven axles where the gearwheel used has grubscrew retention. The whys and wherefores of this are covered in the appropriate section of the 'powertrain' chapters. Here, I'm just reminding you that it needs doing before the wheels are fitted to the chassis.

Fitting Romford Wheels

The most difficult thing about fitting a set of Romford wheels is in finding a set of Romford wheels that fit! For the reasons chewed over at length a page or two back, you will frequently run up against situations where the 'correct' size is too big overall, and the next size down miles too small. What I think Romford *actually* need in their range are nominal sizes like 17, 19, 23 and 25 mm, to give *overall* diameter equivalent to a scale 4 ft 6 in, 5 ft, 6 ft and 6 ft 6 in wheel. However, leaving aside the lack of certain diameters, Romford wheels are stunningly easy to fit. The only tool needed is an 'axle nut screwdriver', which you can buy, or, by attacking a cheap electrical screwdriver with a needle file, make, as in Fig. 7:4.

Preparing a Romford wheel for fitting is but the work of moments. Nowadays, they come drilled and tapped 10BA for the turned screw-in crankpin. I put a drop of Nutlock 242 on the thread to prevent accidental unscrewing, and tighten the pin home with a pin vice. Check over the wheel for any burrs or casting flash (both rare) and make sure that the boss on the back is flat and that the locating 'square' that fits over the axle is clear and undamaged. Oh yes, have a look and check whether it's an insulated or uninsulated wheel; by convention, the 'insulated side' is the right-hand side of the chassis looking forward. Having an aversion to electrically 'live' chassis, I would fit insulated wheels all round.

All that remains is to fit one wheel to each axle, carefully seating the squared key into the wheel-boss. Fit the 10BA slotted cheesehead nut, and screw home with axle-nut screwdriver. Insert an undriven axle into the chassis, and temporarily fit second wheel. Check to see amount of sideplay present – you can measure it easily with an ordinary set of feeler gauges nicked out of the car tool kit (assuming modern cars still have toolkits with such useful implements – Rice's 1967 Rover never goes far without!) Those axles not requiring sideplay will require the excess movement washering out. I use Kean-Maygib's turned brass spacing washers, which come at 0.25 mm, 0.5 mm

Fig. 7:4 AXLE-NUT SCREWDRIVER

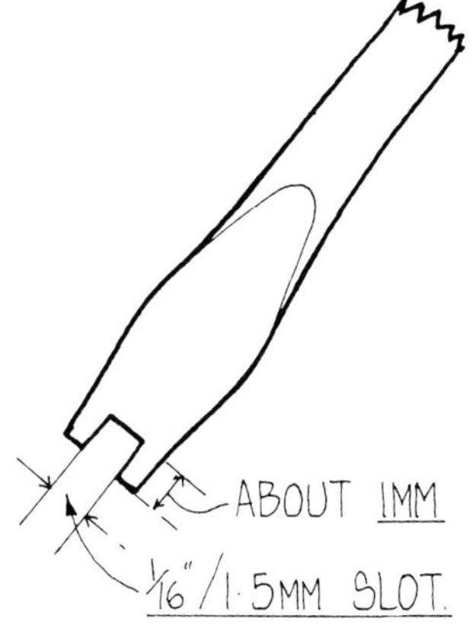

and 1 mm thickness – or, to all intents and purposes, 10 thou, 20 thou and 40 thou, as per the feeler gauges. Don't forget to allow a bit of running clearance – say, 5 thou a side – between the backs of the wheels and the fronts of the bearings, even on non-sideplay axles; if you can't arrive at the right total with the Maygib washers, don't forget the Peco fibre item, which is a bit over 5 thou thick, or Romford's own shim spacing washers, in packs of mixed thickness going in 5 thou steps.

With a suitable conglomeration of washers on each axle, and the final drive gear in place on the appropriate wheelset, all that remains is to fit the second wheel with the appropriate 'lead', and screw it all home nice and tight. Appropriate lead? The normal convention was to set the cranks on the right-hand side of the engine 90° ahead of those on the left – that is, with the left-hand cranks at top dead centre, those on the right would be at front dead centre. There were, of course, exceptions, most notably the LNWR, which did things t'other way about, as did sundry other builders, while 3-cylinder locos made use of 120° crank settings. What you will *never* find is 180° or 0° settings – both possible with the Romford squared axle, but both unworkable. Stick to the convention is my advice; the bloke that can see both sides of an engine at once will have far too many other problems to worry about to concern himself overmuch with a trifling error in crank leads ...

Fitting Kean-Maygib Wheels

The crankpin system for these wheels uses a brass bolt with a smooth head and long neck, which is designed to be inserted into the pre-moulded crankpin hole from the rear, being retained with a flat turned nut which also acts as a spacer to keep the rods clear of the wheel face. The rods themselves run on turned tubular bushes, supplied in two lengths appropriate to single and double rods, and are retained by more of the flat turned nuts. Premounting preparation of the wheels amounts to the insertion of the crankpin bolts and the fitting of the wheel-face retaining nuts; a spot of Nutlock 242 on the threads before you screw these nuts home never goes amiss.

Like the Ultrascale wheels the Kean-Maygibs are a relatively 'easy' push-fit on their axles, and I find that a touch of Loctite 601 is useful insurance against them shifting in service. Those wheels fitted to their axles before being inserted in the frames can be Loctited straight on – run a trace of the magic fluid into the wheel before entering the axle – but the remainder are best done after quartering (see section on quartering push-fit wheels). Otherwise, these are easy enough wheels to install – washering-up and

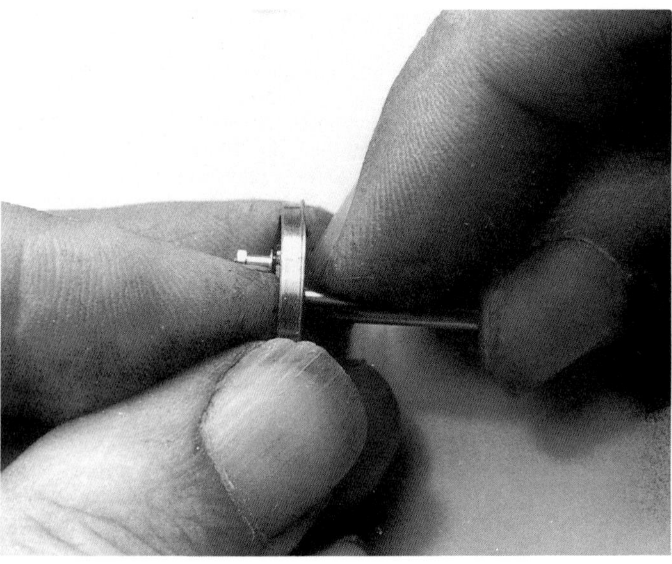

Left: *Mounting Sharman wheels. They can be pushed onto their axles as in the first picture, but the tight fit often calls for the use of a vice, as in the second photo.* Right: *I don't worry too much about the quartering at this stage, so long as I can keep the crankpins from being squashed in the vice!*

the filing of flat 'lands' for gear grub-screws is carried out exactly as for the Romfords. One last job I do undertake with these wheels before the rods and so on get in the way, is to polish the treads of the tyres, removing the chemical blackening and bringing them up to a nice bright steel finish. This I do with fine wet-and-dry, rotating the wheelsets by holding them in contact with the drive-belt of the Cowells lathe – appalling workshop practice, but highly effective! Apart from imparting a more prototypical appearance and improving the electrical performance of the wheels, this Heath Robinson buffing process also serves to check that there are no loose tyres, an occasional fault endemic to wheels with 'pushed-on' tyres. Loctite 601, is, once again, the favoured cure.

Fitting Gibson Wheels

These are very similar in use to the Kean-Maygib, although if anything, a somewhat tighter fit on their axles. I Loctite the tyres as a matter of precautionary course, easy enough to do before the wheel is fitted. Gibson's crankpin pin is steel, which I like, and consists of a long and rather spindly fine metric screw which self-taps its way into the appropriate hole moulded into the wheel. There are turned steel 'top-hat' bushes for the rods to run on (brass would be 'purer' in engineering terms, as on the Sharman wheel), with very nice turned retaining nuts to hold everything in place. These look especially good, giving a convincing replication of a real crankpin nut.

The tightish fit of the wheels on the axles renders Loctite unnecessary, but may call for the use of a vice to squeeze the wheels onto the axles, as described in the next section on the Sharman wheels, which are a *very* tight fit. Gibson wheels generally go on pretty true – if any chronic wobble is apparent, suspect a loose or displaced tyre. As with all these push-fit wheels with cut-to-length axles, simply pushing the wheels right home should set them accurately to gauge, but a quick check with a back-to-back gauge or vernier calliper won't go amiss. Incidentally, if you're working to Finescale OO, don't expect these wheels (which are basically to the EM profile) to give the same 14.5 mm back-to-back as the BRMSB-based Romford. 14.75 or even 15 mm is the likely dimension, reflecting the slimmer flanges as compared to the more chunky Romfords. This will give the correct check gauge across the flange face, which is what matters.

Fitting Sharman Wheels

These are the quickest and easiest of all the push-fits, with their pre-fitted crankpins. All that's needed by way of preparation is to cut off the injection 'pip' sometimes found adjacent to the rim. I also cut or file off the raised figures (the die identification code) often moulded on the rear of the wheel boss, and put a very slight countersink bevel on the axle-hole to ease the entry of the axle – a $\frac{1}{4}$in drill performs this trick, used in the fingers. There is, of course, nothing to do with the crankpins, which are 14BA steel bolts moulded into the wheel during manufacture. A brass 'top-hat' bush, of a length sufficient for doubled rods, is supplied, and this will need trimming to suit the rods before the latter can be fitted. The flange of the top-hat is designed to act as the spacing washer between wheel and rod, while the crankpin retaining nut in this case is a simple brass 14BA hex type – effective but not, it must be said, particularly realistic. A turned retainer as supplied with the other wheel types would be a nice finishing touch – but I have a simple dodge to improve matters as will become apparent in a page or so.

Due to the tight fit of Sharman wheels on their axles, I usually find myself pressing these wheels on in either the vice or the lathe. This isn't as fearsome as it sounds, and the photos illustrate the process; I don't bother about trying to quarter the wheels at this stage, finding it easier to sort this out once the wheels are on the axle. As with all these push-fit wheels, it will be necessary to work out an appropriate combination of washers to take up any unwanted sideplay before the wheels are fitted, this being especially true of the Sharmans which, once on the axle, like to stay put. Measurement is the simplest way to work out the washering requirement – putting the vernier calliper across the outside faces of the bearings will give you the frame width, which can be compared with the proscribed back-to-back dimension to give the sideplay figure. The graduated-thickness shim washers from Kean-Maygib and Romford are especially useful in this context, especially the Romford which run from 5–15 thou. I work on my (pretty accurate) rule-of-thumb conversion that has 1 mm + 40 thou, and I always leave 5 thou a side running clearance. If you're working to fine OO with Sharman's wheels, by the by, you'll be working on a back-to-back of 15 mm – there isn't a gauge, but the axles should give you this.

It's only comparatively recently that Steve Hodgson acquired the machine for axle-cutting, previous to which happy event Sharman wheels were supplied with lengths of axle steel for cutting to length by the user, which used to frighten many folk off. It's not difficult, though, so if you've got stocks of older Sharman wheels, it's worth tackling. The drill is to fit a pair of wheel to a length of the axle rod, with one wheel faced off to the end of the rod, and the other gauged to it, using the appropriate back-to-back gauge or dimension. I then clamp the waste portion of the axle in the vice, and make a nick with a junior hacksaw just clear of the wheel face. Once I have this mark, the wheel is slid back down the axle, clear of the saw, and the cut completed – a little oil on the saw blade will make it easier and keep the swarf in one place. The result of this is an axle which will be very slightly too long. The wheels are gauged-up once again, and the excess of axle carefully filed back flush with the wheel boss. Once I have one axle true to length, the wheels are removed, taking them off the 'uncut' end; the newly-cut end then has its sharp edges bevelled off with coarse emery or a fine file – spinning the axle in drill or lathe makes this easier. This finished axle is now used as a pattern to which the remaining axles will conform.

Even with the current production Sharman wheels, having cut-to-length axles, a back-to-back check is still a good idea, especially in P4 or EMF. Spacing washers to take up side-play must be fitted at the same time as the wheels.

On older Sharmans, axle-cutting was in the user's department, as described in the text. A nice touch is to centre-pop the 'turning dimple' in the axle end, as here on my 'Sandringham'.

Fitting Ultrascale Wheels

You will never, ever find an Ultrascale wheel with a loose tyre. In use, these are very similar to the Gibson tyre already described, the crankpin system using a fine machine screw as its basis, which is designed to self-tap its way through the moulded-in crankpin hole. The Ultrascale version, though, is more complex and refined, with a clever stepped-diameter bush that locates into the face of the wheel, which has a moulded recess to receive it where the pin comes through; this centres the crankpin accurately in the wheel, and also provides the bearing surface of the crankpin. There is a spacing washer, which slips over the bush and keeps the rods clear of the wheel face. Doubled rods are accommodated by a tubular 'extension bush', and the whole lot is kept in place by circular nuts, turned, as are all the other components, in brass. It sounds fiddly but is easy to use and works well.

Ultrascale wheels are an easy push-fit onto their axles, and, as with the Kean-Maygib type, really call for Loctite if they are to remain secure. As already described, half the wheels can be Loctited as they're fitted; the rest will need doing as they're quartered. A swift word on this point on how Loctite works in this context, so as to clear up the common misunderstandings as to its properties. Basically, Loctite (we're talking the 601/602 'retaining compounds' here, not the various other potions now sold under the same trade name) is a chemical which sets and *expands* in the exclusion of air and in the presence of steel. It is *not* an adhesive, attaining its locking action purely by the expansion converting a sliding fit into a force one. The steel is a catalyst to the reaction, which will not occur without its presence. Loctite will not, therefore, work in situations where none of the components being locked are ferrous, so don't bother trying it on brass crankpins in a plastic wheel! For the same reasons, don't ever use a steel pin or a piece of steel wire to pierce the neck of your Loctite bottle, or to withdraw compound from said bottle – as soon as the air is excluded again (lid back on) the lot will go solid, which, at around £5 for a 10ml bottle, is no joke! In the context of keeping driving wheels in place on axles, 601 serves to tighten the grip of an Ultrascale wheel to about the same degree of stiction as a Sharman, which means the bond is not irrevocable and the wheel can still be shifted on the axle if needs be. Even

Ultrascale wheels are more truly a push-fit, and are readily finger-fitted. These EM wheels are equipped with Romford screw-in crankpins rather than Ultrascale's own push-through type. This calls for the wheels to be tapped 10BA – not a problem if you have the requisite tap. Once quartered, the wheels will be 'Loctited' in place.

points or tight spots, in which case congratulate yourself and move on to the next group of wheels.

More likely will be an error of greater or lesser proportions at some point in the revolution. Stop the wheels at this tight spot, and examine the relationship of the cranks on the adjacent wheelsets. The error is usually readily apparent, and is corrected by twisting the 'adjust' wheel to match the datum. The process is continued until the error is adjusted out – when you get to the point where the error is very slight, it will be easier to compare spoke positions, rather than cranks, on the adjacent wheels. Choosing an appropriate spoke and getting it exactly parallel to its equivalent on the neighbouring wheel is easier than fine-judging crank angles, which calls for a good eye and extreme care.

Once you're happy with your first four-coupled group, the adjust axle of that group then becomes the datum for the next pair of wheels, which are similarly rough-quartered, fitted with rods, and adjusted until they, too, run freely. I don't usually take the preceding rods off to do this, reckoning that, as the whole chassis being a free-running entity is the objective, then it's more relevant to consider as much of it as possible at each stage. If you are dealing with undivided rods, they can simply be reversed to embrace all three wheelsets (as I think will have become apparent, I'd never contemplate rods relating to more than three axles under any circumstances).

If the wheels being quartered are to be retained with Loctite, then they are not pressed fully home on their axles, being adjusted for quartering with only half the wheel-depth on the axle so that once all is well, a trace of Loctite in the vacant portion of the axle-hole and the final pressing-home of the wheels (being sure to apply this pressure at right-angles to the wheel and in such a way that the wheel will not be shifted in rotation on the axle) will serve to render all secure.

Finishing Off

Once the wheels are quartered and the chassis is running freely, then a few final jobs need to be tidied up. The crankpin nuts, which should be tightened down hard onto the crankpin bushes, will benefit from a drop of 242 Nutlock, and any excess crankpin will need nipping off and filing down flush. Obviously crankpins that are destined to receive con-rod big-ends at some future stage (such as the next chapter) can't be so treated, but the rest can be finished off and, if necessary, the nuts thinned down a bit if things are likely to prove tight on the clearance front. In the case of Sharman wheels, if you find the hexagonal nuts offensive, it is possible to substitute pieces of brass capillary tube that have been (carefully!) tapped 14BA, as in the sketch.

Fig. 7:5 ALTERNATIVE CRANKPIN NUT

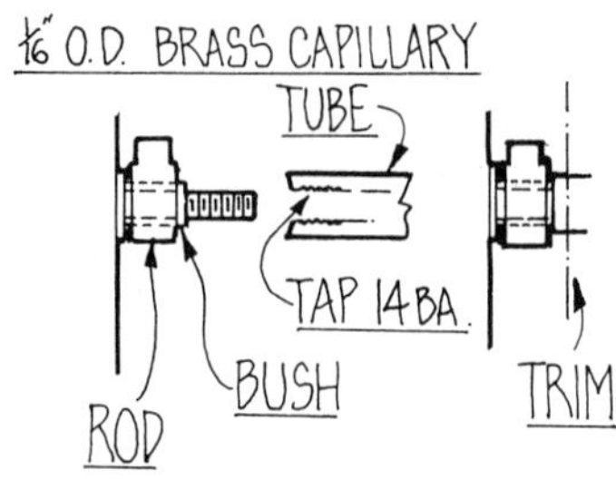

These make a very neat and realistic crankpin nut, easily locked with a spot of the 242 compound run into the tube before it is screwed home. Don't use 601 compound for locking nuts onto steel crankpins unless you are quite certain that you will never, ever need to remove those nuts...

The other finishing job that you will almost certainly need to undertake with plastic-centred push-fit wheels is a spot of 'truing-up', to tease out any wobble in the wheels. First thing to check is that you haven't had a tyre come loose during the fitting and quartering operations, which can happen. If this is the case, run in a smear of 601 and push the tyre back into place. Quite often, however, the problem is that the wheel is not quite square on the axle. Turn the chassis over slowly on the bench, and, using the frames as a reference, note the movement of the rim, determining the point at which the wheel is most out of line with the frames. Using some strong tweezers or, best of all, a pair of flat-nose pliers such as relay pliers, grasp the wheel and give it a tweak in the required direction to correct the offset. If the wheel is a Sharman or Ultrascale, with a moulded-on tyre, you can simply grasp the rim and apply the correcting twist. It may take several goes to get rid of a bad wobble, and it's not really likely you'll get the wheel dead true, but acceptable results don't cause a problem. Obviously, the effect is worst on large-diameter drivers, so take care in the handling of big-wheeled chassis – pick the model up by the wheelhubs, never by the rims.

PLAIN DRIVERS AND OUTSIDE CRANKS

In the case of engines having outside or double frames, the two functions of wheel-fitting and quartering are separated. Actually getting a set of plain (crankless) drivers in place is no more difficult than fitting bogie or tender wheels (indeed, in some cases, you'll end up using the same wheels!). If you're worried about it, the wheels can be matched 'side for side' by sighting through the spokes to get them in the same positions relative to the axle. Axle preparation, of course, amounts to making sure that the length you arrive at is the overall dimension to the outside faces of the cranks. As this isn't a constant – it will depend on the prototype frame width and the thickness of the cranks involved – you will often find that axles for outside-crank wheelsets are supplied as stock for cutting to length. Proceed as described for the older-type Sharman wheels, but working from the distance over the faces of the cranks with these fitted to a 'test' axle, and checked for clearance against the frames of the model. It's wise to give yourself at least ½mm clearance between crank-back and frame face, more if the wheelset has sideplay. Look out for the loading gauge, though, if you don't want your cranks chewing up your platform copings. If clearances are really tight, it may be necessary to thin the cranks themselves down a bit, or to move the outside frames in slightly, wheel clearance permitting.

Fitting the cranks and quartering isn't usually too much of a problem, though it varies with the type of crank being used. In 4mm scale, outside cranks come in three basic varieties: stamped metal/screw fit (Romford); etched metal, laminated, solder-fit (many etched kits); moulded plastic push-on (Ultrascale, Gibson, Sharman). The Romford and Sharman come with pre-fitted crankpins, the rest use some form of fine screw as a pin – usually 14BA to conform with standard crankpin diameter. The Romford crank is designed for use with a special axle having the 10BA thread of the wheel-retaining nut extended sufficiently to accept the outside crank. No 'plain' crankless drivers are available from Romford, and standard drivers are used, giving an unrealistic and redundant crank floating around inside the outside frames. The crank-fitting system uses an ordinary 10BA nut run on to the threaded axle extension, followed by the crank, also tapped 10BA. The axle needs correcting for overall length before the cranks are fitted. Quartering is carried out by exactly the same system of 'trial and adjust' as described for push-fit wheels, and the final settings are 'held' by using the 10BA nuts as locknuts, tightened against the inner face of the cranks – tightened hard, too, if the cranks are not to come loose in service. I usually make sure by lightly soldering the cranks to the axle-ends. The rods are retained by the usual Romford washers, and you will also need a slim spacing washer between rod and crank if binding is to be avoided.

I'm afraid I find the whole Romford outside-crank system tedious to install and bothersome to maintain. Given that the principal Romford virtue – quartering ease as imparted by the 'squared' axle – is lost in this application, I'd always opt for a push-fit wheel such as the Gibson or Ultrascale, and use their force-fit plastic outside cranks. Sharman wheels also have a good, substantial outside crank, which comes with the crankpin moulded in place, as on their driving wheels. The Sharman outside crank also has a longish 'axle sleeve' behind the crank, designed to ensure that the crank goes on to the axle square and true, and that it stays put. Unfortunately, this sleeve is rather large, and often proves too plump for the slots in the outside frames as well as being rather obtrusive. I've found it makes little difference to the functioning of these cranks if you cut it off. Only if faced with the need to accommodate running on coarse-scale trackwork such as Peco Streamline 'universal' would I contemplate Romford outside cranks; and even then, I find you can get away with Gibson wheels if you set them to about 15mm back-to-back.

The moulded plastic and etched metal outside cranks are both used in much the same way. The moulded plastic ones are obviously easier to fit, and can be quartered and Loctite-fitted as for the plastic wheels. The crankpins in the case of both the Ultrascale and Gibson cranks are the same as those for the wheels. As far as I'm aware, Kean Maygib haven't yet got involved with outside cranks and plain drivers. These plastic cranks are all chunky enough to represent the 5–6in thickness of real outside cranks, whereas the Romford item looks distinctly underfed in this respect. To get this sort of thickness, most etched kit chassis designers use up to four laminations of 20-thou mainframe material soldered together, with a crankpin from a 14BA screw nutted in place. Such laminated outside cranks can, if carefully made and finished, look as good as the moulded ones, while the ability to solder them to the axle-ends means that they can be *very* firmly fixed. To this end, it's essential that the axle-holes in the cranks are etched slightly undersize so that they can be reamed to a good push-fit on the axles, one job for which the ⅛in parallel reamer *is* ideal.

Once satisfactorily assembled and reamed, these cranks are fitted and quartered in the usual '4-wheels at a time, adjust one, trial-running basis with the rods in place'. If you don't fancy solder retention of the cranks, then Loctite-fitting works perfectly well.

I've come across some etched chassis 'kits' – notably from Falcon Brass – in which all you get by way of crank components is a few etched crank blanks with some location dimples to give the axle and crankpin centres! The axle-holes, as just described, need to be a true ⅛in fit, and must also be square through the crank if this isn't to run at all sorts of funny angles; and, even with a good drill-press and super-sharp drills, that's not easy. It can best be done on a lathe, but again, this hardly qualifies as kitchen table *kit* building. I'd bin the bits and buy some plastic cranks from Sharman or Gibson if you wish to avoid heartache.

Outside cranks have come on a bit from the old Romford screw-on type, shown on an elderly scratchbuilt 'Dukedog' I acquired recently. These don't look very realistic, and aren't easy to use. They are in stark contrast to the moulded nylon outside cranks fitted to my kitbuilt 'Dukedog'. These are the Sharman items, which come with a moulded-in crankpin, just like the wheels.

These moulded outside cranks are fitted and quartered in the same way as the wheels. The Sharman cranks also incorporate a 'spacing sleeve', which may be too big to fit through the cut-outs in outside frames. I had to cut them off for the 'Dukedog', but could leave them on the six-coupled Kirtley Goods chassis in the picture below.

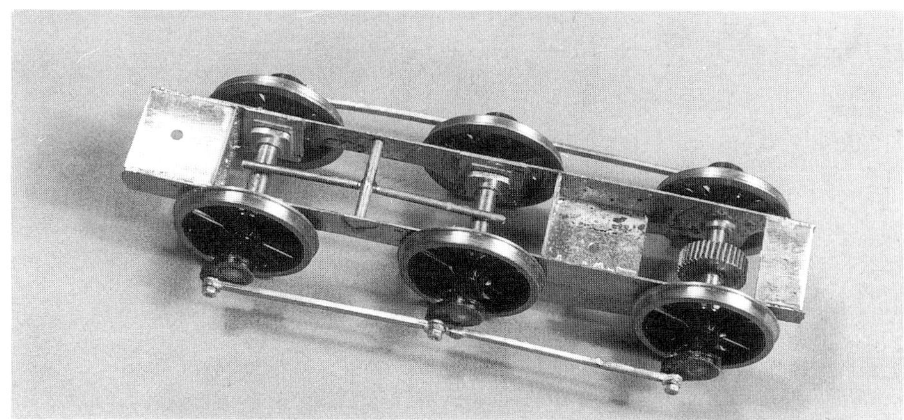

BOGIE AND CARRYING WHEELS

Obviously, everything that I have described in relation to the preparation, fitting and truing of driving wheels can be applied, in simplified form, to carrying wheels. I have found some of these to be a pretty slack fit on their axles, and, while they aren't required to transmit torque in the same manner as driven wheels, they can go out of gauge, with deleterious results in the trackholding department. So it's well worth trotting out the 601 and making sure that they stay put. The only other point of note regarding carrying wheels, particularly bogie and pony truck wheelsets, is in the matter of sideplay, which is irrelevant in such situations. Obviously a bogie wheelset with a lot of sideplay will serve to lessen considerably the guiding action of the bogie, so I aim for the minimum consistent with free running.

THE LAST WORD?

I have dealt with wheels and their fitting in pretty exhaustive detail, but they are so fundamental to both the performance and the look of a model that I felt that they warranted this emphasis. I'll have more to say on the cosmetics of wheels in Chapter 10, but I hope that I've slain all the dragons on the practical front. There is no doubt in my mind that the fitment of a decent set of properly-modelled wheels to a loco is one of the biggest – and simplest – 'fidelity upgrades' that can be applied to a kit-built loco, as I hope the accompanying pictures prove. The next biggest upgrade is to complement said wheels with some equally convincing cylinders and valve gear, which is where we go next.

Inclined cylinders are a subtle but significant feature of Maunsell 'S15' 30506. Note also the 'hidden' slidebar bracket, which is located behind the slidebars between the rear bogie and leading coupled wheels. PHOTOMATIC

Quite a tricky proposition in model form is the Adams single-slidebar. That crosshead needs to be a slop-free fit if you don't want it doing a Heilan' step-dance. L. ELSEY

CHAPTER EIGHT

CYLINDERS AND VALVE GEAR

M & GN Beyer No. 24 carries the characteristic combination of outside cylinders and slipper crosshead between double slidebars – typical of older British locos with inside valve gear. Lovely! AUTHOR'S COLLECTION

Given that, in model terms, cylinders and valve gears are purely decorative items, it might seem surprising that they cause so much trouble. Well, decorative they may be, but there is still a functional aspect to their design and installation, in that model valve gears still have to be able to reproduce the characteristic movement of the full-sized item – which, in the very great majority of case, will be some form of the Walschaerts gear. This may look fairly complex to untutored eyes, but believe me, compared with some of the weird and wonderful conglomerations of levers, cranks and eccentrics that have adorned older or more distant railway locomotives, it's a cinch. Just take a look at a few of Mike Sharman's vintage beauties if you doubt my words.

Once you get to grips with it, Walschaerts isn't so very bad, and the best of the modern etched gears go together very nicely and look very convincing. I'm not going to go into the ins and outs of the prototype gear, but I shall take a look at what moves, and why; as with so many aspects of model locomotive construction, a little understanding of what you're setting out to model helps to make sense of all the bits that come in the kit. However, this is jumping the gun a bit, as before we can consider the ins-and-outs of any valve gear, we first have to provide a set of cylinders for that gear to actuate. And there's more to them than meets the eye.

A set of typical British outside cylinders and Walschaerts or Caprotti gear is by no means the most difficult modelling proposition around . . .

OUTSIDE CYLINDERS

Prototypically speaking, these come in two basic varieties, which are in turn usually associated with particular valve gear layouts. The older designs used an outside cylinder, with the valve and steam chests – and hence the valve gear – between the frames. Typical of this sort of arrangement is the elegant M & GN 'Beyer' 4–4–0 No. 24, which combines these neat cylinders with classical twin-slidebar crossheads. Less common was the association of these simple outside cylinders with a single-slidebar design of crosshead, a partiality of William Adams on the LSWR, and shown to advantage on his classic 'radial tank' design – 30583 is fresh out of the Eastleigh shops for the Lyme Regis branch.

The other basic type places the valve chests above the cylinders outside the frames, and, in Britain at least, is most usually associated with Walschaerts gear. Such cylinders are usually sited high over a bogie or leading truck, and are often inclined to bring the centreline of the cylinder into alignment with the centre height of the driven axle, as typified by S15 No. 30506. If your model is to look 'right', it's essential to get this inclination, which, on the relatively small-wheeled 4–6–0 illustrated is quite subtle, 'just so'. The effect is more exaggerated with 2–6–0s, with their shorter wheelbases, the 'Crab' being perhaps the most extreme example. Not all locos with outside cylinders had them inclined, and many larger-wheeled designs used horizontal cylinders, as on 'Sandringham' 61631, *Selby Hall*.

The GWR, as usual, begged to differ from everybody else, placing 'overhead valve' cylinders outside the frames, but keeping the Walschaerts gear modestly concealed within, much to the relief of generations of GW modellers. Or perhaps that's why they *are* GW modellers? Not content with this aberration, the GW introduced a couple more, by moving the outside cylinders of their 4-cylinder engines (such as the 'King' illustrated) rearwards, to drive the valves from the front, and also by inclining the outside cylinders of their standard 2-cylinder types steeply inward, presumably to suit the geometry of the rocking levers driving the valves. With the progressive enlargement of these outside cylinders (and they were *big*), the limit of the loading gauge was reached, as typified by 'County' 1019, *County of Merioneth*.

Final stop on this whistle-stop tour around outside-cylindered anatomy lands us next to the sole 'BR 8' Pacific, *Duke of Gloucester*, whose distinctive character stems largely from these highly-individual cylinder and valve-gear arrangements – inclined cylinders with rotary poppet valves driven by the rotary shaft-drive Caprotti gear, quite unmistakable. Whilst it's interesting to note the form and location of the actual cylinders, don't overlook the correct relationship with the rest of the loco – again, the 'Duke' is out at the limit of the loading gauge, with the shrouds over the valve drives protruding some way beyond the edge of the footplate – unlike, for instance, the 'Sandringham', where everything finishes flush. This is the sort of thing that, once again, has a terrific impact on the 'look' of a model; cylinders at the wrong distance in or out from the footplate edge stick out like a sore thumb, and correcting any error here is a fidelity 'must'.

A highly distinctive arrangement of outside cylinders, steeply inclined, with a truly massive motion bracket. Getting this right is fundamental to any model of the Hughes/Fowler 'Crab' 2–6–0. AUTHOR'S COLLECTION

This beautiful shot of Gresley 'Sandringham' 3-cylinder 4–6–0 Selby Hall *shows the distinctive features of Gresley gear – the 'behind' lifting links (the engine is in back gear), the three-bar slidebars, and the slender rods resulting from the use of high-strength lightweight alloy steel.* P. H. GROOM

Other details associated with cylinders are obviously of importance in producing a convincing model, and this is especially true of slidebar and crosshead assemblies, often highly characteristic aspects of locomotive design. There are three, slidebar designs, with two, three or four bars, and representing them accurately can be a considerable modelling challenge. Probably the easiest is the twin-bar arrangement, as on the 'S15', the 'Crab', and the GWR types. But note the major differences in the way that these bars are supported, ranging from the almost-invisible inside bracketry of the 'S15' to the gigantic cast effort on the 'Crab'. Again, to produce a good model, you need to represent such features convincingly, but a lot of kits leave you with either a totally non-prototypical arrangement, a rather poor rendition of the correct set-up, or nothing at all. Taking the trouble to modify, correct or make proper slidebar brackets is yet another of those aspects of kitbuilding where an 'average' result can be elevated a peg or two.

Big lungs! The GW Hawksworth 'County' 4–6–0 goes out to the limit of the loading gauge with those characteristic 18½in dia. Churchward cylinders (not quite the biggest – the 2–8–2T of the '72XX', the '42XX' 2–8–0T and the '47XX' 2–8–0s had 19in outside cylinders). Care is needed to get the overall width and inward inclination of these cylinders correct.
AUTHOR'S COLLECTION

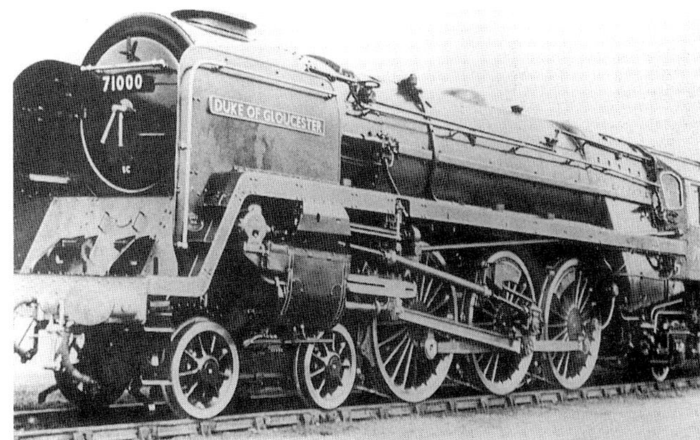

Unique. 3-cylinder Caprotti gear on the solitary BR '8' also gets near load-gauge limits – over the cam-drive shrouds – as well as showing the characteristic massive box-section bracket from which the torque-tube and drive gearbox are suspended. As a modelling proposition, actually simpler than Walschaerts – DJH give you some pretty decent lost-wax castings in their kit for this loco.
AUTHOR'S COLLECTION

CYLINDER AND SLIDEBAR CENTRES

Whilst considering slidebars, it's obviously vital to ensure that they are in the right place, both relative to the cylinders and to the loco wheels and the rest of the motion. And that right place, I would suggest, is on, or as near as practicable to, the correct centres. So far as the relationship of slidebars to cylinders goes, they would in reality be on exactly the same centres, for obvious reasons; however, for models, it can be useful in cases where clearance is at an absolute premium to slightly offset them outwards in relation to the cylinders to gain a few fractions of a millimetre of extra space. This will call for minor modifications to the cylinders, not generally difficult to accomplish. The subterfuge is not particularly apparent, being only really visible from a 'three-quarter rear' viewpoint, and is infinitely preferable to moving the cylinders out, which is not only visually jarring, but probably physically, too, when the overwide cylinder casings clobber the platform copings!

Unfortunately, as already described back in Chapter 2, an awful lot of loco kits come with cylinders arranged in such a way that they will end up in the wrong place if you are trying to build the model for EM or P4. DJH, for instance, use a cast cylinder fitted direct to the mainframes, and arranged so that, with those frames set to their wasp-waisted OO dimension, the outside faces of the cylinders finish up in the right place – which leaves the EM or P4 modeller with cylinders some 2 mm *a side* out of gauge; or, put another way, a foot of error in the overall width of the engine. And, let me tell

Outside cylinders bracketed directly off the mainframes, as on this Brighton Atlantic (from an old Jidenco kit) are a bit of a headache if you need to use a different frame spacing from that 'catered for'. Converting this model to EM was no sinecure!

you, 2 mm a side is an awful lot of filing ... The opposite of this particular nonsense is the case where the cylinders are set out at the correct (to prototype) distance from the frames, but the frames themselves are then set at an incorrect (OO) spacing, with the result that the cylinders are miles too narrow.

The answer, as I noted briefly in Chapter 2, is to design the cylinders as a separate sub-assembly, with their own stretchers and spacers to set them on the correct centres and hence at a correct overall width. This was excellently done on the Peter K chassis for the 1361, as illustrated, and also on the Perseverance GW 'mogul' of a page or so hence; while way back in the dark ages W & H sold cast GW and LMS cylinders paired on a cast stretcher at the correct centres. But it's not uncommon to come across such cylinder assemblies with incorrect centres and unworkable clearances – the Mallard/Blacksmith Brighton 'K' mogul sticks in my mind as a particularly difficult specimen when I tried to build it to EM standards. As the photo shows, I had to cut the cylinders off the stretcher and modify them to bracket direct off the frames at

The right way. The excellent chassis kit for the GWR '1361' 0–6–0ST by Peter K had one of the best outside-cylinder set-ups I've ever come across. The first shot shows the bare chassis with the locating slots for the vertical cylinder stretchers.

This picture shows the cylinders being erected onto the stretchers. Note alternative frame width provision. No clearance problems with these correctly-centred cylinders.

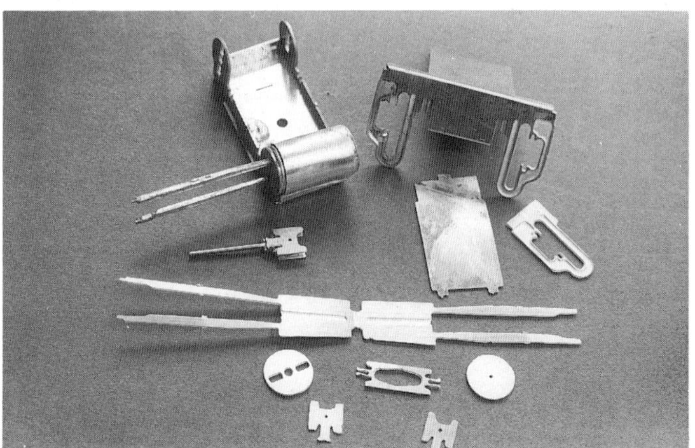

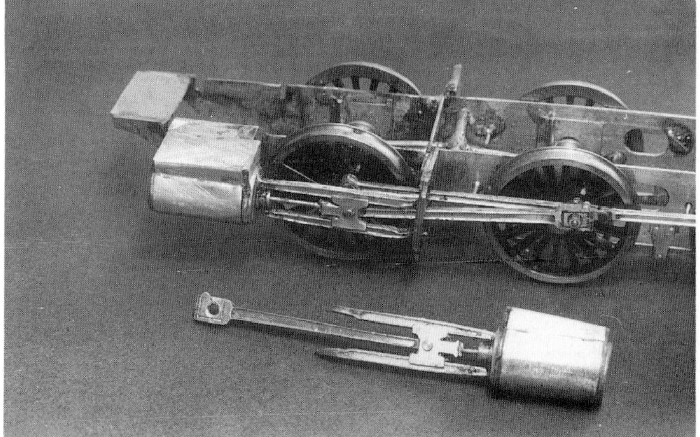

Left: *Oh dear! Here are the cylinders of the old Mallard kit for the LBSCR 'K' Mogul, on an independent stretcher as proscribed, but, in this case, set to centres suited only for OO locos, for all that there are location slots for EM frames!* Right: *The only solution with those Mallard cylinders – and other examples of like ilk – is to abandon the stretchers and locate them correctly in relation to the frames in use, EM gauge in this case.*

And lo! Now those errant 'K' cylinders line up correctly with the footplate valancing. There is is only one correct location for outside cylinders – the prototype location.

something like correct centres, which not only made them look right in relation to the footplate but afforded fag-paper crosshead clearance and enabled the loco to run.

So, I'd suggest, if you find that the cylinders in your kit fetch up in the wrong spot when installed as per instructions, then it will be wise to modify them along the line sketched in *Fig. 8:1*, which is a general arrangement of pretty wide application. It matters not if the cylinders be cast or etched, the principle of the independent stretcher is equally applicable and not difficult to make. I've also come across the odd kit where the cylinders are integral with the body – in some cases, such as the various streamlined types and old-stagers with 'Crewe' front ends, this is unavoidable. The solution in the former case is to split the cylinder assembly between the body (outer casings, shrouding, etc.) and the chassis (main cylinder block with the slidebars attached). This avoids the necessity to take down the con rods and withdraw the crossheads – not to mention stripping half the valve gear – every time the locomotive superstructure is removed. In the latter case, there's no way of avoiding the inclusion of the slidebars, crossheads and cylinders in the superstructure assembly, given that the cylinders are integral with the smokebox. There are relatively few kits of 'Crewe' prototypes – I recollect building a Highland 'Skye Bogie' several years ago, and it was necessary to to have the con rods off the leading crankpins for body/chassis separation. Thank goodness there weren't any Walschaerts-fitted 'Crewe' types – but those design features belong to different eras which, fortunately, didn't overlap. An unaccountable kit design feature I have come across, though, is a perfectly normal set of cylinders attached to the superstructure rather than the chassis. I ignore such nonsense and proceed as in *Fig. 8:1*.

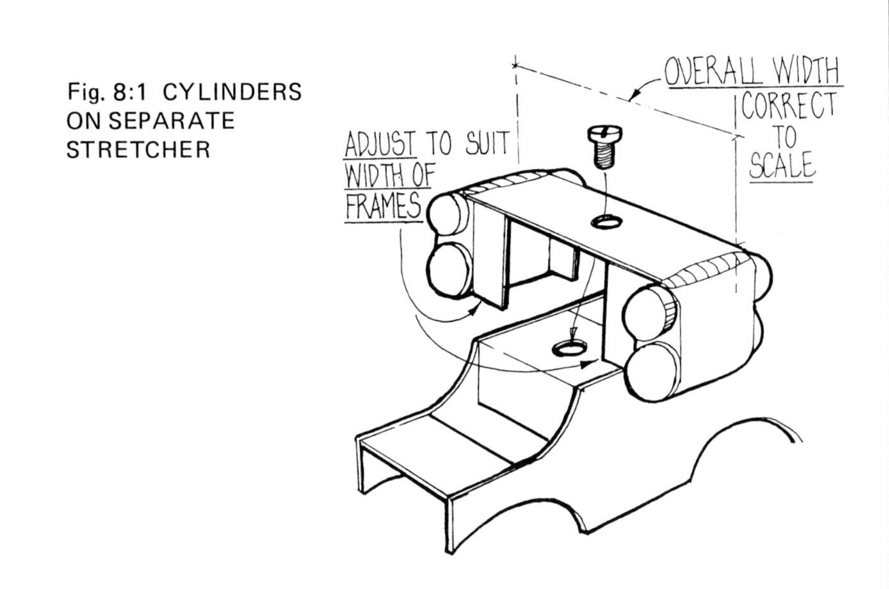

The cast cylinders of the DJH 'S15', fitted direct to the frames. Apart from the width difficulties, whatever happened to the cylinder inclination exhibited by the prototype a page or so ago? That screw-on motion bracket is a good idea, though.

CYLINDER MOUNTING

As I trust will now have become abundantly clear. I'm strongly in favour of mounting cylinders to a separate stretcher, which is then bolted to the main chassis. Quite apart from the fact that the cylinder centres can be accurately set thereby, it makes it a lot easier to assemble, set up and align such things as the slide bars and crossheads if the job can be done away from the rest of the chassis. In fact, I generally try, as far as is possible, to make the whole cylinder/valve gear assembly a self-contained and separate unit, much as Hornby-Dublo always used to. To this end, I'll often arrange to join the cylinder stretcher and motion bracket into one unit, so that all the vital alignments can be set up 'on the bench'. After all, as far as a model is concerned, the only point of attachment of this whole shebang to the rest of the moving mechanism is on the

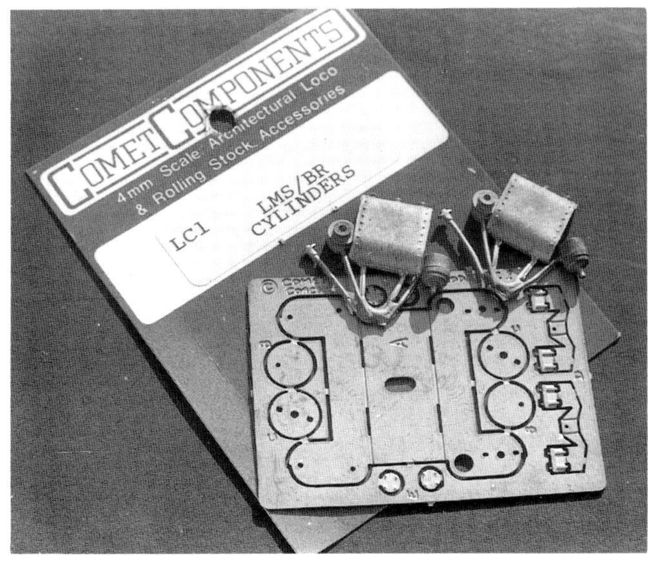

If the cylinders in your kit are simply too gruesome to contemplate, firms like Comet or Puffers will come to your rescue. Here are Comet's splendid LMS type – a substantial fold-up stretcher with correct centres, and cast wrappers complete with bolt-head detail.

crankpin of the driven axle – either by just the con rod big-end, or by this in combination with the eccentric crank. The suspension/attachment points of the rest of any valve gear are all related to either the cylinder themselves, or can be arranged to bracket off the cylinder/motion bracket assembly. More on all this when we come to valve gears in a page or so.

It's obviously wise to plan through as much of this job as you can before you start, and I think a lot of people run into problems with outside cylinders because they don't look far enough ahead when tackling the task. In the case of a Walschaerts-fitted engine, you can't separate the cylinders and their associated gear into compartments – it's always necessary to consider them as a unit. The other vital necessity is to keep checking on the clearance front, at very frequent intervals. Clearance behind slidebars is a very critical factor on a lot of real locomotives, and it needs careful attention – and, often, the application of a few dodges and bodges – to avoid trouble on models, given that we've got an electrical dimension to worry about as well as the purely mechanical problem of keeping things apart that seem intent on colliding, binding or catching.

DJH cast cylinders, from the 'Britannia' kit, benefit from stretcher mounting. Cast detail is beautifully crisp, and castings are of excellent quality. C. J. LANGDON

SETTING UP CAST CYLINDERS

While the actual way in which these are intended to go together and locate onto the chassis varies considerably from kit to kit, there are some general points to consider. The first, and most vital, of these I have already dealt with – the need to get them in the right relationship to the rest of the engine. This will often involve a spot of modification to the raw castings before assembly, whether it be the filing off of an excess of metal from behind cylinders intended for OO to mount them on EM or P4 frames, or the packing-out of those 'scale-spacing from OO frames' types. If you agree with me that a separate stretcher is a better bet than direct-mounted cylinder assemblies, then now is the time to arrange a suitable mounting system. This can range from the simple solution of a strip of suitably-dimensioned brass soldered direct to both cylinders, to the somewhat more sophisticated set-up drawn in *Fig. 8:2*, which is closely based on the system that Hornby-Dublo evolved for the *Duchess of Atholl* back in 1948.

Here, each cylinder is soldered to a 'half-stretcher', which is in turn, bolted to a central cylinder/valve gear 'mounting plate', which will also carry all the other bracketry and pick-up points associated with the valve gear. The idea behind this complication of the simple basic scheme sketched a page or so back is to maintain the overall relationship of the various elements of the

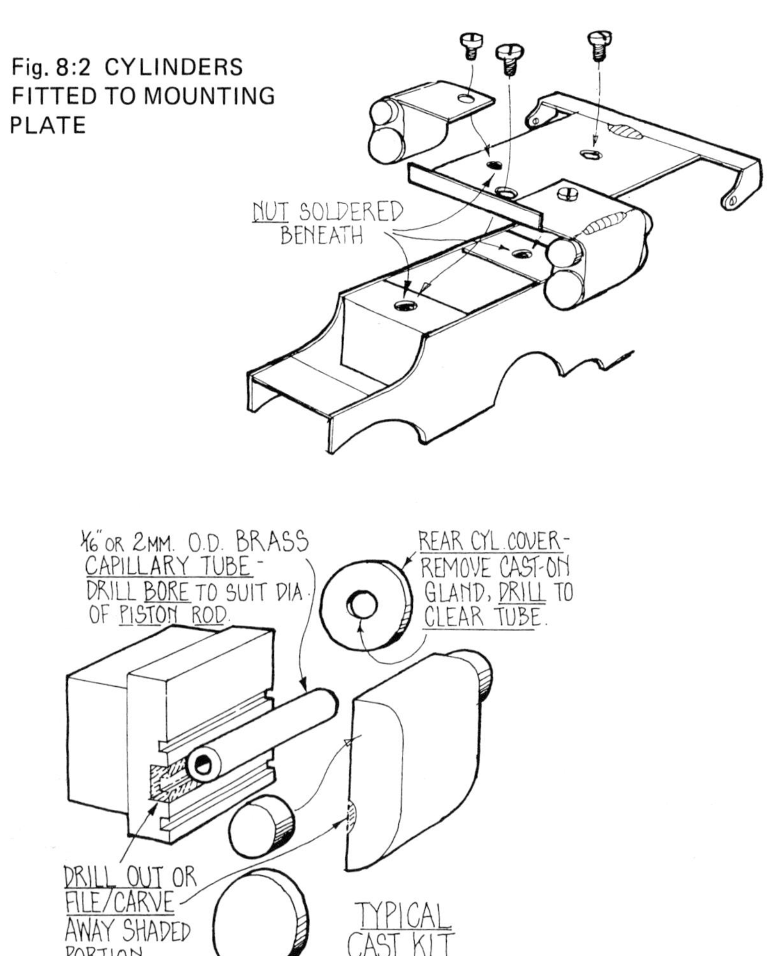

Fig. 8:2 CYLINDERS FITTED TO MOUNTING PLATE

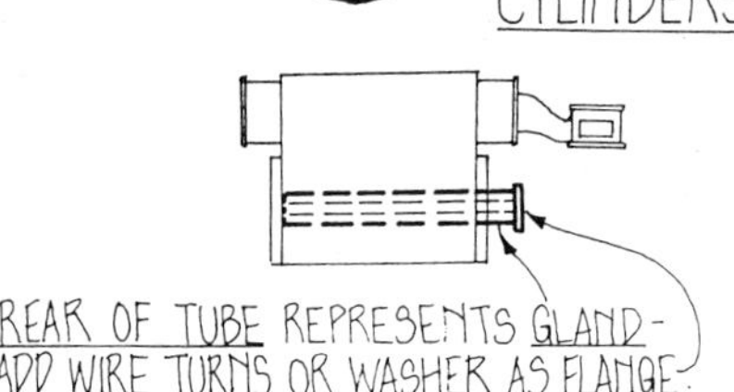

Fig. 8:3 BRASS TUBE PISTON ROD GUIDE

NB:- BOTH METHODS - SET ALIGNMENT BY JIG AS IN DIA. 8:7.

FILE DOWN PIN-HEAD, BUTT ONTO CROSSHEAD. SOLDER IN PLACE FROM REAR

HEAVY STEEL DRESSMAKER'S PIN, FINE PANEL PIN,-OR- 18 SWG. STEEL PIANO WIRE

DRILL TO SUIT, LOCTITE IN PLACE.

Fig. 8:4
SUBSTITUTING PISTON RODS ON CAST CROSSHEADS

cylinder/valve gear assembly, whilst allowing each side to be set up as an individual unit. If you want to do a real 'engineering job' throughout, you can arrange for the other components hung off the mounting plate to be bolted in place, but usually I compromise and tack-solder these in place – apart from anything else, it makes it easier to 'fiddle' things a bit when you find that you've made a slight error in setting out the position of a component.

The other functional point to consider when building-up cast cylinders is the proper location of the slidebars, and the free, smooth movement of the piston-rod and crosshead. Many cast cylinders incorporate slidebar locations in their assembly, and a careful check of this vital 'fit' and the relationship with the crosshead is a prerequisite for a smooth-running chassis. Obviously, a crosshead whose piston-rod has a sticky relationship with the guideway provided for it in the cylinder isn't going to be much use, so this is, again, an important check. I have encountered crossheads that couldn't even be entered in the slidebars due to the piston-rod being bigger than the hole provided for it in the cylinder! I've also encountered the opposite, where there is a massive amount of slop in the fit of the piston-rod to cylinder, leading to a crosshead that waggles up and down like a sword-dancer's sporran.

Neither of these extremes is much help, so I generally prefer to substitute my own arrangement in this area, using a piece of brass capillary tube as a guide, drilled out if necessary to be a nice, smooth, sliding fit on the piston-rod. I then file or drill out the guideway in the cast cylinder to take this rather more elegant set-up. Often, I find that in doing this I end up doing away with the cast-on stuffing gland at the rear of the cylinder – which is of little account, as the tube will represent this quite nicely, and can be dressed-up as needed with the odd washer or turn or two of wire to represent the end flange if the prototype has one. It is simply a matter of making the tube long enough to fulfil this additional role.

Cast cylinders generally come with cast crossheads, some of which are a very dubious proposition indeed. There is an increasing and welcome trend to supply such items as lost-wax brass or, better still, nickel-silver castings, which is a distinct improvement on structurally-weak whitemetal. The real drawback to all these cast crossheads is that the piston-rod is unlikely to be either truly round or truly straight. It is a case of very careful preparation of the castings if problems are to be avoided; we need to ensure that the piston-rods are dead straight and free of flash, bulges, and misregistration. We also need to check that they are the right length; the piston-rod that hits the end of the cylinder a resounding clout before the wheel reaches fore-dead-centre will stop a loco dead in its tracks, while the opposite extreme where the rod falls out of the rear gland ere the wheel-crank is at the aft-end of its travel isn't a lot of help either. While the former case is simply cured with a spot of (progressive) trimming, a rod too short can only be cured by substitution.

In fact, I often choose to substitute a length of steel pin for the cast piston-rod on a cast crosshead, an admittedly ticklish bit of soldering, especially on whitemetal crossheads. If you leave the head on the pin, filed down a bit to make it a tad less obtrusive, it gives you a bit more metal to play with at the point of joining. The odd crosshead is meaty enough to be drilled to take a new piston-rod, when the steel can be neatly secured with a spot of Loctite. I suppose that this is a fairly extreme course of action in most people's books, and, if you are faced with a truly dud set of cast crossheads, it may be worth casting about (!) for something better from the trade – quite a lot of firms produce tolerable lost-wax crossheads which can be fettled to fit most applications, especially on more modern locomotive designs, where such items tended to be 'standard fittings'. All the same, I can't help reflecting that when I worked for Hamblings briefly some 25 years ago they used to sell a very natty LMS

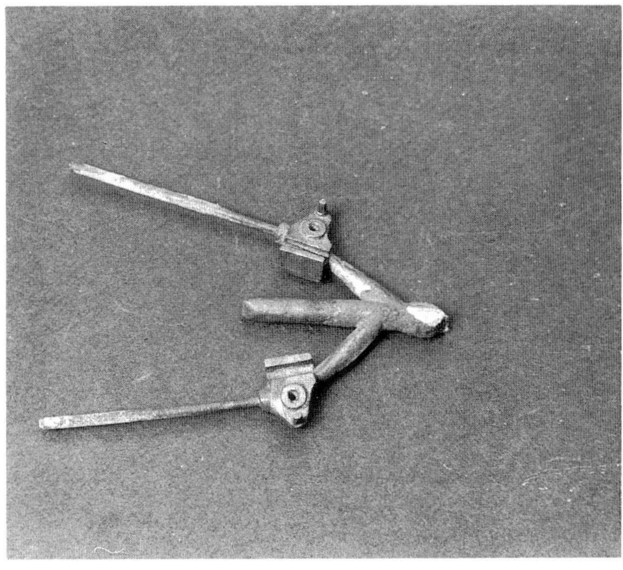

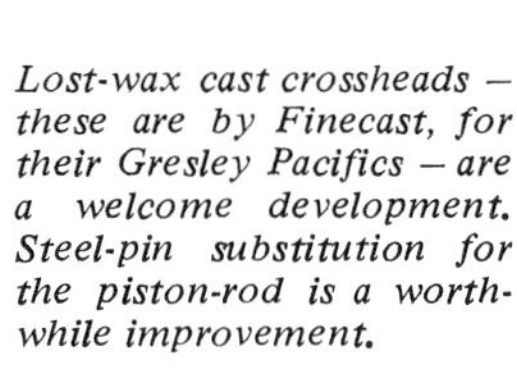

Lost-wax cast crossheads – these are by Finecast, for their Gresley Pacifics – are a welcome development. Steel-pin substitution for the piston-rod is a worthwhile improvement.

crosshead, cast in whitemetal on to a steel pin piston-rod. I can't see any technical problem with this – why does nobody do it today?

THREE AND FOUR-BAR SLIDEBAR SYSTEMS

Thus far, I've been discussing the traditional arrangement of twin slidebars symmetrically disposed above and below the cylinder centreline with the crosshead slipper running between them, and the small end of the connecting rod pivoted direct to this slipper. This was the arrangement favoured by most pre-group designs, by the LMS and GWR during the grouping, and by a majority of BR standard types. The LNER and SR, however, chose to differ, opting for a slide-bar set grouped above the centreline, with the small-end of the connecting rod, the piston-rod and the drop-arm for the Walschaerts valve gear all being offset on a forging 'hanging' from the slipper. The LNER design had three slidebars, a wide top bar and two narrow lower bars, as in *Fig. 8:5*, with a 'T-section' crosshead slipper. The Southern used this design, but also had a 4-bar set-up, as in *Fig. 8:6*. In 4mm scale, these systems look identical, and are usually represented by paired etchings with the crosshead running between them, as on the DJH 'West Country' (actually a 4-bar design). It isn't difficult to model the 3-bar type accurately if you're so minded, using John Flack's milled strip. Otherwise, the preparation of cast 3 or 4-bar crossheads conforms to the same criteria as normal 2-bar types – I still substitute steel pins for piston rods and file the things carefully to a nice sliding fit. The slidebars, too, need the same firm anchorage, though they save you the fag of a bracket – which is why the prototype used them, I fancy.

ETCHED CYLINDERS

An increasing number of kits are being designed with outside cylinders fabricated from etched components and tube, which I have found to produce very good results. Probably the best set of such cylinders I have yet encountered were those designed by Malcolm Mitchell for his mould-breaking GW '45XX' kit, which managed to combine true fidelity to prototype with mechanical sophistication and ease of assembly – no mean feat! The etched cylinders of the Perseverance GW 'mogul' chassis are generally similar, and I have taken this Rod Neep-designed version through a full build in the accompanying photo-sequence. I would say that these are pretty typical of most current production kits, and, if well-designed (which most of them are, praise be), fabricated cylinders, present few problems. The thing that seems to worry most people, actually forming the wrappers around the front and rear plates,

Fig. 8:5 3-BAR SLIDEBAR AND CROSSHEAD

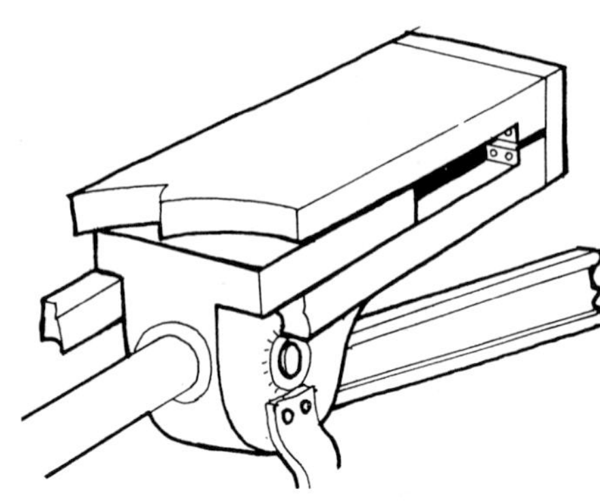

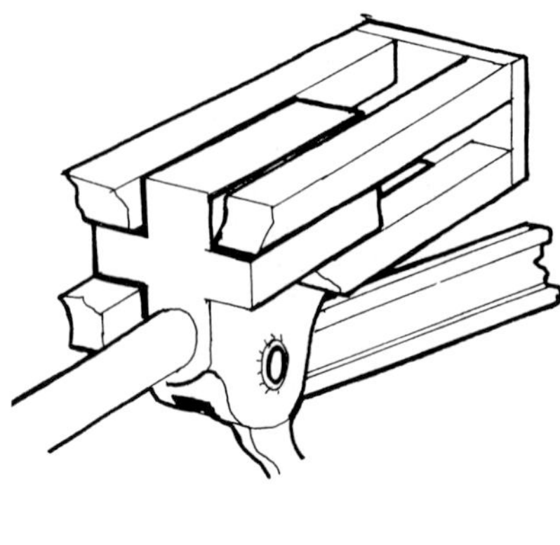

Fig. 8:6 4-BAR SLIDEBAR AND CROSSHEAD

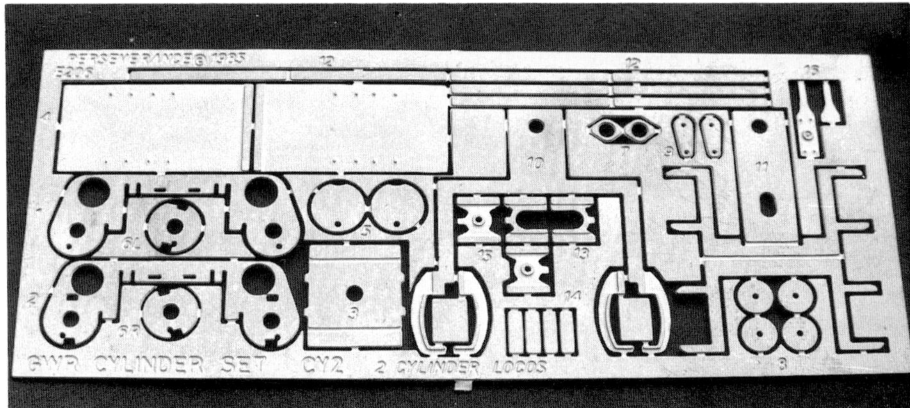

Fabricating a set of etched outside cylinders is not too fearsome a job, as I hope this little sequence will show.

These are the Puffers/Perseverance 'GW 2-cylinder set', intended for the '43XX' Mogul. Most of the components come on a single etched nickel-silver sheet, seen in the first picture. These cylinders are based around front and rear stretchers with brass tube spacers, which also represent valve-chests.

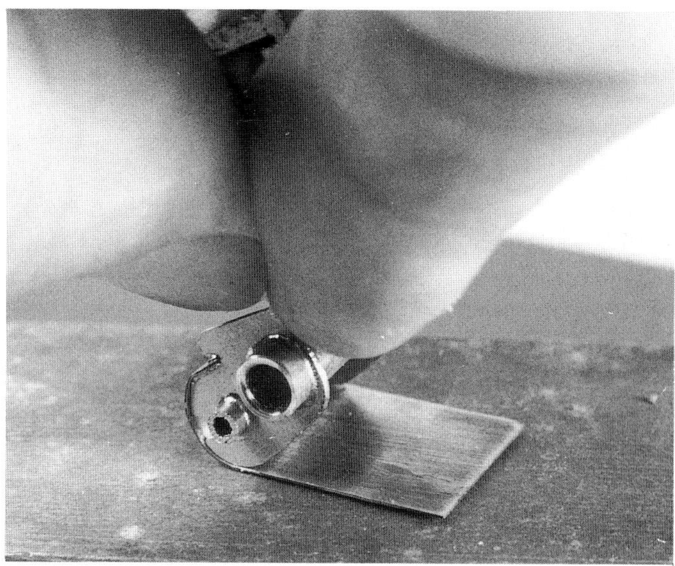

Left: *The cylinder wrapper is half-etched to around 10-thou thickness, and locks into slots in the stretcher, clearly visible in the second picture. Before forming to shape, the wrapper should be annealed by heating to dull red in a flame (gas hob!) and cooling.* Right: *The wrapper is then located in the slots, and formed to shape by rolling on a firm, flat surface; I used the top of my 'V blocks', but it's not critical. Tack at the start, and don't try to go the whole way in one go.*

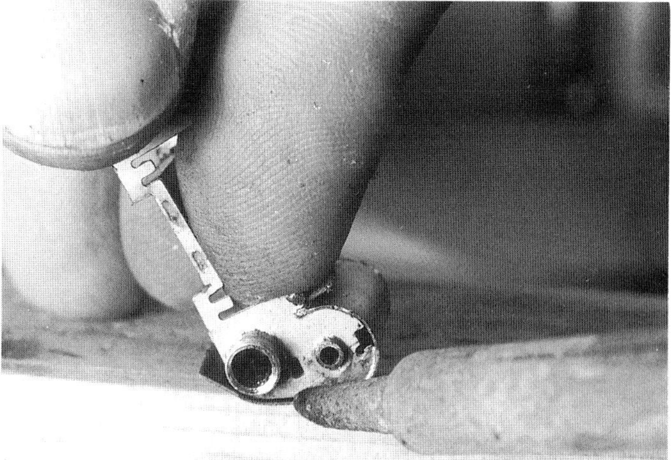

Left: *Initial forming of the wrapper goes as far as the stage shown here.* Right: *The wrapper is then seam-soldered to the end stretchers, and the top part of the wrapper formed.*

Left: *The top can then be 'tidied up'. The wrapper of these 'Percy' cylinders is, very sensibly, etched slightly too wide, calling for some filing to remove the excess, which gives a welcome margin for error. This finishing work has been carried out on the nearmost cylinder.* Right: *Voila! The basic cylinder assembly, complete but for valve chest end covers, is trial-fitted to the '43XX' chassis.*

is actually one of those jobs that are considerably worse in the contemplation than in the execution. For those who would rather not even contemplate, Comet have come up with an ingenious and workable solution by combining a cast wrapper with an etched inner structure/ends, as seen in the photo of their LMS/BR cylinder. I would prefer to see a full tubular piston-rod guide as in the Neep design, but this would be easy enough to add. These cylinder kits are available separately, come with good instructions, and are a recommended substitution for indifferent kit cylinders whether cast or etched.

ETCHED CROSSHEADS

These are a fiddle, but well worth the effort. Basically, they're a soldering exercise in assembling some pretty tiny components, which isn't easy. The Neep design, especially, calls for considerable dexterity and a high pain threshold, for which reason I modify the method of construction as in the photographs, substituting a long piece of strip for the etched-to-length top and bottom piece of the crosshead 'slipper' (part 14 in the Perseverance instructions). This strip (I use nickel-silver fret waste, but John Flack's bound to have something suitable) is bent into a horseshoe shape of appropriate width, soldered in place on the rear of the crosshead, and then used as a handle to keep a hold on the job while the front face of the crosshead is sweated in place. The excess strip is trimmed off once the crosshead is complete, using a piercing saw with a fine blade or a pair of flush-cutting nippers – the 'Xuron' snips sold by Acme Model Co. are ideal for this and any number of other jobs in the assembly of valve gear.

Last job in assembling a fabricated crosshead is to solder in the piston-rod, which Perseverance provide as steel wire, with a sleeve of fine brass capillary tube to bring the diameter up where it enters the 'slipper'.

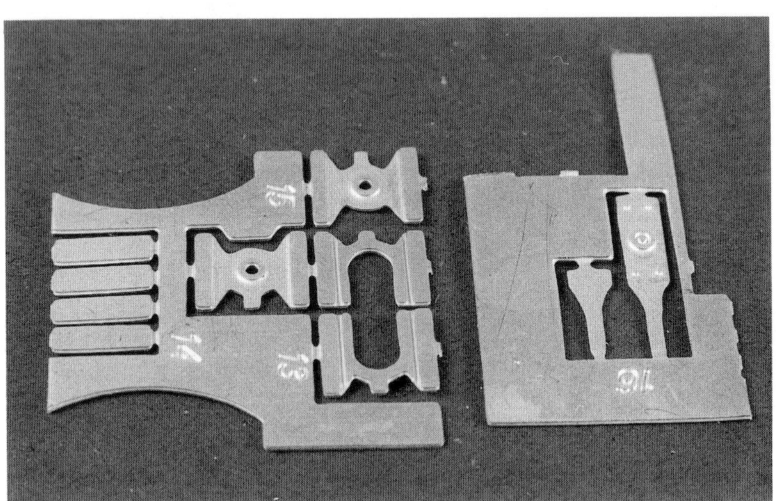

Left: *Etched crossheads have a reputation for being a bit tricky – which they are. The ingredients of the Neep GWR version can be seen in the first picture. The front and rear 'plates' are fine, but the four little strip etchings for the actual guides look ticklish.* Right: *My solution was to forget them, and to substitute a piece of suitable strip – scrap fret from the junkbox – as in the second picture. Much easier!*

Left: *The 'front face' of the crosshead can now be added. Note that I didn't detach this from the rest of the fret until after fitting, to give myself a 'handle'. The rear face was tinned, and the joint made by sweating from the front.* Right: *Once the crosshead assemblies are soldered up, the individual crossheads are parted off with a piercing saw, and cleaned up with files. They can be trial-fitted on the slidebars, and, of course, the piston-rods can be added, either by use of the jig drawn in Fig. 8:7, or in situ as advocated by Rod Neep. The piston-rods here are steel pins, with collars of brass capillary tube.*

I feel that Perseverance's wire is a bit on the skinny side to represent a piston-rod, which is usually of 2–3 in diameter. I usually resort to my 'bit of pin' – either a domestic dressmaking pin or a small steel panel pin – and drill or ream out the sleeve to suit. Getting it all in alignment can be a ticklish sort of a business, which I accomplish with the aid of the little jig illustrated in my sketch, *Fig 8:7*. Obviously, it's all too easy to disassemble the slipper while soldering the piston-rod in place – press a suitable heat-sink down onto the crosshead while the rod is being soldered in place. It helps to scrape a bright contact patch where the rod locates, and to pre-tin the end of this where it fits between the sides of the slipper. Be generous with the flux, use 145° solder and a clean iron, and *don't linger*!

Fig. 8:7 JIG FOR SETTING PISTON RODS INTO CROSSHEADS

LOCTITE - OR - SWEATED JOINT.
1/8" SQ. SOFT BALSA
1/8"×1/16" HARD BALSA
1/16" SHEET BALSA

CONNECTING RODS

Assembling these is generally no problem – they are often a single-layer etching, but at worse should be no more difficult to laminate than coupling rods. Obviously, slop in either the big or little end bearing holes of a connecting rod won't have the same sort of dire consequences as with coupling rods, but it's undesirable nonetheless, for cosmetic reasons; the con-rod that takes half-a-revolution to change direction is scarcely convincing! It's in the location of the small end within the crosshead that problems can be encountered. Note, firstly, that 'within'. Con rods do *not*, ever, fit behind crossheads. A steam locomotive develops enormous torque, which means that the in-line loading on a connecting rod is correspondingly massive. To avoid any shear action, all components of a real engine's drive system are arranged exactly in line – piston-rod, slidebars and con rod all share the same horizontal centrelines, while, as already noted, the cylinders are usually inclined to minimise the vertical 'change of direction' occasioned by the rotation of the big-end. Cranked con rods and other such dubious dodges beloved of model loco-builders would last about as long as the radio aerial of a parked Porsche in the hands of a disaffected skinhead – and would finish up similarly mangled – if tried at full size. The dictates of appearance, never mind those of proper working, suggest that model locos will benefit from some care in alignment of these components.

In order to get the con rod in line with the piston-rod, the actual bearing will need to be either in the front face of the crosshead slipper or, if this is correctly represented with a 'cage' construction, in both front and rear faces with the rod between them. Most model crossheads make do with a single bearing in the front face, either in the form of a rebate in a solid cast crosshead, or by cutting-out the rear face of an etched one.

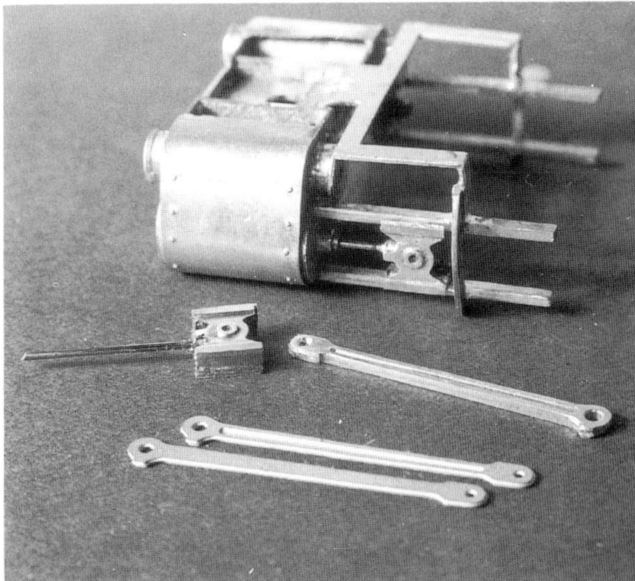

The logical sequence has gone up the Swanee a bit here, as the slide-bars and brackets have, apparently, appeared by mystical means with never a mention. However, we get around to them in a moment; just now, it's connecting rods that concern us.

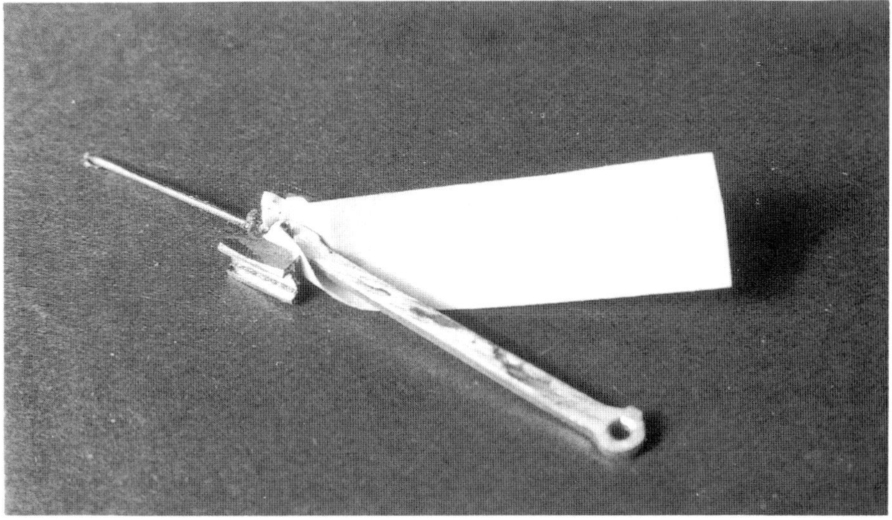

Those of the '43XX', seen in both component and assembled form in the previous picture, are pretty typical – double-layer construction, as for the coupling rods.

I fitted them to my completed crossheads using Exactoscale 'long' valve-gear rivets, soldered to the rod and pivoting in the crosshead. The usual paper spacer keeps the solder in check. The finished job can then be test-fitted to the loco for 'clearance trials'. They did – just!

I have often found that model three or four-bar 'overhead' crossheads, à la Gresley or Bulleid, have a bearing which is cast the full thickness of the piston-rod, leaving the con rod effectively 'behind' the centreline of the piston-rod. This steals valuable – often vital – clearance in what is always a troublesome area, and it's worth filing down the bearing or the rod (or both) to get things as near in line as possible. *Fig 8:8* should show what I'm on about.

Fig. 8:8 CROSSHEADS AND CON-RODS

THE CROSSHEAD CROSS-SECTION

SLIDEBARS

CON. ROD

BIG-END

PROTOTYPE ALL ON ℄

TYPICAL CAST CON.-ROD WELL OFFSET-'ORRID.

IMPROVED CAST-THIN DOWN CROSSHEAD & CON. ROD.

NB:- 4-BAR TYPE SIMILAR.

SLIDEBARS

Slidebars, on real engines, are pretty massive, solid structures. They are, after all, containing and directing the force generated in the cylinders – and force capable of overcoming the inertia of several hundred tons of train takes a bit of containing. Real slidebars do not wobble, vibrate, or leap up and down in concert with the gyrations of the connecting rod; model ones, regrettably, are apt to do all of these things – simultaneously, on occasions! It behoves us, therefore, to undertake a spot of 'beefing up' on many of the etched slidebars which accompany most current kits. A lot of these are far too two-dimensional – most real slidebars are from four to over six inches wide; a bit of etched 20 thou nickel scales out at an inch-and-a-half, so even doubling-up can leave things a touch undernourished, However, we have to take into account the width of any crosshead guideways, which the kitmakers often produce on the narrow side. Some compromise is often inevitable here, as, for reasons already expounded, model locos tend to be short of clearance, and narrower-than-scale slidebars and crossheads can win back a few valuable fractions. I usually find myself taking the width of the slidebars out to the maximum that can be accommodated by the crosshead which, as well as improving the look (and strength) of the bars, cuts out lateral slop of the crosshead on the bars – something else unheard of in prototype circles.

The other area that well repays attention is the anchoring of the slidebars. The better designs fit into cast or etched locating holes in the cylinder rear, and meet up with substantial and firmly located brackets at their outboard end. Etched kits are generally better than the older cast designs in this respect, and slidebar brackets are now often slot-located into the mainframes, which, in combination with a top-anchoring to the 'mounting plate', makes for a commendably solid assembly. Real slidebar brackets tend to be either massive steel castings, or rather smaller and neater forgings. Again, many of the newer generation of kits take the trouble to model these accurately in terms of both outline and any relief detail. Older kits may provide rather more basic components that will benefit from a bit of fettling in this department.

Functionally, it is slidebar alignment that is all-important. The bars must be absolutely parallel to the cylinder centrelines in both the vertical and horizontal planes. Errors here will lead to binding of the piston rod in the cylinder, or to that well-known

Fig. 8:9 BEEFING-UP SLIDEBARS

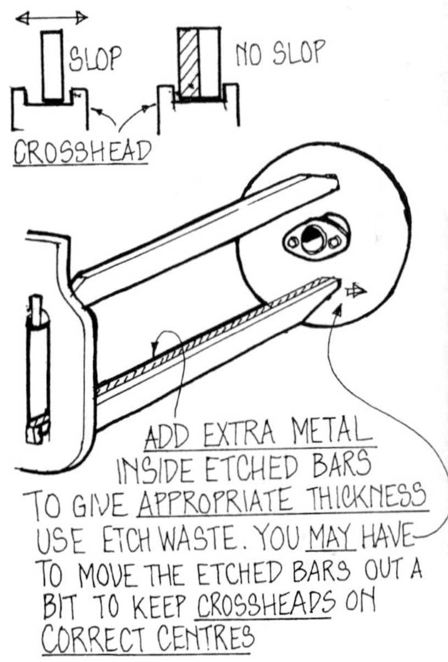
SLOP
NO SLOP
CROSSHEAD
ADD EXTRA METAL INSIDE ETCHED BARS TO GIVE APPROPRIATE THICKNESS USE ETCH WASTE. YOU MAY HAVE TO MOVE THE ETCHED BARS OUT A BIT TO KEEP CROSSHEADS ON CORRECT CENTRES

phenomenon of flexing slidebars as they are forced out of alignment by the action of connecting rods and crossheads. So it is well worth taking considerable trouble to get things absolutely 'spot-on' on the bench before being tempted to install cylinder assemblies on the loco – a good reason for going to the lengths of 'split stretchers' and mounting plates. A good dodge for lining up slidebars is to insert a longish piece of suitably-sized straight wire into the piston rod guide in the cylinder, where it can act as a reference for aligning the bars. The other critical relationship in this area is obviously that between the bars and the crossheads. In most cases, I have found that any error tends to result in the crossheads being a tight fit between the bars, not too difficult to resolve with a bit of careful filing of the crosshead guideways. Excess slop is more of a problem, especially in the vertical

Some etched cylinder assemblies have the slide-bars as integral parts of the structure, as in the Black-smith 'K' Mogul bars seen here.

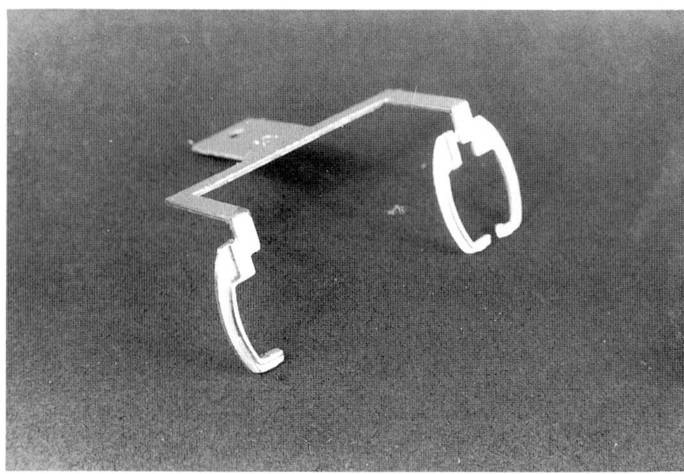

Left: *The slidebars and bracket of the '43XX' are a good example of etched kit practice. The slidebar bracket is a natty fold-up, intended to be fitted to the cylinder stretcher, thus uniting cylinders and slidebars into one rigid unit.* Right: *The slidebars themselves are folded over and soldered up to give double-thickness bars – very strong.*

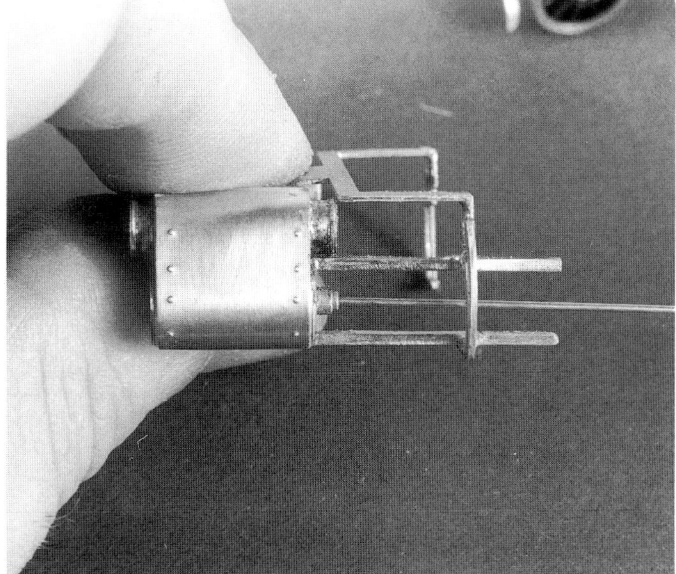

Left: *A bit of filing-out of the slidebar brackets to get the bars sitting level and parallel.* Right: *Test by comparing with a length of suitable-diameter wire fitted into the piston guide.*

The completed assembly is offered-up to the loco, and checked for fit and clearance.

plane. It is usually possible to 'close up' conventional twin-bar slidebar assemblies a touch to take up small amounts of slack, but if there's too much daylight, some packing, in the form of thin strip, may be needed on either bars or crossheads. Three or four-bar designs almost always call for packing if they're sloppy; *Fig. 8:10* gives the recipe.

On some locos, such as the '43', the slidebar bracket has to line up with its continuation – as a boiler stay – above the footplate. Check that it does while adjustment is still easy!

INSTALLING CYLINDER ASSEMBLIES

There are a few things that can only really be sorted out properly with the cylinder/slidebars/bracket/crosshead/connecting rod assembly actually installed on the loco. As it is highly likely that such installation will throw up the need for all manner of minor adjustments, the demountable attachment system described really pays dividends at this point. The two most critical checks are to ensure that the crosshead travel is of the right length and in the right place, and that there is sufficient clearance behind the crosshead. It is wise to make a check on these factors at as early a stage as possible – you don't need to have fitted the slidebar brackets or any cosmetic gubbins.

To take things in order, if the kit is good, the first two of these critical points may not arise. The crosshead travel is set by the wheel crank throw, and if you are fitting correct wheels there should be no problem. However, if you are using Romford wheels, with their nominal 24 crank throw, look out if you are modelling, say, a Drummond loco that only had 18 in of throw – that extra 2 mm of movement could bring the crosshead into contact with the rear of the cylinder. Fortunately, in the vast majority of cases, real slidebars are considerably longer than the actual crosshead travel – the need to position the slidebar brackets behind the leading driving wheels sees to that. If you find that you have crossheads reaching the extreme fore end of the slidebars and hitting the cylinders due to excessive crank throw, it is possible to overcome the problem by shortening the connecting-rod slightly; try drilling a new small-end pivot hole a suitable distance to the rear of the 'true' position, which will bring the crosshead travel back along the slidebars by a commensurate amount. Just don't overdo it, or the cross-heads will 'derail' at the rear end. If you can't get wheels of the correct crank throw for your loco, err on the short-throw side. The naked eye will barely spot 24 in throw cranks on an engine that should have 26 in, but don't try 30in throw GW 5 ft 8 in wheels on, say, a Gresley K3...

If you find that you have a piston-rod hitting the front of the cylinder, or the con rod itself touching the slidebars at their outboard end, the chances are that the

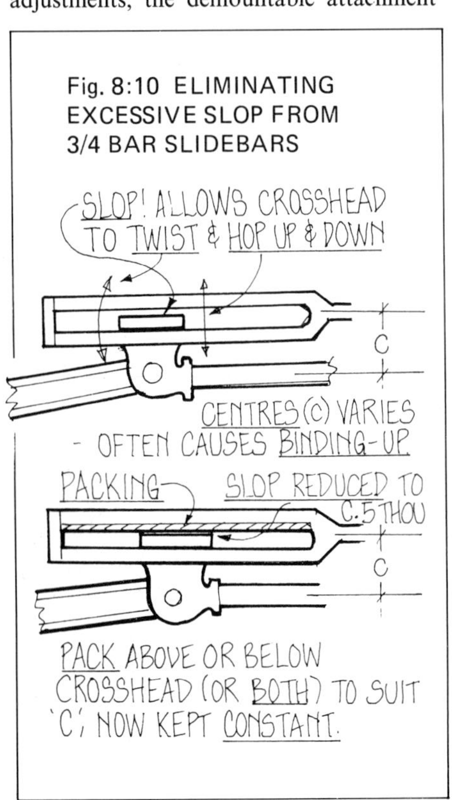
Fig. 8:10 ELIMINATING EXCESSIVE SLOP FROM 3/4 BAR SLIDEBARS
SLOP! ALLOWS CROSSHEAD TO TWIST & HOP UP & DOWN
C
CENTRES (C) VARIES - OFTEN CAUSES BINDING-UP
PACKING
SLOP REDUCED TO C.5 THOU
C
PACK ABOVE OR BELOW CROSSHEAD (OR BOTH) TO SUIT 'C', NOW KEPT CONSTANT.

crosshead travel is in the wrong place in relation to the slidebars. This can be due to the con rod being slightly too long or too short, or it can be due to the cylinders being in not quite the correct location. Check both factors by measurement from a reliable fixed point, such as the centre axle. Again, modifying the connecting rod is the easiest way to correct this error – it will almost invariably call for the rod to be shortened. If the loco you are modelling has a slidebar bracket that embraces the con rod or the coupling rods – or, usually, both – make a careful clearance check here. Fit the bracket in place, and take a close look at its relationship to the movement of these rods. Again, problems can arise where wheel crank-throws are wrong, but hopefully a spot of filing on the bracket itself will win a bit more clearance.

Horizontal clearance behind the slidebars is the other big worry, especially in EM or P4. Check this at the earliest possible opportunity, as if there is a major problem then drastic steps may be needed to effect a cure – and the sooner you know about the need for changes, the easier they are to incorporate. I've already touched on possible remedies, but they can be a life-saver so I'll describe them in detail here. The first step in avoiding clearance problems behind slidebars comes a long way back in the chassis-building process, by severely restricting or eliminating sideplay on any wheelsets occupying this area, as mentioned in the section on bogies and in relation to wheeling-up. The second step applies to the most common problem of all, where the crankpin nut of the leading driving wheels on a 4–6–0 or 2–6–0/2–6–2 fouls the back of the crosshead. The nut can be thinned down, which may be enough to gain the necessary clearance. It can also be replaced with a countersunk retaining system, as in my sketch – that's what the prototype does when things get tight.

If that isn't enough, then we have to start bodging. My favourite dodge is drawn in *Fig. 8:12*, where it can be seen that it consists

Fig. 8:12 OFFSET CYLINDER CENTRES

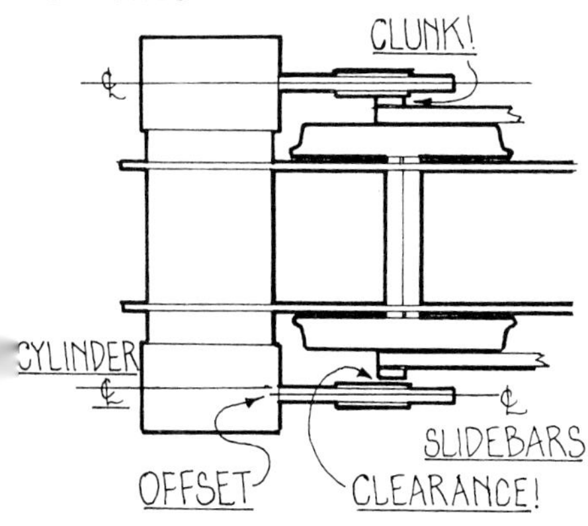

Clearance checking behind the crossheads is vital. On the P4 '43XX' guinea-pig it was of fag-paper fineness. With nil sideplay on the leading coupled axle, this is enough.

Fig. 8:11 COUNTERSUNK CRANKPIN NUT

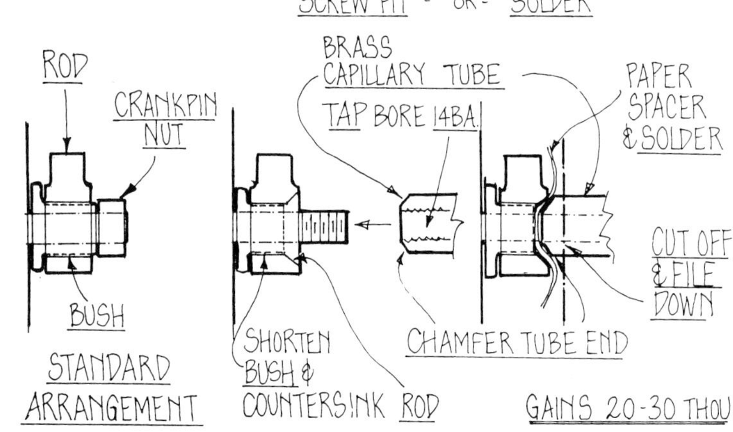

One other clearance to look out for when installing cylinders is wheel-to-cylinder rear – it can be very tight! I had to ease the '43XX' cylinders forward by ½mm to avoid problems.

Left: *While fitting cylinders to the chassis, it's as well to check their relationship with the superstructure. As can be seen from the first picture, mine didn't want to relate at all!* Right: *The cure was quite involved but by no means untypical. I had to lower the cylinder assembly in the frames slightly and, as can be seen in the second picture, carve away some room for the brackets in the underside of the footplate on the Mainline body.*

Left: *The results of this surgery can be seen here, where the front end is now 'sitting right'.* Right: *It's necessary to keep checking as the rest of the slidebar assembly is added, to make sure that nothing fouls and it all lines up. The ride height of the front end is still a bit 'high', but this will be adjusted by bending the compensation beam, as described in Chapter 6.*

of an offset of the cylinder centreline – and with that, the piston rod/crosshead/slidebar centrelines – towards the outside of the cylinder. To execute this solution, it will be necessary to modify the cylinders at the assembly stage to accept the piston-rod guide and slidebars in their new positions. The slidebar bracket will also need fiddling to accommodate – which is why it's best to find out you need to do all this as soon as possible, like before you build the cylinders at all ... Catch 22? You bet – try a dry run, or just tack everything together until you're sure such surgery isn't needed. It *is* effective, though. I've gained as much as a full 1 mm a side without it being *too* apparent on the finished model. Don't forget to washer the connecting rod out on the driven crankpin if you don't want to give the game away with some funny angles between rod and slidebars ...

Only when you are satisfied that all these clearances are acceptable, and that the crosshead moves freely on the slidebars with the correct travel and without slop, and that the bars themselves are correctly aligned and firmly located, can the cylinder assemblies be passed as acceptable. If it's an inside-geared loco (Swindon be praised), then the cylinders and bracketry can be installed on the chassis and attention turned to the next stage of the job. If, however, there's a small matter of Walschaerts gear to be considered, then read on ...

WALSCHAERTS VALVE GEAR

This ingenious mechanism was designed by the Belgian engineer whose name it bears. It's a wonderfully subtle affair, capable of great accuracy in the maintenance of accurate valve events over a wide range of adjustment. Although you don't need to know exactly how it does this, I think it is worth gaining an appreciation of the way the various bits move, and what they're doing. All Walschaerts gears are basically the same, differing only in minor details. I illustrate the main variations in my little gallery of prototype pictures, and I think it should be simple enough to relate the components to my Walschaerts 'key diagram', *Fig. 8:13*.

One of the unfortunate aspects of the Walschaerts gear as used in this country is that some of its parts have acquired more than one name, presumably in translation from the French or Flemish. On the diagram, therefore, I have given the names I am most familiar with to the various components, with alternatives in brackets. The principle on which this gear works is that of moving the pivot points of the various levers in order to vary the stroke and timing of the valve spindle. This happens at two main points, the actual drive pivot of the spindle, which is moving continuously under the impetus of the radius rod, and at the other end of this rod, where the position of its pivot in the die block can be adjusted by the driver. The gear derives its motions

Classic Walschaerts – the LMS variation – double slide bars, lifting links behind die block, valve drive on sliding trunnions, plain eccentric rod big-end.

The Gresley variation – triple slidebars, lifting links behind, conjugated valve gear driven off front of valve spindles, slipper valve guides, roller-bearing eccentric big-end.
F. MOORE

Southern syncopation – 3-cylinder 'Z' class has single slidebars, lifting links behind die-block but passing through footplate to weighshaft above, suspended link valve guides, conjugating gear in front as Gresley, and plain eccentric rod bearings. Note countersunk front crankpin nut.
F. MOORE

Rule Britannia! Bulleid-type 4-slidebar crosshead, lifting links ahead of die block with overhead weighshaft, LMS pattern valve guides and roller-bearing eccentric crank. The best of British!
AUTHOR'S COLLECTION

Fig. 8:13 WALSCHAERTS KEY DIAGRAM

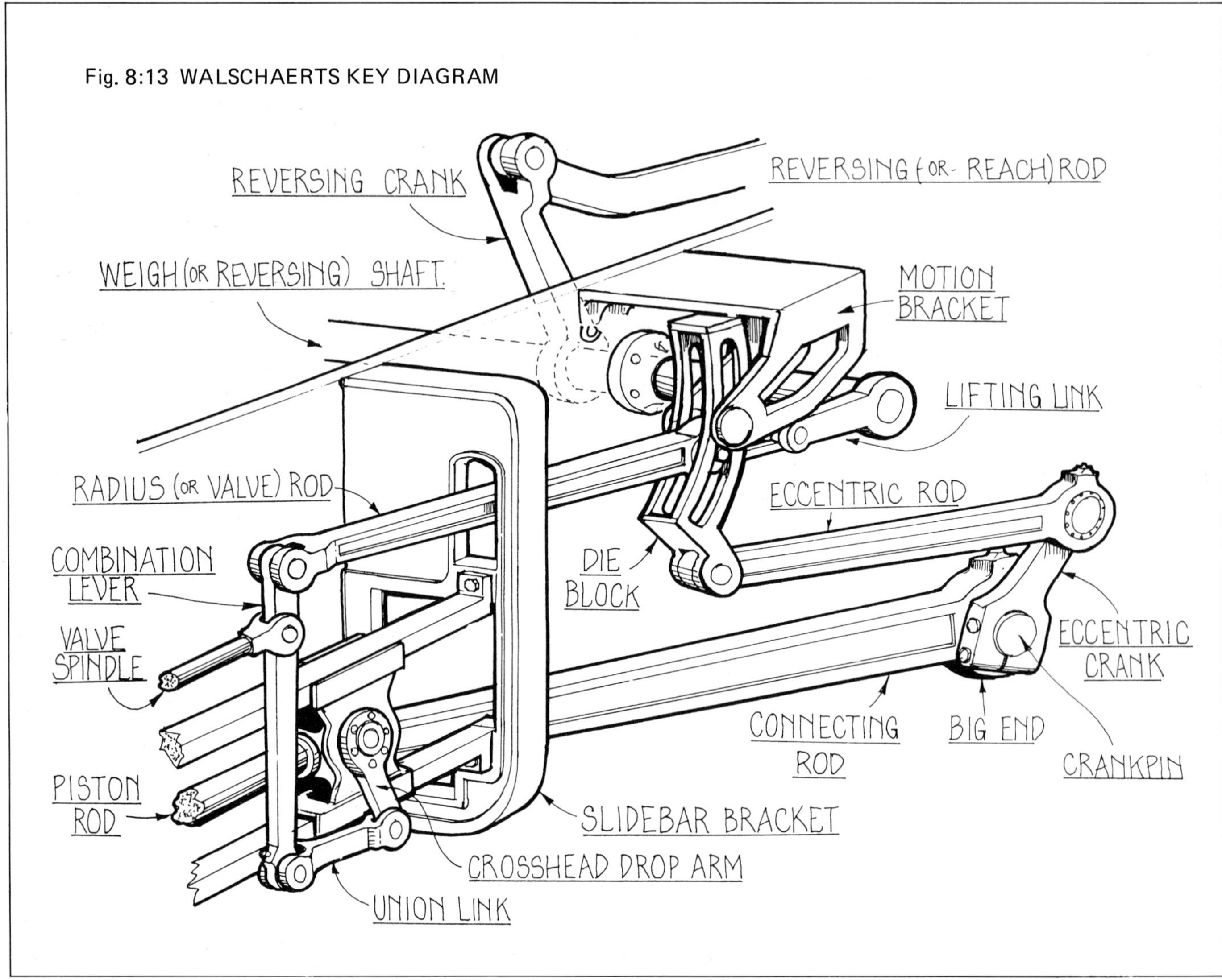

from two points on the engine – the crosshead, at the fore end, where the union link and combining lever provide the 'fixed' element of the drive, and at the rear from the eccentric crank on the centre crankpin which rocks the die block to and fro, and hence, via the adjustable radius rod introduces the 'variable' element of the drive.

It is this latter part which we need to get right on our models if our Walschaerts gear is to look right in motion. The further out from the central pivot of the die block the heel of the radius rod is set, the greater will be the movement of this rod and the longer will be the portion of the valve stroke during which steam is admitted to the cylinder. When the heel pivot of the radius rod is at an extreme end of its travel on the curved path through the die block (which curve is of a radius equal to the length of the rod, hence its name), the engine is said to be in 'full gear', either 'fore' or 'back' as the case might be. When the heel of the rod is at the mid-point of the die-block, then it will not move at all – and neither will the engine. This is described as 'mid gear' and is, unfortunately, the condition reproduced by a lot of model valve gears – most of the etched gears are supplied thus. The pity of this is, of course, that the characteristic compound motion of the Walschaerts gear is largely absent, and, to my eye at least, an engine modelled thus 'loses' quite a lot. Deciding what to do about it is not easy though; fore gear normally calls for the heel of the radius rod to be below the pivot of the die block, while back gear has the rod heel high. If you're modelling a Walschaerts-fitted tank loco such as a Stanier or Fairburn 2–6–4T, Thompson 'L1' or Maunsell 'W', you're going to be wrong about 50% of the time; it's not so bad on tender locos, which at least spend *most* of their time running 'right end forrard'.

It *is* possible to make a working reversing Walschaerts gear in 4 mm scale, given a big enough engine and a touch of electronic wizardry with a couple of diodes and a limit switch or so. You won't read about it in these pages, though... Full gear, with the radius rod at an extreme of its travel, is only used under maximum load conditions such as starting or hill-climbing. With the gear 'linked up' to give free high-speed running, the rod will be much nearer the pivot. I generally opt for a position somewhere between, though if I was modelling a terminus, say, when my locos would be seen starting trains off under load, I'd go for full gear. You get a more satisfying degree of 'waggle' at the valve pivot end of things, apart from anything else. One of the critical factors in designing real Walschaerts is the angle of deflection of the eccentric crank. Nil deflection will bring the rear pivot of the eccentric rod directly over the centre of the driving wheel (the length of the eccentric crank is equal to the crank throw, another little pitfall to look out for if you have an incorrect crankthrow on your wheels, or if the kitmaker has assumed you'll be using the nearest available Romford when you have opted for something spot-on from Sharman). In this condition, the eccentric rod will simply revolve on its pivot on the crank without moving fore and aft at all – which means that none of the gear will work. The greater the angle by which the eccentric crank is offset from this position, the greater will be the movement imparted to the eccentric rod and, hence, the die-block and radius rod. Overdo this movement, and the gear will tie itself in knots, so err on the side of caution – 15°–25° is usual, but it's best to consult pictures of your prototype as this amount did vary a lot.

The other aspect of the Walschaerts gear we need to address if our model is to look right is the actual reversing arrangement, by means of which the heel of the radius rod is moved along the curved slide in the die-block. Basically, this is achieved by linking the pivot of the radius rod to a lever, the 'lifting link' on the key diagram. In the context of a 4mm model, the means by which this is done needn't concern us, but we must ensure that the two *appear* to link up, which means we need the toe of the lifting link to be lined up with the heel of the radius rod, and preferably overlapping it slightly on the outside of the die block. Usually, these lifting links were behind the die block, but some designs – notably the BR standard types – had them in front, working on the radius rod direct. See the prototype photos and the sketch at *Fig. 8:14*. You will also note that the heel ends of all lifting links are joined by a massive (up to 6 in diameter in reality) cross shaft,

Fig. 8:14 LIFTING LINKS IN FRONT OF DIE BLOCK

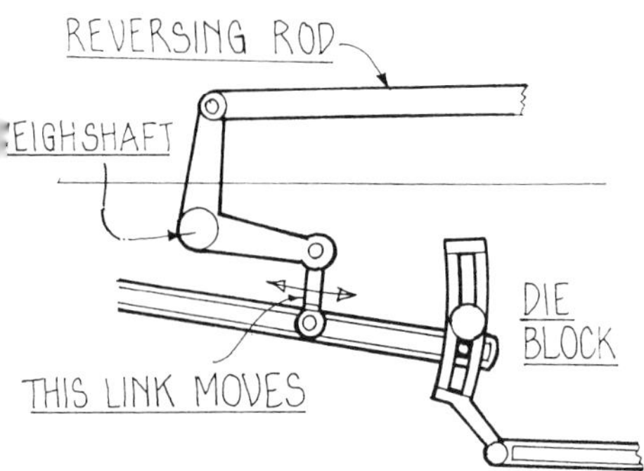

running across the frames and uniting the gear on both sides of the engine. It is quite obvious, therefore, that the heel ends of the lifting links *cannot* come over the driving wheels. Take a look around the next model railway exhibition you go to and see how many model locos you can spot apparently running with a 6 in diameter steel shaft between the spokes of their driving wheels!

The shaft joining the lifting links is known as the 'reversing shaft', and it is rotated – to alter the gear – by means of the reversing rod, usually highly visible above the footplate. This turns the shaft by means of a crank, often also visible, while at the opposite end it will disappear into the cab, where it is linked to the screw reverser or reversing lever by which the driver controls the gear. If our model is to look right, we need to make sure that all these various elements do at least line up with each other, and *look* as if they're linked even if they aren't.

MODELLING WALSCHAERTS

In an ideal world, we should find all we need to make a good model Walschaerts in our kit. Unfortunately, as usual, a lot of kit designers seem totally ignorant of the workings of Walschaerts, and give you only the merest approximation. Undoubtedly the

Nonsense valve gear. This DJH 'Fairburn' 2–6–4T has the engine in mid-gear – fair enough – but with the lifting links 'in line', which has the weighshaft passing, apparently, straight through the wheelrim of the centre drivers! I didn't build this one.

The very similar gear of the BR Standard Class 4 2–6–4T which I built for Chris Langdon's layout, also from a DJH kit. The gear is also at mid-point, but the lifting links have been separated and correctly aligned to miss the wheels. They do, because this engine has a weighshaft.

best set that I've ever met in a kit was that provided by Kemilway in their late and much-lamented BR standard 2–6–2T, possibly one of the best all-round loco kits of recent years. I reckon most of the rest are compromised in some way and often far too chunky, so I'm afraid you're in for a fair bit of work to make a good job of them. If you what you find in the kit box is too horrid to contemplate, then don't despair, as there are some good 'after-market' gears available, the most comprehensive of which is the MRJ-commissioned fret covering all the LMS 4–6–0 Stanier gears. Available in steel or nickel-silver, this isn't cheap but it is exquisite and makes a delightful gear. Almost as good are the rather wider range of valve gears produced by Comet Models. These are very well designed and look as if they result from some years experience in loco-modelling. The actual rods are nice and fine, generally to scale, with all holes etched undersize to allow for accurate fitting. They are good representations of their prototypes, beautifully etched in nickel silver, and come with good instructions. In other words, they are the sort of thing you should get in the kit in the first place! Comet should give lessons.

Assuming you're sticking with a less-than-perfect kit gear, though, what can be done to improve matters? The first thing to do is to compare the fret with a prototype photo and my 'key diagram' to identify the components and determine whether or not they look anything like the real thing. Generally, a bit of aggro with a file will serve to slim down chunky etchings into a reasonable reproduction of reality. One would hope that the various elements of the gear will have the pivots on the correct centres and be of accurate overall length; it's usually in outline that the troubles arise. You'll almost certainly find the radius rod and lifting links etched as one piece, in a straight line (engine in mid-gear). Separate the links from the rod, so that you can align things accurately; quite apart from more esoteric considerations, a lot of gears didn't have the lifting links in line with the radius rod even *in* mid-gear, which is where a lot of those nonsensical 'shaft between the spokes' valve gears come from.

The other component that may need modifying a bit is the die block, which will quite probably have the heel of the radius rod and the pivot of the block itself on a common pivot hole – again, irrevocable mid-gear. To place that heel pivot at a suitable point to give the fore end of the gear reasonable motion will probably call for the drilling of an additional hole at a suitable position as in my sketch at *Fig. 8:15*. You do get the odd etched gear which has the die-block correctly slotted with the curved guides – see the Comet 'Brittannia'

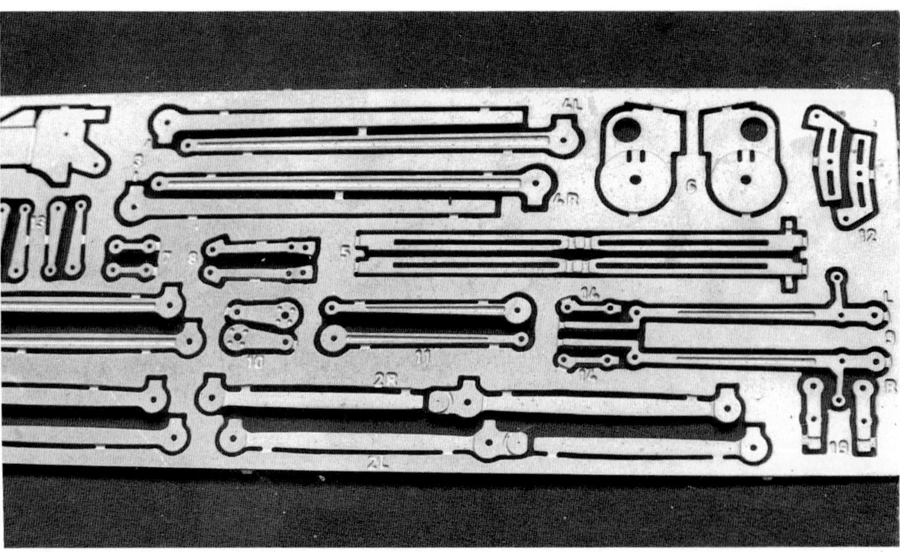

The Comet BR 'Britannia' valve gear is a very well-designed 'after market' gear, though now also available as part of a complete 'Britannia' chassis kit. More please, Mr. Buckenham!

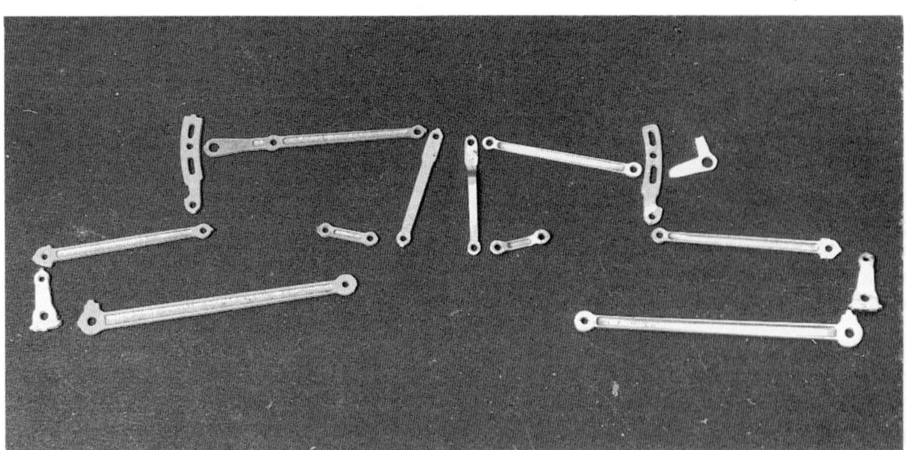

'Refining' valve gear, by slimming down chunky etchings, correcting outlines, shaping and generally tidying-up the etchings is well worthwhile. This is Nu-cast's 'K1' gear, as comes on the left, 'got at' on the right.

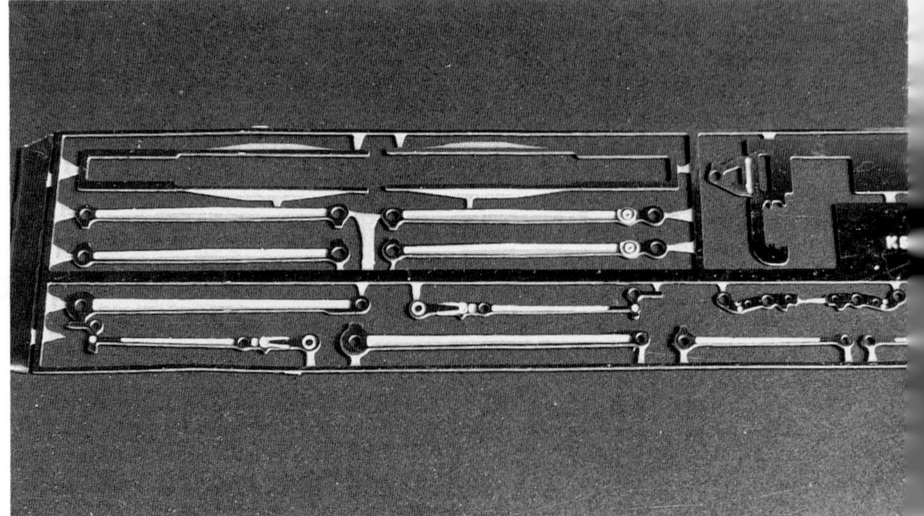

Typical of kit valve gear 'as it comes' is this DJH fret, from the BR Class 3 Mogul – a bit chunky, and with rather generous holes, but susceptible to a bit of reworking for a satisfactory result.

Fig. 8:15 SETTING RADIUS ROD IN DIE BLOCK TO ACTUATE GEAR

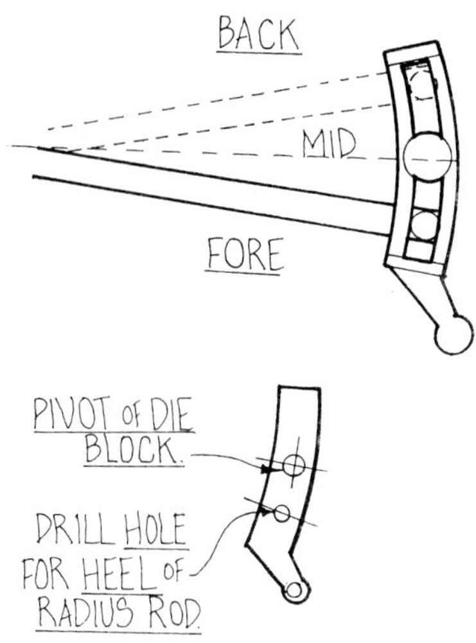

Closing plain rivets. I use a natty little jeweller's anvil and a 1 oz hammer, with a series of gentle taps rather than a single seismic swipe. End result should be neat.

valve gear in the photograph – and this gives you the freedom to set your gear anywhere you like on the travel and even change your mind about it! Others please copy.

ASSEMBLING ETCHED WALSCHAERTS

There are two means of assembling these gears; by riveting, or by pinning-and-soldering. I prefer to rivet where I can, and if the kit doesn't provide suitable rivets, Exactoscale do – superb steel turnings of a delightfully discreet head size and in three lengths. They are my preferred option. Pinning-and-soldering goes back to Ahern, and calls for very small-headed pins if it isn't to look clumsy; try fine brass lace pins – from specialist needlework shops – or entomological pins, not so easy to come by. When soldering, it's essential to interpose thin paper between the various elements, or you'll solder the lot solid. This is one soldering operation for which my favoured liquid flux is less than ideal, and I keep a small tin of 'Fluxite' paste for this particular application. Clean the iron thoroughly after using this flux, or you'll end up with a bit encrusted in a black residue of burnt resin and pocked with more craters than lunar green cheese. If you are soldering the gear together with paper spacers, keep these thin and make sure the joints are reasonably 'tight' so that the gear does not start out with a mass of lateral slop, which can lead to clearance problems once it's installed on the loco.

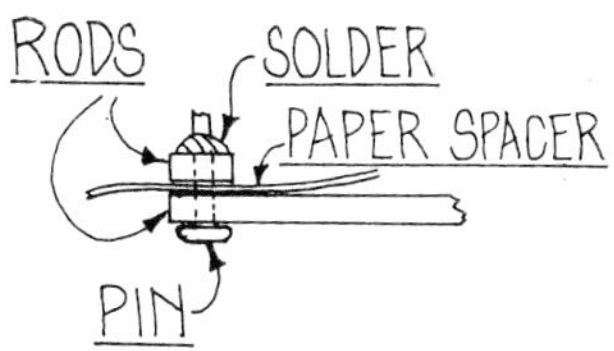

Fig. 8:16 SOLDERING VALVE GEAR

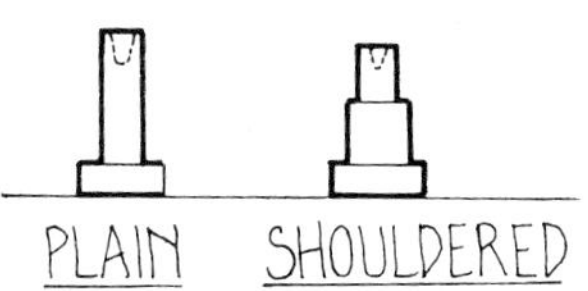

Fig. 8:17 VALVE GEAR RIVETS

It's easier to 'keep things tight' with rivets, one of the main reasons I prefer them. These come in two basic varieties, shouldered and plain (see *Fig. 8:17*). The main difference is that the shouldered rivet, which locates into different sized holes in the two different rods, guarantees a fixed clearance between the two, and can't be made too tight. The snag is that it can often be too loose, again introducing undesirable lateral slop. I prefer the plain rivet as supplied by Exactoscale, which means I can keep such slop to a minimum. The trick is not to get too heavy-handed when closing the rivet – I use a 1oz pin-hammer, and lightly at that. Proceed on the basis that you can always tighten things up a bit with more tapping, on a 'tap-and-trial' basis until the joint moves freely vertically without flopping too much horizontally. If you get things a tad on the tight side – by either solder or rivet methods – don't despair; dredge up some of the sludge from the bottom of an unshaken tin of

Brasso, apply to the joint, and work to-and-fro until it eases off. Wash the Brasso away with meths and oil the joint to keep it free.

ASSEMBLY SEQUENCE
In terms of the 'order of business', I always start at the die-block and work out both ways to the extremities of the gear. So I start by riveting the heel of the radius rod to the die-block. Here again, we usually depart from reality, as real die-blocks are generally hollow, with the radius rod fitting in the middle between the cheeks containing the curved guides. Not many model gears represent this accurately, so the usual compromise is to rivet the radius-rod to the inside of what should be the front cheek of the die-block. The same applies to the 'small end' of the eccentric rod, and this is the next component I fit. I then finish off the rear end of the gear by riveting the eccentric crank inside the big end of the eccentric rod. This last will often need forming to shape to give the correct offset to bring the eccentric rod in line with the die-block (see *Fig. 8:18*).

The fore end of the gear is then built up onto the front of the radius rod. Care and thought is needed here to get the various rods in the right order in terms of what goes inside which. There are prototype variations here, but it helps to remember that the object of the exercise is to drive the valve spindle, which therefore needs to line up with the centreline of the valve chest on the cylinder. The most critical joint is that at the front of the radius rod; almost always, the combining lever dropping down to the crosshead is fitted behind the radius rod, and the valve spindle is in turn fitted behind the combining lever. Look out at this stage if you're modelling a loco with a sliding trunnion valve spindle bracket, which goes over the combining lever, conveniently hiding the actual valve spindle (which only the most fastidious of us will thus need to model) but sometimes resulting in the need to thread the combining lever through the bracket before the last little bit, the union link, can be fitted. The LMS gear, in common with most Gresley gears, has the joint of the radius rod and combining lever *above* that for the valve spindle, with a shrouding bracket. BR Standards used the same layout, with the notable exception of the rebuilt Bulleid Pacifics, where there was an extra fixed pivot for the top of the combining lever, with the valve spindle drive below that, and the drive from the radius rod downstairs again . . .

There are two options with these shrouding valve-spindle brackets; they can be incorporated with the cylinders when these are built, which means that the combining lever needs to do its 'eye of the needle' job,

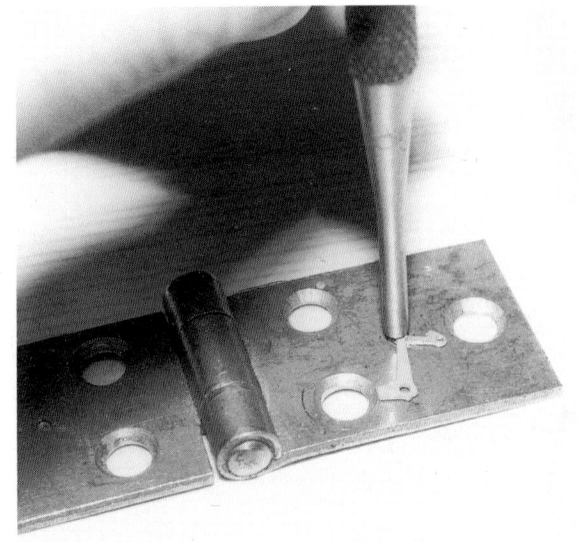

Chris Langdon has a natty alternative by way of an anvil – a steel butt hinge with a shallow recess drilled into it to keep the rivet-head in place. Use of a punch can help accuracy, especially where rivets are close together.
C. J. LANGDON

The valve gear of Chris Langdon's DJH 'Britannia' being assembled on the bench. With the engine in 'mid gear', the die block and the heel of the radius rod (key diagram) can be on a common pivot, so the gear can, as here, be made in two halves, only being united when the whole shebang is installed on the chassis. Note that in this instance DJH have provided the crosshead drop arm as a separate component.
C. J. LANGDON

Here is the 'Britannia' gear being 'test mounted' to the rest of the chassis. The screw through the motion bracket unites die block, bracket and radius rod. Note the locating hole for the weigh shaft in the motion bracket/boiler support casting.
C. J. LANGDON

or they can be added after the valve gear is installed on the loco. I prefer the latter course. What you can't do, if the loco is to look anything, is to leave them off altogether. Quite a lot of kit valve gears do just that ... I have attempted to cover the assembly of this vital fore end of the Walschaerts in one comprehensive diagram, *Fig. 8:19*; I think that the alternative arrangement mentioned can be appreciated from the pictures of the completed valve-gear on the rebuilt 'West Country' – on which more in a moment, when we get on to valve gear faults.

The fore-end of the 'West Country' valve gear as finally assembled – mostly DJH (corrected considerably) with the odd bit of Rice. Exacto-scale rivets used throughout.

Fig. 8.18 REAR END WALSCHAERTS ASSEMBLY

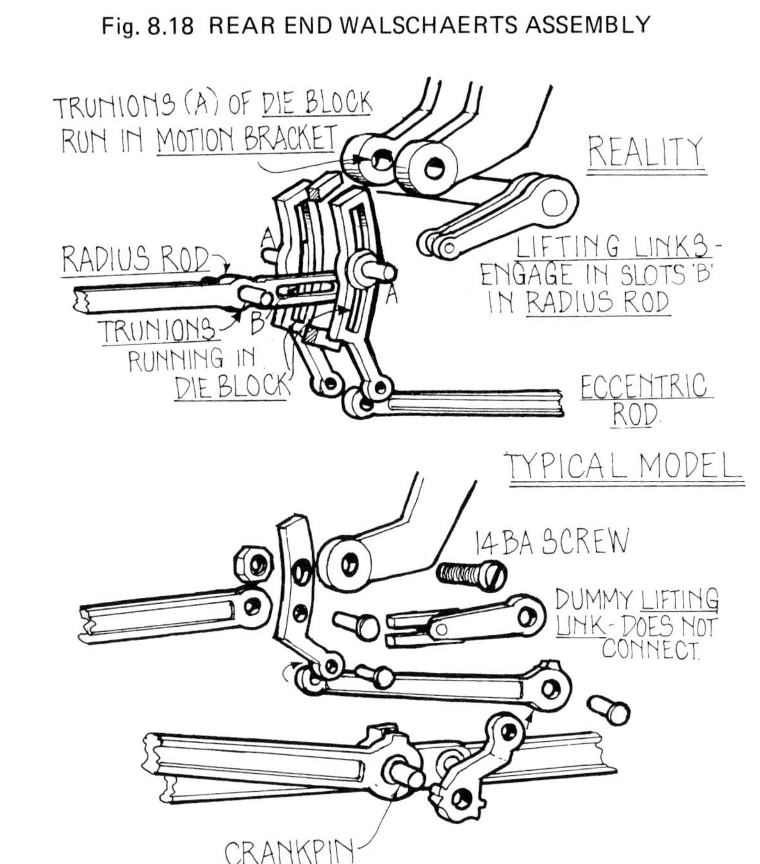

Fig. 8:19 FORE END WALSCHAERTS ASSEMBLY

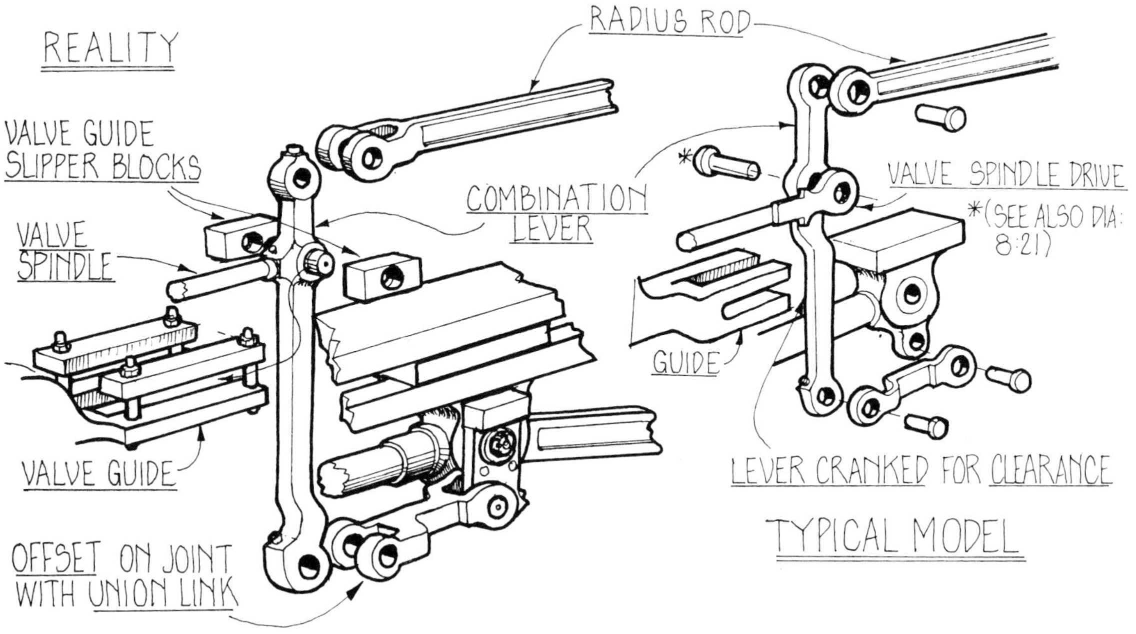

The last, and most ticklish, bit of the valve gear assembly is the fitting of the tiny union link at the bottom of the combining lever. Now, in reality, this joint, in common with most of the others, is a forked joint, with the combining lever sitting in between the two cheeks of the fork of the union link. We don't go to these lengths in 4 mm scale, settling for a fair representation which would often call for the union link to be fitted *outside* the combining lever – which might look OK, but will tend to cause clearance problems where the crosshead passes inside the combining lever at the fore end of its stroke; the prototype clearance at this point is often well under an inch. So I fit the union link 'indoors' and hope nobody notices – even so, it is sometimes necessary to put a slight set in the combining lever to keep it out of the way of the crosshead – rare but not unknown in full-size practice. The last joint of all, that between the union link and the drop-arm on the crosshead, can't be made at all until the gear is finally installed on the loco, so I'll pass over it for a moment, though it figures in *Fig. 8:20*; which, I hope, will help make clear just what I've been on about.

Fig. 8:20 UNION LINK COMPROMISE

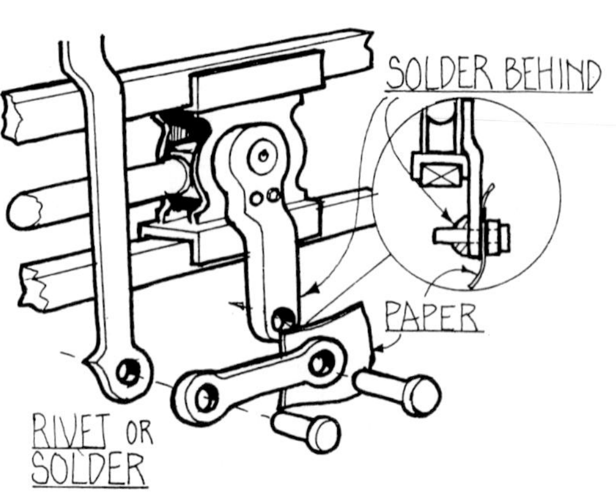

INSTALLING WALSCHAERTS VALVE GEAR

Assuming that we have succeeded in assembling the various components of our model Walschaerts in the correct order and relationship, and with all the joints nicely free but not sloppy, then we can unite this complex sub-assembly with the rest of the loco chassis. It will interface at four points (Jargon! what is the world coming to?); the joint of the union link to the drop-arm of the crosshead, just mentioned; the valve spindle bracket; the motion bracket carrying the bearing of the die block; and the eccentric crank on the appropriate crankpin. One of these points, the valve spindle bracket, we can often ignore, so there are generally three connections to make. I usually employ a pin-and-solder joint between crosshead drop-arm and union link, use a small (14BA) nut-and-bolt to secure the die block, and solder the eccentric crank firmly to the crankpin, using a paper interleaf to give the required running clearance and keep the solder in place. The motion bracket is soldered or bolted to the mounting plate which also carries the cylinder stretcher and slidebar brackets. This maintains the whole cylinder/slidebar/crosshead/connecting rod/valve gear assembly as a separate and self-contained unit which can be removed 'in toto' from the loco chassis by the simple expedient of unsoldering the eccentric cranks from the crankpins and unbolting the mounting plate from the chassis. The need to remove a wheel, say, or gain access to the drivetrain for servicing or replace-

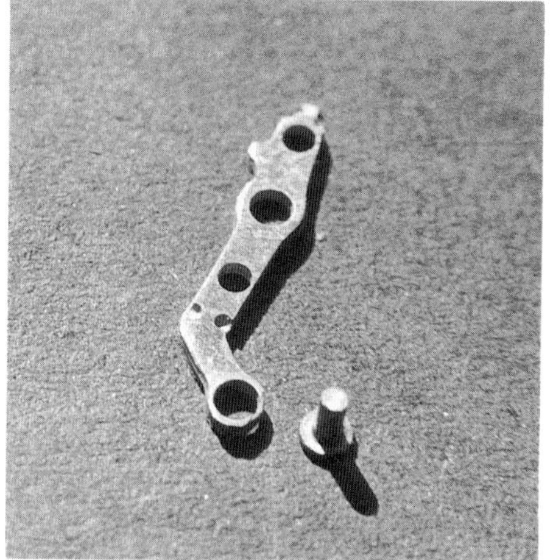

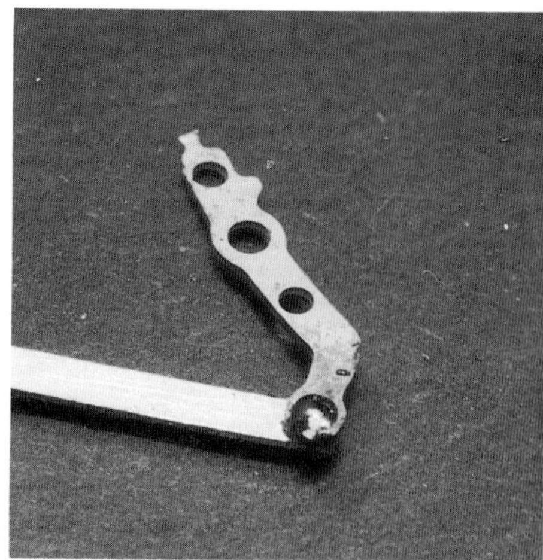

Left: *Hole trouble. As this comparison shows, the holes in the DJH 'West Country' valve gear were decidedly generous compared with the rivet shank!* Right: *This was corrected by soldering some fret waste behind the offending hole, and then re-drilling and reaming to the correct size, trimming off surplus strip.*

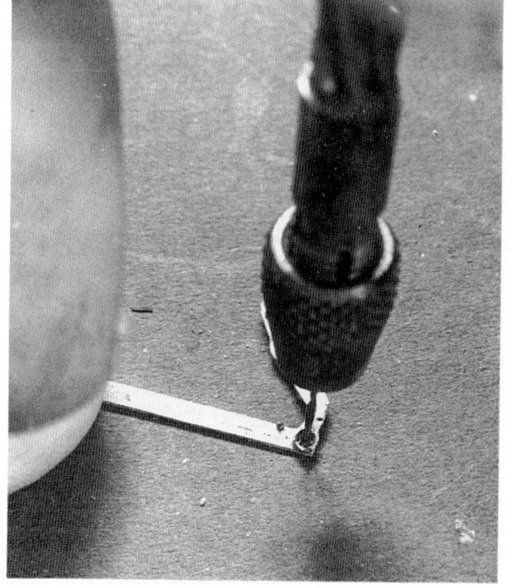

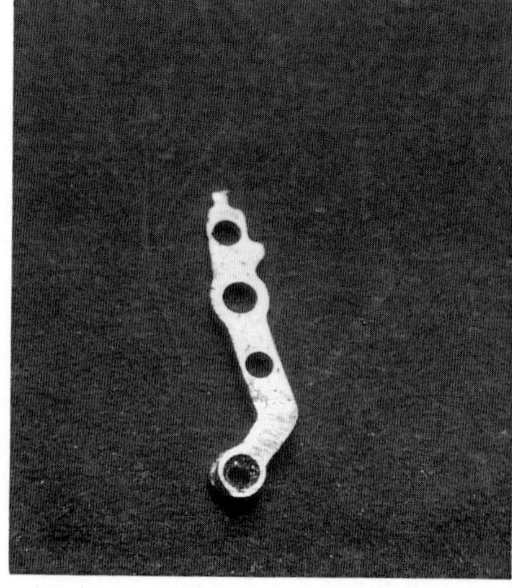

Left: *You can only do this stunt where the additional thickness resulting from the correction will not in itself cause a problem (i.e. rivets not long enough, lack of lateral clearance).* Right: *I got away with it on the Bulleid, but, with eight holes a side to do, it was tedious.*

ment, does not involve any stripping of the valve gear. Phew!

VALVE GEAR FAULTS

Test running of the loco fitted with its valve gear may disclose one or two faults and can result in the loco not running at all, due to binding. If you've fitted a big Portescap you may also tie the gear in a granny if all is not well, so test it under finger power before feeding RG4 grunt through it. The other faults needing correction are those which become apparent during assembly – I've touched on one or two of them, but the worst is undoubtedly oversize holes, so I'll start with that particular headache.

It just so happens that the etched gear supplied by DJH with the 'West Country' which figures from time to time in this epic proved sloppy, as the photos show. I daresay that had I sent this fret back to DJH they would have supplied a better example. As can be seen from the pictures, the rivets supplied were quite slim – so slim, in fact, that I could get two of them into some of the holes, while the (biggish) heads all but passed through; the finer Exactoscale rivets went clean out the back without touching the sides! The remedy, as can be seen from the little photo-sequence, was to solder thin strip fret waste to the rear of the offending orifices, which could then be re-drilled to a more appropriate size and carefully reamed to a nice fit on the rivets. The waste strip was then nipped off and the rod-end filed back to shape; not a five-minute job. One rod, the eccentric rod, was too far gone for even this treatment, and was replaced with a modified eccentric of appropriate length from an MRJ LMS valve gear fret (which gives you alternative-length rods to suit the various Stanier engines).

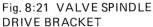

Fig. 8:21 VALVE SPINDLE DRIVE BRACKET

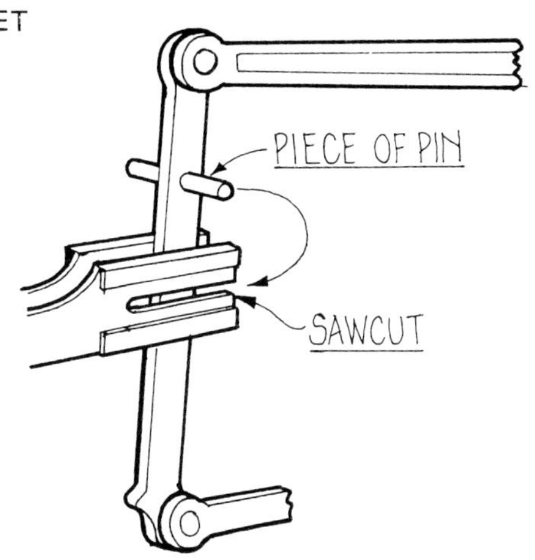

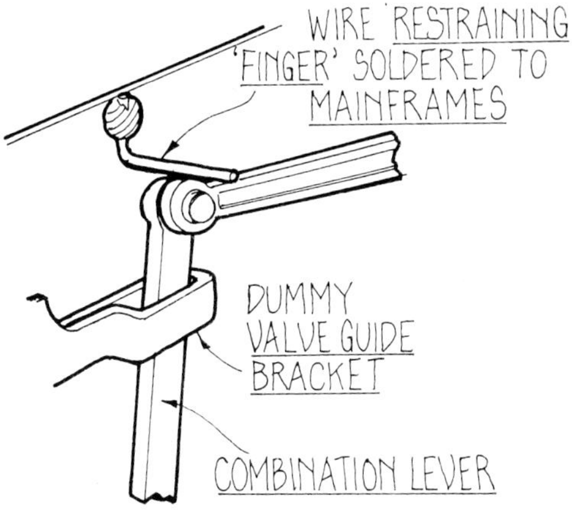

Fig. 8:22 VALVE GUIDE BODGE

Of 'dynamic' faults, which become apparent once the gear is installed and working, three are common and troublesome. I have laid some stress on the need, when assembling the valve gear, to minimise the sideways slop in the joints. It this is not done, it is all too easy to arrive at the situation where a bit that should be waggling fore-and-aft elects to waggle side-to-side instead. The other trauma induced by lateral slop is the loss of vital clearances – I've already harped on about that where the crosshead passes behind the combining lever, but don't overlook the potential for trouble where the connecting rod passes inside the lower end of the die block, where the eccentric rod attaches. It's one reason I like to screw the die-block in place – it's then easy to adjust-out any sideways slop here, retaining the setting by locking the retaining nut with a spot of Loctite 242 'Nutlock'. That eccentric-rod/die-block joint wants to be nice and tight, too, and if it's a pin-and-solder job, make sure you file the back face down flush once the joint is made.

The second dynamic favourite is potentially even more troublesome than bits knocking together, and that is when incorrect travel of parts of the gear can result in some joints (most notably the combining lever/union link) turning 'inside out'. The eccentric rod can also drive the bottom of the die block up over the radius rod if there is too much movement, although this is usually easy enough to cure – you simply reduce the amount by which the eccentric crank on the crankpin is offset from the driving wheel centre. The union link inversion is usually due to excessive crosshead travel or a union link that is too short. Excessive crosshead travel, due to driving wheels of the incorrect crank throw, as already discussed, is impossible to correct, so the remedy is to proceed as in the second case, and make a slightly longer union link. Very occasionally, one meets the opposite situation, where the link is too long, whereupon the bottom of the combining lever clouts the cylinder and can jam the gear solid. A shorter link (and a snotty letter to the kitmaker) is called for. Trouble can also arise if, as described in the section on slidebars and crossheads, the crosshead travel is occurring too far forward on the slidebars, due to an overlong connecting rod. Even if things are not so extreme that the crosshead hits the cylinder rear, there may still not be enough clearance for the union link, so bear this in mind when you're setting up the slidebar/crosshead/connecting rod assembly.

The last persistent fault is the combining lever that hops up and down like the proverbial fiddler's elbow. This is due to the fact that we are not restraining the lever in the area of the valve spindle drive joint, as is done by the spindle drive bracket on the prototype. The most elegant solution to this problem is to make the bracket do its job, by introducing the arrangement sketched in *Fig. 8:21*, which isn't that difficult to incorporate as you build the gear when the bracket is fitted after the valve gear. I make the slit in the bracket with a piercing saw and solder the fine wire into a hole drilled in the combining lever at the appropriate point – I use 0.45 mm wire in a 0.5 mm hole. If you don't fancy this, or if your spindle bracket is a part of the cylinder assembly, then the bodge in *Fig. 8:22* can be called up; the restraining arm is fashioned out of stiff NS strip, and soldered to the mounting plate of the whole cylinder/valve gear sub-assembly. Horrid but effective – paint it black and hope no-one notices.

VALVE GEAR VALEDICTUM

I could write an entire book on modelling valve gears, but in the context of the present volume I think that I've said all I can. I'm not going to pretend that building a Walschaerts is an easy job, because it isn't. But approached logically, taken in easy stages, and undertaken with a clear understanding of what is required to make it all function, it's not as bad as it has been painted by modelling tradition. After all, if you bish it all up at the first attempt, you can always get another valve gear etch, and try again. Or become a GW modeller ... I haven't touched on non-Walschaerts gears or GW/Gresley derived gears here, as they're simpler than Walschaerts or entail only minor cosmetic additions. Just to round things out, then, here are a couple of last sketches, of GW spindle drive and Caprotti's rotary gear which, in 4 mm at least, stays blissfully still. If you want subminiature bevel boxes and working UJs, you're on your own!

Fig. 8:23 VALVE DRIVE FOR GW 2-CYLINDER LOCO (GUY WILLIAMS METHOD)

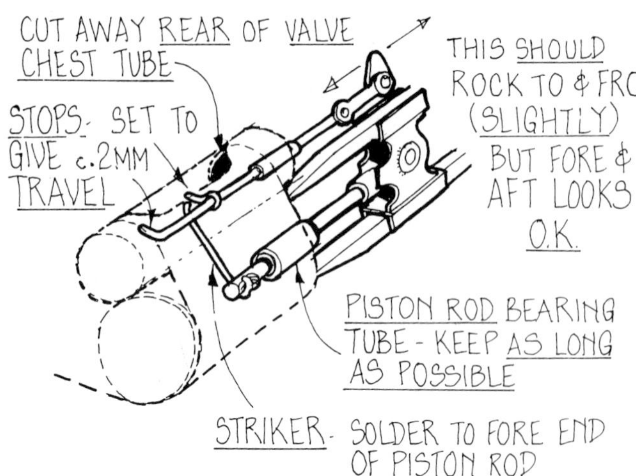

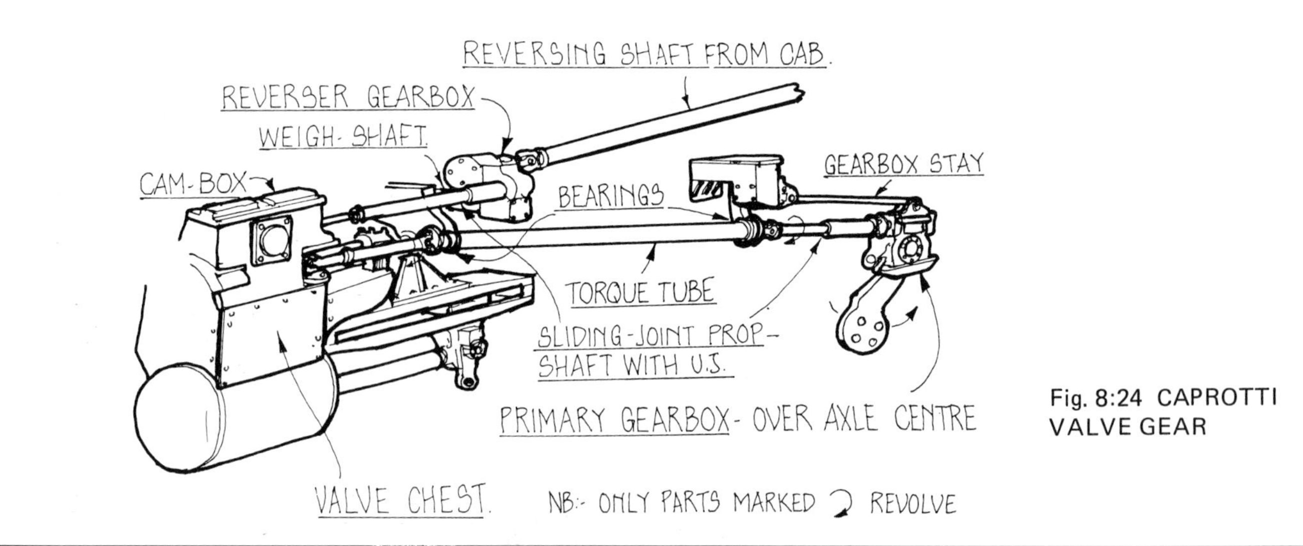

Fig. 8:24 CAPROTTI VALVE GEAR

Caprotti valve gear – in 4mm scale, nothing moves! Here, just to help you, is a close-up of the 'Duke's' offside gear, to go with the nearside shot at the beginning of this chapter. DJH cast the lot in brass, and very nice it is, too!
AUTHOR'S COLLECTION

CHAPTER NINE

Drivetrains: Part 1 – Motors

INTRODUCTION

It is at this point in the consideration of model steam locomotive chassis that we part company with reality – for, while real engines most certainly have frames, bogies, pony trucks, wheels, cylinders, coupling and connecting rods and valve gear, they assuredly do *not* have a thumping great electric motor whirring away in their nether regions. Neither, praise be, do they employ finicky worm-and-pinion gears by way of a transmission, nor have they any need of pick-ups of any sort. We, regrettably, need all these things, designed, selected and installed with care, if our models are to be capable of locomotion.

In company with many other aspects of model locomotive kit chassis design, proper drivetrain installations have been sadly neglected. Broadly speaking, the historical trend was that K's gave you one of their own notoriously variable double-ended motors, while everybody else specified the good old Tri-ang X04, or, latterly, one of its derivatives. It so happens that the X04 was actually a very sound motor design, and for its day (it started out as the Zenith/Gem X3 in about 1948), was pretty well 'state of the art'. So long as the locomotive you were modelling had sufficient bulk and girth to accommodate it, an X04 was capable of giving a very good quality of running, especially if driving through Tri-ang's own gears using the single-start worm for a 40:1 ratio. The snag came, of course, with smaller prototypes, where the X04 could not be coyly concealed, and burst out in all sorts of unseemly places, filling cabs with its magnet, or robbing the daylight from beneath the boiler.

The X04-type motors are designed to locate by lug-and-screw fixing, which is very sound engineering practice. The normal approach is to incorporate the mounting points within the chassis, and, in the context of a good-quality cast or milled block-type chassis, this should give good mechanical alignment with the gears. There are a few older etched chassis around designed to take the X04 family (X03, X04, MW005 or Romford Bulldog, the last two being 5-pole variants), but in the context of such a chassis, the provision of the large cut-outs needed to accommodate a 13mm-wide X04 in a OO chassis often leads to unacceptable weakness. With the arrival on the scene of the far more compact, but comparably powerful, 'D' series motors, which are only 11mm wide overall, the need to incorporate cut-outs in etched chassis has been eradicated. On the 'S15' illustrated here the nether end of a DS10 motor is very visible just where the real loco is uncompromisingly solid. This is avoidable and I would also question the advisability of using a small, low-powered, high-revving motor like the DS10 in a hulking great cast engine like the 'S15'.

I could go on about drivetrain design which often ranges from the indifferent through the desultory to the downright disastrous. I do not wonder that so many kit-built locos run so badly; I only wonder that they run at all! The point must be made that, in drivetrain design, as with so many other aspects of model locomotive kit origination, there are certain fundamentals of engineering practice that *cannot* be ignored. I shall set them out in due course, but I would stress that these are *facts*, not Rice's personal opinions. I hope that my explanations will make clear why these things are so vital, and that an appreciation of the principles involved will suggest ways in which the many thoroughly unsatisfactory chassis kit drivetrains can be corrected and improved. Fortunately, with the more-or-less universal adoption of prototype-based (full frame profile with no cut-outs) chassis design, coupled with axle-hung motors, the problem of poor powertrain installations in model locos is receding. If the kit-designer suggests something daft in the instructions, he can be ignored and something more appropriate devised – and devising something appropriate and installing same is what this chapter and the next are really all about.

DRIVETRAIN DESIGN CRITERIA

The powertrain installation that provides real quality of running is one that optimises a number of factors. There is no 'universal panacea', no single, simple, off-the-peg solution that will suit any loco from a 'Pug' to a 'Princess'. There is a tendency these days to assume that a coreless motor/gearbox will provide top-drawer running almost irrespective of application or installation, but I have found this isn't necessarily the case. For a start, no motor/transmission combination will overcome the sort of binding resulting from an error in the coupling rod-chassis correlation, and it is vital to get the whole chassis as smooth and as free-running as possible before the motor is installed. Hence the stress laid on the need for accuracy in these matters; until you've got the basic mechanics of the chassis functioning properly, there's no point in worrying about such powertrain niceties as gear meshing, motor alignment and sound damping.

If asked to summarise in a single short sentence (some hope!) the ingredients of a good powertrain for a kitbuilt model loco, I plump for something along the lines of 'The best motor you can afford, the biggest motor you can conceal, the simplest possible installation, and gearing chosen to keep it all sweet.' Trite this may be, but I think that is a shot in the right direction – pro-

All-too-visible DS10, due to unnecessary frame cut-outs on the DJH 'S15'. A DS10 is only 10mm wide, so even OO shouldn't call for this sort of compromise.

viding you have some means of assessing just what it is that makes a motor good and keeps it sweet! That calls for a little understanding of motor characteristics and the relevance of correct transmission ratios, matters which occupy much of the next two chapters. Note also that emphasis on concealment; it is, I think, an important one in the context of today's high-fidelity loco kits. These days, a cabful of motor magnet and a highly-obtrusive wormwheel stealing all the daylight from beneath the boiler are no longer acceptable, and given the choice of components now available, there should be no need to contemplate such gross intrusions.

In fact, the cause of concealed motors was hindered as much by one of those 'tablet of stone' conventions we modellers seem so prone to as by any lack of choice of suitable components. This particular commandment decreed that, in the case of a six-coupled engine, the drive must always be taken to the centre axle. Why? No-one has ever given me a rational or convincing explanation. But still the notion lingers on, though I think it is becoming accepted that, provided the basic chassis criteria of axle/rod correlation and accurate quartering are observed, then it matters not a hoot which axle you choose to drive. That choice should, I would suggest, be biased towards the set-up that best hides the necessary evil of the motor from the unclouded gaze.

My last ingredient in the 'drivetrain delight' recipe, that of 'sweet' gearing, is really a matter for Chapter 10, except that it is something that must be considered in the light of the performance characteristics of the motor, as we are also concerned with keeping this turning over at its sweetest speed for as much of the time as possible. This is a subtlety that seems often to pass by the kitmakers' door, and I regularly come across inept suggestions as to suitable motor/gear ratio combinations in kit instructions. This may have been excusable in the old days of 'one make, three ratios, take-it-or-leave-it' gear availability, but nowadays results more from ignorance or indolence. Fortunately, our lot is eased by the generally excellent quality of the components we have to work with, so it's really a matter of a bit of headscratching with a scribbling pad or a (eureka!) soak in the tub. If all else fails, you can always bust open the piggy-bank and buy an Escap RG4, which solves many of your problems for you, except that of possible bankruptcy!

The tablet of stone: thou shalt always drive the centre axle of a six-coupled chassis. Why? Turning the motor round to drive the rear axle of the 'S15' would still have kept the cab clear, and there would have been room for a bigger and more suitable motor, such as a D13.

MOTOR CHOICE – PHYSICAL CHARACTERISTICS

Motor characteristics are assessed under two broad headings; physical, and performance. The physical aspects are easily appreciated, being apparent on inspection; one only has to look at the motor to discern whether it is of open-frame or 'can' design, how big it is, and how it is designed to be mounted. Open-frame motors are regarded as slightly 'old hat' these days, the state of the art inclining toward fully-enclosed 'cans', often of outer-rotor 'coreless' design. However, open-frame motors are often more compact than equivalent enclosed designs, and most of the really small motors are still of this type. The recent trend has been to combine the best of both worlds with flat-sided can motors such as the Mashima 1220/1224 series; these also go some way toward open-frame design practice by having exposed brush-gear, not always a good thing.

Most of the characteristics that concern us in the choice of our motor are dimensional, given that virtually all the motors currently available have more power than the loco that will house them can use. This ignores the way in which that power is delivered, but, if necessary, problems here can usually be addressed in the transmission design. Where the loco to be powered is of obliging disposition, and there is plenty of room for the concealed installation of a wide range of motors, then I would select the motor on performance and cost grounds. This happy circumstance is rare in the life of one who tends to go for older, and hence more restricting, prototypes, although it is surprising what an open mind and a bit of careful measurement will prove to be possible. Vertical 'short can' motors in small Belpaire fireboxes would be a case in point – the RG4/1616 and gearbox will, for instance, fit a 'Dean Goods' in this mode. Normally, though, it's a case of carefully assessing width, height, overall length and shaft length when deciding on suitability. Only when you've found out which motors will fit the basic envelope of your lōco are the running characteristics of those motors of relevance.

The other physical criteria we need to look at are shaft dimensions and bearing disposition. These are very critical factors, given that we are almost always using fine-pitch precision worm-and-pinion gearsets, which need very accurate meshing and substantial support. A motor with a great length of thin and whippy shaft sticking out of an insubstantial front bearing, which is itself held in a flexible plastic frame, does not provide either the location or the support, and may thus have to be discounted on those grounds even if otherwise suitable. Either that, or the necessary support and location will need to be provided by other means, such as a gearbox. But what you cannot do is to ignore the problems that such a configuration poses – and that is precisely what some kitmakers do. The full implications of motor shaft characteristics, bearing location and gear meshing are dissected in Chapter 10, but for now I'll suggest that it's wise to choose a motor that can be positioned with the worm gear as close as possible to the front bearing if you're not prepared to get involved in the provision of extra bearing support. And that, in turn, may suggest a narrow open-frame design in place of a 'can' too portly to fit between the frames.

An obvious first step in 'shortlisting' a selection of motors suited to a particular engine is to relate them to the space available; you never know, the kit designer may already have done this for you, and made some suggestions. Reading such a list in conjunction with the notes on motor performance that follow might be enough to clinch matters, which is useful if you are setting out to buy a motor for a given kit. My own method of working is to keep a small stock of those motors whose performance I have come to respect, and which are of a size and shape affording good general utility. For what it matters, my choice of 'stock' motors encompasses six types: The Sagami or Mashima 1628, Sagami 1620 and 1425 cylindrical 'cans', the Mashima 1224 'flat can', and the D13 and DS10 open-frame designs. The reasons for these particular choices will be evident from the 'performance' notes.

One advantage of having the actual motors to hand is that a suitable choice can be made by trial and error as the loco is built – a process aided by the way in which I choose to use the now-universal fold-up etched motor mounts, which isn't quite the way they're intended to be used ... However, a lot can be done in assessing the suitability of a motor by offering it up to a 4mm scale drawing – as provided in the kit instructions? If you are engaged on such fiddling about and head-scratching, don't forget that there a goodly few ways of killing a cat, and that there is no law which says that you *must* mount the motor horizontally with the worm on top of the wormwheel, or that you have to drive any particular axle (although if you've opted for a compensated chassis it is generally a very great deal easier to drive the fixed axle rather than one of the floating ones). I have sketched some motor outlines to scale in *Fig. 9:1*, while possible mounting schemes are in *Fig. 9:2*.

The up-ended short can motor – here, an Escap 1616 on an RG4 gearbox – suits a great many Belpaire-boilered types. This is a Perseverance chassis for a Mainline '2251' in EM.

MOUNTING SYSTEMS

The almost universal approach these days is to mount the motor on an etched fold-up bracket located on the driven axle. While this system has a number of advantages, it

A neglected drive configuration for many small locos is the steeply-inclined small open-frame (DS10, etc) or flat-sided 'can' (Mashima 12XX series) motor driving the rear axle with the worm in front of, and/or below, the pinion. Here is such an installation of a Mashima 1224 in Don Leeper's LNW 'Cauliflower', built from the excellent George Norton kit.

Fig. 9:1 RICE'S HALF-DOZEN

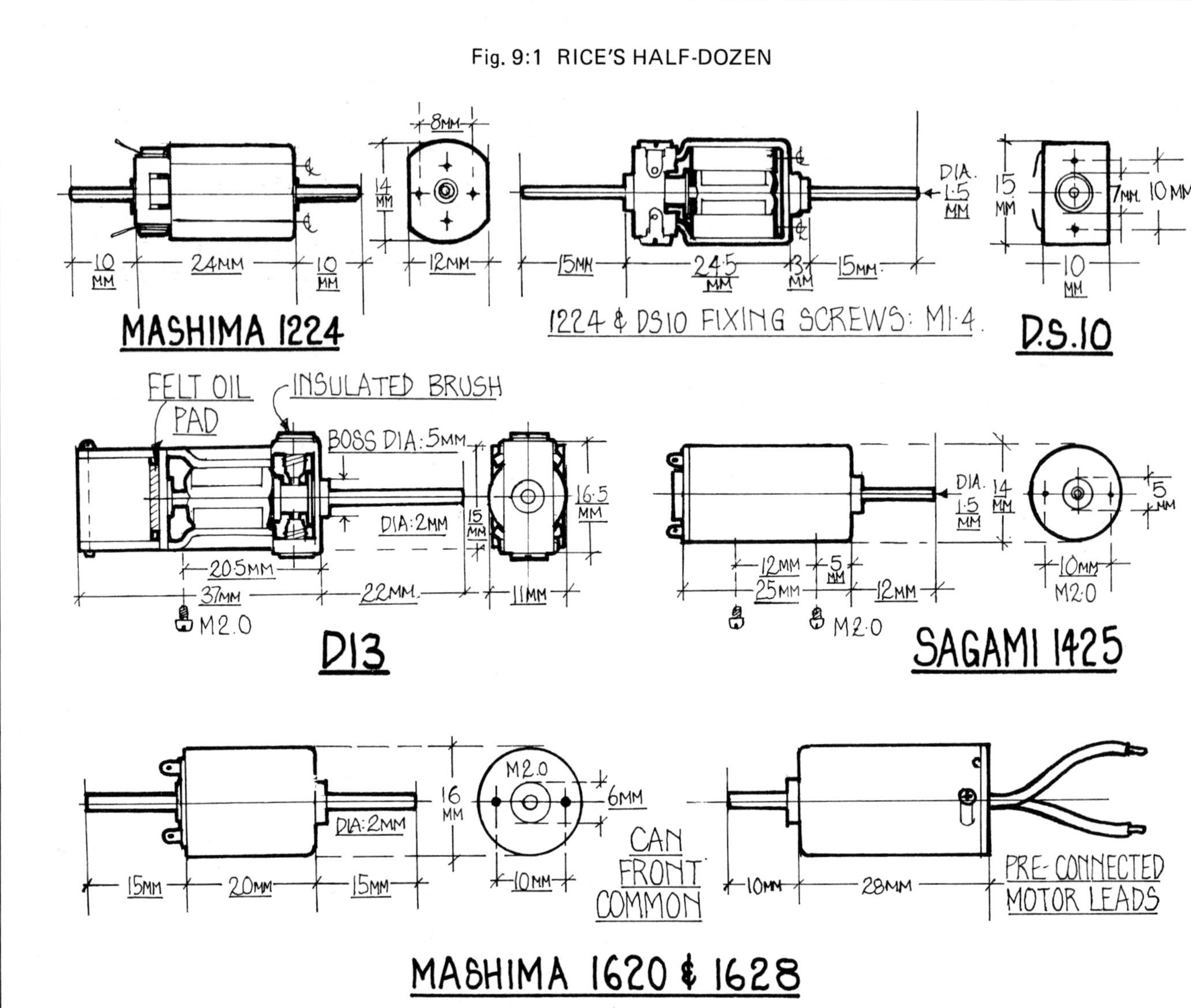

also has some drawbacks, especially in the case of those installations where the motor is held on the bracket by fixing screws on vertical centres, the lower one of which is inaccessible behind the gearwheel once everything is in place. This means that the motor can't be taken off the bracket without the driven axle being withdrawn, which in turn involves quite a major strip-down of the chassis. I have evolved my own modification of these mounts to overcome this drawback. Overall, I feel that they are often the simplest and best choice, especially if you're a bit dubious about the whole business of motor installation. They do need care in assembly, however, if they are to work properly, while the accuracy of some of them leaves a bit to be desired. This isn't so critical with relatively coarse-pitched gears such as the Romford 30 or 40:1 types (although even these need accurate align-

Fig. 9:2 BASIC MOTOR MOUNTING CONFIGURATIONS

ment to give of their best), but the finer types such as the Ultrascale 38:1 and larger reduction-ratio Romfords need 'spot-on' location to work at all.

Some motors, such as the Sagami 1425 'can', give you alternative mounting points, in that they have tapped holes in both the front face (for bracket mounting) and along the long axis (for bottom mounting to a plate or cradle). There are a number of other possibilities for mounting can motors, and rather than gloss over these here, I have incorporated the design of such 'one-off' set-ups in the installation notes which form part of the transmission chapter. (Sorry about all these cross-references, but it underlines the point I find myself making most often in all these essays – that you can't divide the job of model loco-building up into watertight compartments, and that each stage of the job has implications elsewhere.) Such flexibility in the design of a can motor is a boon, as if you find that your first mounting idea doesn't work out in practice, there are options to overcome the snag. This is also true of the traditional open-frame motors, most of which can now be mounted either to an axle-hung fold-up mount, or direct to the chassis.

When considering mounting systems, there are a few other factors to bear in mind. For instance, if you're intending to exhibit your models a lot, and undertake extensive running in public, then a 'quick change' system which enables you to replace an errant motor in short order is quite a life-saver when a key loco expires in mid-exhibition. I speak from experience of such face-reddening occurrences in my erratic career as an itinerant exhibitionist ... You may also wish to try and engineer your drive system to be as quiet as possible, which suggests that either a fully-flexible or fully-rigid set-up be designed – it's the half-way-house jobs that seem most apt to generate noise. There is also the matter of complexity-versus-reliability to be considered, and in that context there's little doubt that simplicity usually pays.

MOTOR PERFORMANCE

Like other types of motor, most notably the internal combustion effort we are all familiar with in our cars, small electric motors have certain marked performance characteristics that we need to take account of and exploit to get the best out of the thing in service. In practical terms, we aren't too bothered about the actual electrical characteristics, as most modern controllers are designed to take care of these aspects of motor performance. What we are really concerned about is the power and, more particularly, torque output of our motor, and the speeds at which these figures peak.

The fold-up mount has become the most widely-used mounting system. Here is the chassis of my NBR 'R' class 4–4–0T, which uses an Impetus mount to unite the 1224 Mashima motor with the Ultrascale 38:1 gears on the driven axle. Part of the upper sides of the mount have been filed back to minimise cab intrusion.

Mounts can be used upside-down, as shown in the 'Cauliflower' chassis under construction.

The Sagami 1425 is a useful 'can' motor that tends to be overlooked in the UK. An unusual feature of this type is a pair of tapped holes in the side of the can, permitting direct mounting to a chassis in conventional fashion, as here on my 'J72'.

'Plug-in' motor. The Sagami 1620 in my '14XX' could be changed in a few moments. It is connected to the drive via a push-on neoprene tube coupling, and is held in place with plastic tape. Swapping the motor leads would be the longest part of the job.

The peak power – strictly, the maximum amount of mechanical energy which a motor is capable of producing – occurs relatively high up the rev. range, and will almost certainly amount to far more 'oomph' than we can reasonably use. What is of far greater concern to us is the quantity of torque (twisting effort) that the motor can exert, and the speed at which it does this.

A real steam engine has the outstanding virtue of exerting its maximum torque on starting, that is, at minimum speed. This is the characteristic which made a steam engine so exceptionally suitable as a means of locomotion for railways, where the outputs required to keep a train rolling are a very great deal lower than those required to get it moving in the first place. Electric motors, like internal combustion engines, have a torque figure that builds fairly steeply from low revolutions, peaks somewhere between one third and a half of the way up the speed range, and declines more or less thereafter. The relationship of these prime characteristics is what most concerns us when deciding the suitability of a motor for a particular application, and it will always be the main factor to consider when selecting an appropriate gear ratio. This makes the whole business sound very complex, which it would be if our model locomotives had to work anywhere as near their ultimate limits as real locomotives do in service. Fortunately, we are almost always going to have at our disposal an excess of power and torque over our strict needs; what we are concerned with is arranging matters so that our motor is running under more or less ideal conditions for most of the time.

I'm not going to go into a great deal of detail on the minutiae of motor performance characteristics. Instead, I'm going to stick to a 'character sketch' of those motors with which I am familiar and have direct experience – which is a fair selection of the currently available types. For the purposes of this book, a generalisation as to their suitability and the determining of an apposite gear ratio are the relevant findings; the various specialist societies publish more detailed data which can be consulted if you find yourself in a particular difficulty. By and large, locomotives that pose really tricky motorisation problems don't come as kits. However, before listing my own assessments, there's a much more general point that I'd like to give an airing to, one which I think we tend to over-look if we get embroiled in too much theory – that of application.

MOTOR APPLICATION

Horses for courses, runs the old cliché – and, like most such trite utterances, it's a truism. So long, that is, as you appreciate the nature of the course. One of the other motor characteristics – beside the power and torque outputs – that we need to consider, is that of heating. Electric motors have no external cooling system (at least, not as we install them they don't), and rely on the flow of air through the gaps surrounding the armature. Obviously, this flow is dependent on motor speed, and if we consistently run a motor under load but at a speed such that there is insufficient airflow for adequate cooling, then trouble is likely to result. On motor data sheets, there is usually a graph containing a shaded area described as the 'Zone of Rapid Heating'. If you consult such sources in respect of popular model railway motors, you will find that this zone often covers the very speeds at which we will want to run our motors during normal operation.

What is rarely put into this particular equation is the time element. If, like Ken Northwood, you are going to expect a loco – such as the '72XX' 2–8–2T mentioned back in Chapter 1 – to run for long periods at a very slow speed, (a scale 15–20 m.p.h.) under considerable load (65 + wagons on 1 in 100 grades), then motor heating becomes of real concern. In fact, in the case described, the boiler top of the '72' becomes too hot to touch after a dozen laps or so. Fortunately, the big Pitman DC66B sitting beneath is a very robust animal that seems able to take such punishment without demur – but try the same trick on a DS10 or some of today's delicate can motors, and the result can be terminal so far as the motor is concerned. Obviously, in the context of a lot of contemporary layouts, where the running is of a far more constricted nature, the effect is never likely to cause a problem. But if you are faced with a situation where you will be calling on a motor to run at a high output for long periods (more than three or four minutes, in this context), then it will be prudent to arrange the gearing so that, at the predominant operating speed of the loco, the motor will be spinning fast enough to keep its cool.

Unfortunately, this cooling requirement is frequently in direct conflict with other desiderata, like keeping the noise level down, and sacrificing power for maximum torque. Generally speaking, low revs equate best with low noise, while the relatively small reduction ratio that serves to keep the motor speed down will also be more efficient. Here is the enormous advantage of the coreless motors, which generate a torque level at or near their maximum figure over a very wide rev range. This enables them to 'make do' with one transmission ratio, a modest 35:1, to cover the entire gamut of duties that they might be called on to perform. These motor/gearbox units also have a very high efficiency, and at full output an RG4/1624 will only be consuming a current of 250MA, around a third of that taken by even a good open-frame motor like the D13, and less than a fifth of the consumption of that hard-worked Pitman in Ken's 72XX. And the current flowing in the armature has a direct bearing on the amount of heat generated, bringing us back to square one.

What rescues us from this drama of conflicting requirements is the general case that, by and large, our model locomotives have a haulage power well in excess of that needed for the type of train that the prototype could manage. In the context of realistic railway operating practice, we should rarely be taxing our motor, which means that we can ignore a lot of these undesirable characteristics and concentrate on extracting the best possible *quality* of running in terms of smoothness and silence. However, one last caveat must be considered, and that is the necessity of ensuring that, under normal conditions, our motor can never stall under load. Put simply we need to make sure that, if the load imposed on the loco by its trains defeats its haulage powers, it does so because the engine 'loses its feet' and slips, and not because the poor old motor can't summon up the grunt to overcome the train resistance; that is the swift road to a nasty niff and a new motor. So, always ensure that you don't ballast a loco to the point where it can't slip even if run up against a stop-block.

An advantage that a properly compensated chassis confers is that the superior grip offered by continuous and consistent wheel-to-rail contact means that you need less weight for a given tractive effort, thus considerably reducing the load on the motor. As an example, my converted-Mainline '57xx' pannier, with a compensated Perseverance chassis powered by a 1620 Sagami driving through a 38:1 gearbox, and an all-up weight of only 180 grams ($6\frac{1}{2}$ ozs) will happily start 25+ wagons up a 1 in 30 gradient – which is a nonsense, as the prototype would have struggled with ten!

The aforementioned Pannier is, in fact, patently 'over motored', and would perform perfectly adequately on something like a 1224 Mashima or even a DS10. It doesn't matter, though – all it means is that the 1620 is never extended, so keeps cool and runs very quietly and smoothly. It's entirely happy in this particular application – but I wouldn't venture it in something like Ken's '72', or any other large, heavy cast-kit loco. Where is the point, when such engines will happily accept bigger and more suitable powerplants such as an Escap RG4 or the 'big brother' Sagami and Mashima 1628 'can' motors? Or even, perhaps, a Pitman DC66 or the very similar KTM DH15? So to sum all this lot up, the rule of thumb comes back to that simplistic 'biggest that will fit', and the converse, resisting the temptation to put in something too small and too puny. I wouldn't put the DS10 in that cast 'S15' (weight 370 grams/13 ozs for loco alone!) – just because it looks easy. Even a whopping great reduction ratio wouldn't

rescue a case like that – and with the 30:1 fitted, the poor little DS10 has a cruel load.

PERFORMANCE CHARACTERISTICS

A few general observations following on from the points raised in the last page or two can suggest the likely performance characteristics of the different types of motor. Firstly, as a rule, the smaller the motor, the lower will be the overall output of power and torque, and the higher the engine revs at which these outputs will peak. The notable exception to this is the Mashima 1224, of which more in a moment. Secondly, the bigger and stronger the magnet, the higher will be the ultimate power output. Thirdly, the larger the overall diameter of the armature (and hence the number of turns and the amount of wire of which it is made up), the higher the torque output. And fourthly, the more 'poles' or 'slots' an armature has, the smoother and more consistent will be its rotation and torque output. There are other, more subtle, design features that affect performance, such as the extent and shaping of the pole-pieces, which determines the nature of the motor's magnetic field, the 'skewing' of armature windings to smooth the path through that field, and the nature and quality of the bearings and brushgear. By and large, the quality and sophistication of motor design are usually reflected in the price, which brings me back once again to my trite summary.

I have dwelt long and in detail on the characteristics that we need to look for in motors, as I have consistently found that the poor quality of running exhibited by so many kitbuilt locos has a lot to do with inappropriate motor choice and poor motor installation. The DJH 'S15' featured on p 107 was incapable of any but a stumbling progress at low speeds, it started like the proverbial jackrabbit, was harsh and noisy at almost any speed, and ran hot into the bargain. A new chassis incorporating a D13, 38:1 gearing and compensation would quite transform it ...

Overpowered Pannier? Re-hashed Mainline '57XX' 5715 has a 1620 Mashima 'can' driving through a Sharman 38:1 gearbox. The motor is very unstressed in this application, giving dividends in quiet, smooth performance at the model's normal operating speeds.

In the context of a kit-based book on chassis design and construction, it is obviously the 'mainstream' motor types that are going to engage our attention. Those few kits that cannot accept the likes of the Mashima 1224 that forms the 'smallest option' of my preferred motor list are likely to be for industrial or narrow-gauge prototypes, where the kit designer will almost certainly have designed the whole thing specifically around one of the ultra-small 'mini motors' now available; with luck, he may even tell you which one it is! So, for my brief 'Who's Who' (or should it be 'What's What?) of motors, I'm sticking to types suited to normal main line prototypes.

A 'WHO'S WHO' OF MOTORS

The brief notes in this section are the result of my own experiences with the motors described. All I'm intending here is to give a broad idea of the strengths and weaknesses of the common types as I have encountered them.

Mashima 1224 (1220 Similar)

This little 'flat can' is a most remarkable motor which 'bucks the trend' in a number of ways. Properly installed, it can give truly excellent performance, and it's my favourite answer for smaller prototypes. It is both powerful and low-revving, the two characteristics most valuable for shunting engines and the like. It has an off-load free-motor speed of only 11,000 r.p.m., and has a remarkable torque output for such a small motor. Having dissected one, I'm not quite sure why it should be so good, as its innards are unremarkable. Among other virtues, it possesses both vertical and horizontal mounting holes on the can-end, while the 1.5mm double-ended hardened steel shaft runs true and has little end-float. The quality of the bearings seems quite adequate, and the motor integrates very well with the excellent Ultrascale 38:1 gearset.

Drawbacks include a certain fragility – it was not unknown for the plastic moulding holding the rear bearing and brushgear to part company from the 'can' on earlier specimens, while it is possible for the fixing screws to contact and damage the front of the armature windings if they're screwed right home without the motor being on a mount. I'm puzzled by the double-ended shaft – I suspect an application in N-gauge American diesels, as for the DS10. Given the low-revving nature of the motor, there's precious little point in sticking a flywheel on it (unlike the DS10), but cutting the shaft back is a tricky business, best undertaken with an abrasive disc in a mini-drill. Don't do it if you don't have to is my advice. The other main problem I've experienced is oil from the rear motor bearing migrating onto the commutator and brushgear, where it can soften the brushes and cause them to disintegrate; this is especially likely to happen where the motor is mounted vertically – I opt for grease lubrication (a tiny spot of 'Tri-Flow') on this lightly-loaded bearing in these circumstances.

There are a number of etched mounts produced for this motor, which I normally modify in my normal heathen manner, described in the installation notes in the next chapter. With the relative abundance of power and, especially, torque produced by the 1224, coupled with the compact dimensions that suit it for so many small engines, there is no need to consider any fancy gear drives for this motor (unless you're Mike Sharman insinuating it into some Crampton with 8ft 6in driving wheels), and I have found that the straightforward 38:1 set-up already mentioned is all that is needed – for an explanation of this, see the notes on 'Choosing Gear Ratios'. It deserves to be a lot more popular than it is, and I now fit it in preference to the DS10 in very many instances, for all that it's smaller. In this particular case, the dimensions give the lie to the performance.

The DS10

This goes under several aliases, depending upon whom you buy it from. It comes out of the same factory in Japan, I'm told, as the Mashima motors, and it certainly has many features in common with them. As already mentioned, it started out powering N gauge Yankee diesels, which explains its double-ended configuration and that long, thin (1.5mm dia.) and over-whippy shaft, which was intended to locate into plastic universal joints driving gear-towers atop the bogies of an EMD SD40. As far as I'm concerned it was most certainly *not* designed to have a fine-pitch (60:1 often suggested) worm-gear hung on the end of so wayward a wand, a trick which British kit designers are oddly fond of; I've found the results are less than ideal, and the life of the motor-bearings (never designed to resist the sort of sidethrust generated by a worm-and-pinion gearset) short.

Take the trouble to understand the DS10's foibles, though, and it makes a useful little motor, the more so as it's a vital couple of mm slimmer than the 1224 Mashima, and hence will fit between frames (OO frames, mainly) that are too tight-waisted for that canned paragon. The DS10 is essentially the right shape to suit a very many smaller prototypes, hence its great popularity; but its performance characteristics are not so clever, and take a little accommodating. The off-load speed, at around 22,000 r.p.m., is double that of the 1224, and the peak torque figure of around 10,500 revs is also a bit on the high side. The DS10, like the 1224, can run pretty hot, but it takes a lot less load to cause the condition, and the revs needed to keep it cool don't make for a peaceful ride. Generally speaking, this is not a motor to fit if you need a high tractive effort; even with sky-high gearing, in my experience it's never really happy under high loadings, while the rather skimpy nature of its bearings and the lightweight frame make for a lot of noise at high revs. Far better to put it in a lightly-loaded application where you can gear it for modest speeds because you aren't bent on extracting a lot of output from it. I'd have no hesitation, for instance, in using a DS10 in something like a '14XX' to haul an auto-trailer, where it would be quite happy with the good old Ultrascale 38:1 gearset that bids fair to become a 'standard fit' these days.

You have to install the DS10 'right' if it is to perform properly – which means recognising the inherent unsuitability of that thin shaft for worm-gear drives; position the worm as close as possible to the motor front bearing, and if this can't be done, arrange some additional bearing support for the shaft close to the gear. Rod Neep recognised this necessity when he designed the Perseverance mount for this motor, which incorporates an 'outboard' bearing to stiffen it all up. If you are calling for a bit more than the sort of minimal 'oomph' suggested from a DS10, it may pay to fit 50:1 gears and a flywheel, which helps to smooth the output at the higher revs that will be involved. For reasons that I'll come on to in the next chapter, I don't like going above 50:1 reduction in one step, and I'm convinced that hanging ultra-fine 60:1 worm-and-pinion sets on as thin a shaft as the DS10's, on a motor with a weak torque output, is about as sensible as cruising a motor-mower up a motorway.

The D11

As with other motors originally imported under the Anchoridge label, the D11 now appears under differing codes from various sources. It is not a motor I like – as far as I'm concerned, it's leagues behind the 1224 Mashima. I have found its torque disappointing and those I've tried have run hot at slow speeds. It seems to draw more current than I would expect for so small a unit, and I regard it as harsh and noisy. Its principal virtue is that it is very easy to mount, having twin tapped holes 8.5mm apart on the bottom plate. It also has a monstrous long shaft sticking the better part of an inch out of the front bearing, a legacy of its original design installation, which I believe was in an early Japanese brass HOn3 model of a Rio Grande C-36 2–8–0. In this loco, the motor sat back in the firebox (which, in best Yankee tradition, was *inside* the cab), and drove the second coupled axle via a chunky cast gearbox. It did *not* have a naked worm-and-pinion gearset waving around on the end of it a country mile from any bearing support, a temptation British modellers and kit designers seem unable to resist.

The D13

Given that the D13 is very closely related to the D11, even to the extent of sharing front frame/bearing/brushgear assembly and cross-sectional dimensions with it, it may seem surprising that I am as enthusiastic about the one as I am dismissive of the other. The D13 is 6.2mm longer than the D11, split roughly 50/50 between a longer armature and a bigger magnet. The difference is of proverbial chalk-and-cheddar proportions. The D13 has peak revs some 5,000

Doing it right by the DS10. Properly installed, as here in Robin Arkinstall's GER 'Y14', this motor gives a very good account of itself. Robin used an Anchoridge cast mount and Romford 40:1 gears in this Gibson-kit built loco, which was a regular performer on the old East Suffolk Light Railway layout.

r.p.m. below the D11, produces over 30% more torque at a correspondingly lower speed, consumes less current, and is generally smooth and quiet. Unlike the D11, it has but a single tapped mounting hole, but otherwise design detail and construction are identical. The D13 has 19mm or so of shaft – as with the D11, of 2mm diameter ground centreless silver steel – protruding from the front bearing, for, I'm pretty certain, an original installation similar to that of the D11, probably in the bigger K-37 2–8–2. Both the D11 and D13 are usefully narrow – 10.5mm over the magnet/frame assembly, 11.3mm maximum over the armature.

D13 drawbacks? Not too many, really. The motor frame can go 'out of true', causing a certain stiffness in the bearings. A good tweak in the appropriate direction usually puts that right. The other main point to watch is the rather exposed nature of the windings where they are led out to the commutator – I've had a couple of D13s killed by these connections being caught, ripping windings from the armature. A rather dated design feature that can tell against these motors is that only one brush is insulated, leaving the motor frame (and hence the rest of the chassis in which it is installed) 'live' to the opposing pole. This can be a real nuisance in some circumstance – you need to think very carefully about which way round and up you install this motor, or you can end up with a loco that insists on going the opposite way to the rest of your stud. There is a further point in relation to the brushes that is worth bearing in mind, not just on the D13 but also on the various other motors sharing this type of 'sprung plunger' brushgear, and that is the necessity of avoiding corrosion to the brush spring. These are wound from very fine phosphor-bronze wire, and if the connection from the pick-ups is soldered in place on the brush housing using an acid flux, either stray flux or flux fumes can enter the housing and corrode the spring to the housing or, in extreme cases, cause the spring to disintegrate. If you have a D13 that ceases to work after some months, suspect this cause; replace the brush, holder and spring (spares are available), and try again. Better still, fit wiring tags as on the DS10, 1224, etc., and avoid the problem in the first place. If you must solder to the brusholder – only ever necessary on the insulated brush, anyway – use a resin flux or cored solder.

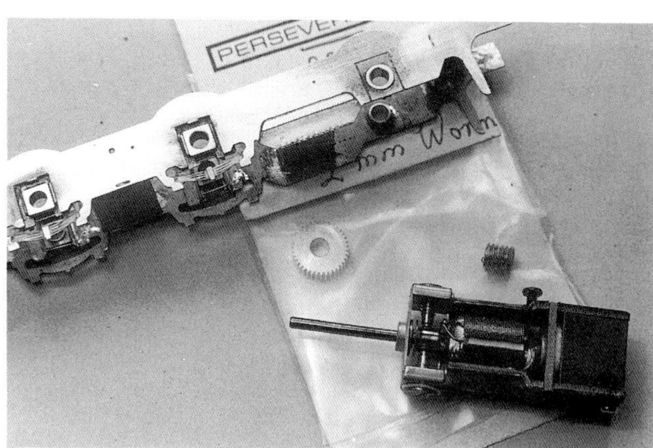

The 'D13' was the chosen motor for the guinea-pig '57XX' chassis, mounted direct to the frames and driving through the Perseverance version of the Ultrascale 38:1 gearset.

The D13's slender hips would permit a low-down, between-the-frames, mounting such as this in a OO version of this chassis – a real boon.

Sagami 1425

As with all can motors, this is simply and unconfusingly classified by the dimensions of the actual 'can' – 14mm diameter × 25mm long. This motor isn't as widely available in the U.K. as most of the others, though it can be had with a little effort – see the 'sources' index. It's worth the effort, and I rate this as one of the very best motors for 4mm locos, with an almost ideal combination of dimensions, power output, high torque and smooth running. Of the nine of my own locos sitting on the shelf beside me as I write this, five of them have 1425 power; the rest would have if it would fit! Only for biggish engines do I normally look to anything larger.

The 1425 has tapped holes in the front of the can at the standard 10mm centres, shared with the larger 1620/1628 types and with the DS10. They can all be mounted on fold-up mounts sold for this latter type, although they will lose the boss location afforded the DS10. If you don't fancy a bodged fold-up mount, the 1425 has two tapped holes on its longitudinal axis as well, and can be 'conventionally' mounted. Shaft diameter, at 1.5mm, is common to the DS10 and 1224 Mashima, and, once again, the Ultrascale 38:1 gearset is an ideal companion. In terms of power output, the 1425 slots in neatly between the D13 and the big 16mm cans; the torque figure seems closer to a 1620 than to the D13. The 1425 is also relatively low-revving, and produces useful outputs right where we need them. Current consumption is modest – a tad less than a D13 at around 600MA on full load – and the 1425 generally runs fairly cool. It is also notably smooth and quiet – a characteristic that seems particularly associated with motors that are relatively 'long and thin'; the 1224, 1425, D13 and 1628 types all seem to compare favourably with 'squarer' designs like the DS10, D11 and 1620.

Sagami 1425, remote-mounted on a rubber pad, fitted with a rather pointless flywheel (not enough revs!), and driving through a Mk I Sharman 38:1 gearbox in a chassis for a Mallard GWR '517' in EM.

Sagami 1620. (Mashima 1620/Anchoridge TA10 very similar)

This is, dimensionally speaking, another very useful motor, having the virtue of brevity, which enables it to be up-ended in the firebox of a great many locos. I use it a good deal these days, and find it powerful and very torquey, although not as sweet as either the 1425 or the bigger 1628. Shaft diameter is 2mm, using high-quality ground and centreless hardened steel. 1620s normally come in double-ended format, which is a bit of a pain if you're bent on mounting the thing vertically in a firebox, which calls for the shaft to be cut off close to the rear motor bearing. Take care to keep swarf away from the bearing, and use an abrasive disc in a mini-drill; these shafts are *seriously* hard, and eye protection should be worn when cutting, as disintegrating discs are not unknown! Fortunately, as with all these Sagami 'cans', the motor is fully enclosed and protected, so there's no danger of debris entering the 'works'. Unlike the 1425, the 1620 has mounting holes only on the front of the 'can', and I either fit it to a modified DS10, mount, or install a gearbox, such as Exactoscale's 40:1 type, directly on the shaft or remotely.

This is a low-revving motor, and is happy producing the sort of outputs we need at really very slow motor speeds. On small-wheeled locos, I have used 30:1 gearing and obtained plenty of haulage power with very quiet running. It is efficient, taking only around 500MA on full load, and runs reasonably cool, although all these fully-enclosed cans – with the exception of the coreless types – tend to run a bit 'warm'; they lose heat more by radiation from the can (hence the usual matt-black finish) than by air circulation through the motor innards. The only real drawback with the 1620 – shared with other 16mm diameter 'cans' – is that it is too portly to fit between the frames of even EM and P4 chassis, while it won't go between the *wheels* in OO. It is thus sometimes difficult to mount with a straightforward direct gear drive to an axle, and may call for either a remote gearbox and transmission shaft, as in the case of the '14XX' chassis illustrated, or for some form of step-down gear-train to get it above the frames or wheelsets, rather as is done by the RG4 set-up.

Mashima 1628

This also goes under the ex-Anchoridge appellation of 'TA12'. There is an exact Sagami equivalent which, for some reason, seems rarely to make it to these shores, and I would expect this to turn in an equivalent performance to this Mashima canned powerhouse. This is 4mm super-power, and in my book, the combination of one of these big 'cans' and a high-quality gearbox such as Exactoscale's or the milled-brass Sharman gives a finer quality of running even than the much-vaunted RG4. A well set-up worm-and-pinion transmission in a good, rigid mounting of the sort offered by such gearboxes is inherently quieter than the largish collection of whirring spurs in the RG4, and while the 1628 Mashima may not equal the daunting torque output of an Escap or Falhauber coreless equivalent, it produces more than enough for all practical purposes. I am not alone in this preference – most of Alan Ketley's big engines, including the '9F' and 'Merchant Navy' featured in my *Whitemetal Locos* book, are powered thus, and have long been regarded as bench-marks of running quality.

The only real drawback of the 1628 is that common to all these 16mm diameter cans, and noted in my comments on the 1620; their relatively generous girth can make for mounting difficulties. The 1628 Mashima normally arrives, praise be, in a single-ended format, obviating the need for shaft-cropping. Like the 1620, it is designed for can-end mounting, with the standard 10mm screw centres and the same 2mm shaft diameter. The other main difference is that the plastic can rear is screw-fitted on the 1628, rather than being held with turn-down lugs as on the smaller cans. This means you can get at the brushes much more easily for cleaning or replacement should the need arise.

It goes without saying that the outputs, like those of a Rolls-Royce engine, are 'adequate'; it is all but impossible to stop the shaft from rotating with the fingers even at 'just off the stop' motor speeds, while further Rolls-like qualities are evident in the almost total lack of noise and vibration, even at full revs. Not that these are many, for the 1628 is another low-revving unit, and is quite happy driving through gears of modest reduction ratio, to the great benefit of both noise and overall efficiency. This is reflected in very low current consumption under normal working, and in a cool-running motor – remarkably so for an enclosed type.

CORELESS MOTOR/GEARBOXES

These arrived in the late 1970s, and immediately took over from high-quality conventional designs like the Pitman at the top of the market. They differ fundamentally from a 'conventional' iron-cored motor (the 'iron core' being the iron or steel laminations making up the armature pole-pieces) in that, rather than deriving their power from an armature revolving more-or-less *within* a magnetic field, the armature is hollow and revolves *about* a magnet contained within it. This makes for far greater efficiency, a very high torque output, and ultra-smooth power delivery, owing to the fact that there is no 'magnetic locking' caused by individual armature poles entering and leaving the magnetic field. The low relative mass of the moving parts keeps

The 1620 cans are very amenable to vertical mounting in Belpaire fireboxes. This is a Sagami 1620 sitting on top of a Sharman Mk II gearbox in my 'J17' (scratchbuilt, but this works well in kit chassis).

The chassis of my 'J15' has a Sagami 1425 direct-mounted to a vintage Sharman milled-brass gearbox. This 14mm diameter motor is, as can be seen, an easy fit between the frames in EM or P4; it will go between OO wheels, but not frames.

noise and vibration very low, but also results in a bearing system that is not able to take side-thrust.

It was this characteristic of the bearings which rendered coreless motors unsuitable for use with conventional model railway worm-and-pinion transmissions (which, as we shall see, develop considerable side-thrust loads). Until Ken Pelham developed the RG4 bevel-and-spur gearbox, few coreless motors found their way into model railway locos, although the Americans were using them successfully with separate worm gearboxes, where the side loadings were taken by the gearbox. The RG4 design also addressed the mounting problem by utilising a 'vertical' geartrain that put the 16mm diameter motors well up above the frames and clear of all but the largest driving wheels. An 'inline' version of this transmission never caught on, and has now been discontinued.

There are three 'coreless' motors retailed on the British model railway market, one employing a 12mm diameter Swiss 'Minimotor' and the other two using 16mm diameter Escap units. All three use the same 35:1 geartrain, although the 1219 has a 'lower' configuration to bring the axle centre/motor shaft height down to a dimension more suited to small-boilered engines. The 'after market' has latched on to the fact that the RG4 geartrain can be re-arranged into a number of different configurations to suit different types of locomotive, and alternative RG4 gearbox side-cheeks are now widely available; they are even incorporated into some kits.

RG4/1219

This is the 'baby' of the range, using the compact 12 × 19mm 'Minimotor'. While exhibiting all the traditional coreless virtues of high torque across a wide speed range, very high efficiency (up to 85%), ultra-low current consumption (around 150MA on full load) and a very smooth output, the 1219 is, in my experience, prone to a couple of notable shortcomings. The first of these is really an 'external' problem, in that I've found the 1219 demands a very 'smooth' power supply to provide good running. This is because the very low inertia of the lightweight outer-rotor armature enables it to accelerate or decelerate extremely rapidly, while the high efficiency and low-current characteristics also mean that a relatively small fluctuation in the supply can result in quite a marked change in motor speed. I found it difficult to get really steady low-speed running with the 1219 when used in conjunction with many controllers, especially feedback designs like the AMR or Compspeed. To get the best out of this motor, I think it's best to use a controller designed to accommodate it, such as Stewart Hine's 'Pentroller'. The popular hand-held version of this incorporates a 3-position output setting switch covering 12mm and 16mm coreless motors as well as conventional iron-cored types.

The second drawback is not unrelated to the first, in that the minimal nature of the armature and the ultra-low current consumption enable these coreless motors to employ very tiny precious-metal commutators and minute wire-wiper brushgear. The current-carrying capacity of these components is *very* low, and they will self-destruct well below the levels at which most controllers are designed to shut down in response to an overload. So, should your 1219 stall under load, for whatever reason, the chances are it will fry before you realise anything is wrong – no joke at thirty-odd

Coreless power – an RG4/1616 Escap, here installed in the chassis of a Vulcan 'Drewry' shunter kit (now available from Alan Gibson). A clear excess of power over requirement! Note the height of the motor above the frames.

A 'Big Portescap' – RG4/1624 in the embryo chassis of the DJH 'West Country'. The RG4 will clear 6ft 6in wheels in OO with Romford flanges.

The rather inflexible layout of the RG4 mounting system has led to a thriving range of after-market 'alternative configurations'. Here, a standard RG4/1219 is compared with the same motor on an MJT 'configuration 1' gearbox, designed to put the gears under the cab floor and the motor in the firebox. The only snag with these is that your guarantee goes out of the window once you dismantle the factory gearbox.

pounds a time! Again, the answer is to use a controller designed to protect such a motor, with suitable current-limiting circuitry. That Pentroller again ... It is also important to realise that coreless motors do not have infinite power, just higher levels than similarly-sized conventional motors. The 1219 is a small motor for lightly-loaded applications and not really suitable for the likes of Westward's cast '28XX'2–8–0.

RG4 1616/1624

The two 'Big Portescaps' come on the same gearbox, being the original 1978 design. They are now firmly established as the 'best fit', and a lot of kits are being designed around them these days. The 1624 was, for instance, the recommended motor for the DJH 'West Country' that features from time-to-time in these pages; an eminently suitable application. To be quite honest, I can never detect a lot of difference between them, and for all practical purposes, either has more than ample power and torque for any 4mm scale loco. I suppose the 1624 must deliver more 'grunt' than the 1616, but it's almost irrelevant. Like a very fast car on a typically British slow road, the ultimate performance is of no consequence, as you can't exploit it.

Apart from the desirable output characteristics already described, all these motor/gearboxes have a further outstanding virtue, that of ease of use. All the difficult stuff is done for you – just install on the driven axle, tighten a grubscrew and – Bingo! Superpower in seconds. I suspect that this is one of the main reasons for the outstanding success of these units, which are not without their drawbacks. Drawbacks? Well, for a start, they cost getting on for twice as much as a conventional motor and separate transmission, and even with the 'alternative configuration' gearboxes, they are a bit inflexible in the matter of installation. The actual gearbox, while of high quality and efficiency (around 65%), can be noisy, and is susceptible to entry by dirt and foreign bodies. And, while the 1616 and 1624 are not as fragile as the 1219, they still need proper protection and suitable control systems to keep them safe and sweet.

I suspect that for most people, the use of an RG4 gives them a better chance of obtaining high quality of running than trying to optimise the setting-up of something like the big Mashima. At the end of the day, it will often come down to a fiscal equation; can you afford Portescap power, and do you consider it worth the extra? Impecunious skinflints like Rice think one thing; a lot of others think RG4 and never consider any other alternative. Oh, yes, one last snippet – the name. The RG4 bit is actually the *gearbox* (reduction gearbox, 4mm scale – there's an RG7 for O gauge use) – the motor description follows normal 'can' designation by dimensions, although Portescap themselves sometimes code them 'C' (1616) and 'M' (1624). Don't ask me why.

MOTOR PREPARATION

Modellers have a tendency to simply stick motors straight into loco chassis without checking them over and setting them up first, which has never struck me as a particularly bright idea. Quite apart from the reluctance of suppliers to take back faulty motors that have had shafts cut short or brackets soldered onto them, it's pretty frustrating to spend ages trying to track down a chassis fault that turns out to be down to a dicky motor. And, like all such mechanisms, motors benefit from a bit of gentle running-in under 'free' conditions before being asked to turn over a brand-new and probably very 'stiff' chassis. When in haste, I've occasionally skipped motor preparation, but somehow the resulting loco never seems to run quite as well as when I take the trouble – and in one or two cases it has ceased to run at all due to premature motor failure.

What you can do varies from motor to motor, but I start by looking the thing over. On open-frame motors, I'm looking to ensure that the frame is square and true, and that the bearings are in line. I also check that the magnet is healthy (small screwdriver, pulled away), that there is no corrosion, that the brushgear is present, correct and clear of obstruction, and that there is no obvious damage to armature windings. On can types, it's not so easy to check these factors, but I do look for excessive bearing play or end float, and check that the plastic rear plate of the can is secure. Once I'm happy that it's all, as far as can be seen, present and correct, then I oil the bearings lightly with clock oil (J. D. Windle's, first prize and medal, Paris Exposition, 1867, 'warranted not to thicken or corrode' – probably no better than any other clock oil, but I *love* the label), and try the thing under power. It probably won't start too easily, or run really slowly, but it *should* run without excessive vibration or noise. It is quite likely that there will be some sparking at the brushes, while if you have an ammeter in the circuit, you'll see fluctuations in the current drawn. Fear not, 'tis only a want of some bedding-in of the brushgear.

RUNNING IN

Almost any motor (except possibly the coreless types) will benefit from some careful running-in. Make sure that the bearings are lubricated (it has never ceased to amaze me that some modellers see a virtue in running bearings – motor, axle, or crankpin – 'dry'), and, if necessary, solder on some pick-up leads, noting the precautions described when discussing the D13 if you're dealing with plunger brushes. Mount the motor on a blob of Plasticine or Blu-tak on the bench, clip on the power leads from a controller, and set the motor running at the slowest speed that it will comfortably maintain. Let it be for about five minutes, checking from time to time that it is not getting too warm. After five minutes, allow it to cool if need be, then reverse the controller, and give it five minutes widdershins. Once again, check the temperature, let it cool a bit, then crank the controller up a notch or so and repeat the process. Keep going until you've given it a total of about 20 minutes in each direction. Then set it to about half-speed and give it a quarter of an hour each way. That usually does the trick – if you do have an ammeter, you'll notice the current consumption dropping steadily as the brushes bed in, while it will start running cooler and probably quieten down into the bargain. I often run-in the motor while I'm fitting the wheels and rods, quartering the chassis and installing the final drive gears; there's a nicely complementary feel about combining the two activities. Once the motor is run in, the chassis and geartrain should be ready to receive it. Geartrain? On to Chapter 10.

CHAPTER TEN

DRIVETRAINS: PART 2 – TRANSMISSIONS

'A noisome, loathsome thing – the work of the very devil'. I think that was Dr. Johnson disapproving of something – or was it Samuel Pepys on a piece of music he didn't like? Even if I can't recall precisely who said it about what, it does sum up very nicely the sort of transmission arrangement that so many model locomotives are saddled with; a miniature worm-and-pinion needs to be understood and properly set up if it is to be anything other than 'noisome and loathsome'. Getting the gearset properly installed and accurately meshed will do more than any other single thing to give your loco a sweet-running mechanism, while failings in this respect will negate the smoothest of motors or the most free-running of chassis. Gears of poor quality, or good gears badly meshed, give rise to a great many of the most common ills to which our small-scale model locomotives are prone – uneven running, especially at low speed; high levels of friction, leading to motor stress; distortion of frames and overloading of motor bearings; and, not least – noise! Horrible rumblings, grindings, graunching, buzzing and screeching – there is almost no aural unpleasantness that lies beyond the compass of an abused wormgear.

WORM GEAR CHARACTERISTICS

As with the motors and their properties, it is of considerable help when trying to get the best out of worm-and-pinion gearsets to understand the whys and wherefores of their workings. Only once you are aware of the factors that affect – usually critically – the functioning of these gears can you hope to design an installation using them, or decide why the set-up the kit has provided is failing to produce the desired results. The fundamental engineering rules which need to be followed to ensure the proper working of these gears are actually simple and straightforward, but I cannot stress too much that these *are* fundamental; ignore them and the result is inevitably compromised.

The basic principle of the worm-and-pinion is quite straightforward. By rotating a threaded spiral rod (the worm) in mesh with teeth of appropriate pitch around the circumference of a gearwheel (the pinion) it is possible to simultaneously transfer a drive through 90° and provide a very considerable degree of reduction. This reduction is expressed as a ratio, so that a gearset of 30:1 will require the 'input shaft', carrying the worm, to rotate 30 times for one rotation of the 'output shaft' carrying the pinion. There are a considerable number of other variables involved, including the skew angle of the teeth and the exact spiral pitch of the worm, the tooth profile, the area in contact at any given time, and the 'tolerance' of the gearset as a whole. Fortunately, with the exception of the last-named, all the other variables affecting worm gear drives are the province of the gear-designer and manufacturer.

Worm gears are capable of transmitting high levels of power and torque with great precision and in near-silence if properly installed. They generally have low levels of 'backlash', or free play between the spiral thread of the worm and the teeth of the pinion. One of the factors that enables worm gears to transmit high torque levels is the substantial contact area between the worm thread and pinion teeth, and the progressive manner in which the drive is transferred from one pinion tooth to another as the gears rotate; this property also gives the exceptional smoothness of transmission that makes worm gears capable of producing really steady running, especially at low speeds of rotation. Other advantages enjoyed by the worm drive include compactness – especially where 'single-start' worms are used (universally, in current model railway applications), ease of lubrication, and relative cheapness.

However, on the 'no such thing as a free lunch' principle, worm-and-pinion gears also have some notable drawbacks. The generous contact area that enables them to transmit high torque has a pay-off in high levels of friction, and this in turn leads to considerable reaction through the gearset. Put simply, this means that the worm gear is constantly trying to climb out of mesh with the pinion, and thus has to be restrained by very firm and precise location of the input shaft. These friction levels and the corresponding reaction vary in direct relationship to the overall reduction ratio of the gears, which are anyway inherently pretty inefficient. A good 30:1 gearset might transmit 35% of the applied power; raise the ratio to 60:1, and the efficiency can plummet to not much better than 15%. Install the gears badly enough, and the efficiency will decline to nil as the gears bind up solid!

There is a further reactive load generated by worm-and-pinion gears that we need to accommodate. For, as well as trying to climb out of the bed with the pinion, the worm is also trying to travel around its circumference. It can't do this, of course, but the result is that there is a force generated in line with the worm, acting in the opposite direction to the rotation of the pinion. This is 'end thrust', and the bearings of the input shaft need to be designed to resist such additional loading. This can be done either by using 'thrust bearings' on the ends of the shaft, or by placing bearings either side of the gear, against which the gear can act. This is one of the principal advantages of self-contained gear-boxes which, if they're properly designed, will absorb all these reactive loads with minimal friction. However, we're often stuck with the use of the motor shaft as our transmission input shaft, so if we are intending to mount worm-gears direct, we need to be sure that the motor bearings are designed to cope with these forces.

Very small errors in the spacing and alignment of worm-and-pinion gearsets have a very substantial effect on the functioning of the gears, and this is the most critical aspect of their use so far as we railway modellers are concerned. The input and output shafts of a worm gear set must be installed *exactly* at right-angles, and precisely the right distance apart to optimise the meshing of the gears. The pinion must be truly concentric, as any ovality will drastically affect this correct meshing – one of the most common causes of unsteady slow-speed running of model locomotives; the same, obviously, goes for the worm, and also for the shaft on which it is mounted. Both input and output shafts *must* be absolutely rigid, and fully and solidly supported by adequate bearings. In other words, the main drawbacks of the worm and pinion gearset are more to do with the rather exacting conditions needed to install the thing successfully than with the actual gears themselves.

There are a couple of further engineering tennets connected with the proper design of worm-and-pinion gearsets that must be observed if they are to give satisfactory service. The first is another fundamental of bearing and gear design practice, which states that where frictional loading occurs between rotating components, then these should be of different metals. In the case of lightly loaded gears such as ours, we could probably ignore that constraint (Tri-ang did for years), but in the context of finer gears, it's most desirable. All the Romford and Ultrascale sets use steel worms and brass pinions, which is fine. Exactoscale go one better, with a phosphor-bronze pinion, theoretically an even lower-friction combination. The second engineering problem is the means by which the gears are mounted to the shafts, where the pure mechanical

Fig. 10:1 PROPERTIES AND CRITERIA, WORM GEARS

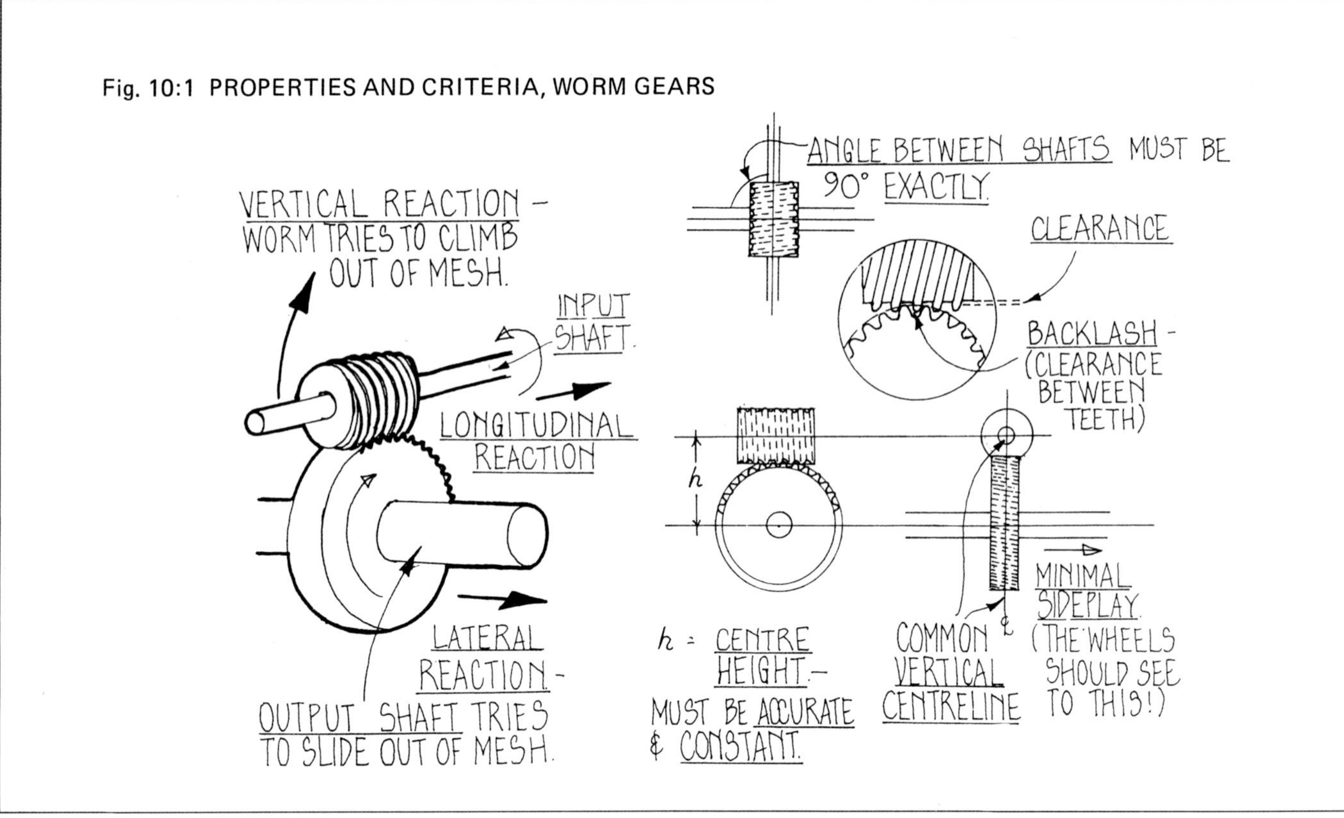

considerations must be balanced against ease of use. Traditionally, ease-of-use always won, with grubscrew mounting being preferred in spite of the concentricity problems that can arise, discussed in a page or so in the 'installation' notes. In the context of the finer-pitch, close-tolerance gears now coming into use, such practice is no longer acceptable, and so many more recent gear designs use a 'Loctite' fit, also covered under 'installation'.

The particular properties and drawbacks listed above are specific to the worm-and-pinion gearset, and are not shared by other types of gears such as bevels and spurs. The worm-gears that we use for our railway models represent, at best, a fairly broad compromise, but our common need for compactness and relatively high reduction ratios have rather dictated the choice. It is that high reduction ratio, needed to make sense of our high-revving miniature motors, that has meant that the gears we use have a pitch angle that prevents torque reversal through our transmission – our worm-gears only work one way. The coarse pitch, wide-angle 18:1 worm gears that served Hornby-Dublo so well have far less inhibition in this respect – but few modern motors can approach the sort of towering torque output of a low-revving Hornby, especially the ring-field design. It's a bit like comparing the engine of a vintage Bentley with the 16-valve turbocharged whizz-wonder in a contemporary 'hot hatchback'. In many ways, we're making the best of a bad job, in that the type of motor we need to use forces on us a rather tricky transmission. It's interesting to note that the R-T-R mass-market has tended to move away from the traditional longitudinal motor/worm drive arrangement in recent years, preferring to revert to the much earlier set-up of a large-diameter, face-commutator motor across the chassis, with a drive of coarse-pitched plastic spur gears of minimal reduction ratio. That must have the wraith of old Airchie Stewart-Riedpath, progenitor of the type, chuckling in the ether, while long-term advocates of the scheme such as Stewart Hine may permit themselves a few self-satisfied smiles!

However, I don't think even Stewart would claim that the face-comm. motor and spur drive system would suit all prototypes, and it is anyway only an option for those people who, like Stewart, have the necessary skill and expertise to design and build their own drivetrains from scratch. The only true alternative to the worm-drive transmission for the rest of us lies within the smartly-blackened side cheeks of an RG4 gearbox, should we be able and disposed to acquire same. There is a sort of 'halfway house' that I shall touch on, where the need to use very high-reduction worm gearsets can be avoided by combining a spur-gear stage of, say, 2:1 with a worm final drive. Thus, ratios such as 60 or 80:1 can be arrived at with 30 or 40:1 worm sets, to the benefit of overall efficiency and less criticality in the installation, but often, it must be said, with the penalty of increased noise levels. This sort of multi-stage gear set-up is very definitely the province of Mike Sharman and if you're interested in such arrangements, his booklet '*Gear Fitting – For the Small Scale Modeller with No Workshop*' (!) is recommended reading. *Having* a workshop does not, apparently, preclude you from perusing a copy . . .

INSTALLING WORM GEARS

I have described the basic properties of worm-and-pinion gears in some detail, and now I would like to relate those properties to the type of gear installation that best suits a kit-built loco chassis. While it is obviously possible, given the time, skill and determination, to engineer almost any type of transmission into a modern chassis using etched sideframes, the older solid blocks are far more limiting in this respect. This is at once their virtue and their downfall – the virtue being that a well-designed, well-made solid chassis should give you very firm and accurate motor and axle location, both essential for successful worm gear installation; the downfall is that, if the thing isn't well-designed or well-made, there's not an awful lot you can do about it! With a careful choice of components, however, almost any etched chassis can be set up to give a transmission that is on a par with the very best of solid block chassis, while the wide possibilities for selecting motors and gearing to suit an application are in stark contrast to the 'one motor type, one gear ratio' option that solid blocks afford. It's not hard to see why the etched chassis is in the ascendant.

The possibilities for motor/gear installations in model locos can be divided into three basic categories: direct mounted gears, axle-hung motor; direct-mounted gears, chassis-mounted motor; and indirect-mounted gears. However, it is important to appreciate that all these alternatives have to take full cognisance of the fundamental requirements of the worm gears, so will need to incorporate the basic engineering solutions that best provide for those requirement.

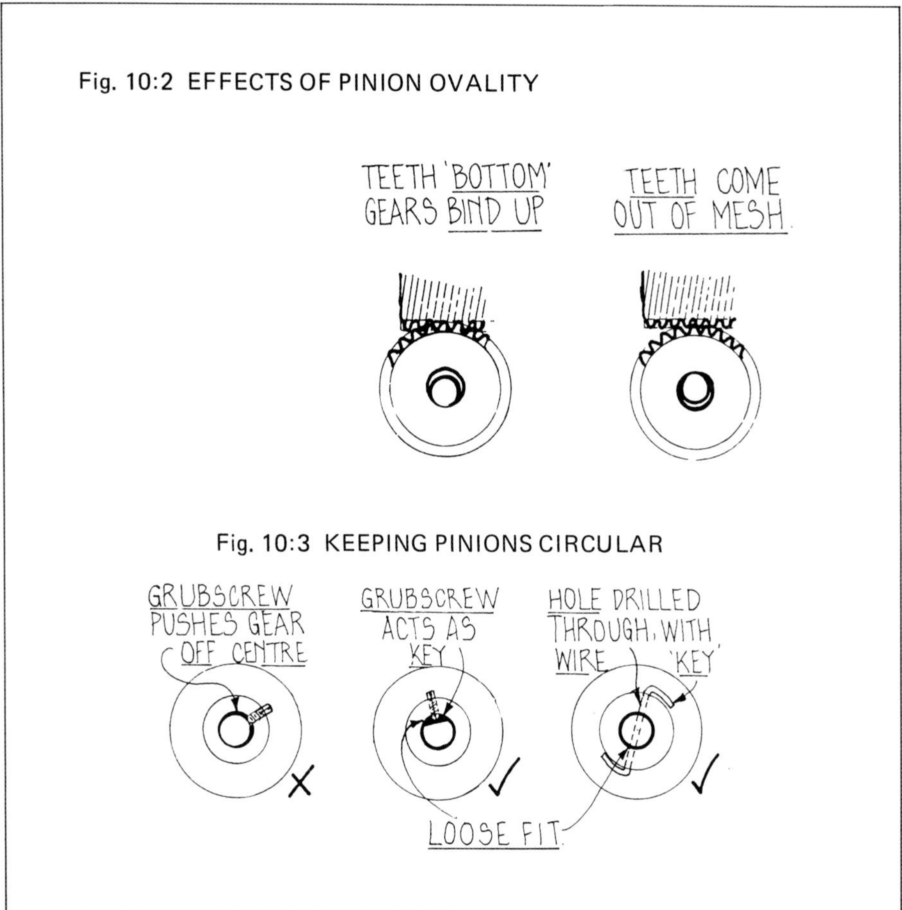

FITTING GEARS TO SHAFTS

No matter whether your gears are to be mounted directly to the motor, or indirectly in some form of gearbox, they still need to be properly installed on their respective shafts. Concentricity is the name of the game, and that means a very exact fit. When we're considering close-tolerance fine-pitch gears such as Ultrascale's popular 38:1 or the higher-reduction Romfords, an error of only a few thou in ovality is more than enough to 'gum up the works', given that the backlash and clearance will be of a similar order. Get the gear 'out of round' by an amount equivalent to, or greater than, the actual clearance between the tip of the worm thread and the bottom of the slot in the pinion, and you've got real trouble – the gear will bind-up enough to stop rotation. The same effect can occur if the bearings supporting the shaft have play in them, or if the shaft itself can 'whip'. This is why motors designed to take worm gears need good, solid, close-tolerance bearings firmly located, and shafts of substantial diameter made from hardened steel.

The traditional means of mounting gears onto shafts has been by means of grubscrews, which is pretty bad engineering in this context. The reason is that a grubscrew, tightened hard against a shaft within a gear (which it must be if any drive is to take place) will inevitably push the gear off centre by the amount of difference between the shaft diameter and the internal size of the gear boss. And, if the gear is not to be a force fit on the shaft (which would make the grubscrew redundant anyway), then there *must* be some clearance, even if only a thou or two, to enable the gear to slide onto the shaft. The trouble is that, by tightening the grubscrew to take up this clearance, the gear is forced tight up against the shaft on the side opposite the screw, hence the eccentricity. You may not think 1 or 2 thou would affect things, but a moment's consideration will show that the error amounts to twice the offset, and that *is* significant. Given that there is a manufacturing tolerance of plus or minus a thou or two in the making of gears and axles, if you're unlucky you can end up with a pinion gear running 10 thou or so 'out' – and that'll foul up even relatively coarse-pitch worms such as the Romford 40:1. Look out for the 'tight spot' every revolution.

Proper engineering design overcomes these problems by using gear retention systems that act concentrically around the shaft, or by providing 'keyways' to transfer the drive from shaft to gear. We can adapt both these approaches to get a better mounting for our model gears, by either using a retention compound such as 'Loctite', or by providing 'flats' on shafts for our grubscrews to bear on. 'Loctite' has the property of running around inside a joint by capillary action before 'going off', and will thus centre a gear as well as retain it. This is the mounting system preferred for fine-pitch gears such as the Ultrascale type mentioned (they do other ratios, intended for a similar mounting system, but the 38:1 is the one that figures in kits), and for the gears included in gearboxes like the Exactoscale. It is also the only practicable alternative to the grubscrews for the majority of worm gears, as you won't get far trying to file a 'flat' on a hardened steel motor shaft!

It's in the fit of grubscrew gears to axles that we have the biggest problem. With the wide 'boss' needed for the grubscrew, it's not possible to offset these while Loctite is introduced, as suggested for the Ultrascale gears and illustrated hereabouts. You can saw the bosses off (I've done it), but a better idea is to file a flat on the axle to take the grubscrew; most axles are only mild steel, so a sharp square or triangular needle file will do the business. I make the flat just wide enough for the grubscrew, so that the rest of the gear is sitting on full-diameter axle. When I'm fitting the gear in place, I screw the grubscrew hard down into the flat, then back it off by half-a-turn, giving a little bit of play that will enable the gear to self-centre on the axle. Once the gear is finally installed, I retain the grubscrew setting with a spot of 242 Nutlock. This is effective for most of the Romford gears up to the 50:1, and for reasons already given I steer well clear of the ultra-critical 60:1 anyway.

Loctite fitting of gears is very simple, and highly effective. I know it seems incredible that a mere drop of blue fluid can both centre a gear on a shaft and lock it immovably in place, but it does. For worms on

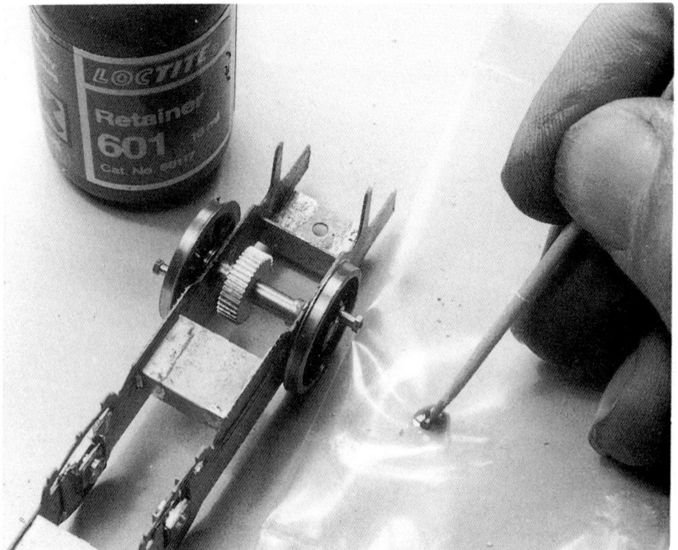

Left: *Loctite-fitting a pinion on an axle. The Ultrascale-type 38:1 gears fitted to the guinea-pig '57XX' chassis are designed for Loctite or solder fitting. I use Loctite 601, as here. A drop of compound is squeezed out onto a suitable base – a scrap poly-bag – and a sufficiency for the job is picked up on the tip of a cocktail stick for transfer to the axle.* Right & Below: *With the gear (which should be a 'stiff sliding fit' on the axle) pushed over to one side, the 601 is applied to the axle. The gear is then centred (you have about a minute). Here, I'm using the 'inside measuring' points of my vernier callipers, pre-set to the correct frame/side of gear dimension, to get the gear plumb on centre.*

As a final check, the motor is dropped into place, with mounts already fitted. The worm should be centred over the pinion. Praise be, it was!

motor shafts, fit the thrust washers as shown in *Fig. 10:4*, slide the worm on, pull it 'half off', and run a drop of Loctite off the tip of a cocktail stick into the bore of the gear. Push the gear home, allowing a few thou of backlash if you're using a full set of thrust washers (see next section), and allow to cure. If you ever need to get it off, heat the worm with a soldering iron and lever off against the motor front. Pinion gears on axles are even easier. Slide the gear onto the axle slightly off centre, place a drop of the Loctite on the middle of the axle, and slide the gear into place. You've got a few moments to check that it is truly 'on centre' – I use a vernier calliper gauge which I've pre-set to the correct 'side of gear to end of axle' dimension. A quick trial from each end of the axle in turn will reveal any error in short order.

THRUST WASHERS AND BEARINGS

The purpose of these is to reduce the friction generated when a revolving gear under 'end thrust' loading impinges onto a fixed bearing surface, such as the face of a motor bearing or the inner side of a gearbox case. By interposing one or more washers, which revolve at speeds intermediate between that of the rotating gear and the stationary bearing, the friction is reduced because the effective areas in contact are increased by the faces of the washers. Such washers are included on the input shafts of all good worm gearboxes, and between the armature and motor bearings of double-ended or 'can' motors (or at least those of the breed designed with the worm-gear in mind).

Single-ended motors, like the D13, go one better by incorporating a thrust bearing at one end of the shaft, where a steel ball between the shaft-end and the bottom of the bearing acts in a similar way, although with even greater effectiveness. This is why so many locos fitted with single-ended motors run rather better in one direction – when the end-thrust is being absorbed by the thrust bearing – than they do in the other, when a simple washer has to cope. The best arrangement of the lot is to have a thrust bearing at each end of a motor or gearbox shaft, but only Hornby-Dublo and Tri-ang (in the XT60/X05) have ever managed this in general commercial production, although vintage specialist motors by Romford and Taycol incorporated such a layout.

There are instances, as when the oft-advocated installation of a worm close to a motor or the use of an outrigger bearing will produce a need for additional thrust washers. In our lightly-loaded applications, these needn't be anything special, and small BA steel or brass washers will suffice. So long as they have smooth, flat surfaces and are an easy running fit on the shaft, they will do. Don't *over*do the washering of motor or gearbox shafts to the point where you take up all the end-float – around 5–10 thou is desirable; indeed, such running clearance is vital in the case of motor shafts, which get hot and expand. Study of the photographs accompanying this section will show such thrust washers in place – there's no limit to the number you can put in, though if you end up with more than three or four, the gear is probably too far from the bearing, or the situation won't call for them anyway as the revolving and stationary components are unlikely to make contact. Don't forget about these friction-frazzling devices come oiling time, either.

DIRECT MOUNTED GEARS

These are the predominant, and simplest, types of transmission. In these arrangements, the motor shaft is the input shaft of the transmission, and carries the worm gear directly mounted on it. This means that the only bearings normally supporting one-half of the transmission are those of the motor, while the location of the input side of the transmission is solely dependent on the rigidity of the motor shaft and the quality of those bearings. A glance at *Fig 10:5* will show where we can anticipate problems with a set-up like this. The main drawback is the 'overhung' nature of the worm, which has bearing support only at the end closest to the motor.

It is to minimise the effects of this poor shaft support that I have laid such stress on the need to keep the gear as close to the motor bearing as humanly possible. This is especially vital in the case of short motors like the D11, DS10 and 1620. The reason for this is that the length of shafting from the 'contact centre' of the worm gear to the adjacent motor bearing acts as a lever, serving to magnify the already considerable upward thrust developed by the reaction of the gearset which, if you recollect, is constantly and busily engaged in trying to climb out of engagement. The only counter to this relentless upward thrust is the rear motor bearing, acting in turn through the leverage of the length of shaft separating it from the front bearing. The longer this 'lever', the greater the restraint available and the more precise (or rather, less imprecise) will be the location of the worm in relation to the pinion. This is, I'm sure, why 'long' motors like the 1425 or D13 give better running than short types when installed in this mode.

If we're honest about it, the only reason that we can get away with such poor engineering at all is that we are operating a long way short of the ultimate transmission

Fig. 10:4 THRUST WASHERS AND BEARINGS

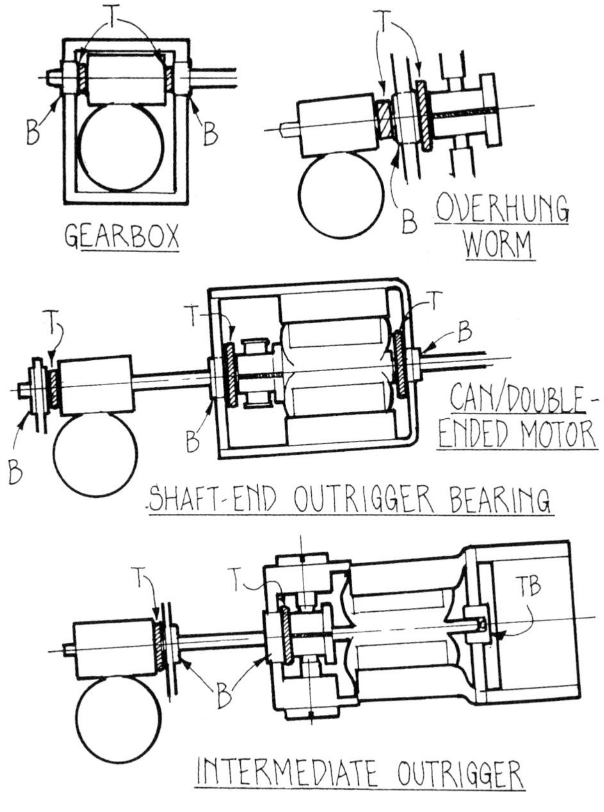

T = THRUST WASHER(S) B = BEARING
TB = THRUST BEARING

Fig. 10:5 GEAR LOADS ON MOTOR

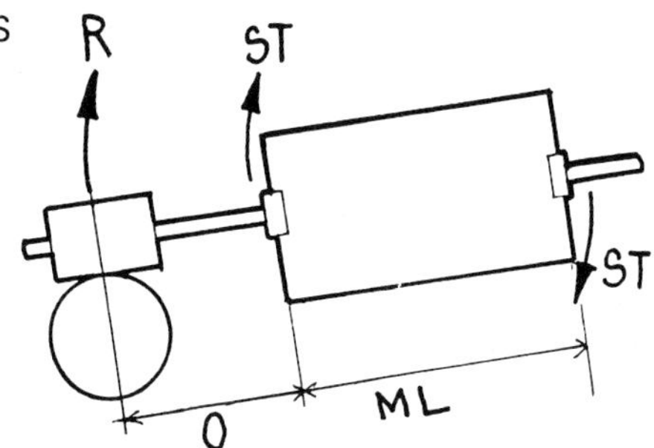

ST = SIDETHRUST; AT FRONT BEARING = R×O UPWARDS; AT REAR BEARING = R×O÷ML DOWNWARDS

R = REACTION O = OVERHANG.

ML = MOTOR LENGTH (BETWEEN BEARINGS)

TO KEEP ST TO MINIMUM, O SHOULD BE SHORT & ML RELATIVELY LONG

potential of the gears. The reactive loads described are a product of two factors – the efficiency of the gearset, and the torque being fed through it. Efficiency is, you will recall, related to reduction ratio in a perverse fashion, so it behoves us to arrange things to get away with as small a reduction ratio as possible, while endeavouring to keep the loads imposed to a minimum. An apt choice of motor, and careful engineering of the chassis for truly free running, will bring rich dividends in running quality and mechanism life. Don't forget the influence of loco ballasting and train resistance on loading, either – the further we can keep the whole of our drive system from its operating limits, the better will be the results in terms of refinement.

FOLD-UP ETCHED MOTOR MOUNTS

The fold-up etched motor mount that seems now to be the prefered means of direct-mounting gearsets to motors and axles has a number of benefits and can, if well designed and accurately assembled, control most of the critical aspect of worm-gear installation. A good mount should give you spot-on centre-to-centre height between

Fig. 10:6 MOTOR MOUNT CRITERIA

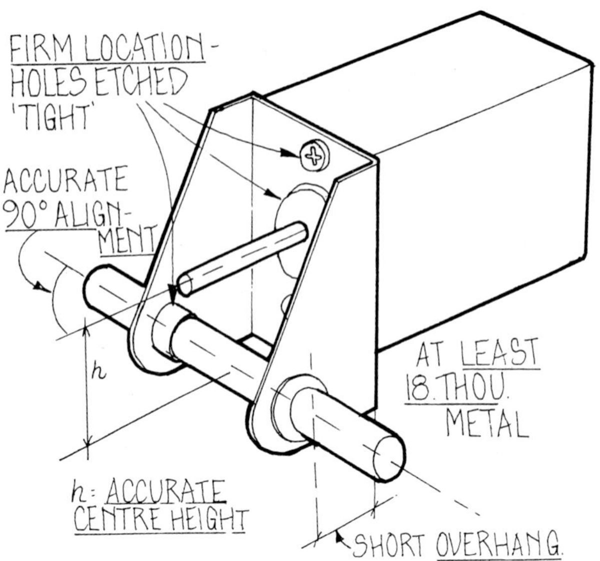

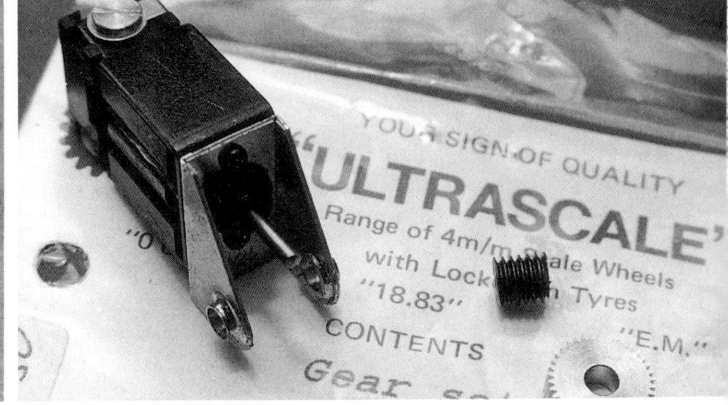

Left: *A typical etched fold-up mount, in this case the Impetus 'short reach' mount for the DS10, using Ultrascale 38:1 gears. This design, as can be seen, seeks to keep the worm as close as possible to the front motor bearing by making the distance from the motor plate to the axle centre as short as possible.* Right: *The mount is folded up and the bearings fitted, using a length of 1/8in axle rod to get it all square. This is a nice substantial mount in 20-thou nickel-silver; avoid any that are thin and flimsy.*

Left: *The tricky bit in fitting mount-hung motors is the need to enter the axle through up to four bearings and the gear in one go. I grip the gear-wheel between my fingertips and locate the axle to ease entry.* Right: *The usual Loctite-fitting procedure was followed to centre and retain the gear. This is a 'narrow' mount, suitable for OO, but there is still enough room to get the gear out of the way for Loctite application. This DS10/38:1 combination was being installed in a rather heavily modified Craftsman 'C12' chassis.*

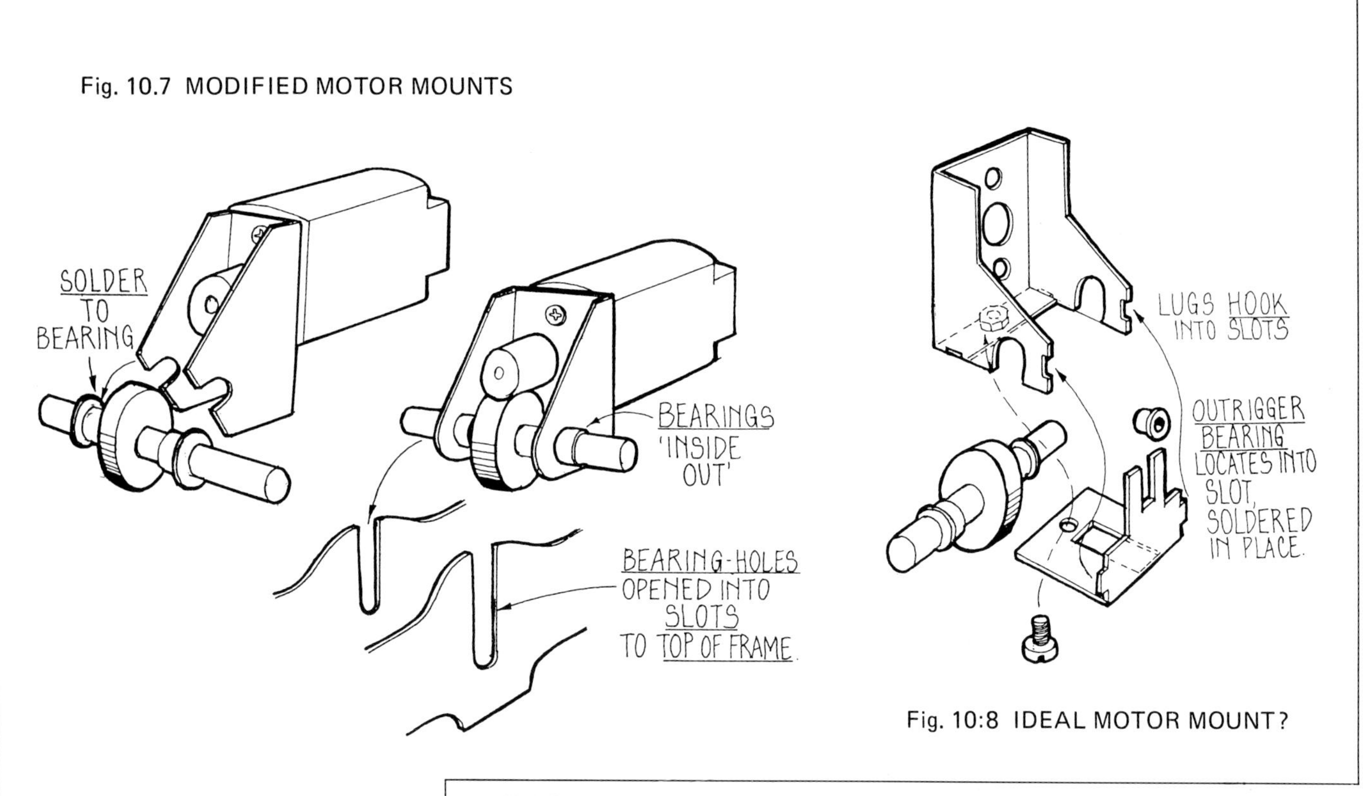

Fig. 10.7 MODIFIED MOTOR MOUNTS

Fig. 10:8 IDEAL MOTOR MOUNT?

motor shaft and axle and, if correctly assembled, will keep these two at right-angles. If you have a mount-based transmission that is 'tight', incidentally, check this as a possible cause; if you haven't got the thing folded up at a true 90° between the sides and the actual motor-mounting plate, then this vital alignment will be compromised. I check this with a square when folding the mount up, and 'lock' the angle with a generous fillet of solder down the insides of the folds. Other potential areas of trouble with these fold-up mounts include the accuracy of retention of the actual motor – the holes locating the boss and mounting screws need to be as tight as possible. The same engineering precept that applied to holes etched for axles or frame spacers is just as relevant here. I also look for a mount design that keeps the 'overhang' of the gear to a minimum – for the reasons just expounded – or which, like the excellent Puffers/Perseverance VMM7 DS10 mount, makes provision for additional, outboard, bearing support. Now *that's* engineering!

The manner in which these mounts are installed to the axle constitutes, to my eye, their main drawback. Suggested practice often runs to retaining the mount on the same bearings that carry the axle in the frames, which is sound enough practice, but often makes for rather tricky installation and setting-up. There are a number of ways around this, a couple of which I sketch in

There are fold-up mounts for the D11/D13 as well – this one was designed by Rod Neep for Finecast, and is seen installed in a pre-production trial build of their new 'Buckjumper' chassis – all typical of good contemporary practice. Note that the rear end of the D13 is sitting on a block of firm foam rubber (camping mat) to help keep things quiet.

Fig 10:7. My own preference is the second of these, where the mount is modified to come off the bearings, to which it is soldered when in place. This rather brutal snipping of the nether extremities of the mount may seem to negate several of the advantages, but in practice it works pretty well, and does at least mean that it is possible to get the motor, mount and worm out of the chassis if needs be. It also offers scope to correct the centre-to-centre height where this proves incorrect – by no means unknown. The ideal design of axle-hung mount has yet to hit the market, but when it does eventually arrive I rather hope it will look something like the bathtub doodle in *Fig 10:8*. Such a set-up would, I fancy, run a pukka gearbox reasonably close in the refinement stakes.

Do make sure that you're absolutely clear which gearset your mount is intended to accommodate – usually either the 'common centre' Romfords of 30, 40, 50 and 60:1 reduction, or the rather smaller Ultrascale 38:1. I have rather definite views on gears, and prefer the Ultrascale if at all possible, which it usually is. The 30 and 40:1 Romfords are pretty reasonable, but I'm not over-convinced by the 50:1 and wouldn't contemplate the 60:1 at any price. A 60:1 gearset of this type has *very* fine tolerances, and needs to be installed in a very rigid and well-engineered gearbox if it is to give of its best. The 'margin for error' with a miniature 60:1 worm set is just about nil in any of the critical alignments. My own feeling is that an apposite choice of motor and application will obviate the need to employ such sky-high ratios in almost any application relating to a normal standard-gauge loco, but were it to prove desirable I would go for a 2:1 spur followed by 30:1 final drive any day.

This brings me back to the same basic precept as applied to an apt motor choice – just because you can physically fit a certain combination of motor, mount and gears doesn't mean that these will necessarily work well. The use of an etched mount doesn't remove any of the loading from the motor bearings, which are still being called upon to support the gear and absorb all those reactive side-loadings. The arrangement which I find particularly wanting is the combination of the DS10 with an 'overhung' mount and a set of Romford 60:1 gears on the end of the shaft. As I explained in the last chapter, this particular motor was designed to power big Yankee diesels in 'N' gauge, driving both bogies through plastic universal joints and truck-mounted gear towers. It is therefore endowed with a shaft and bearings intended to cope with the far more modest loading imposed by such a set-up. It is not intended to have a set of close-tolerance, highly reactive high-reduction worm gears mounted out at the end of its thin, whippy, unhardened shaft. This is poor engineering practice. I would only use the DS10 in applications where it can perform adequately on a more modest reduction ratio.

To the ethereal sounds of Portescap guarantees floating out of windows, an RG4/1219 is dismantled for rebuilding in an alternative configuration, using MJT milled-brass gearbox sideframes.

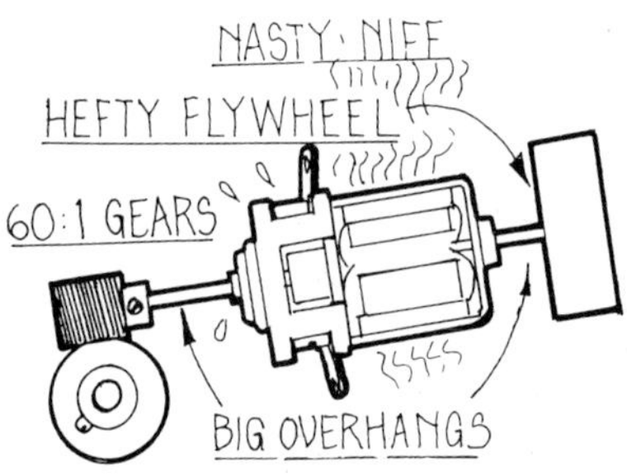

Fig. 10:9 HOW TO KILL A DS10

INSTALLING THE RG4

Never mind the semantics, an Escap coreless can on the RG4 gearbox amounts to a mount-fitted motor with direct-mounted gears, even if we are talking bevels-and-spurs (and so many of them!). One of the joys of this design is, of course, that it's so easy to install – wang the axle through, tighten up a grub-screw and bingo! Job done. There are only a couple of points to watch, the first and most important of which is the need to maintain a spot of clearance between the side of the final drive spur gear and the adjacent large spur that takes the power from the intermediate shaft. I usually site the brass final drive gear with the boss containing the grubscrew close to the bearing on the opposite side, which gives you a full 1 mm of clearance. And, although these spur gears are not as affected by slight ovality as worm pinions, I still seat that grubscrew into a filed axle flat to keep it all as 'true' as possible. As the geartrain is fully reversible, having the gearbox in place on the axle does not impede quartering, so I generally install RG4s during 'wheeling up'. If the motor gets in the way, then the two screws holding the plastic motor mounting block to the gearbox are easily removed. You may, of course, decide that one of the 'alternative configuration' RG4-based gearboxes will be better suited to your purpose, calling for a strip-down and rebuild of the geartrain. Obey the instructions that come with the new gearbox sides, take care, and don't forget that your guarantee from Portescap goes out the window once you take the RG4 to bits . . .

CHASSIS-MOUNTED MOTORS

This is the most traditional system, and is that employed by all the older 'solid' chassis designs. The motor shaft still forms the input shaft of the transmission, with the worm-gear mounted directly on it; the difference is that the motor is fitted direct to the chassis rather than to the axle by the intermediary of an etched mount. This has a number of advantages which seem to have been somewhat overlooked of late, including ease of removal and a degree of adjustability lacking in the axle-based systems. I still tend to mount motors in this manner in many instances, and provided that, once again, you look after the basics in terms of accurate alignment and rigid location, it can give excellent results. It is particularly suited to open-frame motors like the D13, and the DS10 can also be mounted thus with advantage. Given that it is easy to arrange some adjustment of the depth of mesh, a critical factor about which you can do little (other than hope that the designer got it right) in the context of a normal etched mount, it can also offer the chance to 'fine tune' a mechanism to surprising effect.

It's actually very simple to arrange a direct chassis-mounting for most motors, provided that you have some means of fixing the motor to a mounting plate or plates. If there are tapped holes and so on, I use them, but in many instances I simply solder things up – apart from any other considerations, soldered joints don't come unscrewed! A good example is the simple way in which I mounted the D13 into the Puffers '57XX' chassis that forms the 'prime example' back in the assembly chapters, sketched in *Fig. 10:10*. The little mounting plates I used here were actually a couple of the spare 'flat' frame-spacers that came with the kit, which I think are intended to provide screw-locations for body mounts – certainly, they came with etched holes to clear 8BA on their centrelines, very useful in their new roles as motor mounts. I soldered one to the brass framing of the D13's brushgear/front bearing assembly, using the hole as a reference to get it central under the motor shaft. The other was simply screwed in place beneath the motor using the fixing screw provided. With the worm-gear and its associated thrust washers in place, the motor-plus-mountings were offered up to the chassis, aligned for 'right angularity' with the driven axle (easy to do by eye with the entire length of the frames to use as a reference), and meshed with the pinion on the driven axle. To keep the gears from 'bottoming' but provide minimal backlash, I called up the old dodge of interposing a scrap of hard tissue paper between them – it's the one thing in the world that 'Bronco' loo-paper is really good for. (It was a sad day for me when the Devon Fire Brigade went over to something soft and pink – what *will* I do when my last box of manly old-issue 'hard' is exhausted?) This scrap of tissue was 'wound out' once the motor had been soldered in place between the frames, where it fitted exactly as the 'mounts' were obviously to exactly the right dimension.

Many people seem worried by such a comparatively crude method of fitting a motor into a chassis, particularly in that it is, effectively, soldered in place. I suppose it would be possible to screw the front mount to the motor frame rather than soldering it, but if you prefer a more 'readily-removed' variation then the combination of a front vertical plate locating over the bearing boss coupled with an identical rear screw-fixing would give the same rigid and positive location of the D13; the arrangement is sketched in *Fig. 10:11*. The adjustment mentioned can be effected either by unsoldering the tacks holding the rear mounting to the chassis, or by slackening the retaining screw beneath the motor and inserting slips of paper to adjust the mesh. Note that with this latter method, you can only deepen the engagement of the gears, so if you like the sound of that approach, err on the slack side when setting the mesh in the first place. Put in two sheets of 'Bronco'.

I don't often reckon to need to remove motors from chassis, so the soldered-in approach doesn't worry me. Only in the context of a high-mileage 'exhibition' loco would I be tempted to arrange for 'instant' motor withdrawal – and even then I feel that it's better to have a few more locos and not be too dependent on any one of them, which is why my current modest china-clay branch is populated by no fewer than seven assorted Pannier tanks! At all events, the set-up applied to this particular example was extremely quick and simple to install, and ran sweetly and surprisingly quietly from the outset. I have come to the conclusion that to obtain truly quiet running you either need great rigidity or total flexibility (rubber-mounted motor, neoprene coupling and self-contained gearbox); the system applied to this particular loco seems to benefit from the combination of the rigid motor mounting, the

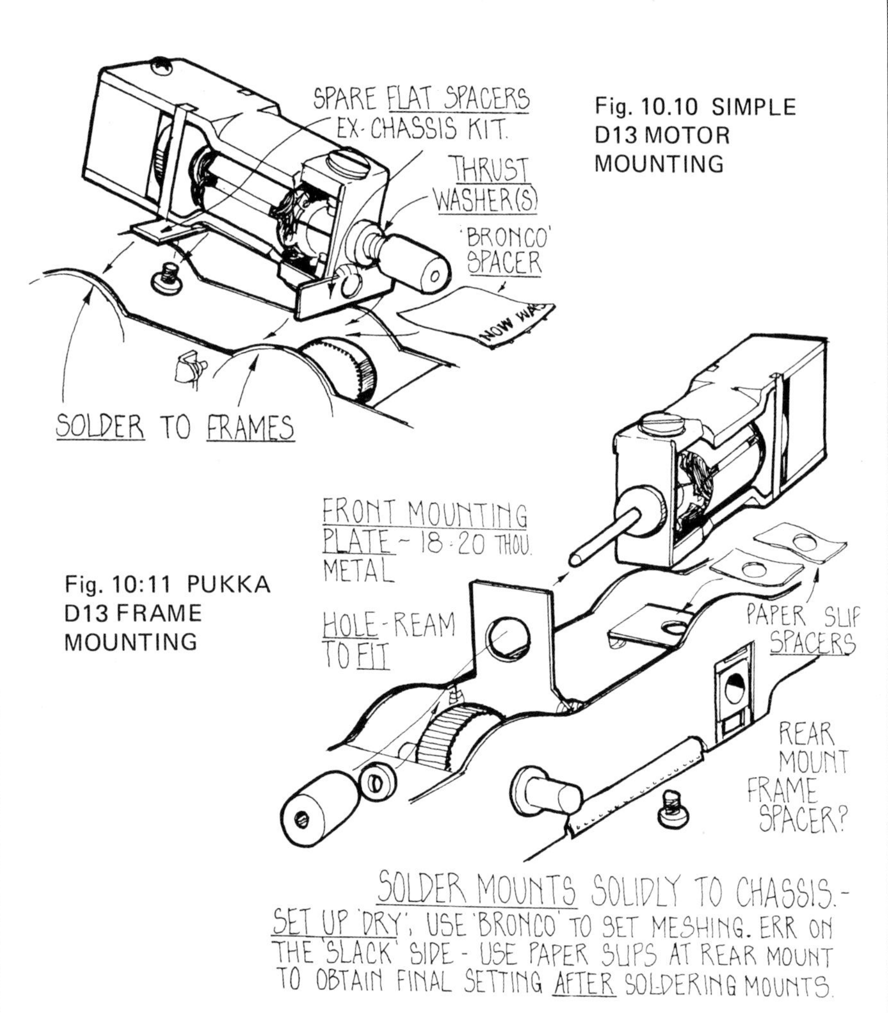

Fig. 10.10 SIMPLE D13 MOTOR MOUNTING

Fig. 10:11 PUKKA D13 FRAME MOUNTING

Tissue-paper gear spacing goes back to Ahern, but still works well today, even with fine-pitch gears such as Ultrascale's 38:1.

The Bronco hard toilet paper (best Fire Service issue) is 'wound out' by rotating the motor armature once the motor is fixed. The result is a well-meshed gearset, giving smooth, quiet transmission with minimal friction.

efficacy of Bronco as a meshing depth guide, and the sound-deadening properties of the K's cast pannier tanks.

Rather than go into endless chapter-and-verse describing a number of possible ways of accomplishing a similar result with other motors, I shall content myself with this description of the basics, amplified with the sketches in *Fig 10:12*. The main point is that, provided you follow the main criteria outlined earlier in this chapter, it doesn't really matter how you achieve the result. So long as the meshing is right (not too deep, shafts at right-angles) and everything's rigidly held in place, it will work. If you've got something wrong, your ears will soon tell you! Indeed, this is the main principle upon which I proceed when adjusting worm-and-pinion drives; experience has shown that the setting that gives the quietest operation is invariably that which also gives the lowest levels of friction and backlash. The sound of the gears can also give away faults such as ovality – if the 'note' changes every half-revolution or so, the pinion is eccentric on the axle.

OUTRIGGER BEARINGS

I have laid considerable stress on this whole business of motor bearings coping with gear-thrust loadings, as it is critical. However, there are circumstances when measures such as close-mounting the gear to the front motor bearing just aren't practicable, due to other, over-riding factors such as the need for motor concealment or necessities like frame spacers dictating a mounting position for the motor well away from the motor front bearing. The lack of support that results when the worm has to be moved out to the end of the shaft can be compensated for by installing an outrigger bearing close to the gear. Just such a system was 'designed in' to the Tri-ang 'TT' chassis, and it works very well in the context of a chassis-mounted motor. I draw the arrangement in *Fig. 10:13*, and there's a picture of Don Leeper's LNWR 0–4–2T 'Webb Dock Tank' showing the system built into a modified M & L kit chassis. It's not so easy to come up with a similar set-up for use in conjunction with a fold-up mount unless, like the Perseverance VMM 7 DS10 mount, it is 'designed in', so avoid the use of mounts if gear support will be compromised. Fix the motor to the chassis and follow one of the schemes in *Fig 10:12*.

INDIRECTLY MOUNTED GEARS

Gearboxes are what we mean here, and there's no doubt that a well-designed worm-drive gearbox can produce a transmission of real quality. That's because such a unit is real engineering, in contrast to the rather 'bodged' approach typified by the direct mounting arrangements. Use of a gearbox

Fig. 10:12 CHASSIS MOTOR MOUNTS

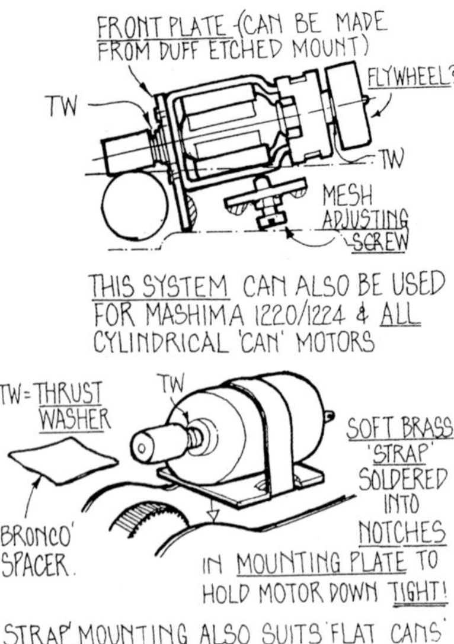

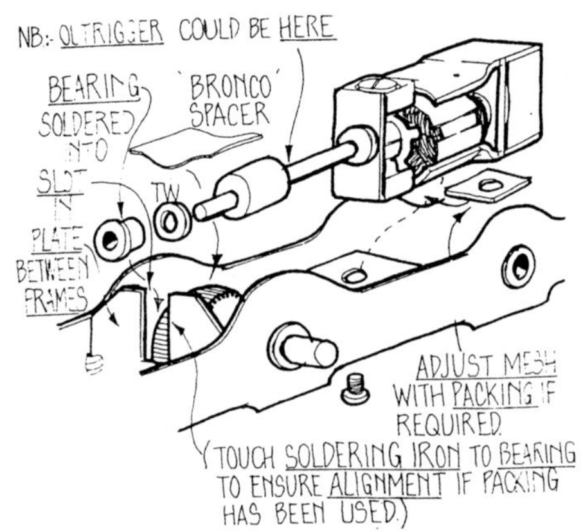

Fig. 10:13 OUTRIGGER BEARING IN FRAMES

An outrigger bearing fitted as close as possible to the gears (old-type Ultrascale 50:1) in Don Leeper's D11-powered LNW Webb 0–4–2PT Dock Tank. This is an arrangement conceived to keep the motor out of sight and to preserve below-boiler 'daylight'. The 50:1 gears on small wheels keep the D11 spinning at the relatively high speed at which it is happy. Note also the 'top mounting' of the D11, needed to leave room for a compensating beam in the modified M & L kit chassis.

means that all the loadings generated by the worm gears are absorbed by the gearbox, rather than motor bearings, while the gearbox casing provides – hopefully with great accuracy – rigid location for both input and output shafts. In other words, we are able to optimise the installation of the gears without having to worry about keeping the motor happy at the same time. The general arrangement of a worm drive gearbox is typified by the Sharman design in *Fig. 10:14*; for optimum results, the casing needs to be as rigid as possible, and the thrust bearings and washers of generous proportions to keep down internal friction. A fully-cased gearbox also means that the gears can be run immersed in lubricant, to the obvious benefit of silence and long life.

You may ask why, if gearboxes are such a 'boon and a blessing to men', they are not in universal use? The reason is that it is not always easy to install them, in that they may have to be built-up in situ between the frames. There are ways around this, but it does call for the chassis to be specifically-designed for use of such a gearbox, or for the pre-built gearbox, already fitted to the driven axle, to be installed in the chassis at the frame-assembly stage. This isn't too much of a problem if the gearbox is designed in such a way that the input shaft can be removed with the box in situ; if this can't be done, it means that it won't be possible to quarter the wheels by the proscribed 'trial and adjust' method, as the presence of the gearbox will effectively prevent the driven axle from rotating. It's also extremely inconvenient if the set-up you need to employ calls for the gearbox and motor to be installed as a single unit, as when a gearbox is installed directly on a motor shaft. I suppose that it can be argued that this isn't an indirect mounting, but it's something I often do, particularly on 'short' motors like the 1620 or DS10, where relieving the motor bearings of gear-loadings brings substantial improvements in running quality.

Fortunately, both my favourite gearboxes *are* designed to give a removable input shaft, which overcomes most of the drawbacks in one. In common with many of the better 'open' gearsets, the pinions of all the currently-available worm gearboxes are designed for force or 'Loctite' fitting, for reasons of space utilisation and to ensure concentricity – a consideration already dealt with. This also dictates a 'pre-assembly' of the gearbox onto the driven axle before the frames are assembled – or, if you prefer, the frames can be simply modified as for 'removable' fold-up mount brackets as drawn back in *Fig. 10:7*. This particular arrangement can also save the day if you only elect to fit a gearbox *after* the chassis has been built.

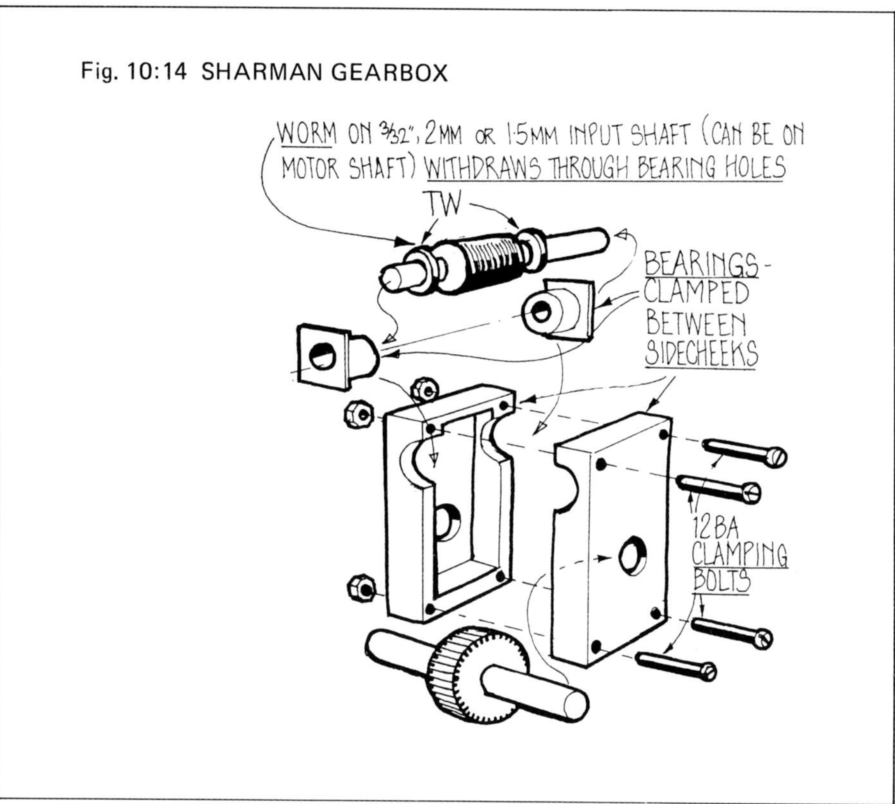

INSTALLING WORM DRIVE GEARBOXES

At the moment, there is not a very wide choice of such devices on the market, and of those I'm familiar with, I can recommend two as being really sound engineering jobs. These are the milled-brass Sharman, and the fabricated Exactoscale. The Sharman design is illustrated in the photos and drawn in *Fig 10:14*. It will be seen to consist of two brass side-cheeks, in which are machined bearings for the standard 1/8 in axle, bolted together using four 12BA cheesehead machine screws and nuts. Trapped between the side-cheeks are a pair of very substantial 'top-hat' thrust bearings, available in 1.5 mm, 2 mm and 3/32 in bores to suit the common motor shaft sizes. These bearings are of a size big enough to permit the withdrawal of the input shaft, complete with worm gear and thrust washers, 'freeing' the gearbox for quartering. These gearboxes are designed around the 38:1 Ultrascale gearset already described, which was, if I recollect

Real engineering at last – a Sharman Mk II milled-brass gearbox mounted directly to a D13 motor in yet another 'Buckjumper' chassis, in this case a scratchbuilt version for my old 'Butley Mills Buck', 68499. In point of fact, this is the actual first-off 'production prototype' of this gearbox, which I tested for Mike Sharman back in 1985.

aright, originally developed for the old design of Sharman gearbox that Brian Brompton used to mill out up at Stroud. A lovely thing it was, but a *pig* to install.

The Exactoscale is a rather more complex animal, sold in kit form for flexibility and economy. It has its origins in the old Protofour gearbox design, and the need to maintain compatibility with the current range of Protofour components dictates the rather odd axle arrangement, which has a 2 mm axle sleeved up to 1/8 in if required. This is because many of the smaller Protofour driving wheels used a 2 mm axle, as closer to scale, and the box had to be designed to accommodate these. Reference to *Fig 10:15* will show how this high-quality unit goes together. There is no engineering compromise in the design, which is why the bearings in the sidecheeks are of large diameter, running on the phosphor-bronze sleeve of the pinion. The cheeks are assembled onto four turned spacers, and the chunky bearings of the input shaft sit on the uppermost of these. The assembly is completed with a U-shaped plate forming the bottom and ends of the casing, and a further plate – incorporating a lubrication hole – which forms the top and retains the input shaft. I solder these components carefully together using 145° solder and a *paste* flux ('Fluxite') – less inclined to stray where it's not wanted than my usual phosphoric acid. Although not as outstandingly rigid as the Sharman box, the Exactoscale unit is more than adequate, and is far more compact. It can be had in three ratios – 18:1, 30:1 and 40:1, incorporating steel worms and phosphor-bronze pinions, all of the finest Swiss instrument quality; a real 'Rolls-Royce' job capable of the finest results.

The unique feature of the Exactoscale box is that use of the 2 mm axle in conjunction with the 2 mm sleeve, already mentioned. In practice, this causes no problems, and once the sleeve has been secured with Loctite 601, the axle can be treated just like any other 1/8 in plain axle, and will happily accept wheels intended for use with such a system. However, for this reason, the Exactoscale box cannot be used with Romford wheels, unlike the Sharman. It is also limited to one size of input shaft bearing, 3/32 in; other motor shaft sizes can be accommodated by use of high-precision turned steel sleeves, but the unit is really intended for truly indirect drives, where the motor is connected by means of some form of shaft or coupling. Exactoscale sell a range of complementary drive components that include shafting systems and neoprene drive tubing; the simplest set-up is shown in *Fig 10:16*, and this works very well. I frequently use this system with can motors, notably the 1620; the only mounting for the motor

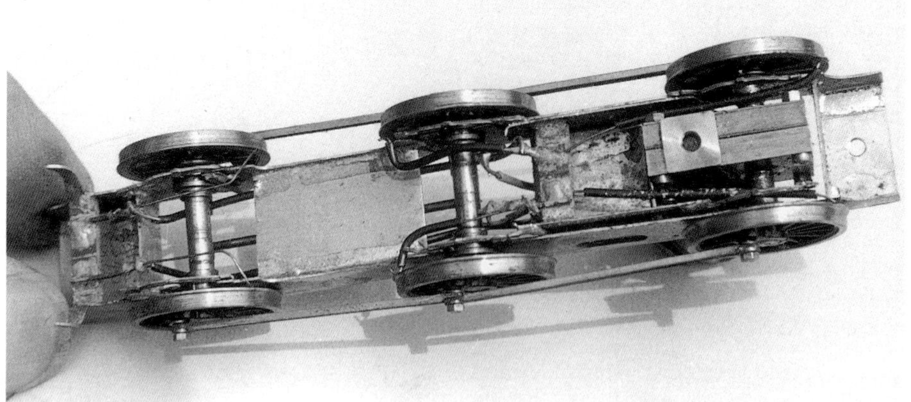

Here is an underneath view of the Sharman gearbox of my 'J17' (which has, you may recollect, a vertically-mounted motor), showing the thumping great thrust bearing clamped between the halves of the split casing. Slackening the clamping screws permits bearings, input shaft, worm and thrust washers to be withdrawn, leaving the pinion and axle free for quartering.

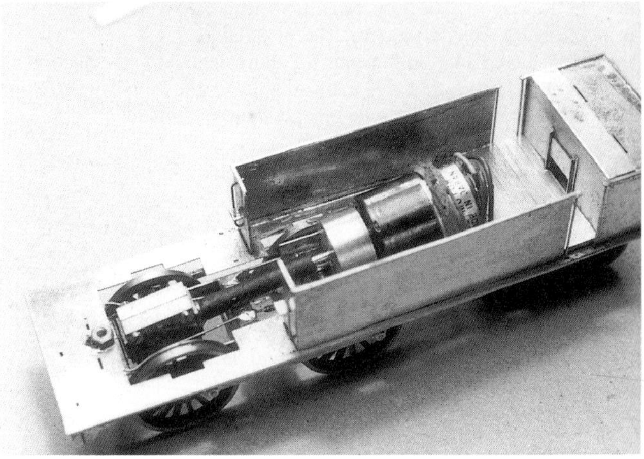

A remote-mounted Sharman gearbox driven by a Neoprene coupling from a flywheel-fitted Sagami 1620 provides a concealed high-quality drive for a Craftsman MR '1P' 0–4–4T. This arrangement preserved the 'daylight', kept the cab clear, and left the boiler free to take ballast. The result was a sweet-running, powerful loco – a happy contrast to many kit-built 0–4–4Ts.

Fig. 10:15 EXACTOSCALE GEARBOX

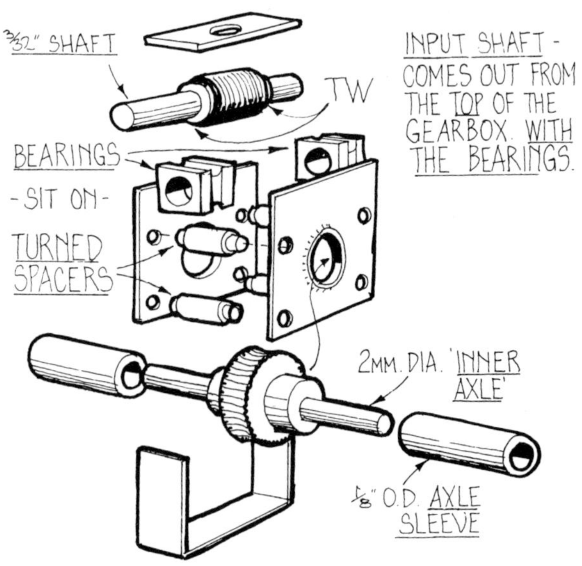

is a simple plate or cradle as in the diagram. I either stick the motor in with a blob of a contact adhesive such as Uhu or Bostik 1, or even tape it in place with insulating tape. If you want to get really refined, try dropping the motor into a little blob of RTV Silicon Rubber (Dow Corning bath sealant or sealing mastic) both available from your local D-I-Y superstore.

If you are using a proper independent drive system with either of these gearboxes, particularly with a 'soft' coupling such as the neoprene tube, you may find that the gearbox tries to rotate about the axle, forcing the coupling out of alignment and producing rough running. This is particularly prone to happen when you're feeding a lot of load through the system, and to counteract it, some form of torque reaction arm is needed. Theoretically, this should incorporate some form of flexible bushing system, but I've found that a rigid set-up seems to have little adverse effect on performance and noise levels. The sketch in *Fig 10:17* shows what I mean.

You don't have to buy one of these proprietary gearboxes to enjoy the benefits of indirect gear mounting, however, as the system that I draw in *Fig 10:18* and illustrate in the context of the latest (Mk. IV) chassis of the hard-worked MRJ 'guinea pig' '14XX' – a veteran of issue No. 1 – is both simple to build and set-up. It still possesses all the virtues ascribed to the more 'pukka' gearboxes, except the lubricant immersion of the whole thing – and that wouldn't be hard to arrange were one so disposed. The bearings used to build such a 'gearbox' (if I may so dignify the arrangement) are available from a number of sources in all the necessary bores – mine came from Sharman Wheels and are the standard 3/32 in diameter. Sharman's can also supply the relevant 3.32 in shafting, while the gears are, once again, the proven Ultrascale 38:1. The results are on a par with the 'proper' gearboxes, and the bearings were set to mesh the gears accurately by the 'Bronco' method. Longitudinal alignment – vital to get the gears exactly at right-angles – was checked by putting a long piece of 3/32 in rod through the bearings and sighting against the frames as a reference.

There are many more possibilities for the design of 'indirect' transmissions, and I could go on to make this chapter even longer than all the others. Within the context of *kit* chassis assembly, however, simpler is undoubtedly better, and I think that I had better content myself with one more set-up, that of a basic two-stage drive as mentioned in connection with high-reduction gearing. This is drawn in *Fig 10:19*, once again featuring the DS10 with which it does make mechanical sense. The necessary gears again come from Sharman, and in this instance it will be necessary to

Fig. 10:16 EXACTOSCALE GEARBOX DRIVEN THROUGH FLEXIBLE TUBE COUPLING

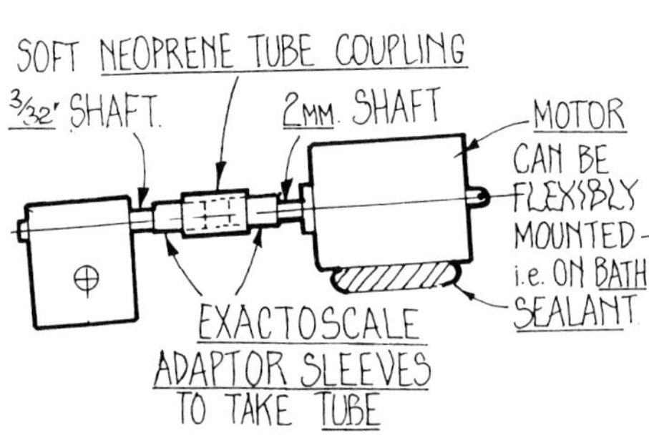

This is Exactoscale's preferred set-up, for which they supply all the components: Sagami 1425 motor, Neoprene tube drive coupling and 40:1 gearbox. Note the torque reaction rod linking gearbox to chassis; this motor is flexibly mounted.

Fig. 10:17 GEARBOX TORQUE REACTION ROD

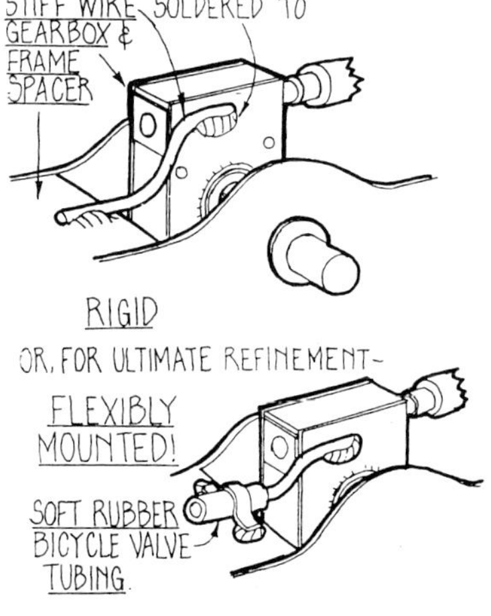

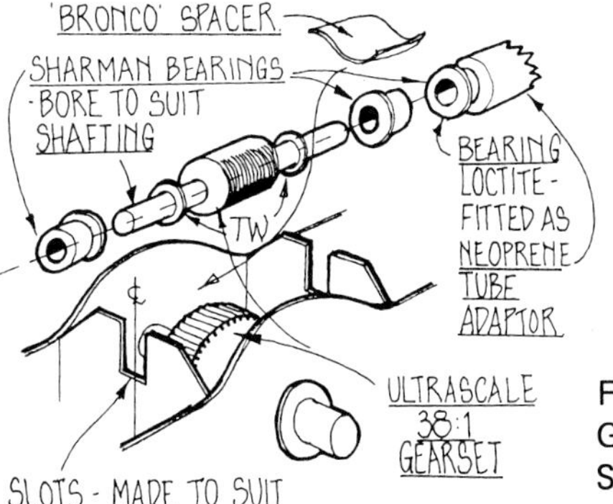

Fig. 10:18 HOME-MADE GEARBOX, MIKE SHARMAN'S PATTERN

use his 1.5 mm bore bearing as a sleeve to adapt the 3.32 in bore spur gear to the DS10 shaft; solder the bearing into the gear, reaming if necessary, and fit it to the DS10 shaft with Loctite 601. The meshing of wide pitch spur gears is a good deal less critical than those of worm-and-pinion systems, so the mounting of the DS10 is not all that finicky. I have used exactly the arrangement shown with considerable success. The worm part of the transmission – a Romford 30:1 – is set up exactly as described for the 'home-made' gearbox in the last section. Simple and effective but not, it has to be said, particularly quiet. I put it in an '08' shunter where it sounded just about right!

Home-made 'gearbox' built into the frames of the '14XX' – once again, Ultrascale 38:1 gears with Sharman bearings and a Mashima 1620. The fine transmission shaft is a piece of steel pin, designed to preserve below-boiler daylight.

CHOOSING REDUCTION RATIOS

I've prattled gaily on for many a page here talking airily of this ratio and that without, so far, explaining how I think they should be selected. The importance of choosing the right overall reduction ratio to keep our motor sweet and happy, and to suit the intended performance of our loco has, I trust, been made clear. So how is it that I can now reveal that, in my experience, for the vast majority of cases I only ever need to consider one ratio, that being the 'median' 40:1? The nub of the matter lies in that qualifying adjective – for what we are really concerned with is the *total* reduction afforded by the gearset *in combination with the driving wheel size.* This is a critical and fundamental factor that is often totally overlooked by modellers, who think only of axle rotation versus motor revs. What really matters is the speed along the track generated by those motor revs, and that is a function of wheel size as much as gear ratio.

Fig. 10:19 2-STAGE 60:1 GEARING FOR DS10, ON MIKE SHARMAN'S SYSTEM

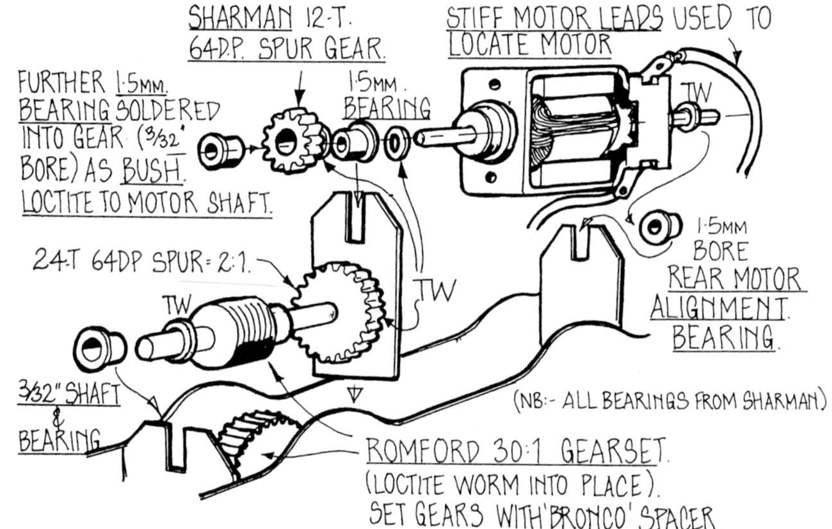

The effect is striking, both in terms of speed and tractive effort. It is, after all, a prime factor in real steam locomotive design, as it is effectively the only form of 'gearing' possible. As a 'worked example', let's look at two engines, both fitted with the same motor and 40:1 gears. One is an express passenger type with 6 ft 6 in drivers, the other a shunter with 4 ft 0 in wheels. For a motor speed of 6,000 r.p.m., not untypical for a small motor, then we will have 150 r.p.m. at the output of our 40:1 transmission. By using the good old formula $C = 2\pi r$ to work out the wheel circumference, we find that for each revolution of its 6 ft 6 in drivers, our 'express' loco will have travelled 81.6 mm, which means that in a minute it will have covered 12.240 metres (and, in my case, would have fallen off the end of the layout after 20 secs or so!). The shunter, on the other hand, will only manage 50.26 mm every time the wheels roll round, and in a minute will be only 7.54 metres from its starting point – just about 60% of the speed of the big-wheeled engine. You'd have to have a pretty massive change in ratio to achieve such a major difference by means of straight gear reduction alone!

There is a way of quantifying this, which is to compare the distance travelled for a given number of motor revolutions, rather as car gearing is often expressed as 'm.p.h. per 1,000 r.p.m.'. Using distance rather than speed comes to the same thing, as the time element (per hour, per minute, etc.) is a constant. On that basis, I do a little sum along the lines of: motor speed of 1000 r.p.m. divided by gear ratio of 40:1 gives axle revolutions of 25 per minute, times the wheel circumference in mm ($2\pi r$ again) divided by 100 (to give an answer in centimetres, which is, I find, the most convenient unit). Thus, in the two example cases, we have results of $25 \times 81.6 \div 100 =$ 20.4cm/1,000 revs for the express loco, and 12.6cm/1,000 revs for the shunter. I have found this a pretty useful measure, and the proportions above are not *too* far out if one were to compare the probable maximum speeds at which similar prototype engines would be running – say, 30 m.p.h. for the shunter, and 65 or so for the express (in the context of the average model railway, where there is rarely room for sustained high speed).

I find that I make great use of this method of determining overall reduction, and I base my choice of motor largely on it. By determining the 'median speed' at which I want a loco to run (that is, the speed that is most typical of that engine performing its usual 'turn'), I can work back through the sums to find out what sort of motor speed this will entail, and whether this falls within the range at which the intended motor is happy. I work out 'scale speed' on the basis of scale distance in real time, and, subjectively, this seems to give a realistic result. In the case of my china-clay layout, where 15 m.p.h. might be seen as a 'median' speed, then I looked to a speed of a scale $\frac{1}{4}$-mile per minute, which translates to 5.3 metres/min or 1 metre in 11.32 seconds. Applying this to my '57XX' pannier, with 4 ft $7\frac{1}{2}$ in wheels,

Fig. 10:20 TABLE OF SPEEDS AND GEAR RATIOS

SCALE M.P.H.	ACTUAL SPEED METRES/MIN	3'0" WHEEL CIRC:= 37.6MM WHEEL R.P.M.	MOTOR R.P.M. 30:1	40:1	50:1	3'6" WHEEL CIRC.= 44MM WHEEL R.P.M.	MOTOR R.P.M. 30:1	40:1	50:1	4'0" WHEEL CIRC. = 50.2MM. WHEEL R.P.M.	MOTOR R.P.M 30:1	40:1	50:1	4'6" WHEEL CIRC.= 56.5MM. WHEEL R.P.M.	MOTOR R.P.M. 30:1	40:1	50:1	SCALE M.P.H.
10	3·520	93·6	2808	3744	4680	80·0	2400	3200	4000	70·0	2100	2800	3500	62·3	1869	2492	3115	10
15	5·300	141·0	4230	5640	7050	120·4	3612	4816	6020	105·6	3168	4224	5280	94·0	2820	3760	4700	15
20	7·000	186·0	5580	7440	9300	159·0	4770	6360	7950	139·4	4182	5576	6970	124·0	3720	4960	6200	20
25	8·800	234·0	7020	9360	11700	200·0	6000	8000	10000	175·3	5259	7012	8765	155·8	4674	6232	7790	25
30	10·600	281·9	8457	11276	14095	240·9	7227	9636	12045	211·0	6330	8440	10550	187·6	5628	7504	9380	30
35	12·500					284·0	8520	11360	14200	249·0	7470	9960	12450	221·2	6636	8848	11060	35
40	14·000									279·0	8370	11160	13950	248·0	7440	9920	12400	40
45	15·900									316·7	9501	12668	15835	281·4	8442	11256	14070	45
50	17·600													312·0	9360	12480	15600	50
55	19·400																	55
60	21·200																	60
65	23·000																	65

SCALE M.P.H.	ACTUAL SPEED METRES/MIN	5'0" WHEEL CIRC.= 62·8MM WHEEL R.P.M.	MOTOR R.P.M 30:1	40:1	50:1	5'6" WHEEL CIRC.= 69MM WHEEL R.P.M.	MOTOR R.P.M. 30:1	40:1	50:1	6'0" WHEEL CIRC.= 75·3MM WHEEL R.P.M.	MOTOR R.P.M. 30:1	40:1	50:1	6'6" WHEEL CIRC.= 81·6 WHEEL R.P.M.	MOTOR R.P.M. 30:1	40:1	50:1	SCALE M.P.H.
10	3·520	56·0	1680	2240	2800	51·0	1530	2040	2550	46·7	1401	1868	2335	43·0	1290	1720	2150	10
15	5·300	84·4	2532	3376	4220	77·0	2310	3080	3850	70·4	2112	2816	3520	65·0	1950	2600	3250	15
20	7·000	111·5	3345	4460	5575	101·4	3042	4056	5070	93·0	2790	3720	4650	85·8	2574	3432	4290	20
25	8·800	140·0	4200	5600	7000	127·5	3825	5100	6375	116·9	3507	4676	5845	107·8	3234	4312	5390	25
30	10·600	168·8	5064	6752	8440	153·6	4608	6144	7680	140·7	4221	5628	7035	129·9	3897	5196	6495	30
35	12·500	199·0	5970	7960	9950	181·0	5430	7240	9050	166·0	4980	6640	8300	153·2	4596	6128	7660	35
40	14·000	223·0	6690	8920	11150	203·0	6090	8120	10150	186·0	5580	7440	9300	172·0	5160	6880	8600	40
45	15·900	253·2	7596	10128	12660	230·4	6912	9216	11520	221·2	6636	8848	11060	194·8	5844	7792	9740	45
50	17·600	280·0	8400	11200	14000	255·0	7650	10200	12750	234·0	7020	9360	11700	216·0	6480	8640	10800	50
55	19·400	309·0	9270	12360	15450	281·0	8430	11240	14050	257·6	7728	10304	12880	237·7	7131	9508	11885	55
60	21·200	338·0	10140	13520	16900	307·2	9216	12288	15360	281·4	8442	11256	14070	260·0	7800	10400	13000	60
65	23·000	366·2	10986	14648	18310	333·3	10000	13332	16665	305·4	9162	12216	15270	281·8	8454	11272	14090	65

I found that it travelled 57mm per wheel revolution, so would need to run at 17.54 wheel revs every 11.3 seconds, giving a motor speed, on 38:1 Ultrascale gears, of 666.5 revs every 11.3 seconds or 3.540 r.p.m. – an entirely reasonable speed for a 1620 Sagami, if a bit low for a DS10.

(In case you get the impression that I have 'got it in' for the poor old DS10, this is not so. It can be a real asset provided you appreciate what it's *designed* to do; the N gauge SD40 in which I first met it (some while before it appeared on these shores) had driving wheels 6.65mm. in diameter and a worm-and-spur reduction of, I recollect, 24:1. At the 50 scale m.p.h. that might be typical of a road diesel on a highball freight (SD40 territory), that DS10 would be turning over at some 10,500 r.p.m. – which is close to its peak torque figure, just out of the 'rapid heating' zone, and right where the motor was most 'in balance'. Horses for courses, you see ...

I hope that all this makes some sort of sense, even if you get a bit lost in the tatty remnants of Rice's schoolroom maths. What I can recommend is the little table of 'design speeds' that appears alongside. The 12 sec/m that I've used for my 'Trerice' locos is in the context of a mineral line where speeds in the 15–20 m.p.h. range would be prevalent. With locos having wheel sizes ranging from 3ft 9in (1366 0–6–OPT) to 4ft 7½in ('57XX'/'55XX'), it can be seen that 40:1 gives me plenty of overall reduction to keep the motors used happy at around 4–5,000 r.p.m. in steady-speed running. Even the D13, higher-revving than the 'cans', gives me plenty of 'poke' at these speeds, and all the engines are well able to haul the dozen or so wagons that is their lot. Extracting more power would call for higher motor speeds, but why bother if you don't need it? I'm much more interested in smooth, quiet running and high-quality control.

What all this comes down to is that I am able to standardise on just two transmissions for almost all my locos – the Ultrascale 38:1 gearset, either naked or in a Sharman milled-brass gearbox, or Exactoscale's 40:1 gearbox. Were I faced with a very small-wheeled loco, which wouldn't accept these types due to a lack of ground clearance, I might have to think again. Similarly, if I was faced with a vintage loco with 7ft 6in drivers, enough room for only a small, high-revving motor, and a need to extract high power or steady slow running, then I might contemplate a high-reduction transmission. Given the choice, I steer clear of them. Pick the right motor, and you can do the same, making the whole job of transmission design and installation a great deal simpler. After all, when the prototype found a need to go faster, they fitted bigger wheels, to up the speed for a given number of wheel r.p.m. (and hence for a given piston speed, on which there is a practical maximum above which the valves can't feed or exhaust the cylinder fast enough, when the engine is said to 'choke'). We're simply following prototype practice to a large extent. And, what is more important in the context of our models, we are avoiding the drawbacks associated with inefficient, tricky, high-reduction gears and screaming motors, as the 40:1 selected is a pretty 'moderate' ratio in all respects. Moderato in locobus, say I!

TRANSMISSION ASSEMBLY

I think that I've covered just about all the relevant aspects of transmission design, performance and installation in this long and rather convoluted chapter except the order of doing. This will obviously vary from loco to loco, depending upon the specification and the components being used. All I really want to do here is to remind you not to forget that bits of the transmission may need to be installed way back in the building process, so, as so often stressed, a bit of pre-planning is needed. A crude 'flow chart' showing how the bits of the chassis come together is a useful aid if, like me, you're a bit absent minded. And now I'm going to have a dram of Edradour and think a bit about pick-ups. Slàinte!

CHAPTER ELEVEN

DRIVETRAINS: PART 3 – PICK-UPS, TESTING, TROUBLE-SHOOTING.

PICK-UPS

This little essay will, hopefully, be as short and sharp as the last one was long and windy. For, so far as pick-ups in the context of kit-built loco chassis are concerned, there are but two alternatives – wipers or plungers. And as I've never had much trouble with the former and nothing *but* trouble with the latter, then you will appreciate that I'm limiting myself to an exposition of but a single, simple device. It's only in the application that things can get a little bit involved, where the prototype is inconsiderate enough to clutter itself up with springs, ashpans, bits of frame or other anatomical details right where it would best suit us to have a wiper. No matter – a bit of lateral through can usually overcome such little hindrances.

TYPES OF WIPER PICK-UP

I find that, in the vast majority of cases, loco kit chassis will accept wiper pick-ups of one of three basic types: Side-acting wipers, fitted below the frames; ditto, above frames; and top-acting wipers. Deciding which is the best bet is really a matter of taking a long, hard look at the chassis. If there are small wheels, bringing the bottom of the frames into close proximity to the track, then some form of top-mounted pick-up is indicated. If the wheels are *so* small that they don't protrude above the frames, then side-wipers are out and top-wipers are the logical choice; if the converse is true, then arranging for side-acting wipers to bear on the tyre backs just above the frames is a neat – and usually unobtrusive – solution. If it's a nice leggy engine, with big wheels and plenty of exposed tyre both above and below the frames, then the world is your oyster. If in this enviable position, then my main consideration is to place the pick-ups in the position that best conceals them from the public gaze; they are not, after all, either seemly or authentic.

In a goodly number of cases, I end up looking to different solutions for different parts of the loco. Just because one axle calls for a top-acting wiper, for instance, doesn't mean they all do. The 1620-powered '57XX' pannier that kept popping up in the last chapter is just such a case, employing top-mounted, side-acting wipers on the two leading axles, coyly concealed within the splashers and mounted on a pair of busbars running along just inside the tops of the frames. This was no good for the rear axle, however, but the fact that the GWR put the hind springs of such engines in the cab (where they got in the crew's way) rather than beneath the frames (so they kept out of *my* way) meant that I could arrange a pair of further wipers, mounted to a PCB block hiding above the brake cross-shaft, bearing on the tyre-backs beneath the frames. Result – reliable pick-up from all six wheels, without any visual intrusion or any possibility of troublesome shorting with pick-ups close to other chassis components.

The need for flexibility of thought as well as flexibility of wiper might be illustrated by the problems posed by another '57XX' chassis, the one featured in the 'frame erection' notes and elsewhere. This more recent example of the genus 'Perseverii' has a 'proper' frame outline, with the semi-circular frame extensions above the hornguide openings, rather than the flat top of its earlier sibling. These frame extensions, of course, completely mask the driving wheel tyres above the 'mean level' of the top of the frames, thus effectively scuppering any repetition of the solution applied to the earlier model. I settled for some very convoluted wipers 'below stairs' that had to thread their way perilously close to the springs beneath the leading two axles. This chassis is, you will recall, fitted with a D13 motor which, due to its use of only a single insulated brush, renders the whole chassis live to the opposing brush. The risk of short

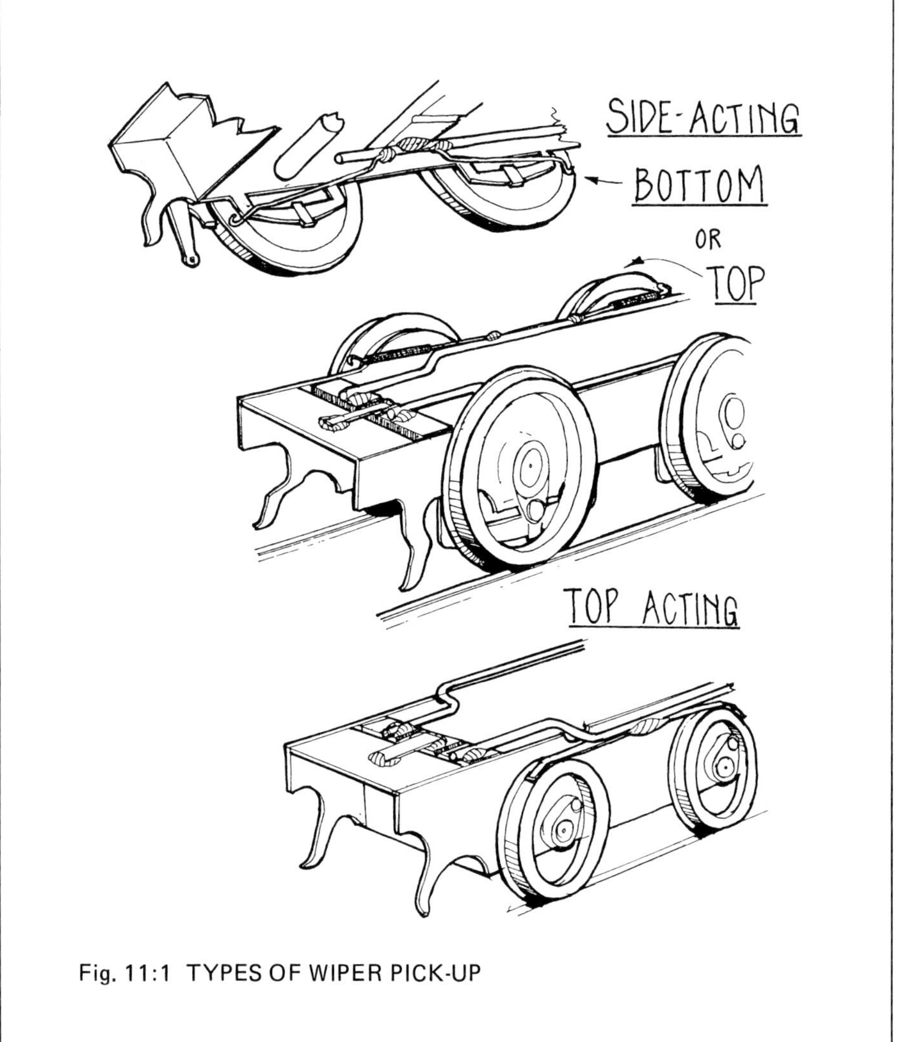

Fig. 11:1 TYPES OF WIPER PICK-UP

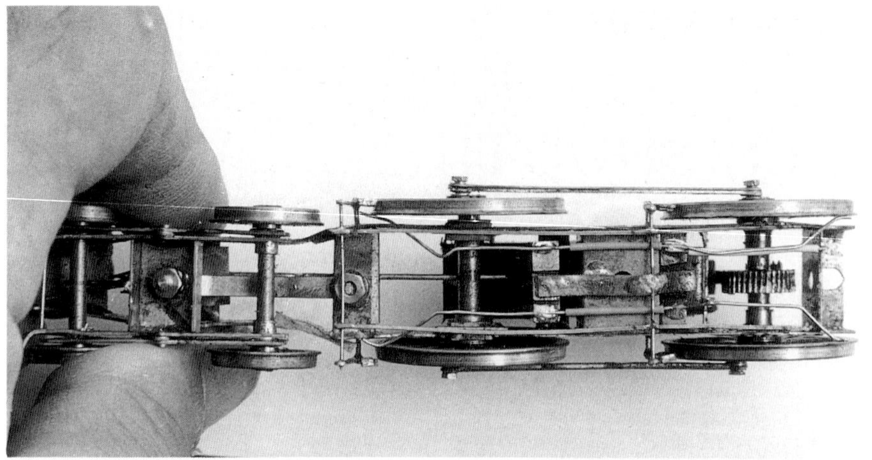

Left: *Wiper pick-ups at their most straightforward, on the driving wheels of an EM 'T9' chassis built from the Westward/Perseverance kit. Twin phosphor-bronze strip mounting blocks fore and aft locate wipers of 0.4mm nickel-silver wire.* Right: *Side-acting wipers on top of the frames are a useful system for a lot of 0–6–0 tender engines, such as this EM '2251'. Normal 'below frames' wipers are used on the rear axle.*

Top-acting wipers are well suited to tank engines such as the Mitchell '44XX' illustrated. The pick-ups and their mountings can be located and concealed within the sidetanks, keeping the crowded and rather convoluted space beneath the frames clear of electrical complications.

Small wheels and deep frames are a classic case for below-footplate top-acting wipers, as on the chassis of my GWR '1366' 0–6–0PT, built from the Peter K '1361' kit. Note busbars running along above wheels. Insulation is by epoxy-soaked tissue paper.

Although such top-acting wipers are, strictly speaking, 'on view', they are pretty unobtrusive, as this shot of my Hunslett 0–6–0DM shunter (from an Impetus kit) shows, or rather, doesn't show; the wipers are, to all intents, invisible.

P4 this time. Note flange-edge location of wipers on trailing carrying wheels.

circuits is thus obviously higher than would be the case with a chassis conforming to more modern practice, where the use of all-insulated (usually plastic-centred) wheels and a motor having fully-insulated brush gear (anything other than a D11/13) will leave the frames and anything attached thereto electrically 'dead'. I overcame the problem in this case by sleeving the relevant wipers with fine PVC insulation stripped from telephone cable.

A third variation is exhibited by the little outside-cylindered 'dock tank' pannier of the '1366' class, which has deep frames and heels only 3 ft 8 in in diameter. Here, top-acting wipers were *de rigueur*, and conform to my normal practice in such matters by employing a pair of stiff wire busbars running along above the wheels but hard up beneath the running plate, from which they are insulated by strips of epoxy-soaked tissue paper (an old Mike Sharman dodge). 'Soft' phosphor-bronze strip wipers bear on the tops of the tyres of the two leading sets of drivers, which are free to move vertically as part of the 'Flexichas' compensation with which all my engines are equipped. These 'extra gentle' strip wipers are used so that their effect on the action of the compensation is minimal; on the rear, fixed, axle, I've installed fine brass wire wipers, to ensure reliable contact, as described in the next section on pick-up design.

The three examples just described are, of course, all 0–6–0T locos, and are picking up from all six wheels. They are also, as noted, compensated, so we can be sure that all six wheels be in permanent contact with the rails and thus able to perform their pick-up function. This is the most often-cited advantage of compensation, and it is probably the most significant; a rigid chassis 0–6–0 would be lucky to be much more than an 0–3–0 in terms of wheels in contact with the track for a lot of the time, given that at the low supply voltages with which we're working, a wheel/rail gap of even 1 thou is enough to break contact. This has led to the sound practice of arranging pick-ups on as many wheels as possible, carrying as well as driven. Indeed, it is one of the principal arguments advanced by the protagonists of split-frame chassis construction, who trade complication in return for the ability to use *all* wheels for pick-up. Such an option is not denied the installer of wipers, either, and it is possible to fit these to some or all of the carrying wheels. I have done so, particularly in the case of 4–4–0 or 0–4–4 *tank* engines, where there is no tender to eke out the driver pick-ups. 2–4–0 and 0–4–2T types are treated as 0–6–0s anyway, but I wouldn't shun the trailing truck of an 0–6–2T, or the radial trucks of a 2–4–2T. Well-designed wipers work well on carrying wheels and also on tenders – but they need to *be* well-designed.

DESIGNING WIPER PICK-UPS

The main drawback of a wiper pick-up is that it exerts a pressure on the tyre of the wheel from which it is picking up, and that creates drag. In the case of drivers, this is of little account, as we have already noted that we have plenty of power and torque to spare (or we have if the drivetrain has been built right), and the amount of drag should be small. However, where wipers are acting on carrying wheels, the drag becomes more critical, as it may be enough to brake the wheel to the point where it skids along the track rather than revolving. To avoid such unseemly behaviour, we need to keep the drag to the minimum possible, consistent with the maintenance of enough contact pressure to ensure reliable pick-up.

Contact pressure is expressed as weight over a given area, and it depends on two things: the force applied by the contact, and the size of the 'contact patch'. I haven't a clue what the actual figures involved in the case of model loco pick-ups are, but I do recall that the 'contact pressure' exerted by top-flight hi-fi gramophone stylii were in the order of tons per square inch, for all that the stylus was operating under a 'tracking weight' of little more than a gramme. The point (!) is that the tip of the stylus is so tiny that the contact area was a minute fraction of a square millimetre, and so a tiny weight acting through this miniscule contact patch was ample to keep the stylus in firm and constant contact with the record. As a firm and constant contact is what we're after to ensure reliable electrical continuity in our wiper pick-up system, then it follows that what we need is a gentle pressure exerted through a tiny contact patch, not a large force acting on a big area. In other words, some fine, springy wire pressing relatively lightly on the wheel-tyre will actually give us *more* reliable pick-up than a thicker, less flexible wire acting over a larger contact area. And it is the actual force multiplied by the contact area that gives the level of friction – so the fine, softly-sprung wiper scores on both counts.

Once I'd worked through this apparent paradox, and junked my thick, chunky wire or strip pick-ups in favour of some thin, springy wires, my pick-up problems vanished. The wires that I use most often are Alan Gibson's 0.33 mm. diameter hard brass, or the similarly-sized gold-plated phosphor-bronze wire sold by Maplin Electronics, apparently for making electric organ contacts. I usually crank the wire at the point of contact, to keep the actual size of the contact patch to a minimum. If I'm forced to fit flat strip 'soft' phosphor-bronze strip wipers in a 'top-acting' capacity, then I reduce the contact patch area by fitting a

Fine wire wipers. These 0.33mm hard brass wire wipers on my 'J15' have put in eight years hard service without problem. This engine has always been a very reliable runner.

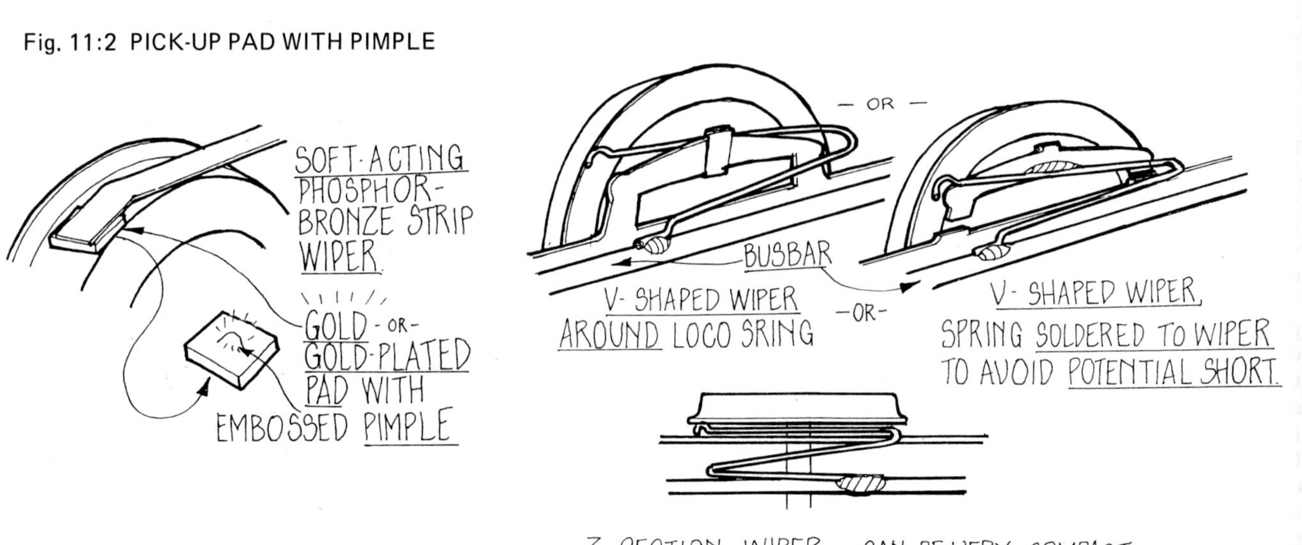

Fig. 11:2 PICK-UP PAD WITH PIMPLE

Fig. 11:3 'V' OR 'Z' WIPERS

'pad' where the wiper meets the wheel. This has a little dimple embossed in it – I simply use my riveting punch, or the tip of a scriber. If I can get it, I make this little pad out of gold or gold-plated phosphor-bronze – the contact strips from old-fashioned computer 'bus connectors' provide a source of suitable material. The reason for using flat strip wipers on top-acting systems in the first place is to prevent them flexing sideways and 'de-railing' on wheels that are free to move, either vertically in tilt (compensated) or laterally (sideplay).

As well as the diameter and stiffness of the pick-up wire, we need to consider the actual length of the wiper, as this will tend to determine the contact force as well as the degree of flexibility afforded to accommodate lateral movement where the wheelset concerned has a sideplay allowance. Many wiper pick-ups I see on model locos are far too short, and nowhere near resilient enough. Obviously, over-stiff pick-up wipers can interfere with the free movement of wheelsets both sideways and in tilt where the loco has a compensated chassis. I always proceed on the basis that the wiper should start off as flexible (and hence as long) as possible, as it's a simple matter to shorten its effective length and increase the contact pressure. But if the thing is too short and stiff to start with, there's not a lot you can do about it, short of junking the whole caboodle and starting again. If you're cramped for room to fit long wipers, don't forget that the effective length can be increased by 'doubling back' in 'V' or even 'Z' form, as in the sketch. I often use a 'V' shaped wiper around an obstructive loco spring, also as drawn.

A variety of wiper forms, including some doubled-back 'V' section, are exhibited on my scratch-built GER Bromley Tank; these are the gold-plated Maplin phosphor-bronze wire.

Fig. 11:4 BUSBARS AND MOUNTING BLOCKS

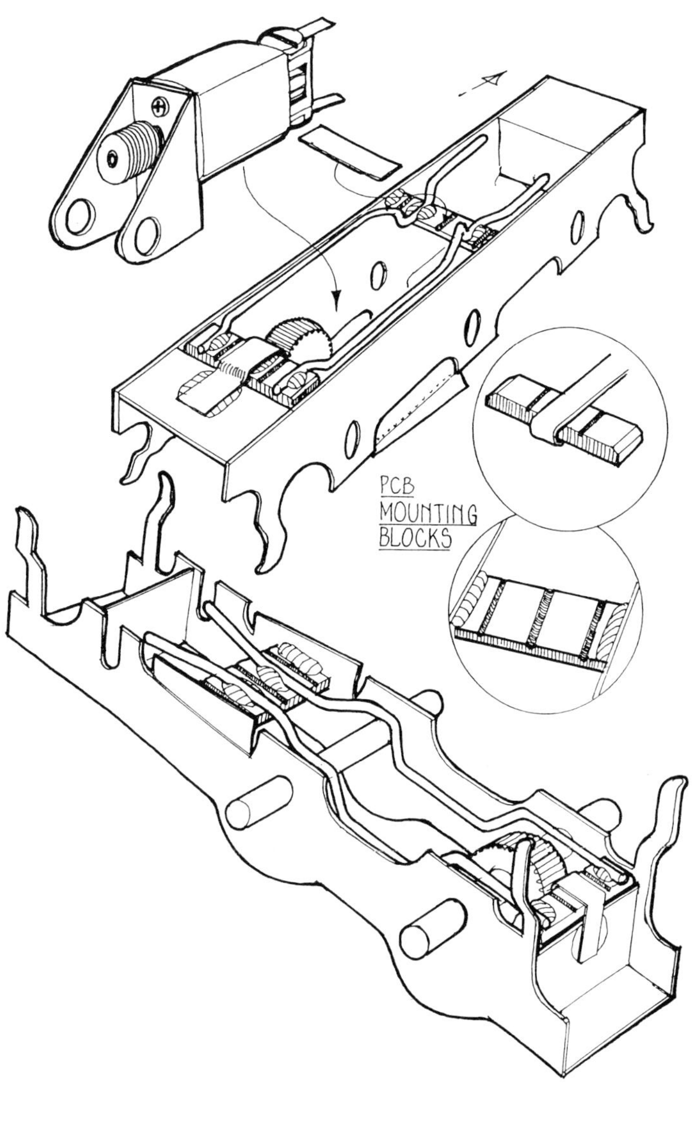

PCB MOUNTING BLOCKS

PICK-UP MOUNTINGS

In the brief descriptions of the pannier-tank pick-up systems with which I kicked off this dissertation, you will have noticed frequent mention of busbars. I omitted to list them in the specification of the second, D13-powered '57XX', but they're there all right, just as they are on virtually all my other locos. Only in exceptional circumstances do I consider any other means of mounting wiper pick-ups. The use of busbars has a number of advantages, among which I would number the freedom to anchor a pick-up at any point along the bar, the ease of installing the wipers individually, rather than 'paired' or emanating from some common mounting point, the ease of attaching motor feed wires, and the usefulness of having some easy point to which test leads can be clipped for wheel-cleaning and other such nefarious purposes. My busbars are simply stiff wire – usually Alan Gibson's 0.7 mm or 0.9 mm brass. It's not critical – I have used 1 mm square or stiff flat nickel-silver strip, and even, in destitute moments unpicked paper clips.

Left: *Fitting wiper pick-ups to the long-suffering '57XX' chassis was a fairly typical operation. It's a job that cannot be undertaken until the chassis is pretty well complete.* Right: *The pick-up busbars were soldered to PCB-strip (modified SMP copper-clad sleepers) mountings, as in Fig. 11:4, located by brackets from appropriate frame spacers, as in the photo below.*

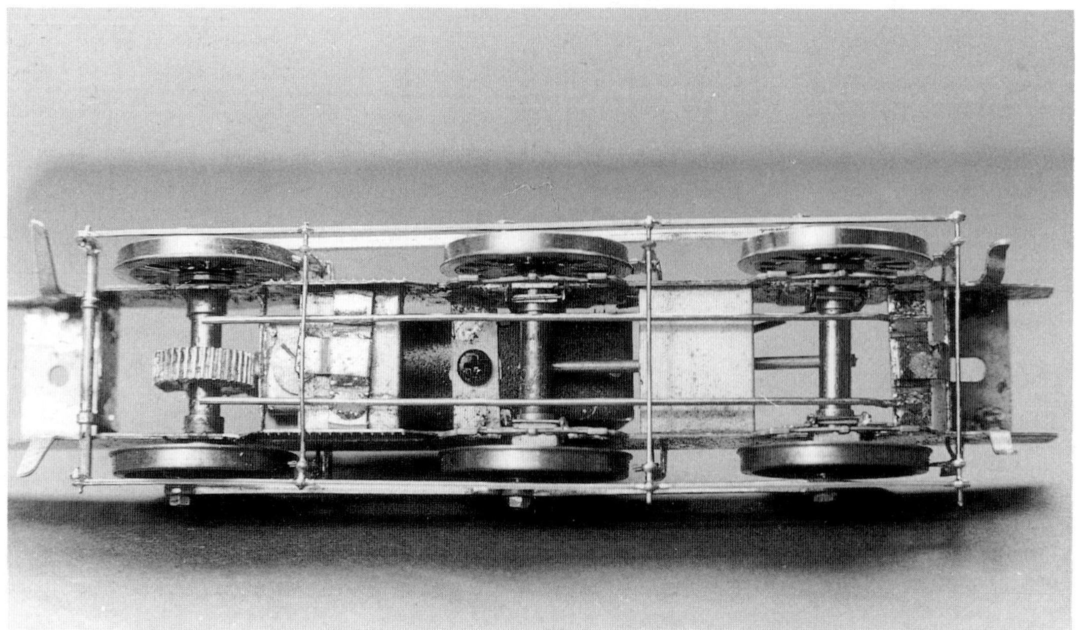

The busbars themselves were, in this instance, fairly straightforward, being fashioned from 0.7mm hard brass wire.

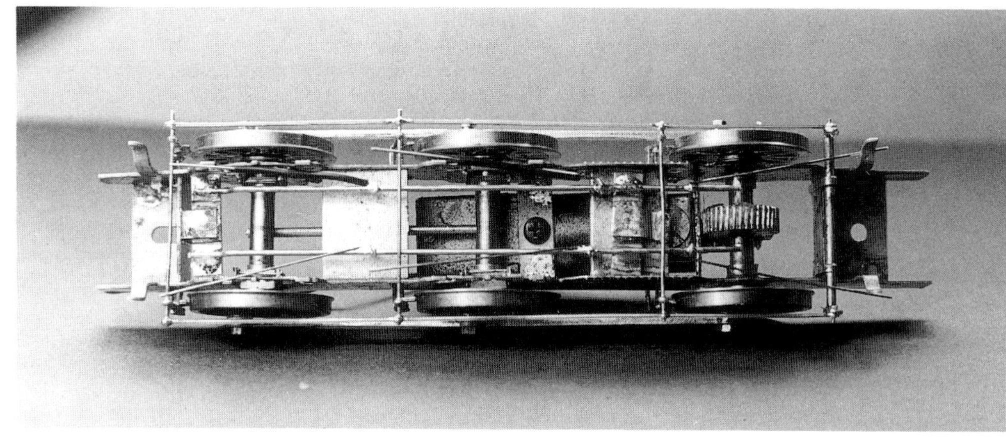

This shot has the short lengths of 0.33mm hard brass wire, from which the pick-up wipers were bent up, soldered in place on the busbars. Note the fine sleeving (ex-Telecom wire) in place on the insulated side. (This chassis, don't forget, uses a D13 motor which has a 'live' brush, hence the chassis itself is similarly live, and insulation is critical.)

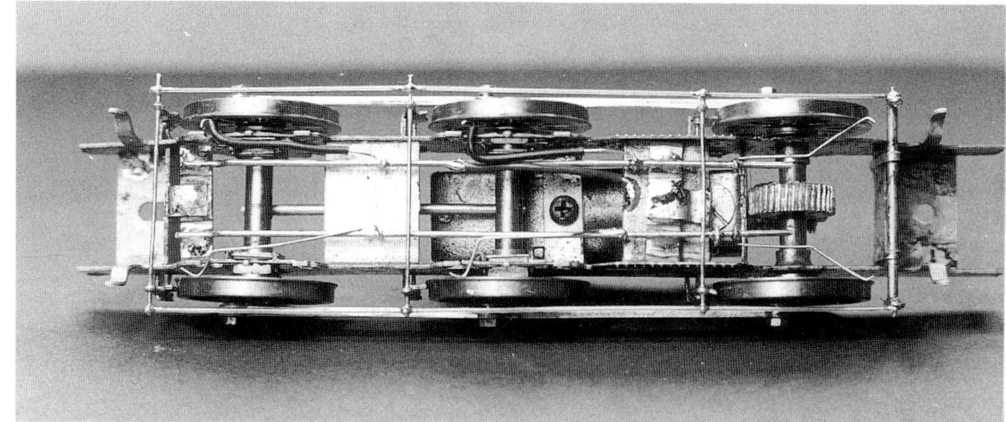

Here is the finished job, with the various wipers formed to shape. Not elegant, but it all works OK.

These busbars need to be long enough to accept all the likely pick-up mounting points needed for the loco, with a gap here and there for the attachment of the motor feeds and those useful croc-clipped test leads. They don't have to be straight – mine rarely are, dodging up and down or in and out to keep out of sight and to avoid springs, ashpans, compensating beams, gears and other chassis impedimentia. I generally get away with two anchorage points, made from sliced-up bits of PCB sleeper. These don't have to be at the extremities of the bars, although I do try and keep overhangs short so as not to compromise the stiffness of the bars and thus their suitability as firm, fixed anchorage points for the wipers. You can't adjust these last with any degree of certainty or consistency if what they're fixed to is waving around in the breeze like old Mother Kelly's washing. It's impossible, obviously, to give a specific bus-bar layout for every application, but as a guide I've drawn some typical installations which should serve to give the idea. Note the detail of the modified-sleeper mounting blocks. A nice alternative is double-sided PCB, which can be soldered in place by the 'back side', leaving nice big firm lands on the face to which the busbars are soldered. Once the busbars are in place, do check the insulation, both one from another and between each bar and the chassis as a whole.

FITTING WIPER PICK-UPS

The one thing I *never* try and do is to pre-shape a wiper before fitting, except in the most general way. My usual technique, illustrated in the photo-sequence, is to attach a piece of the chosen wire of sufficient length to make the pick-up plus a bit, which is then bent to shape *in situ* using fine snipe-nose pliers. Only when I'm satisfied that the wiper is firmly in contact with the wheel but missing everything else do I snip off the excess. The process is then repeated down the chassis until I *think* I've got all the wipers in the appropriate locations, and making what always *appears* to be pretty good contact. The drill then is to clip one test lead to a busbar, and to touch the other to each wheel on the opposing side in turn. That's when you find that wipers that are apparently wiping are actually doing no such thing! So it's out with the pliers, and a tweak here and a tweak there until the loco runs reliably on that particular pick-up, no matter what the antic of the wheel might be in terms of sideplay or compensatory gyrations. Only when I'm happy that I've 'aced' the wiper under scrutiny do I move on to the next one, repeating the process around the whole chassis until I'm as certain as I can be that all the pick-ups are doing the business.

It may be that during this process you discover a propensity of a certain pick-up to misbehave, either by touching something it (Zap! Pow!) shouldn't, or by getting itself out of alignment and 'falling off' the wheel tyre. One snag with wire pick-ups is that they flex equally in all directions, and a wiper that is long and sinuous in the horizontal plane where it bears against the wheel back can be equally sinuous vertically, when it can get up to all sorts of evil. Most of these wayward propensities are harmless enough, but watch out for a pick-up getting between driving wheel spokes, where it can stall the mechanism and, in the case of a coreless motor, lead to a burn-out. If you find that you need to 'stiffen up' an over-flexible wiper, just put a further tack-soldered joint between wiper and busbar to effect the required increase in resolve. Wipers that prove too fond of casual fondling of the chassis or other bits of locomotoid anatomy can be prevented from causing electrical mayhem by sleeving them with a bit of fine PVC insulation stripped

Fig. 11:5 WIPER POSITION

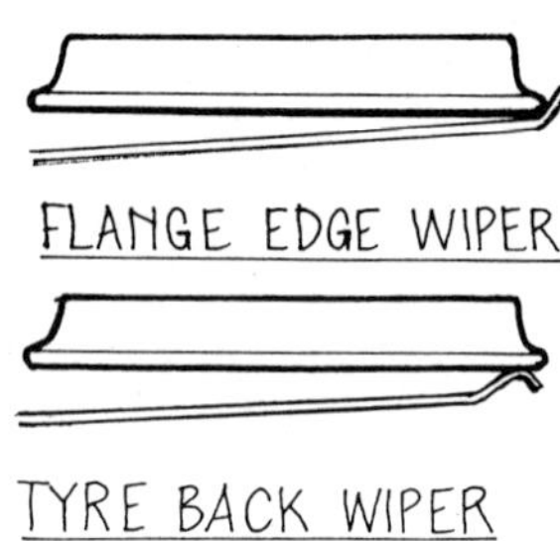

from the skinny GPO (sorry, Telecom; gettin' old) telephone cable – the 4-core stuff that they staple right across the middle of the family portraits when putting in an extension is ideal. Don't overdo this – it obviously affects the flexibility of the wiper, especially if it encompasses any 'tensioning tweaks' put in to adjust the pick-up pressure. A bit more fiddling may be needed to ensure reliable contact once you've added sleeving. I generally try to anticipate where it will be needed and bung it on before bending the pick-ups to shape. If necessary, sleeving can be kept in place with a smear of Uhu on the wiper before you slide it on.

One last consideration in the installation of wiper pick-ups is the exact point at which you arrange them to bear on the wheel. Top-mounted efforts will, obviously, bear on the running surface of the tyre, but the more usual rear-mounted wipers don't lend themselves to such a location. Normally, there are two alternatives – the flat back of the tyre proper, and the edge of the flange. The former is often the simpler arrangement – indeed, on compensated chassis, where the wheel can move in relation to the pick-up, it's the *only* arrangement, as flange-edge wipers inhibit the free working of compensated chassis. The drawbacks of a tyre-back wiper are the need to keep this area of the wheel clean, not always easy, and the inability to paint it. Not many real locos have bright, shiny-clean tyre backs! I generally use both locations on my locos, with tyre-back wipers on the compensating wheelsets, and a flange-edge set-up on any fixed or trailing axles. If you are fitting flange-back wipers, it's worth taking the trouble to set them as close to the edge of the tyre as possible. This makes it easier to keep the 'wiper track' clean, and enables you to paint *most* of the tyre-back. If you're using older Sharman wheels, which used a small hole drilled in the tyre-back as a locking device, you'll be faced with a small plastic 'pip' right in the path of a 'centred' wiper, which can cause an annoying 'clicking' sound. Make sure the 'pip' is filed and sanded flush, and try and arrange the wiper to miss it.

I'm sorry if all this sounds a bit vague, but the whole business of setting up wiper pick-ups really comes down to some persistent fiddling – there's no sure-fire, hard-and-fast recipe that guarantees a result. Bear in mind the requirement for a relatively gentle pressure and a small contact patch, and you won't go far wrong. It doesn't really matter much which type of wiper you're fitting, the drill is much the same. The only real departure comes with flat strip top-acting variants, which call for the addition of the little gold pads with the pips. These are made, as previously mentioned, from the contact strips from computer bus connectors, and I don't cut the pad off the bar until it's soldered in place, so as to have something to get hold of.

PICK-UPS ON TENDERS

Tenders are Good News on the pick-up front, particularly on 4–4–0s and other types with a lack of usable wheels. I very often make use of the 'loaded tender' arrangement for such types, as in the sketch. The combination of the front pair of tender axles floating in a sort of bogie capacity and a relatively well-weighted vehicle means that the rear, fixed tender axle is always in very good contact with the track, and thus forms an ideal pick-up point. In the case of a 4–4–0, taken together with the driving wheels, it gives six-wheel pick-up, which I have found to be the desirable minimum

Fig. 11:6 PICK-UP FROM 'LOADED' TENDER

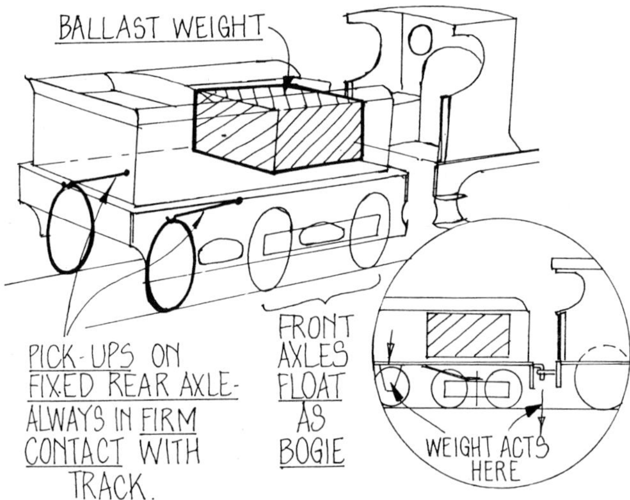

A chassis for a 'loaded tender', with the front two axles lightly sprung (0.33mm brass wire springs each side). Pick-ups are fitted to the rear-fixed axle. This was the tender for the Falcon brass Kirtley Goods.

for consistent and reliable results. I take the power through to the loco with a pair of fine, flexible leads, once again courtesy of BT – taken, in this instance, from the coiled leads fitted to the last generation of dial telephones. These leads are arranged so that they look like the water feed hoses (see next chapter), and the power is transmitted through the simple little home-made plug-and-socket drawn in *Fig 11:7.*

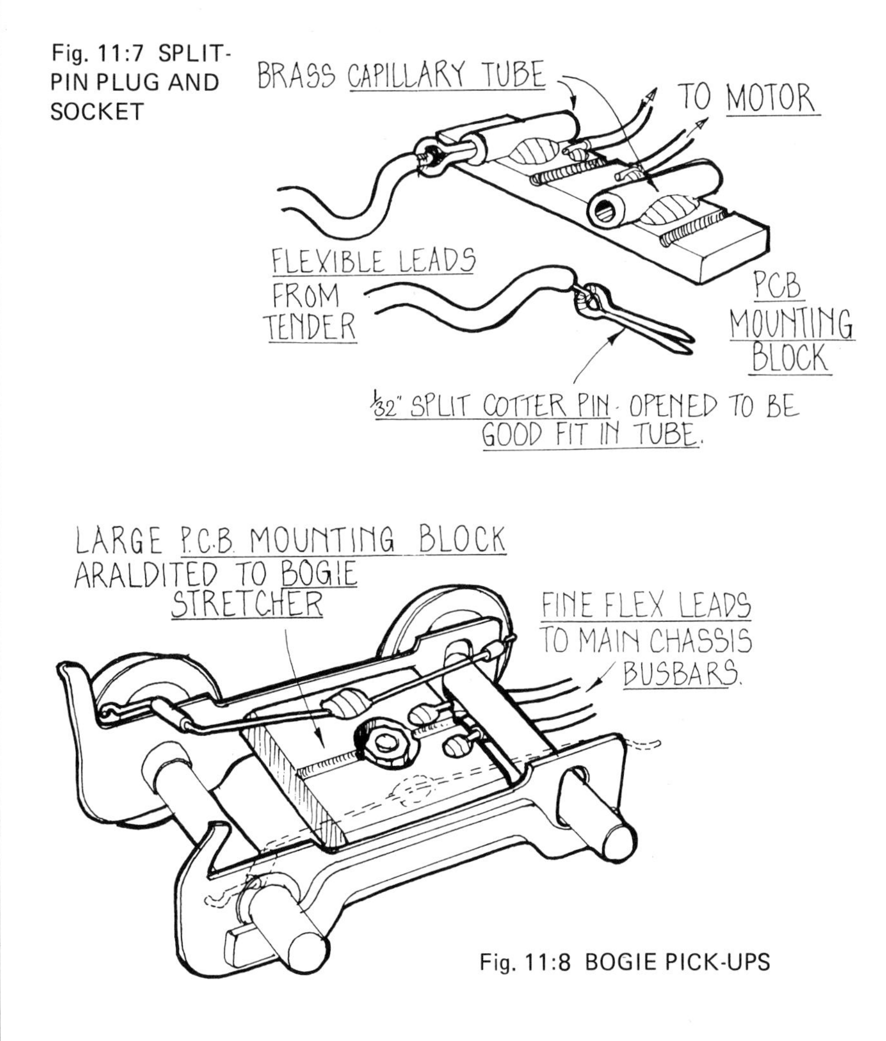

Fig. 11:7 SPLIT-PIN PLUG AND SOCKET

Fig. 11:8 BOGIE PICK-UPS

PICK-UPS ON BOGIES

These are really a bit of a curse, and are inevitably a fiddle to make. I avoid them if at all possible, but on truly awkward engines like 0–4–4 and 4–4–0 tank engines, they can make all the difference between a loco that runs reliably and one that runs like a Gloucester Old Spot. In terms of actual installation, it is a matter of providing some suitable insulated 'lands' to which the wipers can be soldered. There's not really scope for busbars, and the arrangement that I've used is much as drawn in *Fig 11:8.* The criteria for the wipers is reliable contact with the softest possible pressure, to keep the bogie wheels turning freely, not so easy if they're very lightly loaded; it pays to get as much weight as possible onto a bogie fitted with pick-ups, which is usually no problem in the cases noted. Other than the awkwardness occasioned by the general lack of space encountered when trying to sneak pick-ups onto a bogie, the only other little problem to solve is some means of feeding the power back to the motor. Once again, I call on the fine telephone coil-lead flex, and I simply connect this between the pick-up block on the bogie and the fore (or aft) end of the main pick-up busbars on the loco. I can't see any point in getting involved in fancy wiping contact systems to transfer this power.

MOTOR FEEDS

One of the enormous advantages of the fully-insulated chassis with busbar-mounted wiper pick-ups is that you can very easily make it go either way, simply by swapping the feeds from busbars to motor from side to side. All my locos seem to go the opposite way to everybody else's, but at least they all go the *same* way; on the old East Suffolk Light layout, where many of the locos had less sophisticated pick-up systems and several had D13 motors, I ended up with five engines that went one way, and one that was irrevocably wired up widdershins. Well, it kept the operators on their toes! With the general move to axle-hung motor mounts, the motor is often free to pivot about the axle, which it will do under the influence of torque reaction from the gears. The motor feed leads can be used to control this undesirable behaviour. I either fit good, stiff leads from that single-core telephone extension cable, whose sleeving has already proved so valuable, or I use the natty arrangement drawn in *Fig 11:9,* where the leads are used in tension to hold the motor down against a pad of fairly 'stiff' foam rubber – I use a piece of the camping mat on which I lay my track, as described in my 'Finescale Track' book.

These days, we don't have to worry about incorporating all the elaborate TV suppression gear that used to be mandatory if you didn't want to fall out with the neighbours. Modern TV and radio tuners are much more discriminating, and aren't affected by a spot of RFI (Radio Frequency Interference) wafting through the ether. The motors we use these days only produce minimal amounts of RFI anyway, in comparison with the good old days of Romford

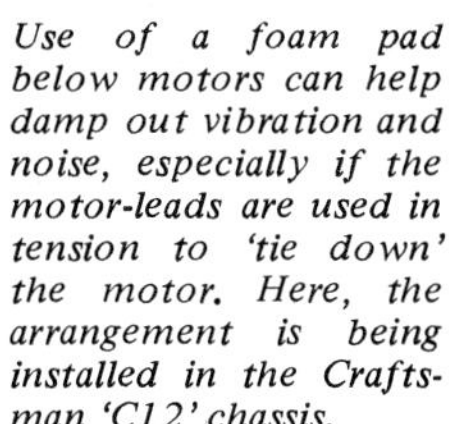
Use of a foam pad below motors can help damp out vibration and noise, especially if the motor-leads are used in tension to 'tie down' the motor. Here, the arrangement is being installed in the Craftsman 'C12' chassis.

Phantoms and the like, which could probably blank out Radio Moscow with a dozen Exeleys in tow! The only motor-feed addition we may wish to make is the insertion of a quick-blow 500MA audio fuse in line with one motor lead, which should give 'belt and braces' protection of coreless motors, no matter what the controller is or isn't doing.

Fig. 11:9 FOAM BLOCK MOTOR PAD

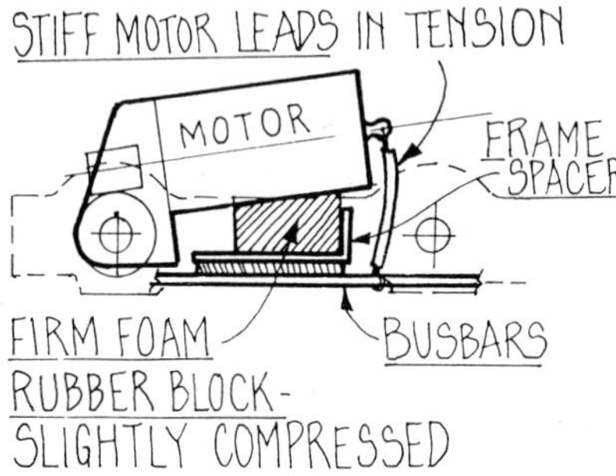

PICK-UP SUMMARY

So, to try and cram this into the proverbial nutshell, I find that I get the most reliable pick-up from soft, springy wire wipers of small section (to give a small contact patch), individually mounted on fully isolated busbars on an electrically-dead chassis (if you're using Romford wheels, cough up the extra and fit insulated all round). Picking up from as many wheels as possible is good insurance, especially on rigid-chassis locos. If you're really after ultimate reliability – compensate!

TESTING

The whole process of locomotive kit chassis construction is really one of continuous evaluation. We fit something, and we test it; until that test is satisfactory, be it the free-sliding of a hornblock, the easy-turning of a new-quartered chassis, or the correct meshing of a gearset, we don't move on to the 'next stage'. I can't impress too much how important it is to be rigorous about this – wishful thinking of the 'perhaps it'll go away when I've fitted the XXXX' variety rarely leads to anything but trouble. It's obviously important when testing to be aware of just exactly which fault you're looking for – all well and good if it's a simple go/no-go situation, not so easy if it's a matter of judgement. Just how free for instance, does something have to be to qualify as 'free running'?

One of the reasons that I have been at pains to give the rationale of the various systems and items of hardware we use to build loco chassis is to, hopefully, provide a basis on which value judgements of this sort can be made. I suppose that, at the end of the day, experience counts for a lot; if, after the thick end of half-a-thousand chassis, I can't decide pretty quickly whether things are OK, or diagnose where a fault lies, then I'm either pretty dozy or the fault is a real stinker – and they still turn up, believe you me! So, what I'm trying to do in this next section is to try and put into words the things I look for when testing and evaluating chassis, and in attempting to get the best out of them.

TEST PROCEDURE

The first tenet that guides me is that I'll learn more about the functioning of the various elements of a chassis using my fingers that I ever will listening to motor or gear notes or watching an ammeter. I *always* check *everything* under fingertip power before considering trying it with real live volts. If asked what I'm really looking for in the context of a sweet-running loco chassis, I think that it would be summed up as 'smoothness'. Something can be 'tight', a bit stiff or sticky – but if that stiffness is consistent rather than intermittent or 'lumpy', then I'm not too worried. A hornblock that jams at one point in its travel every time indicates a fault; one that moves smoothly but none-too-freely up and down the guide just needs lubrication, or a spot of 'running-in' with a drop of Brasso. The same goes for a quartered chassis – if it turns over smoothly but is rather 'tight', then that's fine; probably a good thing, in fact, as it will 'run in' in time and will almost certainly settle down to give satisfactory performance. It's the 'tight spot' once or twice per revolution, the knock or the wobble, and symptoms like crankpin nuts coming unscrewed all the time, that ring alarm bells.

A model locomotive chassis is like any other piece of small precision mechanism – it will have a 'life', over which it will progress gradually from being new and relatively 'tight', to being old and a bit worn, to the final condition (exhibited by a good few of my models) of being ancient and clapped-out. The aim is to maximise the period of the mechanism's life during which it gives the sort of performance we're looking, for; and that period will be substantially shortened if we build-in too much slop when the chassis is 'new'. So, to return to my introductory question, 'how free is free running', I might chance the answer 'when it works smoothly and feels free enough not to overtax the motor'. Once the motor is installed and the gears are meshed, try turning the motor armature over by hand before you even consider putting any power on.

Don't overlook the relevance of lubrication. Metal-to-metal bearings on axles, crankpins and motors are not designed to run 'dry'; there is no virtue in testing an unlubricated mechanism. Worm gearsets, too, need lubrication, preferably in grease form. A smear of 'Tri-Flow' teflon-loaded grease before testing is good practice. If you need to remove lubricants because testing has shown up the need for alterations, for re-soldering or re-Loctiting of components, then a wash with Slater's 'Mechanism Cleaner' or a solvent switch cleaner will do the trick. Meths is also a useful de-oiler in this context, while if you need to re-Loctite an axle that has been oiled and cleaned, a final wipe with some MEK on a tissue will prepare the surface for the fresh compound.

All testing, of whatever type, should be undertaken under conditions of 'minimum load'. Stressing bearings, hornguides or gears will effectively disguise the true state of affairs, so it's a good idea to make your judgement as soon after the installation of each component as possible. Also, do try to test things individually, so that if there is a problem you pinpoint it before it is lost in the interaction of several components. A good example of this is axle bearings – enter the axle in each bearing in turn, and give it a quick twiddle. This will tell you which *bearing*, if any, is 'tight' and in need of reaming, rather than merely that a particular axle doesn't revolve as freely as it should. And if, after testing the individual bearings and finding them satisfactory you still end up with a reluctant axle, you will then know that the fault lies in bearing *alignment*, rather than in a lack of running clearance within a bearing.

Similarly, electrical testing of motors, etc, should be done under 'free' conditions wherever possible. Apart from all other considerations, it is as well to discover a dud motor *before* you've gone to all the trouble of installing it in the chassis and meshing the gears. It's no bad idea, too, to use a 12V light bulb (5W car sidelight bulb with a pair of leads and miniature crocodile clips soldered in place) clipped across the busbars when testing pick-up continuity, rather than having the motor in circuit. The current through the pick-ups is thus limited to a 0.4A maximum, which obviates any possibility of sparking and pitting while ill-adjusted pick-ups are sorted out. This 'minimal load/maximum sensitivity' approach is the bedrock of all worthwhile testing; put paradoxically, if you apply a load to the component under test, how do you differentiate between resistance due to the load, and that occasioned by a fault in the component?

Probably the 'key' test of a newly-built chassis is the first time it turns under its own power. This is the moment at which a number of stages of the build come under scrutiny, and is the point at which it becomes far more difficult to isolate the causes of faulty running. The first thing to say is that it's not realistic to expect too much. There may be nothing fundamentally

Test running – and testing at all stages – is a vital part of the building process. Here is the '57XX' chassis being run 'in air', with the frames clamped in the vice.

wrong with the chassis or the drivetrain, but it will take them a little while to 'settle down'. The whole mechanism is, at this stage, 'brand new', and must be expected to be at its tightest. You will be very lucky indeed if it runs smoothly and sweetly from the outset, although it does occasionally happen, as with the '57XX' chassis illustrated in the 'build' sections of this book. However, if it doesn't run at all, or if the thing is tight and jerky, then I'm afraid it's a trouble-shooting job, which we'll come to in a moment. This key chassis test comes at the point where the drivetrain is first installed in the chassis, and is best conducted with the mechanism 'in the air'. Put it on blocks, or, as shown in the picture, clamp it in the vice.

If the chassis incorporates compensation or springing, you may find you have a situation where it runs erratically with the various axles jumping up and down in their hornguides. This is a function of the rather complex interaction of coupling-rod forces with the suspension, and usually occurs when the hornblocks are free but the rods are a bit 'tight'. It's exacerbated if the hornblocks have generous vertical travel. Don't worry about it – it should only occur with the chassis in 'free air'; sit it on a low-friction surface – plate glass is ideal – and run it up against a stop-block. You may still have it hopping up and down slightly, due to the fact that such compensated chassis need a bit of weight acting through the beam to overcome rod-reaction forces and the inherent friction of the hornblocks. Press down lightly on the chassis, which should stop it; if it doesn't, you need to ease out the coupling-rod clearance a touch.

RUNNING IN

All mechanisms need to 'run in'. All this entails is the bedding-in of the various rotating and stationary components one with another. The surfaces in contact will never be totally smooth, even if they look pretty good to the eye, with all manner of microscopic lumps and bumps, tool-marks and burrs to polish out. As with testing, running-in should be done under conditions of minimum load, much as already described in the context of motors. Ensure *all* bearings and gears are adequately lubricated, and set the chassis up either in free air or on plate glass, as just outlined. I usually undertake running-in in two stages – an initial period immediately after I'm satisfied that the drivetrain assembly is free of faults, and a further stint once it is complete with pick-ups, brake gear and other decorative bits. This latter stage is also a test, to ensure that there are no fouling problems with brake rigging or balance weights, and that the pick-ups are staying put as intended and not touching that which they shouldn't. Once I've given the chassis a good run on its own, I fit the body – or at least the running plate/splasher assembly – and check there are no problems twixt chassis and body.

The drill with running-in a complete chassis (or, if it happens to be independent and self-contained, the drivetrain before installation in the chassis) follows the procedure outlined for the motor alone. Start with a relatively short period at the lowest speed at which the motor is happy turning the whole mechanism over – give it five minutes or so in each direction, with a pause for cooling if required. Gradually increase the speed and duration of the running, taking care to equalise the time spent turning over in each direction. Monitor the motor frequently for overheating, particularly in the earliest stages, when the load will be at its highest. After this first period of running-in, which I usually set at about an hour, I wash off all the original lubricant from the whole mechanism, and replace it with fresh. This should help to flush out any minute metal particles, dirt or oxide that has been displaced from the running surfaces.

Never, under any circumstances, attempt to 'run in' a chassis – particularly the gearset – with any form of abrasive compound. Valve-grinding paste, toothpaste and metal polishes will not help to 'run-in' anything at this stage; premature 'clapping out' is more likely to result from such a process, The careful use of abrasives can help to 'free up' an individual sticky component, such as a reluctant hornblock or a 'rough' crankpin bush, but they should certainly never be applied indiscriminately to a mechanism, and, if used on a 'trouble spot', must be thoroughly washed away once the problem has been sorted; meths or mechanism cleaner flooded on with a soft paintbrush should do the trick. The point is, such remedial operations should be undertaken long before the chassis is complete enough to need running in!

The ideal way of carrying out the second-stage 'complete chassis' running-in is actually to let the loco run on the track, preferably on some form of continuous circuit. So if you belong to a club, or know somebody who has a 'round and round' layout, inveigle yourself some running powers and give your new loco a chance to stretch its legs with some gentle exercise. Again, the procedure of gradually increasing speeds and the duration of run in each direction should be followed, and really the longer you can let the chassis run, the better. It's amazing just how much a new mechanism will 'settle down' and free up given a couple of hours on a test track. It will be necessary to fit some ballast to any chassis for test-running such as this – most 4 mm mechanisms are pretty light, and a certain amount of weight is needed to keep the wheels firmly in contact with the track. If the loco body is not far enough advanced to be used in this role, I clip on the 'test weight' shown in the photograph of that ubiquitous '57XX' running trial. This is cobbled-up out of 45 grammes of lead (stick-on car wheel balance weights) on a springy brass-strip bracket that locates over a frame spacer. Insulating tape beneath the brass prevents short circuits. The alternative is a lump of lead on a blob of Blu-Tak.

If you don't have access to a continuous run (which, in P4, I don't), then the next-best thing is to run the chassis up against a stop-block placed at the end (or both ends) of a short piece of test track. Ballast the chassis to the minimum level that gives reliable pick-up, and proceed with the usual old rigamarole of increasing speeds and durations. Describing this method of running-in reminds me that it can have unsuspected results: many years ago, a chum of mine, who had best remain nameless, was attempting to run-in his latest effort, which was an early attempt at 4 mm super-power. The engine was a OO '9F', built from a Kitmaster kit, fitted with a home-made brass chassis and Romford drivers, the whole being powered by a OO gauge Pitman motor in the tender driving the rear coupled axle through a shaft. In order to maximise the huge power output available, every crevice in the loco was filled with 'Cerrobend', the result weighing almost 3lb. This behemoth was taken to the club test-track, which incorporated a short length of Peco 'Streamline' track fitted with a stop-block, as just proscribed. The '9F' was railed on this, and run gently up against the stop-block, where, not surprisingly, it stalled. My chum reacted to this by giving it a bit of real 'wellie' – whereupon the wheels spun, gripped – and fired the rails of the test-track clean out of the sleepers and half-way across the clubroom! Perhaps those natty little test-rollers that are all the rage these days aren't such a bad idea, after all! They would certainly be a very good way of running-in a chassis, if you can run to the (not inconsiderable) outlay.

With the pick-ups fitted and a temporary ballast weight clipped in place, the guinea-pig '57XX' runs its first track trials. Two fellow 'guinea-pigs', the Kirtley Goods and the '1366', are in the background.

A very nice way of test-running or running-in a chassis is to use rollers in a sort of 'stationary testing plant' configuration, as here; Chris Langon's DJH 'Britannia' chassis is ready to go.
C. J. LANGDON

TROUBLE SHOOTING

Before there is any point in trying to run a chassis in, however, it will be necessary to track down and put right any faults that come to light during the testing procedures. Isolating faults is greatly helped by the suggested procedure of continuous evaluation of the job as it proceeds, but nevertheless there are occasions when all the individual 'stage checks' seem OK, but there is still a running problem. This will usually come under one of three headings: mechanical, electrical, and trackholding. It's the last which I always dread. Mechanical glitches are usually all too apparent, electrical gremlins come down to a short or a lack of continuity, but the reason why an engine dives into the ditch at the least excuse can be hard to divine. It's all too easy to get lured into a false sense of security when evaluating a loco on a test-track consisting of a yard or so of dead-straight, dead level PW. Mine is deliberately kinky, with an evil S-bend and some nasty cants.

MECHANICAL FAULTS

The usual sort of mechanical fault manifests itself by jerky running, especially at low speeds. It's a truism of model loco building that most people can get a loco to blind along all right at the railway equivalent of Warp Factor 5, but find it a good deal harder to achieve a passable result at 5 mph! There are three main possibilities to investigate when your pride and joy develops a stagger worthy of Long John Silver on a rum blinder – a tight spot in the coupling rods, mechanical fouling of some sort, and out-of-round gears. In the first case, the quartering is the prime suspect, and a couple of simple checks may help pinpoint the error. Firstly, equip yourself with one of those small rectangular mirrors that women produce from their handbags

Test-running with the body in place is a vital part of the proceedings, especially if splasher clearances and so on are a bit 'tight'. Don't restrict the test to dead-straight track, either, or you may be in for a nasty shock when you let the loco loose on the layout's curves. Best of all is to test a model over the track on which it will operate, as here, where my Gibson 'J15' takes a testing turn over 'Butley Mills' tortuous trackage.

at the least excuse. Run the loco along the test track at a progressively slower speed until the thing stops on the 'tight spot'. Examine the crank alignment on the side facing you, and use the mirror to check the obverse without taking the loco off the track. The error is often plainly apparent under these conditions, where it would 'lose itself' if you were to pick the loco up. A further check applicable to divided coupling rods is to try and waggle the various sections of rod gently side-to-side or fore-and-aft on the crankpins, again with the loco on the track in the 'sticky' position. If a rod has suddenly 'gone tight', you know where to start looking for a problem.

I've already mentioned the inadvisability of running a compensated chassis 'in the air', where there is no load to make the beams function. Such a practice can be useful, however, when you're looking for just this type of quartering fault, as the axle which hops up and down in its hornguide is most likely on one end of the rod section within which the quartering error lies. If the axle also tilts as it hops, then you're looking for a problem on the 'high' side of that axle. Other indicators pointing to the location of a quartering error include the propensity of a rod to assume a slightly 'skewed' angle in relation to the mean axle centreline, and for the persistent unscrewing of a particular crankpin nut. In all cases the cure is, I'm afraid, to repeat the quartering process. If the error is obvious, it can be corrected by applying an appropriate 'tweak' to the relevant wheel. But if you just can't run it to earth, then I'm afraid it's a case of stripping back the rods a section at a time, until you either get rid of the glitch, or find yourself back at square one. Obviously, on locos with outside cylinders or, particularly, Walschaerts valve gear, it's essential to thoroughly test for, and eliminate, any such errors before you install these appendages. I always get any chassis to be so fitted running as a 'simple' 0–4–0, 0–6–0 or whatever, pick-ups installed and running-in complete, before fitting the extra gubbins, as advocated in my 'continuous assessment' testing approach.

If you simply can't track down a running fault in terms of quartering, and assuming that you have exercised due care and are sure that you don't have a rod/chassis mismatch, then there are some further possibilities to consider. The first of these is to ensure that the jerk, sticky spot or whatever is actually of mechanical origin. It may be due to an intermittent short occasioned by a wheel, possibly with a bit of wobble or very slightly out of round, touching some part of the loco or chassis briefly 'once per revolution'. At high speeds, the short may not be of long enough duration to trigger the controller's cut-out or overload indicator, but slow things down and 'ping' (see the next section for likely causes and cures). The other main causes of slow-speed blues are some sort of mechanical fouling on either body or chassis, and the oval gears already discussed in the last chapter. As I've delved into cures and causes for this condition already, I'll refer you back to Chapter 10, and concentrate on the mechanical fouling.

The first obvious distinction to make is between a fault which occurs when the chassis is run on its own, and one which occurs when the two major sub-assemblies of the model loco are united. A knock or tight-spot occurring when the superstructure is fitted at once directs attention to two very common fouling points; the clearance between crankpin nuts and footplate valancing on locos with wheels large enough to come above running-plate level, and the clearance behind steps. These problems are particularly pronounced on cast-kit locos built to EM or P4 standards, where the combination of 'chunky' footplating and the greater width over the wheel faces often calls for a bit of carving-away of obstructive whitemetal.

Where there is a 'fouling fault' on a bare chassis (rare, in my experience), then we are looking for components that can impinge on the path of the coupling rods, or items that can 'load' wheelsets, causing a tight spot. The most likely culprits for the former case are the connecting rods, slidebars, crossheads and bracketry associated with outside-cylinder locos, or insufficient clearance between the rear of the coupling rods and the face of the driving wheels. This last case is particularly prevalent where you have locos – such as the GWR Churchward 'small Prairies', the pre-1930 GW Moguls, or LNWR Webb types, having an axle-end standing proud of the boss of the driving wheels. The standard crankpin spacing washer, top-hat bush or what-have-you may not be providing enough clearance, causing a tight spot as the rod passes across the axle-end. Look for paint being rubbed off of the axle.

The outside-cylinder clearance problems have already been fairly well covered in Chapter 8, but I would particularly direct attention to the clearance of connecting-rods within slidebar brackets; if you get a hesitation with the wheel cranks at top or bottom dead centre, suspect this cause. Other favourite knocking points are associated with Walschaerts gear, especially the clearance of the combining lever in front of the crosshead, or a slack-fitting die-block waggling laterally to such an extent that it catches the connecting rods. It's usually pretty easy to suss out these sort of faults – for a start, they will usually become apparent as the cylinders or valve gear are fitted. Obviously, if a previously sweet-running loco develops a nasty knock when you hang the canny Belgian's crankwork all over it, you know where to look for the villain. Do be very careful in handling locos fitted with Walschaerts – it's all too easy to bend it a bit and introduce such faults. The main method of detecting a valve-gear-induced 'stiction' is careful inspection, preferably when turning the chassis over slowly by hand. Listen for any untoward clicks or ticks, too. If, as suggested, you have installed the valve-gear in separate assemblies side-for-side, then it is at least possible to narrow down a really tricky glitch by taking off one side at a time. It's when you've taken both sides off that you find the displaced pick-up catching a moulding pip on the back of a driving wheel spoke.

The displaced pick-up is just one possible cause of the last class of mechanical fouling, which is when something interferes with the free rotation of the driving wheels. A few others include brake shoes set close enough to wheel tyres to bind at some point due to slight wheel-wobble or ovality, and balance weights touching outside brake rigging. Fouling inside splashers is another favourite, once again often associated with EM or P4 whitemetal kits. That's often accompanied by electrical fireworks, so should be easy to track down. A lot of these sorts of problems are particularly associated with wobbly wheels, so if you're faced with such a fault, start off by looking at how true the wheels are. And if they're Romfords, do check to see that the retaining nuts aren't coming unscrewed. A loose tyre can also give a similar result. Well, I did warn you!

ELECTRICAL FAULTS

I'd rather have a short or a lazy pick-up to track down than almost any of the mechanical mishaps just described. Shorts are easy to spot – just turn the light out of an evening, and the location(s) of the culprits will be revealed – except, perhaps, when deep within a splasher. I usually take the precaution of lining any 'tight' splashers with my tissue-paper-and-epoxy insulation at the building stage, on the usual 'Murphy's Law' basis that if it can possibly touch, it darn well will. The opposite case, where there is a lack of continuity, will almost certainly come down to a faulty pick-up. This can be simply tracked down by repeating the test procedure outlined during the notes on installing the things, clipping a lead to one busbar, and touching the other lead to wheels on the opposing side in turn.

If *all* the pick-ups appear to be dead, then suspect the motor leads – I've found breaks in Telecom flex before now, invisible from without but revealed by a quick multimeter test. Touch the leads direct to the motor brushes – if it springs into life, a lead is defective, or has become disconnected. If the motor remains lifeless, it's probably because it's dead. Assuming you haven't fried the thing (and you'll know if you have), suspect the brushgear first (a corroded brush spring, perchance?) and the windings second. Only a meter test will tell you their state of health, unless obvious breaks or other damage is visible. And that, I'm afraid, is RIP, dig in the piggy-bank-for-a-new-motor time.

TRACKHOLDING FAULTS

These are, as already intimated, often the most difficult faults to track down. On larger engines, much encumbered with bogies, trailing trucks, tenders and so on, much can be accomplished by Sherlock-Holmes style elimination of possibilities (by removing various bits in turn until the thing keeps its footing), which should hopefully, leave you with the one probability that, however unlikely, is the cause. Probable causes range from the most obvious – that of a wheelset being out of gauge – to the totally mystical where some combination of a slightly skewed axle, flange sidethrust, unequal weight distribution, a touch of wheel wobble, and the moon being in conjunction with Uranus, causes the loco to hurl itself headlong from the metals on a piece of dead straight track. It's difficult, within the context of this book, to do more than list the particular conditions that I have eventually isolated as causes of persistent derailment.

As well as the three conditions already mentioned – wheelsets out of gauge, skewed axles and wheel wobble – favourites include axle tilt due to flange pressure on curves (a speciality of leading bogies and pony trucks), excessive sideplay on drivers, incorrect side-control springing, lack of same, dirt on wheel-treads, damage to flanges, mechanical fouling restricting bogie swing, tenders coupled too close, and sand-pipes and guard-irons close enough to the track to catch stepped rail joints. And those are before we even consider the possibility that there might be something wrong with the track, as happened to a friend of mine newly converted to P4, whose locos persistently turned up their toes – not surprising, as the model shop had sold him a load of C & L EM track. Well, without turning it over and looking at the code on the bottom – assuming you knew it was there – could you tell EM from P4 just by *looking* at it (pointwork excepted, of course)?

The remedies for the various loco faults listed are covered in the various sections dealing with bogies and trucks, compensation and the fitting of wheels. Usually, once you've found the trouble, the cure is self-evident, although I can think of one exception relating to compensated locos that caught me out when I first tangled with the breed – I had an 0–6–0T (a Buckjumper, not surprisingly) that, flexichas or no flexichas, fell off bumpy track with monotonous regularity, for all that it was a paragon of sweetness in all other respects. Mike Sharman eventually identified the cause (over the phone, to whit!), suggesting that I might not have eased the coupling-rod holes out far enough to allow the wheelbase to vary by the tiny amount needed to let the compensated axles move up and down the hornguides. I heeded his advice, eased the holes out by a few thou, and lo! the loco was cured.

MAINTENANCE

The contemporary model locomotive chassis needs, I'm glad to say, virtually no maintenance. With the low current consumption of our motors, brush life is greatly extended; I've worn out locos mechanically without ever wearing out the brushes, and unless they're damaged or contaminated, you can forget them. Lubrication, too, is almost a 'fit and forget' option. Once I've renewed all the chassis lubricants after running-in, I very rarely need to 'top up' – once a year is plenty. I use but two lubricants, as mentioned: J. D. Windle's Clock Oil, and Tri-Flo teflon grease, both from Shestos.

The only other regular maintenance function is the chore of wheel cleaning – and a chore it is. Great care is needed – I've done more damage to my models cleaning wheels than in any other way, including dropping them! Apart from displacing and damaging chassis detail, you can all-too-easily chip off paint (especially from wheelrims) and, if you're a bit heavy-handed, you can 'shift' the quartering. One of the reasons that I so prefer steel wheel tyres is that they stay clean longer, but when I do have to bite the bullet, I usually prefer chemical to abrasive cleaning. I soak a tissue with solvent (Slaters 'Track and Mechanism Cleaner' is good) fold it into a narrow strip, and lay it across the track so that one pair of wheels at a time can be cleaned, power being picked-up from the remaining wheelsets.

Only if things get desperate do I up-end the loco, clip on the test leads, and burnish the wheel-treads with a clean, fresh piece of fine (240 grit) wet-and-dry. I rarely use a fibreglass brush, as I feel that you often put on more dirt – trapped in the bristles – than you remove.

A last point on general running, before I subside thankfully into the detail fittings and the paint-pot of Chapter 12, and that is to do it – regularly, and as often as possible. If I've learned one thing about what makes for good running on a small-scale model railway, it is that the more you operate the layout, the better it performs. And that's my excuse for knocking off from this chapter in favour of trundling the 1366 and a cut of 'clayfits' to and fro by the six feet or so that the current state of 'Trerice' permits; one day I'll build a layout big enough to run a more manly engine, for a decent distance, but any running's better than none. Right away, Dick! (Note for uninitiated: all Cornish goods-train guards appear to be called 'Dick', which led to at least one memorable collision!).

CHAPTER TWELVE

DETAILING AND FINISHING

It seems a long while back in this weighty tome that the concerns of aesthetics outweighed the need for mechanical efficacy, so it's nice to get back to a bit of pure modelling for this last chapter. As I hope I've made apparent, I try to keep in mind throughout the convolutions of the chassis-building process the need to try and make the result *look* right as well as work well. Obviously, correct appearance depends to a large extent on such fundamentals as correct frame outline, the right size and pattern of wheel, and rodwork and valve gear that is both somewhere near scale in size and accurate in configuration. Most of these more basic concerns are properly in the province of the kit designer, aided or improved by a bit of upgrading and correction during construction. However, the finishing-off of the chassis and the application of a realistic paint job do offer the individual builder real scope to 'lift' the appearance of the finished job. All we have to make sure is that these cosmetic additions don't foul-up the workings of the chassis, over which we've gone to such inordinate trouble!

Distinctive chassis detail – most notably those long cylinder draincock pipes – contribute considerably to the distinctive character of the rebuilt 'West Country'.

One of the great bonuses of the modern etched brass chassis kit is that a lot of detail – guard irons, ashpans, springs, lightening or access holes, brake shaft brackets and so on – can (should!) be included in the basic frame etches. So, unless you're faced with a bare cast block, in which case I commend to you the overlays described and drawn way back in Chapter 4, the main chassis detailing work we need to undertake comes down to brake and sanding gear, the addition of wheel balance weights, and the provision of such 'occasional' detail as vacuum or air reservoirs, AWS shoes, injectors and other plumbing, and in some cases sundry stay brackets and gusset plates – all of which may or may not be provided in the kit. In most cases, I fear, it's 'may not', but fortunately there are a wide range of detail fittings available from the trade, while a bit of cobbling up of wire and strip can provide the rest. How far you take the process of detailing the chassis is a personal choice, although to my mind, if the loco as a whole is to look 'of a piece', then the levels of detail on the chassis and body need to be complementary.

BRAKE GEAR

The days when a model loco with brake gear was a wonder to all mankind are, thankfully, long gone. Nowadays, most R-T-R locos are fully fitted, so I would expect brake components to be provided in chassis kits. By and large, they are. A pity, then, that the holes needed to locate brake hanger pivots are so often missed out – but no matter; *Fig 4:4* back in the Old Testament part of this epic illustrated a way of locating same, which needed drilling before the frames are assembled. If working on a cast block with overlays, it's a simple matter to include suitable pivots as part of the overlays. I always make these pivots out of relatively thin wire – 0.45mm brass – as this makes it easy to bend them hither and thither in the entirely likely circumstance of the hole through which they're mounted being in not *quite* the right place to get the hanger sitting 'just so'!

The brakes themselves – consisting of the shoes and either single or double hangers – come in a variety of formats, calling for differing assembly and fitting techniques. The most common approach with etched

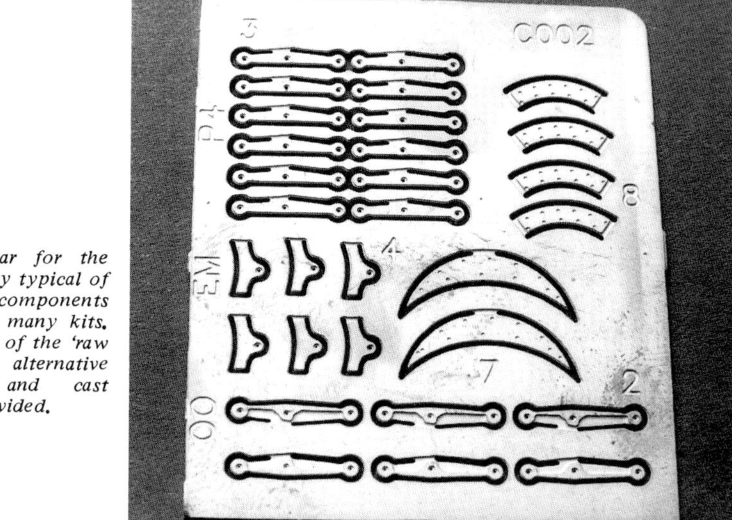

The brake gear for the '57XX' is pretty typical of the etched components now found in many kits. As the picture of the 'raw etch' shows, alternative double-plate and cast hangers are provided.

chassis kits is to include the brakes on the main etches, either as multi-layer assemblies or as single etchings. The Puffers/ Perseverance '57XX' that figures so often in these pages has both, as the kit provides both the original twin-hanger 'sandwich' brakes that the engines had when first built, as well as the later design of cast-steel

My 1950s vintage engine called for the cast-hanger variant, shown being assembled in the second picture. Go easy with the solder to keep these components clean and crisp.

hanger with integral shoe. I used the latter on my 1950s-vintage model, salting the twin hangers away in the scrapbox against a day of need. The trick with laminated brake hanger assemblies is to avoid unsoldering the shoe from the hanger when this last is installed on the pivot, which I accomplish by using one of Shesto's little aluminium heat-sinks as tweezers to grip the brake by when I solder it in place.

Some of these etched brake hangers can be a bit elaborate, as in the case of the vintage GW-pattern twin-hanger design already mentioned. On the Puffers etch, holes are provided for the pivot and cross-rod, together with those for the pin holding the shoe in place. It's thus possible to build up the hanger assembly using wire or pins through these holes to get everything in alignment. I use wire pushed into an offcut of balsa sheet as shown in the sketch (*Fig 12:1*). This is quite a common type of brake hanger on older prototypes, and if the manufacturer has missed off the holes for the brakeshoe pin, I drill them so that I can use this method of holding everything in the right place for soldering-up. Apart from anything else, the real brakes *have* such a pin, and it's a nice touch to include in on the model.

The main dissenter from the etched brake gear camp is Alan Gibson, who, at least on his ex-GE locos that I've seen, provides moulded plastic hangers, shoes included. These are very nice, but you can't solder them in place. There are various other, similar, moulded brake gears about; Slaters do a Midland-pattern 'curved hanger' gear,

This type of brake gear is here shown installed on my older '57XX'; note the large but necessary gap between wheel tyre and brake shoe.

By way of comparison, here is the real thing. Even 'finescale' has some way to go!

Fig. 12:1 ASSEMBLING GW DOUBLE-HANGER BRAKES

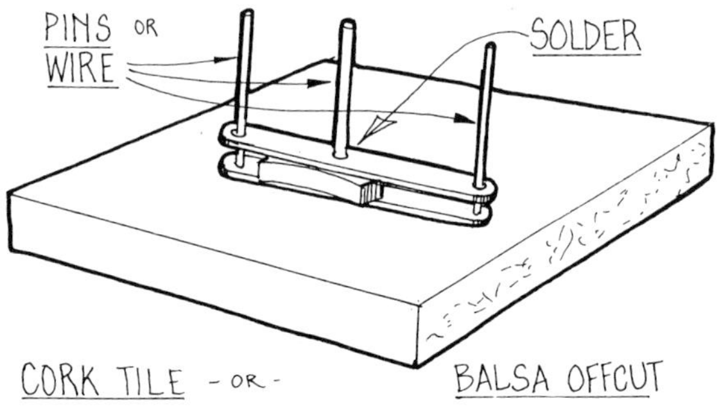

while Cavendish have for some years produced a simple straight-hanger 'typical' brake assembly. With all these, it's a case of drilling a small hole at the pivot location to make them a nice, tight push-fit. A little blob of quick-setting epoxy once the hanger is in place seems to keep them in place well enough – those on my 'J15' are still there after eight long, hard years. The cross-rods connecting the lower ends of the hangers are similarly tight-fitted to the rods and held with epoxy. An advantage of all these plastic brakes is, of course, that they can't cause a short-circuit by touching the wheel-tyres. Don't get complacent, though – they can still produce a nasty 'tight spot' if clearance is lost.

When installing brake hangers, particularly on compensated or sprung locos, it's as well to remember that the wheels will have a good deal more vertical and lateral travel than would those on a real engine; for this reason, it's often necessary to site the brakes with rather more clearance from the tyre than would be deemed desirable were appearance alone the consideration. I generally find it takes a bit of fiddling with the fine-nosed pliers to bend the top pivot into a configuration that puts the brake shoe in the best possible relationship with the wheel, where it looks reasonable and cannot *possibly* come into contact with the tyre. Look out for clearance in relation to the flange and flange root as well – check the alignment from above and below as well as from the side. And, if the chassis is a compensated one, be sure to set the brakes up with it sitting 'on the deck' to keep the wheelsets in true alignment.

The rest of the brake gear – the cross-bars and pull-rods – should also be present, at least in etched kits. Some engines had the cross bars in the form of flat plates, with a single 'pull' acting along the centreline of the loco; many LNWR and LMS types are thus equipped, and the necessary components should be on the etch, or provided as wire of appropriate sections. The other common configuration of flat bar pull-rods either just inside or just outside (or sometimes both sides of) the wheels is usually associated with round cross-bars. These need to be of a wire whose diameter is suitable to represent the often substantial dimensions of these components. I use Gibson's 0.7mm or 0.9mm brass wire. If you're lucky, you may also get the various cranks and brackets associated with this type of brake gear, often very visible on the prototype. Watch out that these aren't too chunky, though – I had to do a lot of filing-down on the DJH brake gear in the 'West Country' kit to make it look reasonable.

If the kit you're using is a bit lacking in the brake gear department, it is possible to provide the missing components from trade

One-piece moulded plastic brake hangers on the Gibson 'J15'. Electrically, a good idea, but you can't solder them in place! Note water-hose detail between loco and tender – these are made exactly as for normal bufferbeam hoses, and soldered to the rear of the loco chassis. They do not make any actual connection to the tender.

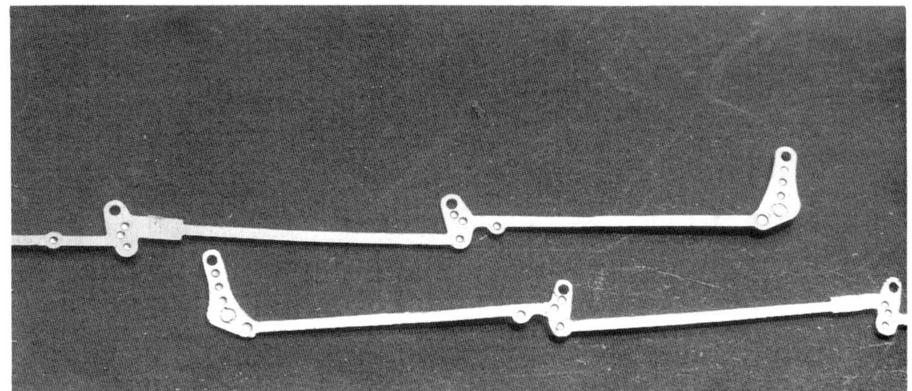

The etched brake pull-rods of the DJH 'West Country' were decidedly chunky as supplied, and called for a few minutes travail with fine files, to arrive at the slimmed-down version at the bottom of the first picture, and installed in the second.

Very distinctive brake gear, such as the big wooden blocks and hefty pull-rods on my North British 'R', forms as important a part of the model as the correct boiler fittings. In fact, in the case of the 'R', chassis components, such as the prominent air reservoir and the sandboxes between the bogie wheels, are as significant as anything above the footplate in terms of character definition.

sources. I've already mentioned the Slaters and Cavendish plastic hangers, but firms like Perseverance, Gibson, Crownline and Comet do make such components available in etched format, while pull-rods and brackets aren't too hard to confect from suitably-sectioned strip and scrap etch oddments. I think that it's well worth taking the trouble to get the brake gear looking as accurate as possible – I feel that it's often a strong contributor to 'locomotive character'. Good photos are a great help when installing brake gear; it's especially important to get things like pull-rods 'sitting right' in relation to the rest of the chassis, and especially so where they pass in front of wheels or ashpans.

Fig. 12:2 STEAM SANDING

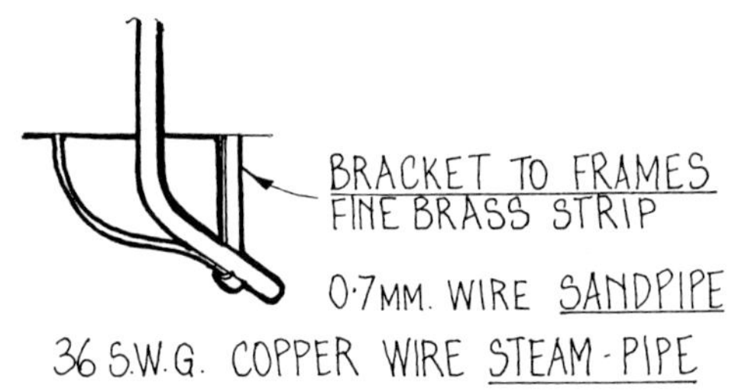

SANDING GEAR

Very often, this amounts – so far as the chassis is concerned – to no more than a couple of bits of appropriately-sized wire to represent the actual sandpipes, the sandboxes being sited 'above the equator' on top of the footplates. Even, in some cases, on top of the boiler! I *always* attach the sandpipes to the chassis, as I found that trying to ensure alignment of body-mounted pipes causes all sorts of problems. I actually make a sandpipe in much the same way as I do a pick-up, simply soldering a length of suitable wire to the frames, and bending it to shape and trimming 'in situ'. Real sandpipes get very close to railheads and wheel-tyres, but that's a recipe for electrical fireworks in small scale, and some modest truncation is a good idea. Many more modern locos have steam sanding, with a small-diameter steam-pipe joining the sandpipe close to its discharge point – easy enough to model with some additional fine wire, as in the sketch. Note also that stay brackets are not uncommon, whilst on a model it often pays to tack-solder sandpipes to brake hangers or other parts of the chassis to 'beef them up' a bit, as they're apt to be rather fragile.

Below-footplate sandboxes tend to come as castings or etched fold-ups, to which sand-pipes have to be added. I solder a length of wire into a cast sandbox before attaching it to the chassis with epoxy. The pipework is bent to shape and trimmed once the epoxy has cured. Fold-ups are best soldered in place, and in these cases I often fit the sandbox first and the pipework secondly and separately, as in the sketch. If I find that the kit gives me no sandboxes, I quite often file them to shape out of bits of $\frac{1}{4}$in 'Perspex', with the pipes cyano-fitted into drilled holes. The completed sandbox is glued to the frames with epoxy – it's best to 'rough up' the gluing face of the perspex to get a good bond. Sandpipes fitted thus have the happy advantage of being electrically isolated. Again, photographs are a great help when fitting sanding gear, and getting the pipe-runs 'just so' is another 'authenticity plus' available for minimal extra effort.

BALANCE WEIGHTS

Again, the better etched chassis kits provide these distinctive fittings as an integral part of the main etchings, and provided the kit-designer is working to the correct 'internal rim diameter' for the driving wheels you're using, all should be well. The etched weights provided for my example '57XX' even had the recessed bolt-heads of the prototype represented, a nice fidelity touch. I usually glue these in place with a reasonably generous dob of epoxy, wiping away any surplus that squeezes out onto the rim or tyre with a tissue soaked in 'MEK'. If the kit doesn't provide any, then I make my own from Plastikard or thick paper, marking the correct outer radius with a compass set from the actual wheel. The 'length' of the weight is easily assessed by counting the number of spokes that it spans on the prototype, and marking direct from the model's wheels accordingly. I cut my weights out with a scalpel, and glue them in place with epoxy. Bolt-heads, if present, can be pressed-in with the tip of a scriber.

Sanding gear and balance weights on the BR Standard 2–6–4T. The rear sandboxes are made from ¼in Perspex, as described and drawn. The sandpipes are about as close as you can go without asking for problems. The brake gear and balance weights are the DJH etchings supplied in the kit. Wheels are by Alan Gibson. C. J. LANGDON

OCCASIONAL DETAILS

There's a lot going on beneath the footplate of many real locos, particularly on more modern engines, where all manner of additional gadgetry can be found hanging from the chassis. I would expect the more prominent items, such as vacuum reservoir tanks, exposed brake cylinders and injectors, to be provided in a modern kit. The better kits come with a very complete range of detail fittings – my Martin Finney '2251' has the characteristics GW-pattern AWS gear, for instance, and the Perseverance '14XX' has all the gubbins associated with the mechanically-actuated auto-gear. All these fittings are represented by castings of one sort or another, with lost-wax brass often figuring for the more delicate items. I find that many of these castings are best attached with epoxy resin once the basic chassis detailing of brake and sanding gear has been fitted and tested.

Chassis plumbing is always a problem area for kit designers – how do you supply it? Cast pipework, of which firms like Crownline are very fond, is apt to be fragile and, to ease the casting process, often ends up rather 'chunky' and overscale. I prefer to find a supply of wires of appropriate thicknesses, together with some clear information as to where it should all go. I make up my own pipe-runs using the techniques described in my previous loco-building books, and summarised in *Fig 12:4*. Taking the trouble to get details like pipe runs right is, I find, very satisfying. Apart from all other considerations, these are the characteristics that gave individual prototype engines their identity, and nowadays I aim to produce a portrait of a particular member

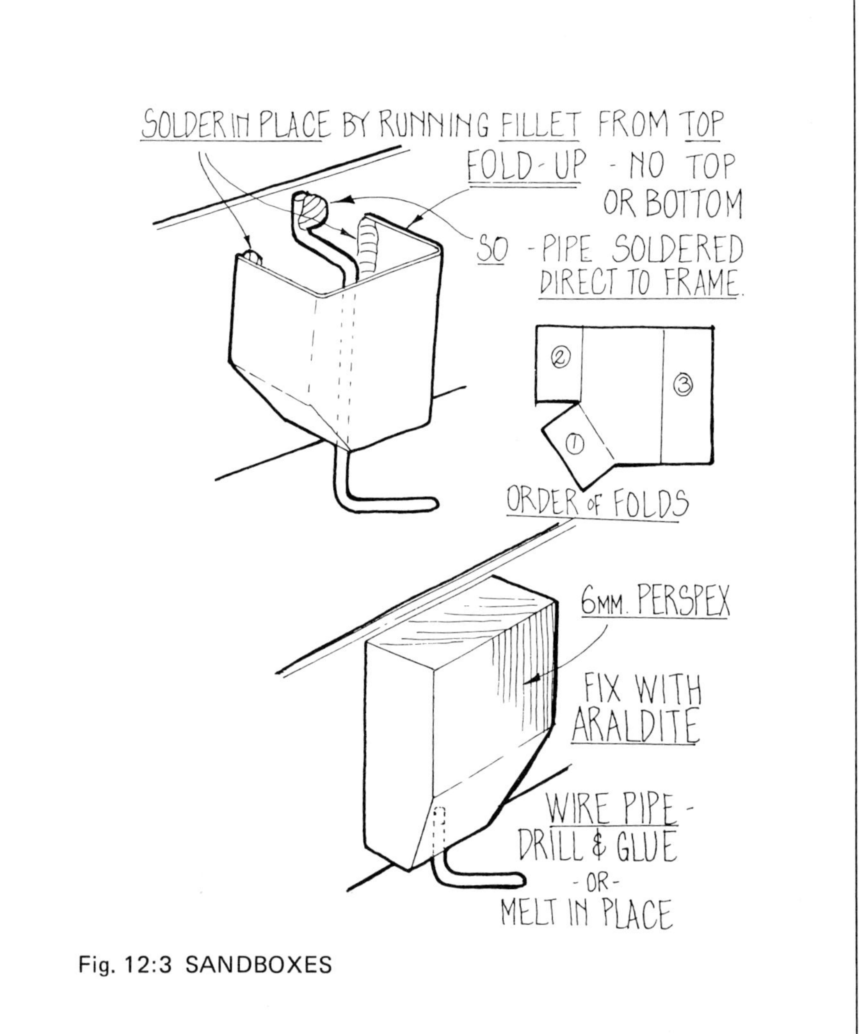

Fig. 12:3 SANDBOXES

of a class rather than a generalised 'common denominator' model. However, you do need a good selection of pictures to do this, not always possible, even for popular classes.

The last class of detail that I identified in my introduction is something that all etched chassis should incorporate, but few do – the various types of stay brackets or reinforcing gusset plates which many real engines have. Some of these are massive and prominent details, fully as significant to the 'look' of an engine as, say, slidebar brackets. But for some reason they seem subject to the same old 'blind eye' convention that ignored motor cut-outs and the lack of chassis detail for so long. It is no problem to provide these components as etchings; after all, the individual modeller can always decide not to bother with them if it isn't the intention to produce a fully-detailed model. The rest of us should have the option! Having said that, it's not usually too difficult to conjure up these fittings from oddments of metal of suitable thickness. Again, I often solder the 'flange' of a stay-bracket to the web, but fix the thing to the loco with epoxy. Typical

Very prominent chassis features such as the massive compensating beam and bracket of the Adams 'Radial' shown here are fundamental to the chassis, rather than being 'add-on' details. If the model is to have any hope of looking convincing, they must be modelled.
GRAHAM WARREN

Fig. 12:4 PIPEWORK DETAIL

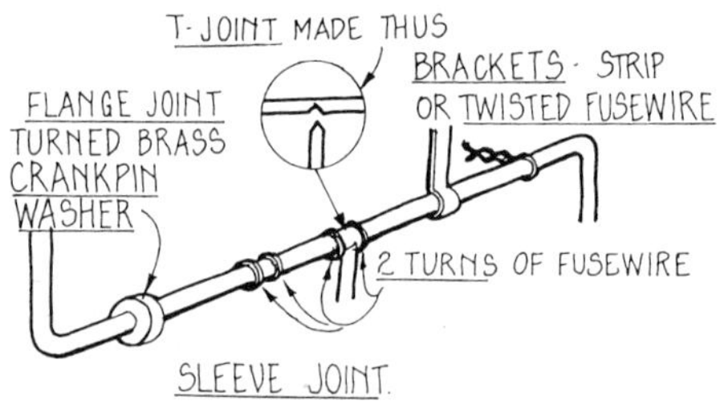

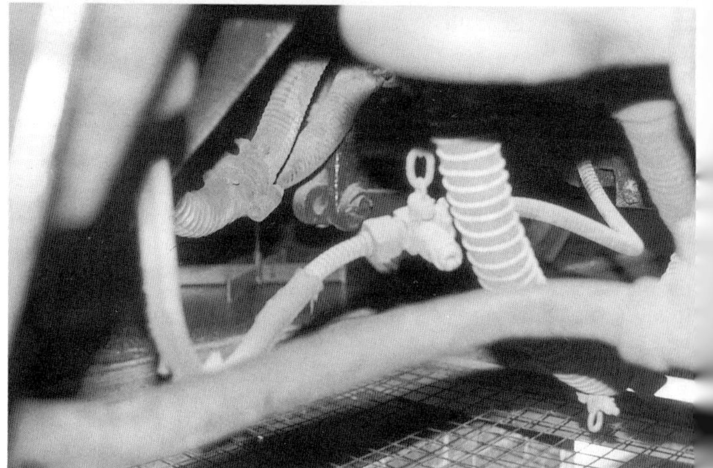

An area of prototype chassis detail often overlooked is the mass of connections between loco and tender. These are on a 'Crab' – water hoses (2), vacuum brake, steam brake, steam heat and a few that have me foxed!

Chassis pipework on the 'West Country', although some of it is attached to the superstructure in this instance. Note the loco/tender connections, and fine damper rods. Such detail is often supplied as etchings that are far too chunky. A bit of substitution for suitable wire and strip helps the 'look' no end.

locations for this type of stay is beneath sidetanks or bunkers, and in the equivalent positions on tender chassis – see any GW 4,000-gallon tender. Another common (and prominent) variation is the horizontal stay bracing the ends of the bufferbeam to the chassis. As with all these chassis details, a few photos will reveal all; stay position and type is one detail that rarely varies between engines in a class.

Plenty of plumbing on 1369's chassis, most notably the vacuum pump, which usually hides coyly between the frames. There obviously isn't room on this tiny loco – they were vacuum-fitted for working boat trains on the Weymouth Harbour line.

CHASSIS PAINTING

The key question relating to chassis painting is – when? Do you paint the frames before the wheels go on, and the rest of it as you go along? Or do you wait until it's all finished and tested, then paint the whole shebang in one hit? There are advantages and drawbacks to both approaches. The 'early bird' catches the worm in terms of being able to concentrate on getting a good finish and good paint adhesion without the wheels getting in the way – but he will have to do an awful lot more work on that painted chassis, and the chances are that the paint will suffer during this process. The latter-day sprayer, on the other hand, knows that once he has painted his chassis, then the only handling it will receive will amount to a touch of cleaning and the fitting of the body. Whatever the painting schedule, both will have to accommodate subsequent 'in service' handling. There is a pragmatic 'middle path' which has much to commend it – that of painting those parts of the chassis that will be obscured by the wheels at the early stage, and the rest at the end of the job.

The approach that I use depends, I find, a great deal on the prototype. Faced with a pre-grouping loco with frames and driving wheels in different colours, I would normally incline to the notion of painting both frames and wheels before they came together; and, in that case, I would re-order my usual sequence of construction to get as much of the chassis work as was practicable, including detailing, done *before* wheeling-

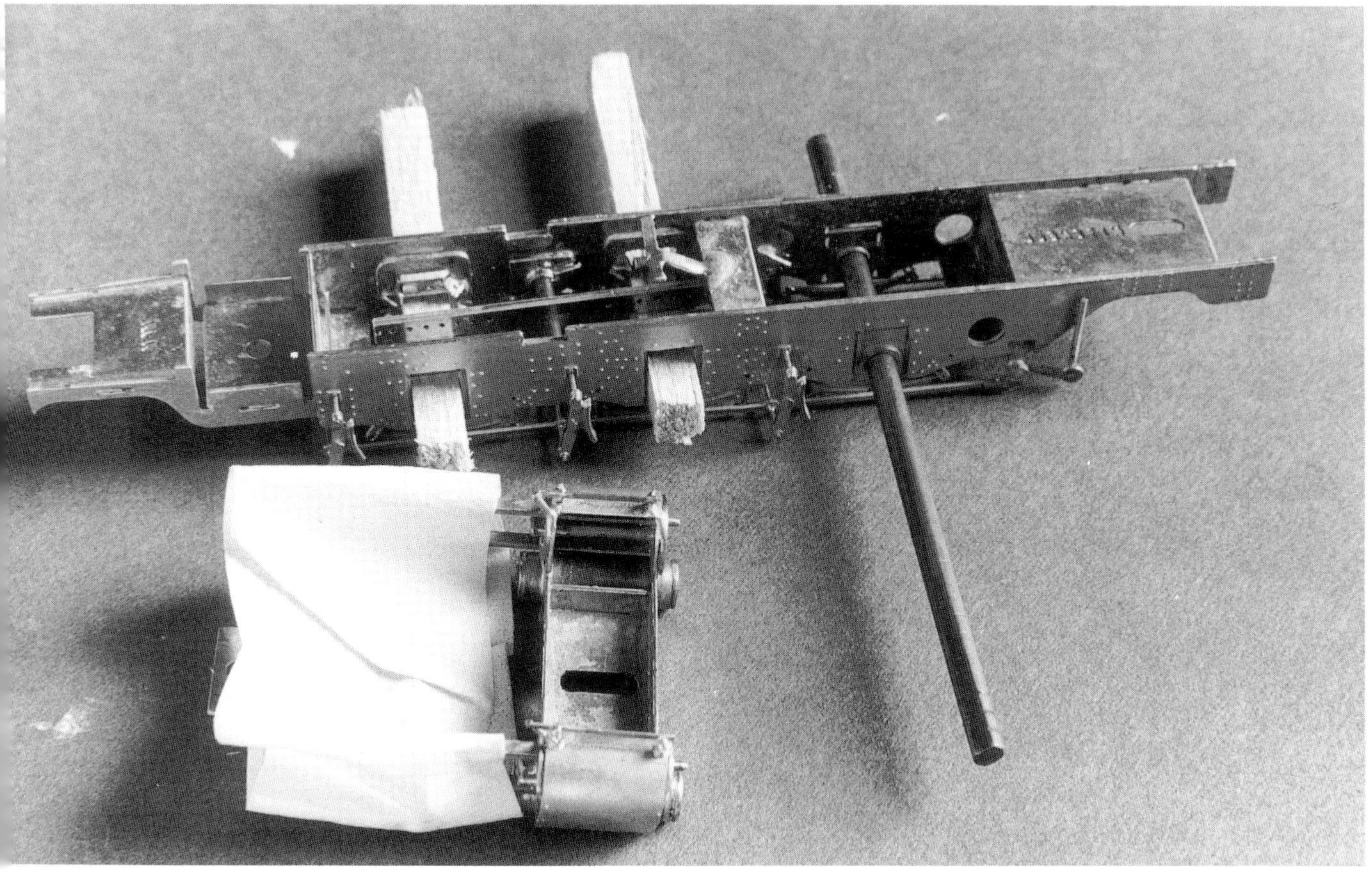

When to paint? Guy Williams likes to paint his chassis before the wheels go on. Here is his '44XX' 'masked up' ready for spraying. The balsa strip and axle rods are to keep paint out of the bearings. R. G. WILLIAMS up. If, however, I was considering an 'all black' chassis, then I would be happy to build it first and paint it last. It is, of course, possible to arrange matters so that the chassis can be dismantled for painting, the wheelsets dropped out and the cylinders and valve gear stripped down. However, very few loco kit chassis are designed for this approach, and a great many of them would need very extensive modification to incorporate such a strip-down capability. I have also found that 'taking down' a chassis like this can upset the assembly work that has been carried out, leaving you with a lot of remedial work, fiddling and fine-tuning to undertake, which will do the paintwork no good at all.

The other painting preliminary that needs deciding upon is the 'aim' of the paint job. There are two approaches to painting small-scale railway models, which I classify broadly as 'layout' and 'showcase'. The former aims at realism, using toned-down colour and incorporating weathering, dirt and 'wear and tear' influences into the paint job. The second approach aims at a 'clinical' finish – all colours as 'correct' as possible, a high degree of finish, and a generally 'brand new' appearance. As all the locos that I build are intended to run on either my own or my friends' layouts, then I aim very much for the former approach, and I find that my 'retro-painting' technique suits it very well. If you're bent on a showcase model, then you're going to have to go to a lot more trouble in the preparation of the chassis before painting, and in the application of that paint. Good luck!

The aim of the paint job must be determined. In the case of my 'J15', as with most of my locos, I was after a 'natural' look to the model. I'm always anxious to make sure that the loco looks 'all of a piece', so I don't paint the chassis in isolation, but very much as part of the whole loco.

MATERIALS

These days, I use a combination of paint types on model locos, with usually a cellulose-based primer, a synthetic or cellulose 'body coat', and acrylic paints for details and weathering. In most cases I find that I don't need the airbrush, as modern aerosols are very good and give a fine spray pattern. As a primer, I normally use one of the 'primer/surfacer' sprays sold for D-I-Y car body repairs – either grey or red oxide. The basic matt black that I now use for chassis work (and a lot of bodies, too) is Humbrol 'Krylon', a synthetic (xylene) based spray that is wonderfully fine, and of a lovely 'soft' shade that looks most realistic. It's ozone-friendly (but not person-friendly, containing toluene and propane as well as xylene), and costs about the same as cellulose. I get it from my local D-I-Y/hardware shop. The acrylics are the normal Humbrol hobby paint, widely available and, I find, quite excellent.

Spraying a chassis under power – Rice's heathen, yet effective, method of painting completed loco chassis. Motor is masked off with a paper sleeve, power applied by clipping leads to pick-up busbars.

SPRAY TECHNIQUE

The way in which I spray my models is really pretty horrifying, but it's effective. Basically, I paint loco chassis complete *and running*, which gets around the problem of the wheel spokes 'shading' the frames. I have a pair of long, lightweight leads fitted with miniature 'croc clips', which are used to extend my normal test-leads so that, with the power-pack on my desk, I can spray out in the garden. The drill is to mask off the motor and gears with paper and masking tape, making sure that the running of the chassis is not impeded. I then fit a 'handle' to the chassis by clamping on a small, cheap hand-vice, usually to the front or rear frame spacer. The chassis is then cleaned, using a small, stiff hogshair paintbrush and Slater's 'Mechanism Cleaner' to remove grease, oil, flux and dirt from the face of the frames and any areas where I want the paint to stick. I do *not* remove the lubricant from gears, axles or crankpin bearings as it wi effectively keep the paint from 'gumming up' the running parts of the mechanism. I also lightly grease the coupling rods and valve gear with a film of petroleum jelly, which will stop the paint from sticking to these components. I don't usually bother to try and 'mask' the wheel-tyres, as they're easy enough to clean with a tissue and a drop of thinners when it's all over. If you're worried, try painting on neat metal-polish with a small brush, and letting it dry. It'll polish off after spraying and bring the paint with it – but make sure no polish gets in the 'works'.

With the chassis duly 'prepped', I do the two-minute aerobic routine with the can of primer, don some disposable surgical gloves (scrounged off the local vet), and retire outside with the chassis, turning over at a moderate speed courtesy of the leads clipped to those so-useful busbars. It is but the work of moments to spray on a light coat of cellulose, which only needs to provide a 'key' for the Krylon and the acrylics. I come back indoors, give the chassis a couple of minutes airing with the hairdryer to 'bake on' the cellulose, and limber up for a while with the can of Krylon black. Then it's back out into the wide blue yonder for several light passes with the second aerosol, keeping the chassis turning steadily and letting each pass 'flash off' before coming back. The idea is to gradually build up a paint layer just sufficient to 'cover' without getting excessive build-up on wheel-rims or cylinders.

Once I'm happy that this is achieved, I come back in to give the whole chassis (still running) a really good going-over with the hairdryer. The Krylon paint is very soft until it's thoroughly dry, so I find it best to leave the chassis in a warm place overnight, and do the cleaning-up in the morning. A tissue and small brushes, used with the 'Mechanism Cleaner', will take the paint and grease off of the rods and valve gear. The wheel-tyres will respond to a touch with a fibreglass brush under power if you've applied metal-polish masking. If you haven't, soak a scrap of tissue in cellulose thinners or MEK, grip it as a ball in the tip of some fine tweezers, and apply to the tread of the rotating wheels. Keep changing the pieces of tissue as each one becomes contaminated, and be careful to keep it on the tread rather than taking paint off the tyre face as well. It sometimes helps to have a small brush handy, to flow extra thinners onto the wheel-tread if your tissue goes 'dry'. Once you've got rid of the worst of the paint, give the wheel treads a good burnish with fine wet-and-dry, and a final wipe-over with Mechanism Cleaner. Oh, don't forget the tyre backs if that's where your pick-ups are bearing. Re-lubricate the rods and valve gear, and check out the pick-ups on the 'one by one' basis to make sure you've restored continuity. Finally, test under power on the track.

The chassis of 'West Country' Clovelly *was painted by the 'spray under power' method – but that wasn't the end of the story. The wheels were overpainted in a harder, slightly glossy black, as were the cylinders. Detail such as the brake gear is also separately picked out, and the whole is lightly weathered with dry-brush acrylic and powders.*

DETAIL PAINTING, WEATHERING

Once I've got my chassis basically painted a nice, even flat black, the fun can start. Real loco chassis aren't just black, they're a wide a subtle range of dark greys, browns, reds and yellows. Ashpan sides get hot and go rusty, as do brake blocks. Brownish grease-bound dirt builds up on wheel faces, slidebar brackets, cylinder backs and motion. Water and steam leaks can cause lime-stains, while steam oil/water emulsion has a distinctive greeny-yellow hue, often found around piston-rod glands or drain cocks. Observation of real preserved engines can help, but the increasing colour archive of the later days of steam, now becoming more widely published, is a good guide. These effects are subtle, so don't overdo things. The acrylics are ideal for this – water-based, simple to mix from a wide range of basic colours, and easy to apply sparingly by dry-brushing or stippling techniques. Proprietary weathering materials, such as Carr's powders, can also be sparingly used to suggest rust and trackbed dirt.

You may be faced with the problem of painting wheels or other details that are 'proud' of the frames, without getting any paint straying onto the chassis behind. A simple paper mask – a piece of stiffish writing paper with a narrow slot cut in it to clear the axle – will prevent such mishaps, and it's not difficult to tackle chassis needing wheels painted in 'livery' colour even by the 'overall spray' method with such an aid. Even where there are cylinders etc. to paint in a different colour, I rarely find it necessary to get involved in complex masking; on small areas, brush-painting livery colour on a sprayed base will usually give you a finish comparable with an all-sprayed finish on the body. As for lining-out chassis components – well, it's no better or no worse than lining out the body, with the possible exception of wheels, which can be lined with a fine brush while revolving (slowly!) under power.

I often carry out the final stages of chassis painting with the chassis united with the body, which I always paint first. The rationale for this is to obtain consistency of finish and colour between the major assemblies of the locomotive, to help the finished result look 'all of a piece'. I'll often apply the weathering process over the whole loco in 'one hit', to finally tie the various elements of the model together. And, generally speaking, that's the end of the job – I don't really find that I can bring any part of a loco to *total* completion ahead of the other parts of the job, so I tend to build and paint everything in concert so far as I can. The result, let it be hoped, is a model that, no matter what its origins in terms of kit used, is individual to the builder, realistic, satisfying – and, if this book has made any sense at all, sweet-running, reliable, and suited to any duty that may be asked of it. I just hope that my approach to building loco kit chassis works as well for you as it does for me!

SOME SUPPLIERS OF TOOLS, KITS, COMPONENTS AND MATERIALS

Tools and workshop consumables:

Shestos (Nathan Shestophal Ltd.)
Unit 2, Shapcote Trading Centre,
374 High Road,
Willesden, London NW10 2DH.
Tel. 081-451-6188

Metals, wire, strip, milled sections, etc.

John K. Flack
107 Hillcrest Road,
Bromley, Kent. BR1 4SA.
Tel. 081-857-4611
(Shows, very good mail order.)

Eileen's Emporium
55 Reedsdale Gardens,
Gildersome,
Leeds, Yorkshire. LS27 7JD.
Tel. 0532-537347
(Shows in north, mail order, very helpful.)

Motors and gears

Branchlines
PO Box 31,
Exeter,
Devon. EX4 6NY.
Tel. 0392-437755 (also Fax)

Impetus *(see under Kits)*

Sharman Wheels *(see under Wheels)*

Exactoscale Ltd. *(see under Valve gear parts)*

Puffers *(see under Chassis kits)*

Chassis Kits (as opposed to chassis included in complete loco kits)

Impetus
PO Box 1472,
Coggeshall,
Essex. CO6 1UQ.
(Excellent state-of-the-art chassis kits, including BR 08 shunter and ex-WD 'Austerity' 0–6–0ST.)

Puffers (Perseverance, Westward)
134a Kenton Road,
Harrow, Middlesex, HA3 0HG.
Tel. 081-907-3521
(The extensive Perseverance range of chassis kits, together with full range of components including hornblocks, motors, mounts, gears and bearings.)

Comet Components
105 Mossfield Road,
King's Heath,
Birmingham, B14 7EJ.
Tel. 021-443-4000
(A growing range of basic [accurate outline, but not highly detailed] chassis kits. Excellent etched valve gears, and a good range of basic components such as cylinders, bogies, etc. All components in chassis kits available separately.

Alan Gibson (Workshop)
The Bungalow,
Church Road,
Lingwood,
Norwich, Norfolk, NR13 4TR.
Tel. 0603 715862
(Wide range of milled brass mainframes – need spacers and hornblocks, but a good basis to work on. Driving wheel range, and a wide selection of other chassis components.)

Some complete kit suppliers will sell chassis separately:

South Eastern Finecast
Glenn House,
Hartfield Road,
Forest Row, Sussex, RH18 5DZ.
Tel. 034-282-4711
(The etched chassis produced for their wide range of cast loco kits are available separately, and are recommended. The chassis of their new LNER 'K3' sets new standards, especially in the matter of the valve gear, the best in a cast kit since the demise of Kemilway's BR 2–6–2T.)

Peter K
Hillcroft School,
Walnut Tree Manor,
Haughley Green,
Stowmarket, Suffolk, IP14 3RQ.
Tel. 0449-673390
(The chassis of the GWR '1361' kit is excellent; where's the body, Peter?)

Malcolm Mitchell
Marsh House
Howard Lane,
Stratton,
Bude, North Cornwall, EX23 9TE.
(Chassis and motion parts available separately; also excellent GWR bar-frame leading bogie.)

Valve gear parts, gearboxes. Sagami 1425 motors:

Exactoscale Ltd.
29 Couchmore Avenue
Esher, Surrey, KT10 9AS.

Wheels

Kean-Maygib Precision Engineering
Wendover Road,
Rackheath Industrial Estate,
Norwich, Norfolk. NR13 6LH.
Tel. 0603-720792

Alan Gibson *(see under Chassis Kits)*

Sharman Wheels
Hen Efail (Old Smithy),
Glan-Henwy, Golan,
Garndolbenmaen,
Gwynedd, LL51 9YU.

Ultrascale Wheels
Gear Services Letchworth,
10 Longmead,
Letchworth, Herts, SG6 4HW.
Tel. 0462-684764

Romford Wheels are widely available through the general model trade.

General Component Stockists:

Challis Models and Hobbies
50B High Street,
Shepton Mallett,
Somerset, BA4 5AS.
Tel. 0749-343527

George Norton & Co.
100 Thorne Road,
Doncaster,
South Yorkshire, DN2 5BJ.
Tel. 0302-323803

ACKNOWLEDGEMENTS

I have many people to thank for assistance with this marathon effort, especially: Chris Challis, of Challis Models and Hobbies, Shepton Mallet, for having such a good stock, and for the loan of all manner of things for photography as well as for vital supplies of all kinds; Terry Cole, Chris Langdon, Robin Arkinstall, Don Leeper, Malcolm Mitchell and Henry Tasker for the provision of guinea-pigs; Ken Northwood, for the wisdom of forty-plus years of hindsight, generously passed on; Tony Smith, who miraculously manages to extract good prints from my indifferent negatives; Paul and June, for making sense of it all; and, of course, Rosalind and the girls, who have had to put up with the whole thing for the better part of this last year. Thank you all very much.